Picturing Tolkien

Picturing Tolkien

Essays on Peter Jackson's
The Lord of the Rings
Film Trilogy

Edited by
JANICE M. BOGSTAD *and*
PHILIP E. KAVENY

McFarland & Company, Inc., Publishers
Jefferson, North Carolina, and London

LIBRARY OF CONGRESS CATALOGUING-IN-PUBLICATION DATA

Picturing Tolkien : essays on Peter Jackson's *The Lord of the Rings* film trilogy / edited by Janice M. Bogstad and Philip E. Kaveny.
    p.   cm.

Includes bibliographical references and index.

ISBN 978-0-7864-4636-0
softcover : 50# alkaline paper ∞

1. Lord of the rings films — History and criticism. 2. Jackson, Peter, 1961 — Criticism and interpretation. 3. Tolkien, J.R.R. (John Ronald Reuel), 1892–1973 — Film adaptations. I. Bogstad, Janice M., 1950– II. Kaveny, Philip E.
PN1995.9.L58P53   2011
791.43'75 — dc23   2011021595

BRITISH LIBRARY CATALOGUING DATA ARE AVAILABLE

© 2011 Janice M. Bogstad and Philip E. Kaveny. All rights reserved

No part of this book may be reproduced or transmitted in any form or by any means, electronic or mechanical, including photocopying or recording, or by any information storage and retrieval system, without permission in writing from the publisher.

Cover image: Elijah Wood as Frodo in the 2003 film *The Lord of the Rings: The Return of the King* (New Line Cinema/Photofest)

Manufactured in the United States of America

McFarland & Company, Inc., Publishers
  Box 611, Jefferson, North Carolina 28640
  www.mcfarlandpub.com

In memory of Dr. Fannie J. LeMoine,
Professor of Classics and Comparative Literature
at University of Wisconsin–Madison,
a respected and much-loved mentor
and friend to Tolkien scholars herein —
an Elvish-spirit taken away far too soon

Acknowledgments

Many thanks to the University of Wisconsin–Eau Claire and University of Wisconsin System, which provided Dr. Janice Bogstad with the sabbatical that allowed her time to initiate this project and allowed both Philip Kaveny and her access to library and computing resources, including the skilled assistance of the LTS staff at Eau Claire, especially Beth Krantz, for negotiating some of the more arcane aspects of Word. Thanks also for the patience of various staff at the McIntyre Library who listened, commiserated and thus contributed to the completion of the project. Credit is also due to Catherine Currier, Josh Lang, Hank Luttrell, and Richard C. West for their various editorial efforts. The kind consultations of Douglas Anderson and Robert Woosnam-Savage, the latter of whose telephone calls and encouragements were a welcome interruption on many grim and dull days in the winter of 2009 and the spring of 2010, were much appreciated. Thanks to Robert E McKiernan, Jr., for the gift of his insights and friendship. Finally, the ongoing cooperation of authors found in this work was much appreciated by Janice and Philip in their first attempt to edit a collection of this type. It has been an often exciting, sometimes exhausting, generally educational, and ultimately very satisfying journey from conception to execution (we liked to watch the "making of" film where Jackson talks about the final days of filming pickups for inspiration).

Table of Contents

Acknowledgments	vi
Preface by Janice M. Bogstad and Philip E. Kaveny	1
Introduction	5

I. Techniques of Story and Structure

Gollum Talks to Himself: Problems and Solutions in
Peter Jackson's Film Adaptation of *The Lord of the Rings*
  KRISTIN THOMPSON — 25

Sometimes One Word Is Worth a Thousand Pictures
  VERLYN FLIEGER — 46

Two Kinds of Absence: Elision and Exclusion in Peter Jackson's *The Lord of the Rings*
  JOHN D. RATELIFF — 54

Tolkien's Resistance to Linearity: Narrating *The Lord of the Rings* in Fiction and Film
  E.L. RISDEN — 70

Filming Folklore: Adapting Fantasy for the Big Screen through Peter Jackson's *The Lord of the Rings*
  DIMITRA FIMI — 84

Making the Connection on Page and Screen in Tolkien's and Jackson's *The Lord of the Rings*
  YVETTE KISOR — 102

"It's Alive!": Tolkien's Monster on the Screen
  SHARIN SCHROEDER — 116

The *Matériel* of Middle-earth: Arms and Armor in Peter Jackson's
The Lord of the Rings Motion Picture Trilogy
  ROBERT C. WOOSNAM-SAVAGE   139

II. Techniques of Character and Culture

Into the West: Far Green Country or Shadow on the Waters?
  JUDY ANN FORD *and* ROBIN ANNE REID   169

Frodo Lives but Gollum Redeems the Blood of Kings
  PHILIP E. KAVENY   183

The Grey Pilgrim: Gandalf and the Challenges of
Characterization in Middle-earth
  BRIAN D. WALTER   194

Jackson's Aragorn and the American Superhero Monomyth
  JANET BRENNAN CROFT   216

Neither the Shadow nor the Twilight: The Love Story of
Aragorn and Arwen in Literature and Film
  RICHARD C. WEST   227

Concerning Horses: Establishing Cultural Settings from Tolkien
to Jackson
  JANICE M. BOGSTAD   238

The Rohirrim, the Anglo-Saxons, and the Problem of
Appendix F: Ambiguity, Analogy and Reference in Tolkien's
Books and Jackson's Films
  MICHAEL D.C. DROUT   248

Filming the Numinous: The Fate of Lothlórien in Peter Jackson's
The Lord of the Rings
  JOSEPH RICKE *and* CATHERINE BARNETT   264

About the Contributors   287
Index   291

Preface

JANICE M. BOGSTAD *and*
PHILIP E. KAVENY

More than a decade has passed since the beginning of cinematic production on *The Lord of the Rings* (hereafter *LOTR*) films in Wellington, New Zealand. Yet the websites persist, fan and scholarly commentary continues and so does the general fascination for the fate of its prequel, *The Hobbit*, as negotiations continue with directors and rights management people. Thus our little book has a place, between two periods in the controversy over cinematic renderings of J.R.R. Tolkien's *The Hobbit* and *The Lord of the Rings* (hereafter *Lord*), novels near and dear to the American Baby Boomer generation and to most of the rest of the world. We had at first anticipated difficulties in finding contributors, but we quickly discovered that a lot of people in a lot of different critical circles still have a lot to say.

It has been a singular pleasure to work with the varied group of authors finally selected for our essay collection. The homogeneity sometimes found in collections of this kind may not be immediately apparent because our essayists come from many different critical traditions. For example, we have film critics, critics of folklore and Tolkien fandom, literary critics and a weapons specialist among our group. We have essayists who have published entire books on Tolkien and entire books on subjects such as the history of cinema as well as those who have not yet published on Tolkien. Yet the essays intersect, contrast, converge and diverge in significant and telling ways. So, for example, where Drout presents the noncontiguous relationship between the culture of Tolkien's Rohirrim and historical Anglo-Saxon culture, an area of expertise for both him and Tolkien, Savage references Anglo-Saxon arms and armor as only one of the many sources for weapons created in the film.

Also, the tendentious issue of written narrative versus cinematic narrative emerges in at least a third of the essays, both around the strength of language over the visual in its evocative powers (Flieger, Ricke and Barnett, and Rateliff) and the uniqueness of the cinematic in conveying such experiences as a visceral connection to characters (Walter). Some, such as Croft, Kaveny, and West, have chosen to focus on character and others on background, such as the physical and cultural setting of the Rohirrim (Drout), the Elves and Lothlórien (Ricke and Barnett) and arms and armor of Elves, Men, Hobbits, Dwarves, Uruk-hai and Orcs (Woosnam-Savage) or the potential reality of "the West" (Ford and Reid). It is especially exciting to see how similar cinematic gestures have been interpreted differently, for example in the controversial absence of all reference to Tom Bombadil and chiefly to the "Scouring of the Shire" in the films. While some, like Flieger, criticize this absence as oversimplifying the story, others, such as Rateliff and Thompson, elucidate cinematic reasons for its absence. Several authors acknowledge that, to most fans of Tolkien, the Jackson films are "another road to Middle-earth." And this group includes literary as well as film critics.

What should emerge in considering all the essays is that the films have a large, enthusiastic audience and that there is a significant overlap between those who love the films and those who love (and have for a very long time in some cases) the books. Many enthusiasts and scholars relate that Tolkien got them interested in the study of languages, in alternative history, in medieval studies or one of its many branches, such as Anglo-Saxon studies, and that Tolkien has inhabited at least a corner, if not a significant portion, of their lives. That is of course the reason that the Tolkien films will be influential for a long time to come: they draw yet another group of people, those who might not otherwise have been visitors to Middle-earth, into this complex and, yes, liminal realm which the rest of us have cherished. For many "bookfirsters," Middle-earth was more like an alternative reality than an escape fantasy. It influenced the careers we chose and helped us chart our niche in the complex world of the present. And these "many" are not all Anglo-American or even European. Scholars of Tolkien can attest to the many languages in which translations of the books and now the films are being experienced by readers young and not so young. When we mention Tolkien to our Chinese friends, old and young alike, they attest to having read the novels or seen the films, most often both. And the books offer such richness — of knowledge, of the spiritual, of literary sophistication, of the nature of history and historical cultures — by giving examples of how they can be built in a literary form. While we don't agree with all the conclusions in these essays, we agree with their core of understanding, that exposure to Tolkien and the many sub-creations he spawned are akin to what Dewey and others of his time called a public good. And according to many represented in this collection, Jackson's efforts cannot diminish Tolkien's accomplishments, they can only deepen them.

Please note that in an effort to emphasize differences in the discussion between films and novels, we will be using abbreviations for all but first references to Tolkien's work and initialisms for Jackson's work. (*Lord*=Tolkien's *The Lord of the Rings* and *LOTR-TR* or *LORT-EE*= Jackson's *The Lord of the Rings Saga* theatrical release or special extended edition, respectively. In some cases, where the distinction between theatrical release and extended edition is irrelevant, only the initialisms for the title are used (*LOTR, FOTR, TT*).

Other abbreviations used in the following pages include:

LOTR	Jackson's *The Lord of the Rings*, theatrical release or special extended editions need not be distinguished.
LOTR-TR	Jackson's *The Lord of the Rings*, theatrical release.
LOTR-EE	Jackson's films of *The Lord of the Rings*, special extended edition.
FOTR-TR	Jackson's *The Fellowship of the Ring*, theatrical release.
TT-TR	Jackson's *The Two Towers*, theatrical release.
TT-EE	Jackson's *The Two Towers*, special extended edition
ROTK-TR	Jackson's *The Return of the King*, theatrical release.
ROTK-EE	Jackson's *The Return of the King*, special extended edition.
Lord	Tolkien's *The Lord of the Rings* (full titles are used for the first occurrence in any selection).
Fellowship	Tolkien's *The Fellowship of the Ring*.
Towers	Tolkien's *The Two Towers*.
Return	Tolkien's *The Return of the King*.

Introduction

The Cinematic Tolkien

It is well known that several attempts were made to turn *The Lord of the Rings*, as well as *The Hobbit,* into cinematic productions. These attempts, along with the several radio and stage plays, are referenced in John Rateliff's article found herein. But since there is evidence that at least one production, the cartoon/rotoscoped version by director/producer Ralph Bakshi in the 1970s, had some influence on Jackson's *LOTR*, and that the early sale of film rights made it possible for New Line to make the film in the first place, their review of books into film at the beginning of this volume bears some attention. Rateliff notes that there have been eight media adaptations of *LOTR*: three audio/radio plays, four film scripts (two produced, two unproduced), and one full-scale stage play. Look to Rateliff's essay, as well as those of Mays and Sibley, for a brief explanation of Tiller's radio play.

Versions of *The Hobbit* became stage plays in schools as early as 1953, and scripts for plays and musicals as early as 1968 paved the way for attempts to obtain film rights to *Lord* in 1957. Carpenter's *Letters* as well as his biography of Tolkien and many subsequent articles) document that Forrest J Ackerman and Morton Grady Zimmerman contacted Allen and Unwin, Tolkien's first publisher, in late 1957 with the proposal to create an animated feature film of *Lord* (for a condensed version of the story see http://faculty-staff.ou.edu/C/Janet.B.Croft-1/three_rings_for_hollywood.htm). Another individual, Al Brodax, had contacted them in mid–1957 with the same prospect in mind. Their first efforts produced a cartoon treatment, by Ron Cobb, of which Tolkien largely approved and a script by Zimmerman, of which Tolkien largely disapproved.

Ackerman, known for his involvement in special-effects films, and Zimmerman visited Tolkien in Oxford to present him with Zimmerman's script and Cobb's visualizations. This is also the point at which Allen and Unwin, along with Tolkien, whose financial situation was quite dire as he prepared to retire from Oxford, settled upon their credo of "Art or Cash," the idea that Tolkien would allow the production of a film if he either approved of its artistic rendering as both image and script or if the funds offered were sufficiently abundant. In the end, neither of these conditions was met. In a year-long correspondence with Ackerman and Zimmerman, both on Tolkien and Rayner Unwin's parts, it became clear that Tolkien could not approve of their plans to convert the books into film nor could they pay enough for Tolkien to overcome his displeasure. He commented on changes he would require in the script but no agreement was made that would render it acceptable. Ackerman and Zimmerman were given a six-month option to create an acceptable film treatment, but in the end Ackerman allowed his option on the film to expire by 1959. Tolkien's oft-quoted letter of response (one of several in April and May 1958) gives us more details, and all of them are summed up by the following: "In fact, the whole construction, especially towards the end, has been extremely roughly handled. And I am not convinced that any limitations of time and space can really justify the confusion and violent alterations of the original narrative that are to be seen in the latter part of Series II and Series III. The 'interleaving' of the events in the two main threads, Frodo-Sam and the War, which was deliberately avoided in the original with good reason, produces a jumble" (*Letters*, 272).

The Beatles were also interested in making the film in the late 1960s with John as Gollum, Paul as Frodo, George as Gandalf and Ringo as Sam. But United Artists was already negotiating in 1967 with Allen and Unwin for rights to *The Hobbit* and *Lord*, so the British quartet could not carry through on their plan. Perhaps the Beatles' attempts—in addition to Tolkien's need for funds—was a motivating force that led to the deal made between Tolkien, Allen and Unwin and United Artists in 1969. But then UA's first attempt to make a film, one directed by John Boorman, seems to have run afoul of sixties counterculture iconography. Boorman's script included many elements deemed by Tolkien to be unacceptable, or even seriously heretical, such as the intimations that pipeweed was more like marijuana in its effect than was tobacco. Next rights went to the Saul Zaentz Company in 1976; Zaentz turned to Ralph Bakshi.

Bakshi's treatment of *The Fellowship of the Rings* and a little less than the first half of *The Two Towers* was the first film to actually reach production; it was released in animated form in 1978. It aroused some interest because of the media hype concerning his rotoscoping of key battle scenes, a technique where existing live-action film was used as a basis for animation. For example, horse-mounted riders from the famous Russian classic *Alexander Nevsky* received animation overlays in garish red-based colors in Bakshi's *Wizards*, and a similar technique appeared at several points in the Tolkien-based animated film. But the true failure of the film was that it was largely incomprehensible to anyone not already familiar with the books; yet it was so different from the books that familiarity bred contempt in knowledgeable audiences.

A script initially created by Chris Conklin and then heavily edited by the otherwise successful author Peter Beagle formed the basis for the film. Beagle is a well-known fantasy author whose sense of Tolkien's work contributed much to the minor success of the film. Unlike the first attempt by Ackerman and Zimmerman, it seemed that the visualization was more at fault than the script and Bakshi was not able to secure backing for the "second half." The conclusion of the "story" was later picked up by Rankin and Bass, who had done an animated feature of *The Hobbit* in 1977; their production was even less well-received and aired on television in 1980. Nevertheless, videocassette and DVD versions of *The Hobbit* (Rankin & Bass), *Fellowship of the Ring* (Bakshi) and *Return of the King* (Rankin & Bass) are all currently available for purchase by devoted fans, who might also want to visit the following websites: http://www.ralphbakshi.com/ and http://www.imdb.com/name/nm0000835/ and http://www.imdb.com/title/tt0077869/ (complete with trailer). Critics of the Jackson version will want to see this film, despite its flaws, in order to consider its effect on his efforts, as, among other things noted by Rateliff, such as that Tom Bombadil is left out of both. In addition, also several pieces of scenery—such as the large statues on either side of the river as the Fellowship boats from Lothlórien towards Mordor—are remarkably similar, even if the full plot is not. An online search of Bakshi produces both biographical information and detailed commentary on *Lord*. The website http://flyingmoose.org/tolksarc/bakshi/bakshi.htm is in fact rather amusing, if heavily opinionated.

Several essayists reference the other attempts to dramatize Tolkien—to offer his work to the world in a form other than the novel—perhaps out of deep respect or out of the notion that some people may not be able to read and appreciate the books without some mediation. For further information on adaptations of Tolkien's work into other media, including taped readings, none of which he produced in any total text during his lifetime, check Hammond and Scull's *Reader's Guide* under "adaptations," although the list of audiocassette productions is not complete.

The editors hope it will become clear that in elucidating these attempts they are also acknowledging Jackson's accomplishment in creating the films, imperfect as they are. He even notes himself that the Tolkien novels will be important long after people have forgotten his films and that perhaps they can be made better by someone else when more sophisticated filmic techniques are available. But to this point, his is the "gold standard" for Tolkien's cinematic presence. It should also be noted that the UA original purchase has been interpreted by the Tolkien estate to provide a limit to what can be incorporated in cinematic renderings of the Middle-earth material in the entire Tolkien corpus, now known as the Legendarium. Only that material found in *The Hobbit* and *Lord*, and none of the subsequent material published by Tolkien or his heirs, is available to filmmakers. Thus *The Silmarillion* and the twelve books of *The History of Middle-earth*, published after Tolkien's death, are off limits. This restriction must have had a significant effect on how Jackson approached the production of his films. At the same time, both his background as a filmmaker and his supporters' understanding of the cinematic audience were significant influences on the final form of *LOTR*.

While Jackson carefully courted the large existing body of fans for the Tolkien books, he also rewrote the plot itself to appeal to the wider audience necessary to support a cinematic production of this magnitude. In fact, at least three books and several articles discuss differences between the films and books. In the case of Janet Croft's collection, the films are found wanting. And while there are websites that praise the films, encouraged by New Line and Jackson for their promotional value, others detail the exact places where the films depart from Tolkien's story. Croft's collection speaks both to and from the sizable body of Tolkien scholars and enthusiasts who do not believe this film series succeeded, and/or that any film version could succeed. On the other hand, there are at least two scholarly studies more focused on the realities of modern filmmaking as it relates to Tolkien's literary accomplishment and Jackson's cinematic one. Kristin Thompson, in *The Frodo Franchise*, examines many details of the marketing efforts, called "franchising," that surround what are expected to be blockbuster films. She compares and contrasts the *LOTR* franchising efforts with such recent phenomena as the *Harry Potter* and *Star Trek* experiences, although I doubt there will ever be a Tolkien theme park or an installation in Las Vegas devoted to Middle-earth. The franchising efforts are nonetheless comparable because many of the same marketing techniques were applied to audiences for the films as well as to the secondary markets for DVD productions. Differences are also significant, as the *Harry Potter* and *Star Trek* phenomena are much more recent and began their existence in a commercial setting in many ways that Tolkien's work did not.

Yet another work, *Studying the Event Film*, presents the results of studies done on the Tolkien franchise by mostly New Zealand scholars, with several in Wellington or Hamilton, NZ (plus one each from New York, Kansas City and Australia). Margolis' essay collection arose out of studies of economics and how much impact the Jackson film trilogy had on its development as part of a corporate, global, consumerist culture. Like Thompson, several of these scholars point to the plethora of footage documenting many details of the film's production, and they assert the expectation that Tolkien fans would want to see all these details and more. Tens of hours of feature-length documentaries can be found on the various DVD productions, including entire movies attached to the special extended edition.

Fan insatiability is manifest in even a casual examination of the herculean efforts exerted to keep fans away from the filming and in the many websites that sprang up in the late 1990s. The One Ring (Theonering.net) is the official website of *LOTR*, sanctioned by New Line and Jackson, but many others exist, including those that celebrate and those that decry the films, as well as those that focus on individual characters and even on individual horses, such as Brego (not in Tolkien's novels) and Shadowfax (central to Tolkien's plot in *Towers* and *Return* as well as in *LOTR*). Even Sam's friend, the lowly pony, Bill, has his fans. A short list of some efforts might be of interest. There are several releases and versions of the films on DVDs, games, picture books, calendars, republication of *Lord* novels with pictures of the films' actors on the cover, and even bobble-head dolls (http://www.wbshop.com/The-Lord-of-the-Rings-Gandalf-Wacky-Wobbler-Bobblehead/LOTRFNGABB.default.pd.html?cgid=prodnew).

Introducing the Selections

These essays have been organized into two groupings to reinforce the additional intersections of their topics in key areas. The first set, "Techniques of Story and Structure," comment on the overall rendering of the Tolkien's six books into a cinematic narrative, focusing attention on the structure of the narrative in each medium, as well as speculating on reasons that may inform changes from book to film. The second set, "Techniques of Character and Culture," outline the transformation of characters, cultures and settings as found in cinematic form and closely examine individual characters and the cultural constructs within which they are set, including setting, moral systems, and ideals.

While a few of our essays are more critical of the Jackson films in both their theatrical and extended editions, Thompson, along with Fimi and Woosnam-Savage, celebrate the films and the filmmaker's choices in identifying a version of Middle-earth that Jackson and his production team were able to create. In fact, essays focus more on the films and books as they relate Middle-earth and its stories than on ways the films fail or succeed based on faithfulness to the book.

Techniques of Story and Structure

Thompson, a film critic who has published on many topics in film history, technique, and theory, examines cinematic approaches to the spirit of the stories of Middle-earth and especially that of this particular period in the history of Middle-earth. While she does address differences in the books and films, that is by way of explaining how the film handled certain problems, and in some cases, in her estimation, why they were handled in those ways. For example, the first problem is the length of the book(s): over 1000 pages and 55 hours of audio turned into 560 minutes of film. The Bakshi film illustrates the folly of attempting to reproduce all episodes in Tolkien's novel by compressing each section. One recognizes elements of the story, but the overall effect is often cute, incomprehensible or stultifying. Thompson especially addresses the many places in which Tolkien's dialog was moved elsewhere in the cinematic storyline or put in the mouths of other characters to preserve Tolkien's celebrated dialog when scenes from the book were cut. Her essay provides a counterpoint to a focus on the books as having primacy of expression and renders them rather as primary texts from which a secondary universe is created. She focuses on Jackson's intention that the environment of Middle-earth and its peoples appear real and historical for his more discerning long-time Tolkien enthusiasts, a goal that motivated the many technical people creating scenery, costumes, special effects and computer-generated imagery (CGI). Jackson admitted to accepting the need to change the narrative structure to appeal to those not familiar with Tolkien's story, so he focused on making the setting of Middle-earth as realistic as possible for "book-firster" Tolkien fans. Thompson's use of "book-firsters" and "film-firsters" is especially useful and is documented in discussions on TheOneRing.net. While foregrounding film theory, she still represents the problems and issues of literature as converted to a cinematic rendering, including the often-neglected difference of each as an economic property.

Flieger's article is more oppositional to the films, and to Thompson and Fimi (whose paper will be discussed later). Flieger asserts that there are many reasons why the film could not measure up to the books, and these are related, as Drout asserts in the broader context of representing cultures, to the necessity in choices to represent the textual, whereas a written text allows the reader a range of imagined characters and settings. In a related area, other essays argue further that literature, more easily than film, can represent the ineffable, the transcendent, the numinous, or the spiritual. Flieger offers this explanation of why the "Tom Bombadil" episode was left out of the film. The ways that Tom and Goldberry are represented in the written narrative evoke vivid images, but the filmmaker must make choices that either render the text as is but violate the spirit, or vastly alter the narrative. In fact, Flieger believes this can't be done in film. In effect, if Jackson tried to film Bombadil and Goldberry, both would become merely ridiculous instead of liminal. This is also, she asserts, behind Jackson's choice to make Gimli something of a buffoon, because he could not be believably represented by an actor as he appears in the written narrative. She privileges the strength of the written word in creating an "other place," a fantastic ideal, and as something film can never achieve. We see this perspective on cinematic limitations in the essays of Ricke and Barnett when they critique Jackson's Lothlórien and especially the character Galadriel.

Like Flieger, John Rateliff explores what has been left out of the cinematic version of *LOTR* and what has been added. He lists four excluded scenes: Crickhollow, The Old Forest, Tom Bombadil and the Barrow-wight adventure of Frodo, Sam, Pippin and Merry. Like Flieger, he starts with the Tom Bombadil and Barrow-wight chapters of *Fellowship* but uses them to make comparisons with other attempts to render Tolkien in dramatic media, including a play, audio productions and earlier film scripts. For each media iteration, he briefly identifies the inclusion or exclusion of Tom Bombadil. The body of his paper is an exploration of what has been elided or added to the Jackson films, and what "could not" happen in the film because of these changes. For example, in Tolkien's *Fellowship*, Aragorn carries the broken sword of his ancestor, Isildur, from the first meeting with Frodo and co.

By contrast, the cinematic story shows the sword's shards on display in Rivendell as part of a scene reinforcing the love of Aragorn and Arwen. As a symbol of Aragorn's reluctance to accept his rightful kingship, Aragorn leaves the still-broken sword behind when the Fellowship leaves Rivendell. Hence Jackson must invent a scene in which Aragorn receives the reforged sword from Elrond late in the cinematic saga, once he has fully embraced his role as a "leader of Men." The cinematic story makes use of the reforged sword, which is held in shards in Rivendell, to reinforce the love of Aragorn and Arwen and to reinforce Aragorn's reluctance to accept his rightful kingship. He must receive the sword from Elrond late in the cinematic saga so he cannot have it before *ROTK*. In other words, scenes left out lead sometimes to other scenes added and the integrity of the cinematic plotline must be preserved by multiple changes in the original narrative. Rateliff's conclusion references what Tolkien himself called narrative debts, scenes that must occur late in the narrative in order to match up with things promised earlier in the story, reducing the number of loose ends and unresolved elements.

Like Flieger, Rateliff concludes with the statement that prose narrative is better at conveying this intertwined set of stories than is film. Film as a medium simply must tell a story differently. Both Rateliff and Flieger discuss the necessity in film of making choices between visualization, characterization and dialog, where all aspects of written narrative are, in the end, narration. One can argue that narrative is a combination of plot, character and setting; but these are always narrated, so there is at once a homogenous and a nonspecific quality not possible in film. For a film to represent a book, more choices than absence or elision must take place. The script writer must choose which narrative elements to represent visually through characters, sets, props, actions and dialog.

Risden addresses structural differences in plotline for film and texts using, for instance, the medieval concept of interlace, to foreground Tolkien's familiarity with complex medieval narrative forms such as we find in *Beowulf* and Dante's *Commedia*. As with these other texts, plot elements that may be seen as "asides" to the main narrative also contribute to or comment on the whole story in ways that Tolkien found enjoyable and important. Rather than advancing the main plot towards its narrative conclusion, as was Jackson's motive in leaving out some episodes and putting others in a different order than in the books, Tolkien used Tom Bombadil, the Barrow-wight, Rivendell, and Lothlórien in parallel narratives in the second and third books to advance and deepen the readers' understanding of Middle-earth, of the characters in the work, and of his themes. Tolkien saw *Lord* more as romance, aiming at different emotions than, say, the modern realistic novel. Additionally, Risden explores *Lord* through the use of two structural metaphors: the fractal, a visual image with a mathematical as well as a natural basis (it appears, for instance, in the variable shape of snowflakes) and the structure and visual experience of the Gothic cathedral, especially in its use of the idea of sacred space. He argues that Tolkien's narrative is complexly nonlinear and so cannot be reproduced in cinematic form; Peter Jackson had inevitably, necessarily, to make choices that minimized some of the spiritual and historical thematics in Tolkien's original. Because of the difficulty in producing a literary interlace narrative in a film, books and films must remain separate but artistically complementary experiences.

For Fimi, folklore studies are relevant to *Lord* and Jackson's *LOTR* films in at least two ways: the folklore incorporated in both Jackson and Tolkien's story and the folklore of their fandoms. For her, the essential relationship lies in the social function of folklore and its historic, as well as its contemporary, creation. Tolkien's novel is rooted in Northern European folklore, the lore of Anglo-Saxons, Old Norse, Celts, and Finns, but also Victorian popular culture. Fimi cites examples in Tolkien. But there is also the fandom of Tolkien's fiction which influenced Jackson's films as well as the fandom produced by Jackson's films. Fimi gives examples of each. The Mythopoeic Society and Tolkien Society, in scholarly as well as popular realms, have existed for many decades, and the films gave rise to websites and fandoms even before they reached the screen. Two versions of the films (theatrical and extended), when produced as DVDs, included hours of commentary on the filmmaking process—films about the filming that satisfied the more avid fans' desire to know as many details as possible and to prolong the Middle-earth experience. In another example, Fimi contrasts Tolkien's Elves, drawn from both Anglo-Saxon and Victorian "faerie" culture, with Jackson's embodied Elves. The latter were influenced by Alan Lee, one of two artistic directors, both of whom had long illustrated scenes from the Tolkien books. Lee influenced the view of Elves on the screen by evoking costumes as an amalgam of several medieval styles lovingly elaborated by costume designers.

Fimi also identifies two scenes in the film that resemble John Duncan's Celtic Revival painting of the Sidhe (the Irish Elves). Then she cites examples of the influence of global cinematic fan-folklore, specifically "Paths of the Dead" visual sequences in Jackson's *ROTK* with only Aragorn, Gimli and Legolas as heroes of the cinematic piece. In the novels, Aragorn is with his ranger troupe, and thus less centralized. Additionally, while Tolkien was extrapolating from the Medieval Latin tradition of the army of the dead, Jackson uses somewhat generic filmic ghost tropes that have caused "originality" disputes with other current film producers. When such techniques cost billions of dollars and result in billions of dollars in profit, establishing "ownership" of intellectual property is a much more contentious question than it was for Tolkien, who felt in 1967 that such films would never be made. Also, both Tolkien and Jackson, in their respective periods, gave rise to fannish folklore. Thompson references "book-first fans" and "film-first" fans. Fimi places both into the context of folklore as culture of the folk (or, contemporarily, the fans).

Kisor then returns to an analysis of Tolkien's plot structure as entrelacement of the *Arthurian Vulgate Cycle*, which is a pattern typified by 13th century narrative or the interlace *Beowulf*, with which Tolkien was very familiar, having done translations from both sets of texts. Her point is that Jackson cannot reproduce this narrative form in cinema. In a sense she is referring to some of the same differences alluded to by Risden; but she asserts that Jackson substitutes a filmic technique called intercutting, one which Thompson also references, in attempting to achieve a similar narrative effect, that of different story lines that are nevertheless connected, and in fact converge, at different points in the overall story. For example, Thompson represents the simultaneous actions by different sets of characters in Jackson's *TT* and *ROTK* by cutting back and forth, cutting between stories which occur simultaneously in the overall chronology of Jackson's *LOTR* but are found in widely separated sections of Tolkien's written narrative. Kisor highlights an important difference in audience perceptions produced by the film and books; readers often share characters' bewilderment, but in the cinematic production viewers often don't.

The most prominent cinematic example is seen during the conversation between Sauron's mouthpiece, Gandalf, and Aragorn, near the end of Jackson's *ROTK*. When the Mithril-shirt is produced by the "mouthpiece" at the gates of Mordor, Frodo's friends don't yet know that he is alive but we, as the cinematic audience, do. We saw his capture and his rescue by Sam. Kisor also references Sam earlier in the cinematic scene in *ROTK* where he's sent away by Frodo, whereas Sam is with Frodo in Tolkien's novel during the battle with Shelob. Consequently, Shelob's scenes are longer in the film than might be expected. Is this another chance for Jackson to explore his interest in monsters? Or is it, as Kisor suggests, to provide visual confirmation of the mental connection with Galadriel, reinforced by the light of Elendil she gave to Frodo, a reasonable technique to contrast forces of good over evil?

Alternatively, Schroeder foregrounds the monsters in Jackson's *LOTR*. Like other essayists, she references Jackson's background in producing monster and zombie movies. But Schroeder particularly argues that Tolkien and Jackson both employ Frankensteinian methods of sub-creation: she links the Frankenstein myth to Tolkien and Jackson's ideas about the ethics of making and destroying their creatures. Like *Lord*, *Frankenstein* exists in novel and film versions with independent identities. Schroeder claims that Tolkien's books and Jackson's films exhibit Frankensteinian influence in the portrayal of artistic sub-creation, creator responsibility, and questions of humanity and monstrosity. Whereas Schroeder finds Tolkien's ethics of creation in *Lord* to be more closely connected with Shelley's novel than with *Frankenstein* films (as one might expect), she notes that Jackson celebrates film portrayals of the monster and his creature.

In Tolkien's Middle-earth, evil is never inherent in the creature; evil results from the desire to create for the wrong motives. Melkor, Sauron, and

Saruman are condemned for their desires to create wrongly. Their monstrous creations are, like Frankenstein's creature, "a filthy type" of the good, corruption rather than creation. But while Tolkien and Jackson both blame their villains for creating/corrupting creatures, they never quite reconcile this condemnation with their own role as monster-creators. Tolkien wrestled with the question of his Orcs' apparent irredeemability long after *Lord* was published; Jackson adopts and expands upon the purely evil Orc apparently without recognizing the conflict. While these monsters are used purely for cinematic grandeur, at other moments Jackson follows and expands upon Tolkien's uncertainty about the distinction between the monster and the human. Particularly in the relationship between Frodo and Gollum, the difference between the human and the monster is unclear. Other authors in this collection note Frodo's developing sympathy for Gollum as Frodo begins to understand the consuming power of the ring. Schroeder points out how Tolkien uses Gollum and Frodo's language to blur the line between hobbit and monster. Tolkien plays with perspectives: Frodo at one point sees Sam as an orc. At another point Tolkien tells the story from the monster Shelob's point of view. The resultant text abounds with monstrous uncertainties.

Jackson both re-creates and expands upon the role of the monster in *Lord,* and his sub-created monsters become perhaps more problematic than Tolkien's. Jackson condemns Saruman for playing God, but Jackson creates the Uruk-hai Lurtz in order to kill him. Through an examination of characters such as Lurtz, the cave troll, Shelob, Frodo, Gollum, and Sam, Schroeder notes that Tolkien and Jackson face the same difficulty Mary Shelley's Frankenstein faced. If the monster has a voice, will that voice persuade?

"Build me an army worthy of Mordor": Woosnam-Savage cites Sauron's injunction to Saruman in *FOTR*. He then represents in detail the ways in which the real craftspeople worked to create not only the Uruk-hai' army, complete with prosthetics, arms and armor, but also the arms and armor for all actors and actresses in the Jackson films. Woosnam-Savage has a unique perspective as the curator of edged weapons — real edged weapons — at the Royal Armouries Museum in Leeds. The same Royal Armouries encourages consultations with moviemakers and hosted one of the few exhibits where pieces of Jackson's *LOTR* arms and armor were displayed. In the course of Woosnam-Savage's articulation of weapons props made for the film, he identifies several types: hero weapons, extras' weapons, stunt weapons, and multi-scale weapons (like those in the reduced sized boat containing a Boromir as the boat went over the falls in the Anduin and those made for smaller-sized stunt doubles of hobbits and Dwarves). He foregrounds the skill and creativity of the many Weta Works players which went into the film props. For example, the Weta Works team — complete with artists Howe and Lee, technical supervisor Taylor, and sword smith Lyons — focused on evocative conceptual design concerns as well as on the practicalities of creating hundreds of weapons and suits of armor. Not only did they examine many actual historical weapons, they also tried to create a logical history for the development of weapons, so the Elves of the Second Age in the opening sequence of *FOTR* look something like those of the Third Age in the battle of Helm's Deep, but in the sense of logical historical developments. This kind of detail is not found in Tolkien's books as direct description. The arms and armor of the Elves match their conception of elfish grace in design. Additionally, each race had its own consistent types of weapons and armor. And then the actors' needs had to be considered. Fortunately Bean and Mortenson were strong enough to wield the "hero weapons," which were real, individually-forged swords; but these could not be used in all scenes. This paper relates similar respect for the range of minds and talents that went into the production of *LOTR* films, as does that of Bogstad when she discusses the tremendous amount of training and attention given to making cultures, large battles, and horses appear realistic. With Woosnam-Savage's considerable knowledge of the actual, as well as the "reel" creation of edged weapons, he is amply suited to introduce us to the wonders of reel weaponry in *LOTR*.

Techniques of Character and Culture

Ford and Reid foreground the multiple endings of the cinematic story. They document differences in the concept rendered by Frodo's departure from Middle-earth in *LOTR*. One contention, that the film simplifies the religious and spiritual dimension of the written text, they see as somewhat inevitable: film limits the perceiver's imagination to one possibility. They focus especially on the imagery of "the land of the Elves," or Valinor, which is actually mentioned only once in the films, and that once only when Elrond is speaking in Elvish. Ford and Reid look at other texts which explain the nature of Valinor, *The Silmarillion*, the history of the Second and First Age, the story of Ilúvatar, the Valar and the Ainur, as informing our literary understanding of Frodo and Bilbo's trip from the Grey Havens "into the west." In the novels, they argue, the language is ambiguous. It does not allow the reader to know, or Frodo to know, if he is really going somewhere or if he is dying. And the novelistic narrative is told from Sam's viewpoint. Sam cannot see where Frodo is going because the ship disappears first into a bright light and then into falling shadows; it is a truly numinous destination, which we have seen elsewhere as challenging to cinematic representation. In the film, however, it seems clear that both Frodo and Bilbo are going on another adventure to another place, along with the Elves and Gandalf. The film presents a more certain and more optimistic portrait of both the afterlife and the survival of a "good" Middle-earth. Ford and Reid also note that Annie Lennox's closing song — a post-visual voice-over with the closing credits — brings back more of the spiritual ambiguity of the written narrative. By extension, one might consider it as written for a different sector of the intended audience. The visual ending is optimistic for the larger number of viewers who are not already Tolkien enthusiasts; the Annie Lennox song speaks to committed Tolkien fans — those who will probably stay through the closing credits in order to prolong the Middle-earth experience — as well as devoted film-goers who respect a director's complete production.

Kaveny pursues a reinterpretation of Gollum's role by reflecting on his ability both to survive 500 years as the ring's keeper and to finally succeed in destroying the ring (along with himself) where men and hobbits could not. Kaveny casts his observations into a religious framework through appeals to our knowledge of the Old Testament story of the "sacrificial lamb" substituted by God for Abraham's son. Whether we interpret his final act, which resulted in the destruction of the ring, as an accident or something supernatural with the power to intervene with the ring's evil intentions, we must concede that neither the historical Isildur nor the immediate Frodo could bring themselves to destroy the ring and Bilbo could not have given it up without the help of Gandalf (*FOTR*). It is as if one needed an imperfect being, or as Kaveny argues, a sacrificial lamb. In a sense the majority of either Sméagol or Gollum's life was a sacrifice, one to which he was doomed when the wiser and more powerful Elves and men and even wizards failed to keep track of and destroy the ring after the end of the Second Age of Middle-earth. But he also details a depth of narrative-history created through Gollum, as the vehicle for a larger historical context in both books and films that would not hold readers' or the viewers' attention as a sustained narrative on its own. The ambiguity which Tolkien and Jackson imbue in Gollum/Sméagol as both monstrous and human is discussed elsewhere, especially by Schroeder (from the perspective of monsters and evil) and Thompson (from a technical perspective). Gollum has both a spiritual and a technical function. Thus Jackson incorporates the cinematic version of both; but Kaveny focuses on the spiritual and those character traits Sméagol, especially, shares with Frodo.

Where Kaveny addresses cinematic character-development in the specter of Gollum/Sméagol, Ricke and Barnett describe Lothlórien, and thus Galadriel, and West on Aragorn and Arwen, Walter's focus is Gandalf the Grey and Gandalf the White. He contends that the Gandalf of the film is both a more social and more humble character throughout than he is in the novels, even though he agrees that differences related to effects unique to cinematic narrative do enter into the characterization of Gandalf in the films. This difference is more pronounced in the books, where Gandalf's supernatural insight and powers are more central, where he is always right and knowledgeable, and, after he becomes "The White," also more remote from those lesser beings around him. However, Walter offers the suggestion that Gandalf must be humbled in the film in order for Aragorn to receive a hero's focus. Frodo's destruction of the Ring and Aragorn's resumption of kingship are the focus of the film where Frodo and Gandalf were, in Tolkien's own words, the two foci of the novels. In fact, he asserts that Gandalf in the film is "inevitably more sensual and visceral in nature" and that "the angelic spirit shrinks in telling ways on screen," with substantial benefits to the character tension of numerous scenes and to the fuller and richer depiction of numerous other characters. Gandalf's own spiritual power, an essential aspect of his character in the books, is reduced in favor of physical prowess, a quality perhaps easier to demonstrate on film. The cinematic substitution of Aragorn for Gandalf can be seen in the scene before the Black Gates of Mordor. Instead of Gandalf confronting the debased human who is the Mouth of Sauron — a depiction used to give a more visceral view of the "great eye's" power — Aragorn challenges him. Perhaps this gives us a better way of seeing the hobbits' friend at the beginning of the film turn into the fierce warrior of Helm's Deep near the middle, and the substitute-leader for Denethor in the defense of Minas Tirith. But since this is Aragorn's story, Gandalf cannot be the same savior of Middle-earth in the films that he is in the books. This is not the war of the rings but the return of the king, Aragorn, to kingship.

Croft views character development in both novel and films within a mythic framework, based primarily on Tolkien's understanding of Anglo-Saxon myth. But she places this insight within Campbell's articulation of the classic monomyth for Tolkien and an American monomyth for Jackson, and especially the "hero monomyth." In its classical form, the hero ventures forth to overcome the overwhelming forces of the enemy and returns triumphant and lordly, having won a decisive victory after many tribulations. The American monomyth of the hero (Lawrence and Jewett) is more contemporary and is largely represented in American film. A community in a harmonious paradise is threatened by evil or attack and a selfless hero emerges to win a decisive victory. But he is a common man in the beginning and returns to that status at the end. He is, or can be, anyone who is viewing the film. Frodo and Aragorn enact parts of the hero saga in the book as classic heroes, but they cross back and forth in enacting the role of the American monomythic hero in the films. Croft asserts Jackson, who was raised on American films, enacts more the American monomyth — which also privileges the common man and is counter to the idea of kingship — probably largely because he feels the need to appeal first to expectations of an Anglo-American audience.

West, in articulating the filmic version of a love story of Aragorn and Arwen, feels he must first acknowledge the original novelistic source for this story; these are events that are not in the story proper of *Lord*, but in Appendix A, after the end of *Return*. West introduces the issue of the larger Legendarium that is Tolkien's allusive and referenced basis for *Lord* as only one of many possible stories, that of the War of the Rings in the Third Age. Why, he asks, did Jackson pull in not only the story but also imagery from this appendix when he left out other major episodes from the books, episodes such as Bombadil and the Scouring of the Shire mentioned by several other essayists? Of course, the most obvious reason is that it's easier to "sell" a hero with a love interest to a wider cinematic audience. This sort of critique has, however, more accurately been applied to the gratuitous battle between Gandalf and Saruman (*FOTR*) that Jackson discussed as "wanting to see what it would be like for two old men to fight with each other." But it was also a prefiguring of their battle of wills on the mountain and later, in *TT*, for the soul of Théoden. Rather than articulate the "elision" criticism found in Flieger and Rateliff, West looks to the spirit of the story, the representative relationships between men and Elves, and the iconic Legendarium reference to Beren and Lúthien. In presenting Elrond's agony over marriage between man and Elf, Arwen and Aragon and Beren and Lúthien also contrast the essence of Elves and Men that was so important to Tolkien, who even referenced it specifically in "On Fairy-stories." Men die and Elves do not. Elrond fears his daughter's choice of life with Aragorn in Middle-earth because Aragorn, through a member of the long-lived Númenórean race, will nevertheless die long before she does and so her devotion to him will eventually cause her much loneliness and suffering. But in the film, this man/Elf contrast also informs Elrond and Galadriel's choice to send Elves to defend Helm's Deep. In the books, they are off defending the rest of Middle-earth. In defending men, the Elves will die untimely deaths after uncharacteristically short lives. West also identifies a compression of their love story into what seems a relatively brief period, whereas it spanned several decades in the chronology of the novel. So we have not just the love story — to appeal to a young, female demographic, a concern of the publicists — but also a reinforcement of both the vastly different lifespan of Elves and men, as well as an allusion to changes in Middle-earth once The One Ring, and consequently all other rings of power, no longer endure. Elves that stay behind in Middle-earth will eventually die, and men will no longer live as long as the Númenóreans from which Aragorn has descended. While they represent the love story of a man/human and woman/elf, the reward for the hero as mentioned with the hero monomyth, they also represent the friendship between Elves and men and the end of the age of Elves that is the beginning of the fourth age of Middle-earth. So their union is also about reinforcing the march of history and the depth of historical detail which stands behind Tolkien's novels and is otherwise so difficult to create in cinematic form.

Bogstad takes up another synecdoche for vast cultural phenomena, the many instances of horses, individually and in large groups, as represented in both Jackson's films and Tolkien's novels. She argues that Jackson's *LOTR* privileges horses over the many sentient animals, birds, eagles and even insects in the novels. Horses, which often seem part of the background, have multiple narrative functions, and these are foregrounded in a more unique set of roles in the films. Tolkien implies they are one of many special animals, but Jackson expands on their functions. Bogstad looks principally at two of the four plot foci clustered around horses: they are characters in interpersonal relationships with individual hobbits, men, Elves and wizards, they act as synecdoche for a vaster cultural phenomenon, and they represent a currently lost technology of war with which Tolkien himself, a World War I veteran, had some familiarity. In Tolkien horses are both part of the relational and background articulations for character development and social indicators in both (historical period) and are specific to the Rohirrim or horse lords of Rohan, inheritors of the Mearas. In Jackson's film the portrayed relationships between people and horses as well as the embodiment of "horse culture" and "pre-industrial society with horse transport" and "timeless society and Elves' special relationship with animal" is more central to the story. Some have been puzzled as to why Jackson invented the horse Brego, who had a supernatural relationship with Aragorn, along with the entire filmic episode with warg riders that were only alluded to in the books. For Jackson this scene was a way to reintroduce Arwen as Aragorn's love interest and inspiration. In fact Arwen herself operates as did women in medieval courtly love culture, a tradition with which Tolkien, as a medieval scholar, would have been familiar — the unattainable object that inspires noble behavior. Therefore the love interest is more than a Hollywood convention, whether intended or unintended by the filmmaker. Bogstad makes some suggestions about the cinematic parallels created between Frodo and Strider/Aragorn that can be documented for consistency with the iconic functions of horses in *LOTR*.

Drout offers yet another perspective on Tolkien's use of horses and horsemanship, one that relates to his interest and expertise in Anglo-Saxon culture and its surviving texts. While some have argued that Tolkien's cultural creation in *Lord* was primarily Anglo-Saxon, it is nowhere an accurate portrait of historical Anglo-Saxon culture, more details of which are available to us now than in Tolkien's lifetime. For example, Anglo-Saxons didn't ride horses into battle, and Tolkien's Rohirrim speak an older dialect of Anglo-Saxon derivation, while their visual culture is more recent. In Tolkien the Rohirrim wrote no books, but the real Anglo-Saxons did have written language, hence the existence of *Beowulf*. Tolkien borrowed elements from Anglo-Saxon culture, but he did not recreate it. Tolkien could also be more ambiguous in language than can be done in the visual medium of film. Jackson created a visual Anglo-Saxon culture closer to the original than that in Tolkien. One must follow literal interpretation to create visual images. He relates Eomer's helmet in *LOTR* to the Sutton Hoo helmet from the actual Anglo-Saxon hoard discovered in the early 20th century. These helmets are similar in structure, but the Sutton Hoo version has a pig crest, where Eomer's has a horsecrest. The Rohirrim village of Meduseld in the book is related to William Morris' House of the Wolflings (which are not Anglo-Saxon). But Jackson's Meduseld is both Norse and embedded in a somewhat numinous horse culture. Jackson sees them as Vikings of the plains, for example, and the pillars in Meduseld are festooned with Anglo-Saxon and Celtic interlace patterns. Film is more susceptible to disambiguation than literary narrative.

Finally, Ricke and Barnett remind us of the more serious reduction of Tolkien's vision of Lothlórien. Many who have viewed, especially, the theatrical version of *LOTR* have criticized the reduction of Lothlórien and Galadriel and the expansion of death and battle scenes on minor and major scales. Ricke and Barnett remind us first that those of us who remember the text from our early readings perhaps largely ignored the battles and reveled in the homely spaces of The Shire, Bombadil, Rivendell and Lothlórien. The battle scenes, death and danger are there. Indeed they seem more immediate and invasive in the films than in the books. After all, in books we can ignore sections, but this is difficult to do when watching a film. Yet these authors look for different reasons and focus rather on Lothlórien as a numinous space where one can experience transcendence. Transcendence is a very personal experience and thus very difficult to represent in a film. One can talk about personal transcendence, but its outward appearances are minimal. We may see tears of joy or rapturous demeanor, but we cannot really understand transcendence unless we've experienced it. These authors argue that transcendence can be approached through language but not through visualization as in a film.

It is hoped that the reader can now approach the works of the many talented essayists with some background in Tolkien's filmic history, the many perspectives on its success and failures as an enterprise, the history of filmic audiences in the 20th and 21st centuries, and a sense of filmic and written narrative as different expressive forms. Consider the above descriptions as our attempts to show contrasts and intersections in the many authors' writings, rather than as any official reading of those pieces. We firmly believe that reading these papers together will result in a whole understanding of the cinematic rendering given by Jackson to the fundamental literary vision of Tolkien's original works.

WORKS CITED

Alighieri, Dante. *The Vita nuova of Dante. Translated with an introduction and notes by Sir Theodore Martin*. Translated by Sir Theodore Martin. Freeport, NY: Books for Libraries Press, 1972.
Brego.net. 2004–2010. http://www.brego.net/lotr/brego.php (accessed June 13, 2010).
Carpenter, Humphrey. *J.R.R. Tolkien: A Bibliography*. Boston: Houghton Mifflin, 2000.
Croft, Janet Brennan, ed. *Tolkien on Film: Essays on Peter Jacksons The Lord of the Rings*. 1st Edition. Altadena, CA: The Mythopoeic Press, 2004.
Margolis, Harritt, Sean Cubitt, Barry King, and Thierry Jutel, ed. *Studying the Event Film: The Lord of the Rings*. 1st Edition. Manchester: University Press, 2008.
Official Ralph Bakshi Website. 2010. http://www.ralphbakshi.com/ (accessed June 13, 2010).
Peter Jackson, Fran Walsh, and Philippa Boyens. *The Fellowship of The Ring (extended edition)*. DVD. Directed by Peter Jackson. New Line Cinema, 2004.
_____, _____, and _____. *The Fellowship of the Ring (theatrical Release)*. Directed by Peter Jackson. Produced by Peter Jackson. New Line, 2001.
_____, _____, and _____. *The Return of The King (extended edition)*. DVD. Directed by Peter Jackson. Produced by New Line Cinema. New Line Cinema, 2004.
_____, _____, and _____. *The Return of the King (theatrical release)*. Directed by Peter Jackson. Produced by Peter Jackson. New Line, 2003.
_____, _____, and _____. *The Two Towers (extended edition)*. DVD. Directed by Peter Jackson. Produced by New Line Cinema. New Line Cinema, 2004.
_____, _____, and _____. *The Two Towers (theatrical release)*. Directed by Peter Jackson. Produced by Peter Jackson. New Line, 2002.
Conklin, Ralph, and Peter Beagle. *The Fellowship of the Ring*. VHS. Directed by Ralph Bakshi. Produced by Saul Zaentz. 1978 (2001).
Scull, Christina, and Wayne Hammond. *The J.R.R. Tolkien Companion and Guide*. Boston: Houghton and Mifflin, 2006.
_____, and _____. *J.R.R. Tolkien: Artist and Illustrator*. Boston: Houghton Mifflin, 1995.
TheOnering.net. 1999–2009. http://www.theonering.net/ (accessed June 13, 2010).
Thompson, Kristin. "TheOneRing Forums: Who Invented 'book-firsters?'" *theonering.net*. June 23, 2010. http://newboards.theonering.net/forum/gforum/perl/gforum.cgi?post=265624.
_____. "TheOneRing Torwp." *theonering.net*. August 22, 2008. http://www.theonering.net/torwp/2008/08/22/29545-tolkien-lawsuit-update-from-kristin-thompson/ (accessed July 11, 2010).

_____. *The Frodo Franchise: The Lord of the Rings and Modern Hollywood.* Berkeley: University of California Press, 2007.
Tolkien, J.R.R. *The Letters of J.R.R. Tolkien.* Edited by Humphrey Carpenter. Boston: Houghton Mifflin, 2000 (1995).
Tyler, J.E.A. *The Complete Tolkien Companion.* 1st Edition. New York: Thomas Dunne Books, St. Martins Press, 2003.

I. TECHNIQUES OF STORY AND STRUCTURE

Gollum Talks to Himself
*Problems and Solutions in
Peter Jackson's* The Lord of the Rings

KRISTIN THOMPSON

Another Version of The Lord of the Rings

By now numerous essays written by Tolkien scholars have decried the changes made in the adaptation of the novel into the film. It's an interesting phenomenon, since numerous literary works get adapted as films without such essays being published, let alone published in such quantity as to become a genre unto itself. It's also an odd topic, since, as I have pointed out elsewhere, there's no apparent readership for such essays. Those who dislike the films presumably don't want to read about them, and those who love the films won't be convinced by a group of scholars to stop loving them.[1]

Scholars seem particularly irked by the films' enormous popularity, not just among fans but also among reviewers. The latter could have dismissed Jackson's trilogy as a mere fantasy film enlarged to blockbuster proportions, and yet many of them treated it with respect. Indeed, the rough-and-ready measuring system on Rotten Tomatoes had "top critics" giving *The Fellowship of the Ring* 92 percent approval, *The Two Towers* a rare 100 percent, and *The Return of the King* 98 percent.[2] Add the many Oscars and other awards heaped upon the film, and some long-time Tolkien experts might resent the trilogy as a work that undeservedly overshadows its source.

Moreover, the film seems all too eager to pander to the broad audience that it attracted, with prolonged battles, monsters, matinee-idol Elves, and comic relief that runs roughshod over the dignity of Gimli, Treebeard, Merry, and Pippin. Elsewhere I have argued that it is precisely these popular-genre elements, albeit, perhaps, at times taken a bit far, that prevent the film from becoming another staid, respectable adaptation of a classic.[3] My view is that it's better to have a film with energy and entertainment value that takes liberties than one that sticks to the original with bland respect.

Yet some Tolkien scholars have simply accepted the changes and can enjoy the film for what it is. To me, a film adaptation of *Lord*[4] is somewhat comparable to illustrations created for the books, calendars, board games, and other material associated with the novel's franchise. The paintings of John Howe, Alan Lee, Ted Nasmith, and others may give us different versions of the same characters and locales, yet we can accept and admire them all. If we consider the film as a very elaborate sort of illustration of the book, it might be easier to look at it a little more patiently and tease out its virtues.

Tom Shippey has done just that in his insightful comparison of the novel and film, "Another Road to Middle-earth: Jackson's Movie Trilogy." Shippey is as respectable a scholar as one could find in the field. He focuses on how the scriptwriters, while necessarily cutting and reworking the book's events and dialogue, found thematic and narrative equivalents for them and created another version of the tale. References to some of his main points are in order here, since I shall try to avoid going over the same ground but am heartily in agreement with many of the points he makes.

Shippey assumes that one key precept of narrative construction in both visual and verbal arts is "show, don't tell." He points out the talkative nature of many of Tolkien's scenes, such as "The Shadow of the Past" and "The Council of Elrond." Although the film devotes an unusually lengthy scene to the Council, it also avoids overburdening it with exposition. Instead, earlier scenes, in particular the prologue, provide us with much of the information from the Council. Shippey also emphasizes Tolkien's propensity to elide scenes and later have characters relate these events after they have happened, as with Merry and Pippin's description of the destruction of Isengard and the tale of the Paths of the Dead episode told later by Legolas and Gimli.[5] Jackson was right, he opines, to show such events directly and in their proper chronological order.

Shippey also examines how Jackson's team transposed actions or dialogue in an attempt to "foreground or bring back quiet but important scenes which might otherwise have been suppressed." These include Gandalf's much-quoted line, "All you have to decide is what to do with the time that is given to you" (*Fellowship*, disc 2, 23:24). With slightly different wording, the book's version comes early on, in the chapter titled "The Shadow of the Past" (*Lord*, p. 51). In the film the conversation occurs during a rest on the way eastward through Moria and is repeated near the end as Frodo's memory of that conversation. Shippey suggests that, for readers of the novel upon its initial publication, the line would have recalled Neville Chamberlain's notorious "peace in our time" declaration of 1938. In the film, he writes, "Jackson gives the words a renewed emphasis by moving them to a different place and moment."[6] Indeed, the conversation is an amalgam of several key ideas propounded by Gandalf during his lengthy exposition in the book, most crucially on pity, on the idea of other forces being at work, and on Gollum having a crucial role still to play. In the film, delivered in extreme close-up by Ian McKellen in a privileged quiet pause in the action, each line takes on considerable weight. The tale of Gollum's early life that Gandalf tells during "The Shadow of the Past" also gets compressed and transposed. It appears as a flashback at the beginning of *Return*.

Shippey refers briefly to Tolkien's well-known set of responses to the 1957 film treatment by Morton Grady Zimmerman, responses which were excerpted in *The Letters of J.R.R. Tolkien*. It is notable that almost none of the things Tolkien objected to in the treatment are present in the Jackson trilogy. One thing did impress Tolkien: a set of photographs of American mountain and desert landscapes that would-be producer Forrest J Ackerman had provided. Tolkien did not find such landscapes mentioned in the treatment: "Z does not seem much interested in seasons or scenery, though from what I saw I should say that in the representation of these the chief virtue and attraction of the film is likely to be found."[7] Decades later, the use of New Zealand landscapes, combined with the miniatures and full-size sets created by Weta Workshop, came to be one of the chief virtues and attractions of the Jackson version.

Still, the question is not whether Tolkien would have approved of the three-part film created by Jackson's team. No doubt he would have been impressed by some elements of it and annoyed by others. The same is true of Tolkien scholars and fans. In essence, Jackson admitted that he didn't expect anyone who knew the books well to approve of all the changes he and his collaborators made:

> We felt we would become derailed very quickly if we attempted to write these scripts to please every fan in the world. You realize that the only way to really do this is to say, "Well, we're fans and we're just going to write for ourselves and not for anybody else." So we took a fairly selfish attitude toward it right from the beginning. It's an interpretation... These movies have the same title, but they're not *The Lord of the Rings*. It's not like on the day *The Fellowship of the Ring* opened there was a meeting where everyone in the world had to burn their copy of the book. Eventually these films will become dated and the book will live on.[8]

Perhaps this modest prediction will come true, but so far, the two versions exist side by side, both with huge numbers of devoted fans, a great overlapping portion of them valuing both.

So far, most of the academic writing comparing the versions has been by literary scholars. I propose to offer a film scholar's view of the ways in which Jackson's trilogy adapted Tolkien's original, using the techniques of a different art form. My purpose here, then, differs from Shippey's in that I want to examine how specific moments and scenes were translated into cinematic terms. Adaptations of books into films can be viewed as an extremely complex activity of problem-solving. An incident that the book renders strictly through words must be represented in images and sounds, and the transfer is not always straightforward, as we shall see. Like other fans, I certainly feel that some decisions which the filmmaking team made in changing Tolkien's book were unnecessary or perhaps not the most successful possible choices. Still, there are a great many effective solutions, even some brilliant ones. In some cases the filmmakers have not been given credit for these; in others a scene may have been admired without the commentator knowing how the effect was achieved. I'll start with the most general changes and move on to more specific problems and their solutions.

The Structural Changes

The most basic constraint faced by the filmmakers, and one largely beyond their control, was that they needed to turn a 1000+ page novel into a set of three films short enough for people to sit through. Of necessity they had to cut, trim, condense, rearrange, and generally shorten the action in ways that they hoped would be the most effective in telling the same basic story.

Nearly as important was the fact that many elements in Tolkien's richly realized world would have to be created from scratch. One of Jackson's motives in deciding to make a film of *Lord* was his hope to stretch the new possibilities of digital film technology in one of the most challenging projects imaginable. The filmmaking team needed to utilize and even invent special-effects methods adequate to the task of realizing Tolkien's trolls, Fell Beasts, and armies of orcs. They also decided to create physical props, costumes, and settings that were handcrafted and realistic to a degree that went far beyond Hollywood's norms. As a result, the film's budget ended up being somewhere in the neighborhood of $330 million, roughly half of which was spent on the computer effects. Just for the studio to break even, it needed a vast audience reaching far beyond the number that had already read the book. This had to be a film with broad appeal, and some of the changes made in the process of adapting the novel were done with the aim of investing the trilogy with such appeal.

Despite also being a "trilogy" and despite totaling about eleven hours (not counting the credits), the film had to shorten the narrative. One unabridged audiobook of Tolkien's novel runs about 55 hours; so the film has only about a fifth of that time to deal with the narrative, the theatrical version (560 minutes) about a sixth. What seems remarkable is how few major events in the book were eliminated entirely, even though there is seldom a sense of the action being rushed.

Tolkien himself wrote that the way to approach an adaptation was to cut material rather than compress it. At one point he remarks, "If both the Ents and the Hornburg cannot be treated at sufficient length to make sense, then one should go. It should be the Hornburg, which is incidental to the main story."[9] To some degree the filmmakers have taken this approach, though their main excisions are only two: Tom Bombadil and the bulk of the action after the destruction of the Ring.

However much some readers may like Bombadil, the whole Old Forest and Barrow-wight section has a mainly thematic function in the book. Its contribution of causal events to further the plot is limited to allowing Gandalf nearly to catch up to the Hobbits and thus narrowly miss them at Bree; to providing the Hobbits with weapons, one of which will eventually play a role in destroying the Witch-king; and to setting up the idea that trees can be dangerous. Gandalf does not follow the Hobbits in the film but goes straight to Rivendell. The weapons are supplied by Aragorn. Thanks to these changes, such a large cut is easily made. The only remnant of these chapters comes near the beginning of the Fangorn episode, when Merry reminds Pippin about legends concerning the Old Forest and how the threatening trees there are said to come alive (*Towers*, disc 1, 28:34). His speech preserves that particular function of the Bombadil episode.

The cut in the epilogue is more extensive, but clearly necessary. Tolkien's daring decision to sustain the novel for a full six chapters past the climax was executed brilliantly. It not only wrapped up loose narrative ends but extended the pervasive theme of diminution to the Shire itself, hitherto the only spot untouched by decline. But it violates the obvious convention of not allowing the defeat of the secondary villain to follow that of the primary villain. The film turned the journey home into a description by Frodo heard over a shot that moved across a map, and it eliminated the Scouring of the Shire altogether. Despite such changes, even reviewers sympathetic to the film found fault with its lengthy epilogue.

Saruman's attempt to damage and foul the Shire is not vital to the film, since the diminution theme is less prominent here. Keeping the Scouring of the Shire would have meant eliminating or compressing some other substantial action. As it is, Saruman dies earlier, allowing the primary villain to be defeated last. At least Gríma is allowed his revenge — a moment well prepared for by the tear he sheds at Orthanc upon realizing the terrible power he has helped Saruman to unleash. Apart from these two sections of the book, no other significant characters, locales, or events are entirely eliminated for the film, though in many cases dialogue or the way those events occur have been changed considerably.

An abridgement of the story was a given. In many ways a more significant decision in the adaptation process was one that might appear less inevitable. The protagonists were changed. I would argue that the book has two major plotlines, each with its own protagonist. The destruction of the Ring centers on Frodo, while the War of the Ring is organized and led by Gandalf. Overall, the book is about the end of the Third Age, and these two characters are the ones who manage to make that end a triumphant and peaceful one, despite the decline that has necessarily accompanied that triumph.[10]

The film is not about the end of the Third Age, though that event is acknowledged briefly. It also has two plotlines and two protagonists, one the destruction of the Ring centering on Frodo and the other the rise to kingship of Aragorn. Gandalf, who is quite an unconventional wizard in the book, becomes the standard wise helper figure, at least as long as he is the Grey. Once he returns as the White, his link to the war emerges. Still, his explicit second goal in the book, that of helping to put Aragorn on the throne, is downplayed. Instead, he merely realizes early on that Men will be the hope of the future and expresses his confidence in Aragorn when Elrond doubts him. The film jettisons Gandalf's overall strategies of using stealth to bring the Ring to Mount Doom and of distracting Sauron by pushing him to a premature attack on the West. Now his principal contributions are limited to helping save Rohan and later replacing Denethor as commander of the troops in Minas Tirith. After those battles, he inexplicably loses hope, and it is Aragorn who proposes attacking the Black Gate to draw forth Sauron's troops.

The decision to bring Aragorn forward as the protagonist was no doubt in part made on two assumptions: that for a broad portion of the potential audience, an old man would not be effective as the protagonist and that a more conventional sword-and-sorcery hero with a love interest was necessary. Hence the greater prominence of Arwen, which many lovers of the book find justifiable on the basis of the material on her and Aragorn's story in Appendix A. There are other changes, however, designed to dramatize their relationship:

the threat of her departure from Middle-earth and the elevation of Éowyn to a plausible love interest for Aragorn. Other obvious changes from the book are due to the greater role of the romance. The scene on the road to Helm's Deep where Aragorn tells Éowyn that the woman he loves is going to the Undying Lands establishes the idea that Aragorn believes he will never marry Arwen. Not long after this moment there occurs the warg-rider attack and his apparent death. This seemingly gratuitous event has a key function, which is to reaffirm Aragorn's connection and commitment to Arwen. Even though Aragorn believes his engagement to Arwen to have been severed, the film must not set up the real possibility of his falling in love with Éowyn. The moment when Arwen mystically appears to him and apparently helps save him ensures our realization that Éowyn's love for Aragorn is hopeless.[11]

Thus the fact that numerous changes, both structural and local, were made during the adaptation process is not at issue here. Everyone, including the filmmakers, acknowledge such changes. Shippey has argued that many of the changes preserve the spirit of the book — its major themes, its locales, and the traits of its characters. A closer look at some of the cinematic solutions to adaptation problems posed by the book bears him out.

Two Recognition Moments

Numerous fans, including those who have long known the books extremely well, have declared that Jackson's film replicated their own mental images on the screen. Given how many changes of plot and dialogue there are in the adaptation, this seems hard to take as fully true throughout the three parts. I suspect that such sweeping declarations refer largely to the appearances of the characters and of settings like the Shire and the Gates of Argonath, which are close enough to the book's descriptions to seem familiar. Even the film's harshest critics credit it with impeccable casting and superb design elements, including settings, props, music, cinematography, and special effects.

As a film scholar, when I read novels I tend to see the action as mental movies, and of course, my imagined version of *Lord* is extremely faithful to the book. Whole chapters of spoken exposition and recitations of lengthy poems, at least as Tolkien writes them, do not bore me. Still, strange as it may sound, at times I insert little changes that would make for clearer or more visually interesting viewing for someone unfamiliar with the novel. Upon seeing *Fellowship* for the first time in a theater, I was startled to see two of those changes in the film as well. The first came during the farewell birthday party. For the filmmaker, there is a problematic moment in Bilbo's speech as given in the novel. The old Hobbit remarks, "I don't know half of you half as well as I should like; and I like less than half of you half as well as you deserve." As the narration comments, "This was unexpected and rather difficult. There was some scattered clapping, but most of them were trying to work it out and see if it came to a compliment" (*Lord*, 30).

It *is* rather difficult, since it drips with sarcasm. Bilbo admits that his relatives and neighbors deserve to be liked — but he doesn't like them much, which rather undercuts the plausibility of his finding them deserving of such affection. The reader can linger over the sentence and realize that it's not terribly complimentary. In a film, the viewer does not have that option. My mental movie's solution is simple. After Bilbo says his line, there is a reaction shot or two of puzzled Hobbits, and then a cut to Gandalf quietly laughing. He, after all, is the only person present likely to be able to catch the sarcasm right off; and his amusement would cue the movie spectator that the Hobbits, were they to grasp what Bilbo had said, would have cause to be miffed. In the book, Gandalf isn't mentioned from the point where he puts off his fireworks to the moment when he comes into Bag End to have his farewell conversation with Bilbo. My imagination takes advantage of his implicit presence to bring him in for a reaction shot, thus helping the viewer with a moment that could be potentially less comprehensible than it is in the book.

While watching the party scene in *Fellowship* for the first time, I realized that the filmmakers had solved the problem of the "difficult" line in exactly the same way, cutting to Gandalf's amused reaction to tip the viewer off to Bilbo's backhanded compliment (*Fellowship*, disc 1, 24:38). Seeing things that are in the book replicated on the screen was one thing, but to see a change made that was just like the one I had made in my own mind years before, and for the same reason, was startling.

Another recognition moment came to me as the Fellowship entered Moria. In the book, the collapse of the entrance plunges the group into utter darkness, which lasts for about half a page as the characters discuss the situation. In prose, the actions, thoughts, and dialogue can be described in the same way they would be in an illuminated scene. From the clause "all light was lost" to the moment when Gandalf says "Follow my staff!" there is little to indicate that the characters cannot see anything, apart from the line "They heard Gandalf go back down..." (*Lord*, 309). Utter darkness is not an obstacle in a book since we cannot help thinking of what the characters and setting look like. Otherwise we wouldn't be able to follow the action.

For that very reason utter darkness is, however, a problem in film. Confronted with a black screen, we lack the author's description to help us along. There is a widespread convention in cinema of using very low light in scenes that are to be taken as pitch dark. That convention is used, for example, in the portion of the sequence in Shelob's cave before Frodo brings out the Phial of Galadriel, a scene which Tolkien describes as completely lightless. The filmmakers' decision to leave the scene after the collapse of the doors black even for a brief time is unusual.

In the novel, the return of light happens in this way: "As the wizard passed on ahead up the great steps, he held his staff aloft, and from its tip there came a faint radiance." In reading, we pass over this. Of course they require light, and we don't need to know how Gandalf gets his staff to start glowing. (We already know from the first chapter of *The Hobbit* that his "magic staff" can emit a "blue light" and "firework glare" that Gandalf is described as having "struck.") We assume that the "faint radiance" is enough to get the group through Moria, since we don't have to think constantly about how nine people could manage with such a dim light.

In the film, there needs to be some representation of how the wizard lights the staff, and ideally the method should be visually interesting. The actor must make a gesture. Simply lifting the staff and having a light appear would be possible but bland. In my mental movie, Gandalf blew on the tip of the staff to light it up. Again, the filmmakers chose the same solution, which I have to admit is a pretty obvious one. They elaborated upon it by having the wizard hold one hand cupped on the far side of the crystal, as if to concentrate his breath upon it. They also have the moment perform another function, since the sudden look of horror that comes over Gandalf's face as the light appears is our first hint that the area is littered with corpses from a battle.

The staff's design also elaborates the moment. Tolkien's few sketches of Gandalf for *The Hobbit* (none of which appeared in the published book)[12] show a plain staff with no carving at the tip, and that's how it looks in my mental movie. In the film, it gains a more convoluted tip. We discover as Gandalf enters the mines that it can hold a detachable crystal, which he inserts into the tip. Thus the fact that the staff glows more brightly than "a faint radiance" is motivated.[13] Given Tolkien's fundamental motif of gems capturing light, the use of such a crystal seems to be in the spirit not only of the book but of the whole legendarium. To allow the cinematographer more flexibility in lighting the Moria scenes, the filmmakers depart from the book and have a few other characters carry torches. Our ability to see all the characters clearly, irrelevant in the book but vital in the film, becomes more plausible.

There were no additional startling scenes of the film containing the same changes that I had envisioned. Still, these two correspondences doubtless inclined me to accept other moments when the filmmaking team departed from the original book. They had clearly studied *Lord* carefully.

Two Cinematic Solutions

As I've mentioned and as these moments of recognition suggest, adapting a novel into a film involves a huge amount of problem-solving. Actions or descriptions that work well on the page may seem flat on the screen or may simply be impossible to represent. Many solutions that Jackson and company made are small in scale and fleeting in their consequences. Others are more dramatic and important. Some may seem like arbitrary changes if one does not think them through. I offer two examples, one brief and one extensive.

Gandalf and Bilbo are sitting on the Hill near Bag End at sunset, smoking and looking out over the ongoing preparations for the birthday party in the field below. Bilbo blows a creditable smoke ring, but Gandalf tops him by producing an elaborate ship of smoke which sails through the center of the ring and disperses it before itself fading away—a change from the book, but a minor one that is unlikely to draw much criticism.

Examined more closely, the moment indicates considerable ingenuity on the part of the filmmakers. In the novel, Gandalf's propensity to blow smoke in shapes is mentioned only once, upon his return to the Shire after a lengthy absence. The narration reveals that the wizard looked slightly older but that "he smoked and blew smoke rings with the same vigour and delight" (*Lord*, p. 46). The reference to Gandalf's delight in smoke rings goes back not to earlier scenes in *Lord* but to *The Hobbit*. There the first chapter describes Thorin blowing smoke rings that go where he tells them to and Gandalf blowing smaller ones that fly through Thorin's and turn green before returning to hover over the wizard's head. In a later scene, he sends smoke-rings zipping around Beorn's great hall as they change shape and color. That is all we know about the peculiarities of Gandalf's smoke rings.

Having him blow several traveling and transmuting smoke rings in the film would take much precious screen time. In contrast the ship appears and fades within a few seconds. It is also more visually compelling. The first two times I saw *Fellowship* in theaters there was an audible gasp from the audience as the ship materialized. It quietly indicates, for the first time in the film, that Gandalf is a magical being. The boat is not an arbitrary choice of shapes but derives from a specific moment in the opening chapter of *Lord*, where some of Gandalf's fireworks are described as "pillars of coloured fires" that turn into various shapes, including "sailing boats" (27). Moreover, the swan head on the ship's prow initiates a motif that will return with Galadriel's smaller boat at Lórien and the similar sailing ship at the Grey Havens. Indeed, the destruction of the Ring leads to the departure of that final ship from the Havens, so that the little scene looks forward to the end in a striking but unobtrusive way.

My second example involves a more important challenge. How could the filmmakers present the dialogues between Sméagol and Gollum, the good and wicked sides of this character's personality? In the book, Tolkien conveys the contrasts of Gollum's shifting moods through descriptions of his expression and voice, as well as through subtle contrasts in his diction. We know both Sméagol and Gollum speak aloud, since Sam sometimes overhears "them."

The film uses a variety of methods to render the character's debates with himself. In some cases, he simply changes voice and expression back and forth abruptly within a single shot, most notably in a tracking movement near the end of *Towers* where Gollum moves through the woods, arguing over whether to kill the Hobbits. This virtuoso shot lasts nearly two minutes and has Gollum moving through a wooded area that casts shifting shadows over his body—a difficult thing to render in CGI (computer-generated imagery). In a scene in *Return*, the dialogue occurs between Sméagol and his reflection in a pond.

Perhaps the most celebrated scene in the entire film, however, comes as Frodo and Sam sleep in Ithilien and Gollum ponders whether to keep his oath to help them.[14] This is another moment which, in my experience, draws gasps from audience members, specifically at the first cut to Sméagol as an apparently separate character facing himself as Gollum. The moment's subtle combination of framing, camera movement, editing, and character glances is difficult for even an experienced film analyst to grasp on first viewing. Indeed, it requires going through the scene frame by frame at times to understand just what Jackson (and Fran Walsh, who directed the scene based on detailed instructions from Jackson) has done to suggest the conflict between Gollum's two sides. The precise technique used here is one I have never seen in another film.

The scene depends upon one of the most common conventions in mainstream narrative cinema, shot/reverse shot. This device is used most frequently during conversation situations. Usually after a distant framing that establishes the space of the scene and where the characters are, there will be a cut to one of them, often a three-quarter view that clearly shows the character's face looking at the other character, who is usually at least partially offscreen. (Often the second character's shoulder and perhaps the side of their head are visible at the side of the frame.) Another cut then reverses the camera's position, showing the other character, usually also in a three-quarter view framing; he or she will be looking in the opposite direction—that is, if the first character faces left front, the second one will face right front. The direction of eyelines is a powerful spatial cue in cinema, and shot/reverse shot has been a staple of conversation scenes since the mid–1910s. What the Gollum scene does is to shoot the same character from two different angles, cutting the resulting shots together in alternation so as to appear as if the series of shot/reverse shots show two separate bodies.

The scene begins (*Towers*, disc 1, 98:36) by using a few close shots to establish that Frodo and Sam are asleep and that the Ring is in Frodo's hand. We hear Gollum's voice muttering from offscreen. In a more distant view, the camera tracks slowly backward to reveal Gollum in the foreground, reviling the Hobbits. A cut to a closer framing of Gollum follows; he is seen in a three-quarter view facing right. He initially has his angry Gollum face and says, "Wicked, tricksy, false!" As he speaks and then lowers his head, the camera tracks in a short arcing movement to his other side, so that we see him in three-quarter view facing left as he shakes his head and looks up with his milder "Sméagol" expression and begins to protest: "No, Master —." Without a cut, the camera arcs back to its original position as the character switches quickly back to his Gollum scowl and snarls, "Yes, Precious, false! They will cheat you, hurt you, lie!" This shot establishes the two framings on the same body, with one end of the tracking movement showing "Gollum" facing right and the other end showing "Sméagol" facing left. By the time this shot ends, Gollum is leaning forward and looking downward.

At this point, there is the first cut to the "reverse shot," apparently showing Sméagol sitting opposite Gollum and carrying on a conversation. The cut carefully matches the position of the character's head, looking down and in the process of switching from his Gollum to his Sméagol face. He looks up and off left, saying "Master's my friend." Although we are simply back to the framing of the character from the middle of the arcing tracking shot, we irresistibly perceive two bodies facing each other.

During eighteen further shot/reverse shots the pair argue. So powerful are eyeline cues that even if one realizes that the reverse shots are merely variant framings of the same body, it is virtually impossible to force oneself not to perceive the entire series of shots as showing two separate bodies. After the first cut the filmmakers don't match the character's position or expression at each subsequent shot change, probably because such precision would be distracting. Finally, after Gollum growls angrily, a close view of Sméagol has him speaking directly into the camera as he repeats, "Leave now and never come back!" Abruptly his smile disappears and he looks around doubtfully. A cut returns us to the initial longer view of him with the Hobbits asleep in the background.

Whatever one may think of other choices made during the adaptation process, this scene's ability to make us apparently see two characters arguing with each other when only one is actually present creates an eerie, even astonishing moment that transcends the presentation in the book.

More Solutions, Faithful and Less So

Apart from these two scenes, there are many other types of solutions used in the adaptation, ranging from those that stick to the book fairly faithfully to those that change it, sometimes to the point of adding entirely new scenes.

Clearly some moments in the text offered no problems in their translation to the screen. Apart from Sam's initial absence and Gollum's brief reappearance, the Shelob episode resembles that in the book. Although it is shortened, the scene where the disguised Sam and Frodo are caught up into a marching Orc band in Mordor is well done. Sam's famous line — "I can't carry it, but I can carry you!" — is a slight variant of what he says in the book, but the rest of the speech is rightly cut in favor of allowing us to watch his actual struggle to lift Frodo. The episode of the Forbidden Pool resembles that in the book, though the unnecessary cruelty of Faramir's troops to Gollum is exaggerated to make it, rather than Sam's distrust, cause the return of his evil side.

Occasionally a faithful rendering of a moment in the book enhances the original in some way. Tolkien's description of the scene where Aragorn, Gimli, and Legolas encounter the Riders of Rohan includes this sentence: "With astonishing speed and skill they checked their steeds, wheeled, and came charging round" (*Lord*, p. 421). It is one thing to read of such a movement, quite another to see it happen with real riders and horses wheeling with the speed and skill described, as they do in the film. Central Otago, with its striking, dark outcroppings of schist, does not adhere to Tolkien's descriptions of Rohan's largely featureless, rolling grasslands, but it provides an immediately striking way of distinguishing a new country that will henceforth be vital to the plot.

The same is true for some characters. In general, I find both Legolas and Boromir to be more vivid characters in the film than in the book, in which they are rather difficult to visualize. Orlando Bloom's stance and gestures, which he described as having tried to make feline, pin down the Elvish grace that Tolkien had to describe in evocative terms and leave to our imaginations. (To be sure, Bloom's abrupt rise to stardom led the filmmakers to exaggerate his superhuman fighting abilities in the second and third parts, but he is admirably restrained in *Fellowship*.)

Boromir actually does relatively little in *Lord*. Once it is established that he is tempted by the Ring, he basically goes along with the Fellowship until the point where he yields to temptation. In the film, Boromir's resistance to the idea of a king returning to Gondor may not be true to the book, but it creates the drama of his gradual acceptance of Aragorn as his sovereign.

The transfer of the battle with the Uruk-Hai from the beginning of *Towers* to the end of *Fellowship* makes sense, with Boromir's death scene providing a high emotional moment for the war plotline as the film draws toward its close. Given the decision to make Aragorn reluctant to pursue his destiny as king, Boromir's death also functions as a spur to make him swear his commitment to saving Minas Tirith.

Even scenes that seem to be gratuitous changes intended merely to create suspense and excitement may have functions not wholly unfaithful to the book. Take the abyss below the Bridge of Khazad-dûm. In the book, Tolkien describes it briefly and in simple terms: "Suddenly Frodo saw before him a black chasm. At the end of the hall the floor vanished and fell to an unknown depth" (*Lord*, 329). The film must establish the space more fully, and it does so in part by inserting a scene immediately before the battle. The giant section of an elevated stone stairway that collapses as the Fellowship tries to descend it resembles nothing in the book (*Fellowship*, disc 2, 37:11). Yet it serves to give the viewer a visceral sense of the great depths below this section of the mines in preparation for the battle with the Balrog. Up to this point in the sequence we have primarily seen the group fleeing across vast horizontal surfaces or through narrow tunnels. Just after we get our first distant view of the bridge, the stairway appears and acts as a transition away from the horizontal to the vertical, establishing this area of Moria as riddled with hugely deep chasms and preparing for the moment when Gandalf and the Balrog plunge into the main one.

One of the changes in the film that has drawn the most ire is the presence of Elven warriors from Lothlórien at the Battle of Helm's Deep. Yet the writers decided to include these warriors through a desire to preserve one of the book's main themes, that the peoples of Middle-earth must unite in order to defeat Sauron. The scriptwriters have said that the archers stand in for the other battles that were happening during the late part of the War of the Ring, when Orc armies attacked Lothlórien and Erebor, events alluded to only in the appendices. The filmmakers wished especially to emphasize the notion of the past alliances between Elves and Men, in part to lead up to Théoden's decision whether to honor Rohan's alliance with Gondor.

The dispatch of the Lothlórien archers to Helm's Deep is set up in the scene where Galadriel and Elrond communicate telepathically (*Towers*, disc 2, 25:28). This has no parallel in the book. Galadriel tells Elrond of two major developments: Faramir's capture of Frodo and potential seizure of the Ring, and Saruman's impending attack on Helm's Deep. "Do we leave Middle-earth to its fate? Do we let them stand alone?" she asks.

The "conversation" between Galadriel and Elrond brings in the notions of obligation and interracial cooperation that are so central to the novel. Near the end of the scene, Elrond stands before a mural we had seen earlier that depicts Isildur in the moment before he cuts the Ring from Sauron's hand. Aragorn and Arwen had stood in the same spot when he said that Isildur's weakness flows in his veins, which in turn recalls Elrond's statement to Gandalf that "men are weak," an assessment partly based on Isildur's claiming of the Ring.

We also know that Elrond himself was present at the scene in the mural and that he failed to persuade Isildur to destroy the Ring. The battle had been set up in the film's prologue as the Last Alliance of Men and Elves, so Elrond's pondering of the painting presumably leads him to agree to the sending of the Elves to Helm's Deep. Haldir's line about honoring the old alliance links back to this moment. Thus the brief scene between Galadriel and Elrond is surprisingly dense in its thematic and causal implications. The motif even returns subtly in the *Return* scene where Théoden must decide whether to go to Gondor's aid. A series of shots shows the other main characters watching him anxiously. Just before he decides, there is a cut to Legolas, who is narrowing his eyes sternly (*Return*, disc 1, 67:38). The implication surely is that Legolas is thinking of the Elves' recent willingness to honor old alliances, even at great danger to themselves. Théoden presumably also remembers their arrival at Helm's Deep, a thought that makes him decide to ride to Gondor's aid.

Another change was the substitution of Arwen for Glorfindel as the rescuer who rides out from Rivendell and helps the wounded Frodo escape from the Black Riders. Apart from the fact that the introduction of a new character just to fulfill this purpose would be weak dramatically in a film, the scene substitutes for the much later scene in the book where Arwen comforts the wounded Frodo and tells him that he may cross the sea in her place, going to the Undying Lands. The film's scene after the Baranduin floods has Arwen embracing Frodo and saying, "What grace is given me, let it pass to him." In the book, every positive character who encounters Frodo aids him, and this scene by the river allows Arwen to do so as well.

History, The Legendarium, and the Melancholy Ending

One thing for which the filmmakers do not get much credit from the naysayers is their decision to retain Tolkien's view of his novel as "feigned" history (*Lord*, p. xxiv). Jackson has said, "It's not fantasy. It's history, and Tolkien himself thought of this as a prehistory and mythology of Europe.... We built on that and based everything in the movie in reality. Rohan is based on Scandinavian culture. Gondor is more Roman with its big white marbled city. We tried to base it on things that seem familiar rather than foreign."[15] Thus the scriptwriters avoided one thing that would have displeased Tolkien enormously. They did not turn his Elves and Hobbits into pixies or Disney creatures. The design team took enormous trouble to suggest historical changes within the various cultures of Middle-earth, providing ruined buildings and fallen statues that the Fellowship members encounter along their route. They hired David Salo, an expert on Tolkien's invented languages, to write dialogue and song lyrics, necessitating the use of subtitles in a film aimed at the broadest possible audience.

Tolkien has written affectingly of the glimpses into the legendarium that he put into the novel but left undeveloped and unexplained. In early 1945, his son Christopher, who had been reading the drafts of *Lord*, had apparently written to him mentioning that he had been moved by the name Celebrimbor, a character mentioned only briefly in *Lord* though he features in various other draft manuscripts. Tolkien replied: "There are two quite diff. [sic] emotions: one that moves me supremely and I find small difficulty in evoking: the heart-racking sense of the vanished past (best expressed by Gandalf's words about the Palantír).... A story must be told or there'll be no story, yet it is the untold stories that are most moving. I think you are moved by *Celebrimbor* because it conveys a sudden sense of endless *untold* stories."[16]

One would expect the filmmakers to avoid all such references to irrelevant characters, places, and events. Yet they, too, have characters mention similar things without explanation: the Undying Lands, the Valar, and particularly Númenor and the Dúnedain. There are also references to Bilbo's adventures: the "business with the dragon," the glimpse of Thorin's map of Wilderland, and Gandalf's reputation for luring Hobbits into adventures. At the time Jackson's trilogy was being made, there was no plan to adapt *The Hobbit* as well, so these tantalizing bits take their place as more glimpses of the legendarium — at least until the planned two-part film of the earlier novel appears. There are far fewer of these tantalizing hints than in the book, of course, but for those who saw the film without having previously read the novel, such moments may have a similar effect in deepening the suggestion of a larger world and its history.

One might also expect the filmmakers to opt for a more epic ending for such a blockbuster — most obviously the moment of the huge pull-back from Minas Tirith as the entire population bows to the Hobbits. It was certainly a moment that many reviewers initially assumed to be the ending, and they complained about what they saw as the multiple endings that the film then provided.

In writing his novel, somehow Tolkien successfully sustained the lengthy journey homeward, with its wrapping up of loose ends and sad, gradual dispersal of the Fellowship and their friends. He even held the reader's attention for the unexpected cranking up of the action for another battle, and one in which there is never any real doubt about the outcome.

The filmmakers could not extend *Return* by perhaps an hour or so in order to include all these events. Instead, they skipped to the end of the journey home; and once the Hobbits are back in the Shire, the filmmakers provided enough action to suggest something of the melancholy of the book's ending. This happens most effectively in the brief tavern scene, where the locals ignore the returned heroes while marveling over a huge pumpkin, and in the Grey Havens scene. At that point, the shot of the ship moving away into the West must have been another tempting image on which to end the film. Instead it closes almost exactly as the book does, with the bittersweet reaffirmation of the ordinary life that the Quest and the War had saved.

Even more remarkable, though, is the film's undercutting of a happy ending to the Aragorn-Arwen romance. In order to persuade Arwen to leave Middle-earth for Valinor, Elrond foretells her final sorrow at Aragorn's death (*Towers*, disc 2, 22:28). In the book there is no scene of any such urging on his part, nor is there any suggestion that Arwen would leave. She and Aragorn have already plighted their troth, and that is that. In the film the scenes that accompany Elrond's prophecy are not a fantasy but a flash-forward. They reveal the literal truth about what will happen to her. Snatches of his speech come directly or as slight paraphrases from the last portions of "The Tale of Aragorn and Arwen" in Appendix A, though there the description is in third person, told after the fact. Aragorn in death will be "an image of the splendour of the Kings of Men in glory before the breaking of the world." Arwen's doubt will become "as nightfall in winter that comes without a star." She will walk alone "under the fading trees ... until all the world is changed and all the long years of [her] life are utterly spent" (*Lord*, p. 1063).

In the book Arwen apparently becomes embittered by her choice of mortality once she realizes what death truly means. She leaves behind her son and daughters to dwell and die alone. The film offers no softening of this doom. There is the child whom she sees in a vision, the joy to counter the grief predicted by her father. The moment causes her to repent her decision to depart, and she returns to wait for Aragorn. Yet the child's existence will not change the future that Elrond foretold. The implication is that she will face the sorrow imposed by mortality in exchange for the joy of having children — yet no child is present at Aragorn's bier to comfort her. This grim little montage stresses the loss and grief, not the joy the two will share before Aragorn's death.

The brief scenes of desolation depicted here are perhaps forgotten by the time Arwen and Aragorn are reunited at the coronation ceremony. Yet some may remember the implications, and those who watch the film again will be reminded and less likely to forget again. The scene is one of the strongest of many elements that the filmmakers could have chosen to avoid or soften, especially since it is not part of the novel proper.

The People Have Spoken

I don't expect that what I've said here will make much difference to those who strongly dislike the films. But for devoted readers who grudgingly like some aspects of the films, what I've pointed out might suggest why there is something here to admire. To those who liked them quite a lot despite the many changes, it might explain more as to why they felt that admiration.

Those who dislike the film and feel it has somehow sullied the novel might consider the nature of the film's popularity. From the time *Fellowship* was released, I have been struck by how people who have seen only the film seem to describe it in terms strangely similar to those used by fans who had loved the book long before the adaptation. They find the characters appealing in similar ways; they recognize the themes of friendship, loyalty, and sacrifice, along with the newly relevant environmental one. Just as many fans of the book have traditionally read it repeatedly, fans of the film watch it over and over, in theaters and on various forms of video. For many, their devotion is just as great.

The films brought new readers to the novel in the hundreds of thousands, perhaps in the millions. They were everywhere in the months after *Fellowship*'s premiere. I happened to be traveling to Egypt and decided to take the novel as my leisure reading, sort of to reassure myself that the book was still there. On my first flight there was a man sitting across the aisle who looked like he was flying on business; he was reading *The Return of the King*. I had a long layover in Amsterdam, which I spent in the airport lounge. In the little square of chairs where I ensconced myself for the wait, there were three more businessmen. I sat reading *The Fellowship of the Ring* while they labored over their computers. As they finished their tasks, two of them brought out volumes of *Lord*. The third started reading something else. Three out of four strangers reading Tolkien! As Gandalf (the one in the novel) would say, "Surely you don't imagine that such a 'chance meeting,' as we call it in Middle-earth, happened entirely through coincidence, do you?" No, I think it was the movie.

Many people who dearly love the film, however, will never read the book. Don't they deserve a version of *Lord*? Isn't it rather condescending to say to these millions of people that these films should never have been made because they do not conform more closely to the books?

Many fans of the books don't seem bothered by two different versions. They have termed the resulting two varieties of fans "book-firsters" and "film-firsters." They coexist peacefully on places like the Message Boards of The OneRing.net, the main popular Tolkien Website. Often in discussions they solicit information about how book-firsters and film-firsters initially perceived certain things in the movie differently. In fact, there was an interesting thread where a book-firster expressed downright fascination with film-firsters' initial reactions to the movie. One of the contributors listed some relevant books, including Jane Brennan Croft's anthology *Tolkien on Film* (cited earlier): "The Croft book has a mix of pro/con articles related to the films, mostly con, though as I recall."[17]

In a way, the condescension and dismissal that the film has sometimes met with in scholarly circles reminds me somewhat of the disdain many of Tolkien's colleagues felt for his fiction. To them the question wasn't really whether the novels were good or not. They were broadly popular and hence frivolous. They drew Tolkien away from the academic work that they automatically assumed was more worthwhile. The two situations as a whole are not parallel, of course. Still, if *The Lord of the Rings* belonged to a large public before, its two versions belong to a vastly larger one now.

Notes

1. Several such essays appear in Croft, ed., 2004. I reviewed this volume in *Tolkien Studies* III (2006), 222–228.
2. Rotten Tomatoes (accessed December 27, 2009.)
3. Thompson, 2007, Chapter 2.
4. To differentiate book from film, I shall refer to Tolkien's novel as *LOTR* and cite pages from the 50th Anniversary Edition (Boston: Houghton Mifflin, 2004); the three parts of the film will be *Fellowship*, *Towers*, and *Return*, and all analysis and DVD timings are based on the extended editions.
5. Shippey, 2007, 370–71.
6. Shippey, 2007, 375.
7. Carpenter, ed. *Letters* 1981), pp. 261 and 274.
8. "The Lord of the Rings: Return [sic] of the King," 62.
9. Carpenter, ed., *Letters*, 276.
10. I do not have space here to elaborate on this and other claims I make about the novel. I am at work on a book about *The Hobbit* and *The Lord of the Rings* where I will discuss such points as who the protagonists of *LOTR* are.
11. Shippey, 2007, also remarks on this scene as a way of linking Aragorn's and Arwen's fates in, 375.
12. Hammond and Scull, 1995, 97, 98 and 109.
13. In *Fellowship*, Gandalf has two staffs. The first has a complex tip incorporating, among other things, a socket to hold his pipe. Saruman deprives him of that

staff during their fight. Presumably the Elves of Rivendell make him a new staff, which is the one he carries on the Quest and loses during the battle with the Balrog. (In my mental movie, Saruman does not dare take Gandalf's original staff, for fear of provoking him to defend himself in a fight during which one or both might be seriously injured.)

    14. *Empire* magazine listed the ten most memorable scenes in the film trilogy, and Gollum's schizophrenic conversation was placed at number one. See "The Classic Scenes," *Empire* 187 (Jan 2005): 134. On page 378 of the essay cited above, Shippey declares, "The Jackson handling of Gollum/Sméagol is masterful all through, with an especially good and original scene in which Sméagol argues with and exorcises his *alter ego* Gollum."

    15. "The Lord of the Rings: Return [sic] of the King," 62.

    16. Carpenter, ed., *Letters*, 110.

    17. OhioHobbit, "I have this strange obsession..." *TheOneRing.net* (March 6, 2007). On June 23, 2009, I started a thread, "Who invented "book-firster" and "film-firster"? on *TheOneRing.net*. Ataahua, a long-time moderator on the site's message boards, recalled them as being in use shortly before *Fellowship* came out, "mid-to-late 2001." Possibly they had originated in another fandom. See http://newboards.theonering.net/forum/gforum/perl/gforum.cgi?post=265624 (accessed July 6, 2010).

WORKS CITED

Carter, Humphrey. *The Letters of J.R.R. Tolkien,* Boston: Houghton Mifflin, 1981.
"The Classic Scenes," *Empire* 187 (January 2005).
Croft, Janet Brennan, ed. *Tolkien on Film: Essays on Peter Jackson's "The Lord of the Rings."* Altadena, CA: Mythopoeic, 2004.
Hammond, Wayne, and Christina Scull, *J.R.R. Tolkien: Artist and Illustrator.* Boston: Houghton Mifflin, 1995.
"The Lord of the Rings: Return of the King [sic]." *Creative Screenwriting* 11, no. 1 (January/February 2004).
OhioHobbit, "I have this Strange Obsession..." TheOnering.net (March 6, 2007) http://newboards.theonering.net/forum/gforum/perl/gforum.cgi?post=8061 (accessed December 28, 2009).
Osborne, Barrie, prod. Peter Jackson, Fran Walsh, Philippa Boyens, writers. *The Lord of the Rings: The Fellowship of the Ring.* New Line: DVD Special Extended Edition, 2002.
_____. *The Lord of the Rings: The Return of the King. (New Line: DVD Special Extended Edition, 2004).*
_____. *The Lord of the Rings: The Two Towers.* New Line: DVD Special Extended Edition, 2003.
Rotten Tomatoes, http://www.rottentomatoes.com/m/lord_of_the_rings_the_fellowship_of_the_ring/?critic=creamcrop; http://www.rottentomatoes.com/m/lord_of_the_rings_the_two_towers/?critic=creamcrop; http://www.rottentomatoes.com/m/lord_of_the_rings_the_return_of_the_king/?critic=creamcrop (accessed Dec. 27, 2009).
Shippey, Tom. "Another Road to Middle-earth: Jackson's Movie Trilogy." In *Roots and Branches: Selected Papers on Tolkien.* Zollikofen, Switzerland: Walking Tree, 2007.
TheOneRing.net (March 6, 2007). http://newboards.theonering.net/forum/gforum/perl/gforum.cgi?post=8061 (accessed December 28, 2009).

Thompson, Kristin. *The Frodo Franchise: "The Lord of the Rings" and Modern Hollywood*. Berkeley: University of California Press, 2007.
Tolkien, J.R.R. *The Lord of the Rings*. 50th Anniversary ed. Boston: Houghton Mifflin, 2004.
_____. *The Hobbit*, or *There and Back Again*. London: Unwin, 1981.
"Who Invented 'book-firster' and 'film-firster'"? TheOnering.net (June 23, 2010). http://newboards.theonering.net/forum/gforum/perl/gforum.cgi?post=265624 (accessed July 6, 2010).

Sometimes One Word Is Worth a Thousand Pictures

VERLYN FLIEGER

> *The radical distinction between all art (including drama) that offers a visible presentation and true literature is that it imposes one visible form. Literature works from mind to mind and is thus more pro-genitive. It is at once more universal and more poignantly particular. If it speaks of bread or wine or stone or tree, it appeals to the whole of these things, to their ideas; yet each hearer will give to them a peculiar personal embodiment in his imagination. Should the story say "he ate bread," the dramatic producer or painter can only show "a piece of bread" according to his taste or fancy, but the hearer of the story will think of bread in general and picture it in some form of his own. If a story says "he climbed a hill and saw a river in the valley below," the illustrator may catch, or nearly catch, his own vision of such a scene; but every hearer of the words will have his own picture, and it will be made of all the hills and rivers and dales he has ever seen, but especially out of The Hill, The River, The Valley which were for him he first embodiment of the word.*
>
> J.R.R. Tolkien, "On Fairy-stories"

Asked to comment on the prospect of a film version of *The Lord of the Rings*, Christopher Tolkien responded: "*The Lord Of The Rings* is peculiarly unsuitable to transformation into visual dramatic form." Christopher was reiterating what his father, J.R.R. Tolkien, had said at greater length and many years earlier in his essay "On Fairy-stories," from which my epigraph is taken. Discussing in particular the unsuitability of drama for presenting Fantasy, Tolkien declared that "Drama [and by extension film] is naturally hostile to Fantasy," his rationale being that "fantastic forms are not to be counterfeited." He gave an example: "In *Macbeth*, when it is read, I find the witches tolerable: they have a narrative function and some hint of dark significance," whereas "they are almost intolerable in the play" for this reason — "that the characters, and even the scenes, are in Drama not imagined but actually beheld — Drama is, even though it uses a similar material (words, verse, plot), an art fundamentally different from narrative art" (*Monsters and Critics*, 141–42I). Not everyone would agree with Tolkien. Some people prefer to "behold" the fantastic rather than to imagine it. The success of the Peter Jackson films has only fueled the debate, with proponents on either side vigorously defending each point of view and with equal vigor attacking the opposition.

I do not deny that there are arguments for and against "transformation into visual dramatic form." Sometimes it does work. Film can vividly translate pictorial elements such as landscape from evocative words to concrete pictures. Moreover, the visual nature of film is ideally suited in certain instances to get maximum impact from images without words. As a good scenic example I offer the landscapes of Jackson's Middle-earth as translated from New Zealand (though Jackson's Hobbiton unfortunately puts me in mind of the set for Teletubbies). And for an example of effective and moving image enhanced by the absence of words I suggest Boromir's magisterial funeral journey down the river, a sustained overhead long shot that is both dignified and poignant. Both examples, however, are more realistic than fantastic, and in general I agree with both JRRT and Christopher that a work like *The Lord of the Rings*, a story so reliant on the right word for its impact and one whose genesis, after all, was its author's invention of languages, is best left to word rather than picture.

The very pictographic opportunities of film, the ways in which photography can both enhance and manipulate reality, frequently tempt filmmakers to extend the visual beyond what the story needs simply because it is feasible to do so. The attitude seems to be that if it can be done it must be done — and all too often with computer-enhanced technology, done to death, resulting not infrequently in effect for the sake of effect rather than to support the story or the theme. The capacity for computer-generated fantasy actually results in a constraining literality. It would be well to remember that less is often more, and that the right word in the right place can be worth any number of computer-generated orcs.

Precisely because film as a medium emphasizes the visual over the verbal, because its job is to translate words into pictures, to present the viewer with a finished image rather than to allow the reader's imagination make what it will of a word, there are some effects that film cannot successfully pull off but which words can successfully create. I offer two small examples. In Fangorn Forest, Gandalf delivers a greeting from Galadriel to Gimli: "Lockbearer, wherever thou goest, my thought goes with thee. But have a care to lay thine axe to the right tree!" Gimli, desperately and uncharacteristically in love, is filled with joy at her message (*Towers*, III, v, 107), and Tolkien's word to describe his physical reaction is *capering*. Gimli, the dour and rugged Dwarf, "capers." Now caper is an odd word to use in conjunction with such a character. It connotes a kind of antic, almost childish agility, a quasi-dance. My *American Heritage Dictionary* defines caper as "a playful leap or hop; a skip," and the act of capering as "to leap or frisk about; frolic, gambol." The OED defines it as "a frolicsome leap, like that of a playful kid; a frisky movement, *esp.* in dancing; said also of horses: a fantastic proceeding or freak."

Try to picture Gimli capering. While Tolkien clearly meant his description of the stolid Dwarf gamboling to be humorous and to provoke a smile, the image thus created would be difficult to put on the screen without getting not a smile but the wrong kind of laugh. It is not just out of character for Gimli to frisk or gambol, doing so would be physically awkward, even clumsy. It would make him look not joyous but ridiculous. To depict onscreen the burly, bearded Dwarf frolicking like a lamb or a horse, an action kinetically unsuited to his stocky body, does violence to what we have been told of his character, his race, and his dignity. It is ludicrous. Yet the word on the page works, for the word can conjure Gimli's ecstatic joy in the reader's imagination without having to choreograph it. On the screen, however skillfully performed by an actor, it would be close to embarrassing.[1]

What Jackson chose to do instead was to play Gimli entirely for laughs and make him a figure of fun. This is easier to do than to create unexpected sympathy. And it's certainly possible that Jackson felt that some episodes, such as the increasingly somber passage in Moria, would benefit from a little comic relief ("nobody tosses a Dwarf") to contrast the growing seriousness of the plot and the darkening mood of others in the Fellowship. As a choice for a filmmaker with a heterogeneous audience to consider, this would certainly be an option. But it is an option that robs the moment from the book that I have described of much of its poignancy, making Gimli a less rounded character and reducing his personality to a stereotype. This is the approach typified by the caricature dwarfs in Walt Disney's *Snow White*, for whose films across the board Tolkien had "a heartfelt loathing" (*Letters* 17). The temptation to such stereotyping is great in a film which by its nature is severely limited in real time and relies more on the visual image and immediate response than on the imaginative mind of its audience.

Equally challenging, though in this case not comic, is Tolkien's description of Goldberry welcoming the hobbits at the door of Tom Bombadil's house:

> About her feet in wide vessels of green and brown earthenware, white water-lilies were floating, so that she seemed to be enthroned in the midst of a pool....
> Before [the hobbits] could say anything, she sprang lightly up and over the lily-bowls, and ran laughing towards them [*Fellowship* I, vii 121].

On the page this works just fine. The verbal picture is appealing, the river-daughter enthroned in a flower-filled pool. But try to work out the physics of her move from a sitting position over an obstacle course of water-filled pottery and you wind up with athleticism, not grace. Goldberry would have to be either a gymnast or an animated character with a cartoon drawing's capacity to transcend gravity. Instead we have the words "she sprang lightly up and over the lily-bowls." The words fuel the imagination, which then does all the work.

But these are minor instances. I propose to offer two major examples which capture the unsuitability of film to convey in pictures what words cannot just describe but create. The first is the episode in *The Fellowship of the Ring* featuring Tom Bombadil, an episode entirely omitted from the Jackson film. The filmmakers have offered their own rationales for this omission, noted and protested by fans of the book. Peter Jackson has been quoted as saying that he purposefully left Tom Bombadil out of the film because he felt that Tom's meeting with the traveling hobbits did not advance the story but rather held it up. For a director who held up endless minutes of screen time for the wholly unnecessary (to the plot) lurching of a computer-generated troll in Moria, this is, to say the least, disingenuous; and I suggest there is more to it than simply the consideration of narrative momentum.

Even on the page, Tom Bombadil comes dangerously close to whimsy, indeed to exactly the sort of thing that people who hate *The Lord of the Rings* hate about *The Lord of the Rings*. On his first appearance Tom is described as hopping, dancing, bounding, "stumping along," "charging though grass and rushes like a cow going down to drink" (*Fellowship* I, vi, 117). Smaller than a man, bigger than a Dwarf, charging like a cow, he is at once human-like and nonhuman, an imaginative hybrid, a crossover between worlds. Even in a story that includes hobbits, Dwarves, Elves, and walking trees, Tom as a character would be next to impossible to make visual without spilling over into buffoonery and downright silliness. Put on the screen, an actual actor engaged in hopping, dancing, and bounding would run the very dangerous risk of disrupting what Tolkien called Secondary Belief, the acceptance by the audience of the behavior of a Secondary World, for such actions would be difficult to enact without eliciting the wrong kind of laughs from the audience. Even Robin Williams would be hard put to play Tom straight without falling into parody.

If *The Lord of the Rings* had been translated into ballet using a stylized vocabulary of movement and pantomime, the hopping, dancing, bounding might conceivably have worked. But Tolkien is so stubbornly realistic in presenting the unreal — and Peter Jackson must perforce follow his lead — that a real actor charging like a cow, chanting in rhythm "leaping in the air" at news of Old Man Willow and speaking lines like "Don't you crush my lilies!" would come across as either camp or comic or both. Yet the words, if left to themselves, evoke precisely the kind of hurly-burly and noise that Tolkien needed to break the sleepy enchantment of the Withywindle Valley and the sinister spell of Old Man Willow

Jackson's avoidance of the problem by excising the whole episode, however, simply points up the larger issue of book versus film, the word versus the picture. Setting aside the fact that Tolkien obviously felt that the Tom Bombadil episode was important and the ancillary fact that as the author of the story he may have been striving for an effect other than "advancing the story" (part of his argument for *Beowulf* was that the poem was structured for balance rather than "steady advance"), it might still be useful to explore what Tom actually does for the story rather than what he doesn't do and wasn't intended to do, for he plays an essential role in embodying Tolkien's theme.

Tom's importance to the story, I submit, resides in theme rather than plot, for the fact is that Tom is there to do what no one else can do, which is to demonstrate to the audience by his actions just what the Ring does not do, which is to have its expected effect on him either visibly or psychologically. Tom is immune to the Ring and the Ring's power; he does not become invisible when he puts it on, nor does he fail to see Frodo (invisible to everyone else) when Frodo puts it on. This is not just a conjuring trick on Tolkien's part; the episode is there for a purpose — to underscore the relationship of the Ring to human nature and human psychology.

From the beginning of the story, whether in book form or film presentation, we have been told that the Ring not only *has* power, it *is* power, power in its most naked and explicit form. Conferring invisibility is the least of its effects. Its real power is to give its wearer power over other wills, with the concomitant, cumulative, and corrosive effect of eroding the willpower of whoever wears or carries it. The desire for power is usually seen as one of the unfortunate characteristics of human nature, hence Lord Acton's dictum that "power tends to corrupt, and absolute power corrupts absolutely." It is a theme in *Macbeth* and *Julius Caesar* and *All the King's Men* and *The Silmarillion*, and it is a major theme in *The Lord of the Rings* as well, evidenced by the steadily weakening struggle of the very human Frodo against the power of the Ring, and his final and complete surrender to it.

The Ring has no power over Tom because Tom is not human, and that is exactly Tolkien's point and exactly why Tom is essential to the theme, if not the plot, of the story. If Tom were the subject in a game of Twenty Questions, we would have to describe him as vegetable, for he is certainly not animal or mineral. Tom embodies vegetative nature. Tolkien described him in a letter as "the spirit of the (vanishing) Oxford and Berkshire countryside" (*Letters*, 26). A countryside does not desire power, nor do its constituent elements — hills, trees, grasses, flowers — though those who own or pretend to own these certainly do. It is precisely because Tom does not respond to the pull of the Ring that we as audience can see clearly what that pull is.

If Sauron the Dark Lord has an opposite number in *The Lord of the Rings*, that opposite number is neither Gandalf his spiritual nemesis nor Aragorn his political adversary. It is the non-spiritual, nonpolitical Tom Bombadil, whose blue eye peering through the circle of the Ring is the counterpart of and response to the Eye of Sauron. Tom is not Lord but Master and the distinction between the two words is central to Tolkien's intent. The one, from Anglo-Saxon *hlaford* from A-S *hláf*—bread, food, a loaf" — plus *weard*— a guard, warder, watchman" — is defined in Bosworth-Toller's *Anglo-Saxon Dictionary* as "a lord, dominus," expressing the relation of the head of a household to his dependants and implying domination, while the other, from Latin *magister*, "teacher," denotes help or guidance. The Withywindle Valley does not belong to Tom, as Goldberry is quick to tell Frodo, nor does he have power over it. "He is," she says, "as you have seen him" (*Fellowship* I, vii 134). Tom has no hidden agenda, no covert desire or plan of operation. He does not hide ambition behind rhetoric, like Saruman, or indulge in disinformation, like Wormtongue. What you see is what you get. Tom is one who guides but does not dominate, who has things to do — making and singing and walking and watching the country. "Tom has his house to mind," he tells the hobbits (*Fellowship* I, viii, 156), and his "house" is the countryside that Tolkien saw vanishing in his lifetime. With Tom out of the picture, all this is missing from Jackson's film. It is missing, I suggest, precisely because of the nature of film, a medium subject not just to the need for narrative momentum but to the constraints of real time (how many hours can you sit in a theatre before succumbing to fanny fatigue?) and the apparent freedom (which brings its own constraint) of a visual rather than a verbal medium.

And that brings me to my second major example, the mighty Ring itself. In the narrative, Tolkien takes care to clothe it in magic and mystery. In the chapter where it is introduced, "A Long-Expected Party," it remains out of sight while its effect is ratcheted up from Bilbo's initial reluctance to part with it to his suspicious possessiveness and paranoia to his unreasonable rage when he thinks Gandalf wants it. We never see it, but we see and feel its effect on

Bilbo. Our first view of it comes up a chapter later, in "The Shadow of the Past." As Frodo takes it from his breeches pocket it feels "suddenly very heavy, as if either it or Frodo himself was in some way reluctant for Gandalf to touch it" (*Fellowship* I, ii, 58). Receiving it out of the fire from Gandalf, Frodo notes that "it seemed to have become thicker and heavier than ever" and he sees "fine lines, finer than the finest pen-strokes running along the ring, outside and inside." They "*seem* [how often this word is used!] to form the letters of a flowing script ... piercingly bright, and yet remote as if out of a great depth" (59).

This passage is immediately followed by an inset of the ring inscription, pictured in Elvish script but in the language of Mordor. The difference in treatment between the Ring and the inscription is significant. The Ring itself is presented obliquely and by indirection, through Frodo's perception rather than by concrete description, whereas the inscription is described in detail, pictured, and then read aloud. Tolkien gives us words as pictures for the inscription, but no picture in words for the Ring itself. He saves that for later, after its effect has been fully established, when Frodo, challenged by Gandalf to damage the Ring, takes it out of his pocket and looks at it:

> It now appeared plain and smooth, without mark or device that he could see. The gold looked very fair and pure, and Frodo thought how rich and beautiful was its colour, how perfect was its roundness. It was an admirable thing, and altogether precious [70].

This is description, to be sure, but it is conveyed at secondhand, limited to one sensibility. It is Frodo's perception of the Ring that is described, not the Ring itself. It is Frodo, not the narrator, to whom the Ring appears *plain and smooth*, who sees it as *fair, pure, rich, perfect, admirable*.

Its next appearance is in the house of Tom Bombadil when Tom commands Frodo to "show [him] the precious Ring!" (*Fellowship* I. vii. 144). The phrase "a circle of gold" is the extent of its description, but the narrative focus is not on the Ring but on Tom's eye gleaming through the circle. Here again, Tolkien uses Frodo's perception to characterize what is after all a pretty ordinary-looking object:[2] "It was the same Ring, or looked the same and weighed the same; for that Ring had always seemed to Frodo to weigh strangely heavy in the hand" (*Fellowship* I, vii, 144).

We next see the Ring at the Council of Elrond, where the narrative does tell at least the reader that it "gleamed and flickered" as Frodo held it up to view, but then it immediately shifts attention to Boromir, whose eyes "glinted as he gazed at the golden thing" (*Fellowship* II, ii, 260). Again we have our attention deflected from the Ring to its effect, this time on the susceptible Boromir.

By directing attention *around* the Ring rather than *on* the Ring, Tolkien has created a vacancy which is immediately filled by the reader's own imagination. He has built up an *impression* which conveys more powerfully than could any picture the psychological attraction of what is after all a plain gold band with a rather lengthy inscription. Such indirection presents a problem for the filmmaker, forced by his medium to show the artifact itself, which however artfully photographed, cannot transcend its own physical limitations It is round, it is gold, it is (except in special circumstances) plain, and no amount of computer-generated glints and gleams can enhance its appearance beyond its corporeal nature. It is just a ring. Everything else about it is in the eye (or mind) of the beholder-possessor.

One is reminded of the Dashiell Hammett/John Huston Maltese falcon (also an artifact translated from book to film) sought so obsessively in the film of that name by Sidney Greenstreet, Peter Lorre and Mary Astor, that turns out when at last it appears on screen to be a shabby black bird around whom a complex mystique of human greed has been woven. It is, in the words of Sam Spade, "the stuff dreams are made of." Tolkien knew, none better, what stuff dreams are made of, and by not depicting the Ring, he enabled his readers to see it for themselves.

"Seeing for themselves" is clearly what Tolkien wanted his readers to do. It is the process he described in the epigraph at the head of this essay about visual presentation and the imposition of visible form as over against literature that works "from mind to mind." All who read the book will come away with their own private Gimli, Goldberry, Bombadil, Ring — mental pictures forged in the fire of our reading experience and produced by the perpetually renewed and renewable collaboration between the author's imagination and our own.

NOTES

1. There is only one actor I can think of—now, alas, long dead—who might have come close to saving Tom as a screen presence. This is Walter Huston, whose performance as the old prospector in John Huston's *The Treasure of Sierra Madre* (another tale about greed and the lure of gold) captures the ornery, acerbic, unsentimental tone that could keep Tom from slipping into whimsy and cuteness.

2. My daughter-in-law, who saw the film but did not read the book, remarked at the Ring's first appearance on film, "Is that what all the fuss is about? I could get something better at Target."

WORKS CITED

Bosworth, Joseph, and T. Northcote Toller. *An Anglo-Saxon Dictionary*. Oxford: Oxford University Press, 1980.
Tolkien, J.R.R. *The Fellowship of the Ring*. 2nd ed. Boston: Houghton Mifflin, 1965.
_____. "On Fairy-stories." In *The Monsters and the Critics and Other Essays*. Edited by Christopher Tolkien. London: George Allen & Unwin, 1983.

Two Kinds of Absence
Elision & Exclusion in Peter Jackson's The Lord of the Rings

JOHN D. RATELIFF

We don't know that they didn't go into the Old Forest. We don't know that they didn't meet Tom.... We just don't mention it. It's just left untold
    Scriptwriter Phillipa Boyens, "From Book to Script"[1]

I prefer to say it's not so much that they never happened, as that those parts of the story just aren't told in this film version.... [T]o the actors and director, meetings with such characters as Bombadil surely took place. We just don't meet them.... [T]hose characters could (and do, in one's imagination) easily live within the movie's vivid world.
        Interview with Fran Walsh and
        Philippa Boyens, by Bob Verini[2]

One of the most difficult decisions facing director Peter Jackson and his screenwriters Fran Walsh and Phillipa Boyens in adapting J.R.R. Tolkien's massive *The Lord of the Rings* to film form was "what to leave out." Even ten hours of screen time proved insufficient to convey all the story, setting, characters, and incidents in Tolkien's twelve hundred pages, as Tolkien himself had long before foreseen (see his 1957 letter regarding "the necessary reduction or selection of the scenes and events that are to be visually represented" for any film version of his story).[3]

Accordingly, Boyens and Walsh adopted a strategy whereby they maintain that scenes from the book which did not appear in the movie had nonetheless happened in the film world, simply taking place offstage or off-camera. This claim found strong support when the expanded edition/director's cut of each film was released on DVD roughly a year following the debut in theatres of the original, and invariably shorter, version (the "theatrical release"). In each case, new scenes were smoothly segued into the existing story, proving that absent scenes could easily be integrated into the whole, just as Boyens and Walsh had claimed.

One might therefore imagine that, given enough time and resources, Jackson and his crew might have included the whole of Tolkien's story into their film adaptation. However, closer consideration reveals that this cannot be the case. While some scenes could easily have happened off-screen — for example, the four hobbits passing through the Old Forest — others are excluded from the film world because their inclusion would contradict material already in the films, newly invented scenes or incidents added precisely to compensate for the omission of original material. For example, the hobbits cannot have gained their swords from the wight's barrow, as in the book, because in the film they are given them by Strider at Weathertop.

Thus we can see an intriguing tension between two categories of material appearing in Tolkien's book but not in Jackson's film: that which, by elision, could have taken place within the film world but is not actually shown on screen, and that which, by exclusion, could not have occurred because of the paradoxes this would incur. For my purposes here I will focus on a sequence of four closely linked absent scenes which fall into these two categories: the "conspiracy" at Crickhollow, the passage through the Old Forest, the encounter(s) with Tom Bombadil, and the Hobbits' capture by the barrow-wight.

Prior Treatments

> *So, you know, what does Old Man Willow contribute to the story of Frodo carrying the Ring? What does Tom Bombadil ultimately really have to do with the Ring? I know there's ring stuff in the Bombadil episode, but it's not really advancing our story & it's not really telling us things that we need to know.*
> — Peter Jackson, "From Book to Script"[4]

Rather than examining in isolation the decisions reached by Jackson's team, it's illuminating to compare his treatment of these points with those of other (mostly earlier) adaptors of Tolkien's story. To date there have been eight such adaptations, including Jackson's: three audio/radio plays, four film scripts (two produced, two unproduced), and one full-scale stage play.[5] In chronological order, here is a quick survey of whether each included the Bombadil/Barrow-downs material (indicated by Yes or No) and how each treated this portion of Tolkien's book.

Terence Tiller's Radio Play for the BBC (1955–56): YES

Coming as it did shortly after the book's publication (1954–55), Tiller's production testifies to the immediate impact of *The Lord of the Rings* and the early interest in adapting it to other media. While no recording is known to survive, we do know that despite its relative brevity (twelve half-hour episodes, the first six devoted to *The Fellowship of the Rings* and the final six to *The Two Towers* and *The Return of the King* together) this version did include both Tom and Old Man Willow, since Tolkien expressed dismay over how the two were presented and in particular over its depiction of Goldberry as Tom's daughter rather than his wife (*Letters* 228).

Morton Zimmerman's Unproduced Script (1957): YES

Another relic of the initial enthusiasm for Tolkien's book, this time from American science fiction fans, this first film treatment tried to compress practically everything from the book into a single 55-page synopsis, resulting in a hectic, helter-skelter breakneck pace. The four hobbits no sooner reach Crickhollow than Fatty Bolger rushes out to warn them of danger, only to be ridden down and killed by a Black Rider (the first they have encountered). Fleeing into the forest, they are captured by the Old Willow and freed by Tom, who promptly escorts them across the Barrow-downs, on the way passing a waterfall from behind which Goldberry waves (her sole appearance). Frodo is dragged screaming into a barrow, and after his rescue they arm themselves with grave-goods before proceeding onward to reach the road — all apparently taking place in the course of a single day![6] Tolkien thought the resulting "compression" only made for "over-crowding and confusion" and stated that he would have preferred "abridgement" (*Letters* 261).

John Boorman's Unproduced Script (circa 1970): NO

Brilliant but bizarre, this second film script stands alone, owing nothing to the earlier Zimmerman effort and having no discernable influence on the Beagle/Bakshi effort that followed. Boorman clearly saw his audience not as those who read the books over and over again but instead took as his constituency the hippy/drug culture that embraced the hobbits as "pipeweed"-smoking counterculture heroes (I'm certain, for example, that unlike Boorman

Tolkien never thought of Sauron as looking like Mick Jagger). As part of its general air of surreal loopiness, Boorman drops virtually all the recognizable encounters between Hobbiton and the Ford, including even the Inn at Bree, in favor of new scenes such as the hobbits getting high on mushrooms or being chased through a hayfield by human farmers with scythes. The Old Forest does appear, but it is so entirely transformed that in Boorman's version the trees help the hobbits escape their sinister pursuer. Neither Bombadil nor the barrow makes an appearance, the latter's wight being more or less replaced by another Nazgûl attack from which they are rescued not by Tom but by the sudden advent of Strider.[7] All in all, given that Boorman's story resembles the spirit of Barbara Remington's covers to the Ballantine paperbacks and *Bored of the Rings* more than it does Tolkien's work, it's perhaps fortunate that we're spared the mini–Woodstock that his Bombadil and Goldberry would no doubt have become.

Peter S. Beagle/Ralph Bakshi Production (1978): NO, BUT...

This, the best-known of all adaptations predating Jackson's, completely omits any mention of Crickhollow, the Old Forest, Tom and Goldberry, or the Barrow-downs, skipping from a brief "conspiracy unmasked" discussion on the open road following the first encounter with the Black Rider to the four hobbits' arrival in Bree, with only a brief exchange of dialogue ("Will we be stopping at Bree tonight, Mr. Frodo?" "I think so, Sam...")[8] to bridge the gap. However, I think it interesting to note that the original script for this film, by Chris Conklin (1976), *does* include the Old Forest (though there is no Willow-Man). Here the Withywindle Valley is combined with the Barrow-downs (!) and the hobbits are overtaken by fog and captured by the wight while still in the forest. They meet Tom only when he happens to pass by the barrow, hears their cries for help, and rescues them; as with the Zimmerman effort two decades before, Goldberry puts in only a brief smile and a wave from the distance. Unfortunately, all this disappears in Beagle's rewrite (jointly credited to Conklin and Beagle and dated May 3, 1977) and the final script (February 14, 1978; rev. September 21, 1978), which is largely Beagle's work.

These deletions have exercised a disproportionate influence because the Bakshi film, for all its obvious shortcomings (it was after all, universally derided by Tolkien fans both upon release and for years thereafter and did so badly at the box office that the accompanying film that would have finished the story was never made, while the VHS quickly went out of print and the film remained unavailable for years before being rereleased on DVD in the run-up to Jackson's releases) was the best-known adaptation before Jackson's, and the one seen by the largest number of people. It was also, incidentally, Peter Jackson's first exposure to Tolkien's story (he saw this film as a teenager before he'd read the books). Therefore its omission of this block of chapters was seen retroactively as providing a precedent for Jackson's similar deletions.

Bernard Mayes' Mind's Eye Theatre Radio Adaptation (1979): YES

Coming fast on the heels of the same cast's adaptation of *The Hobbit* (1979, six hour-length episodes)— the best adaptation of that story to date[9]— this version's relatively faithful script was badly undercut by uneven performances by its cast (the best among them being holdovers from their earlier *Hobbit* shuffled into new roles). Originally broadcast on National Public Radio, it was later widely circulated in wooden boxed sets of twelve one-hour cassettes (and, later, nine CDs). If the Bakshi film may be said to have had a mediocre script savaged by inept animation, in the Mind's Eye adaptation we have a good script badly let down by some of its voice actors. While the actors playing Bilbo, Gandalf, and Aragorn turn in fine work, Frodo is uneven and many of the other performances (such as Sam's belabored falsetto) so eccentric that it's sometimes difficult to make out what they're saying. And, in the end, just as an animated film is seriously handicapped if its actual animation is of poor quality, so a radio play suffers grievously from poor performances by its vocal talent. Significantly, as the most faithful adaptation so far of Tolkien's tale and one that takes pains to retain as much of Tolkien's own wording as possible, this version does retain the Bombadil scenes and the Barrow-down sequence. Unfortunately, the performance of Bombadil is one of the worst in the entire radio play, being strongly reminiscent of a bad impression of a village idiot. Even more regrettably, this would mark Tom's last appearance in any of the major adaptations of the story.

Brian Sibley's BBC Radio Adaptation (1981): NO, BUT...

This widely regarded radio adaptation, originally broadcast in twenty-six half-hour episodes but later reedited into thirteen hour-long episodes, remains the most lengthy adaptation to date, running slightly longer than either its American rival from Mind's Eye (about twelve hours) or the combined expanded editions of the three Jackson films (about eleven and a half hours).

As with the other radio play, Sibley's script is considerably more faithful than any movie adaptation — which makes it rather surprising that this adaptation in its original form omits any mention of Bombadil but moves directly from the four hobbits' departure from Crickhollow to their arrival in Bree. In fact, so short is their journey that they strike up a song upon mounting up at Crickhollow and reach Bree before they finish singing it ("oh, that's Bree up ahead"). As with a similar omission of much the same material from the Bakshi film, Sibley's deletion of the whole Old Forest–Bombadil–Barrow-downs sequence has been used by some as providing not just a precedent but also a justification for Jackson's omissions.

Of particular interest is the fact that a dozen years later Sibley went back and dramatized the missing Bombadil scenes as part of the BBC's *Tales from the Perilous Realm* (1993), a collection of audioplays based on several of Tolkien's shorter stories.[10] Despite the title, "The Adventures of Tom Bombadil" in this collection is not an adaptation of the poem of the same name nor of the book of poems of that title but is rather the missing chapters of *The Fellowship of the Rings* presented as a short stand-alone play. Although cast with different voice actors, it in essence forms a "missing episode" that could easily be inserted into the existing radio play at the appropriate place. In other words, Sibley retroactively decided to treat the Bombadil chapters as a case of what I am calling elision rather than exclusion. The ease with which he was able to later provide the missing episode in the style of the original offers a strong example in favor of Boyens' point about omitted material fitting seamlessly into the existing production.

Peter Jackson Film (2001): NO

We will take a closer look at Jackson's treatment of the Bombadil chapters in the next section. For now it is enough to point out that, prior to his project, an equal number of earlier treatments had embraced and dramatized the Bombadil material (Tiller, Zimmerman, Mind's Eye) as had rejected and omitted it (Boorman, Bakshi, Sibley). Matters were complicated slightly by Sibley's later adaptation of those chapters as a possible indication of second thoughts on his part, suggesting that his earlier omission was purely for reasons of space, and by Bakshi's project having also included these characters at one stage). There is no sign that Jackson and his scriptwriters benefited by consulting the (superior, more faithful) radio scripts; but he was influenced at specific points by all three previous film treatments, especially by the Beagle/Bakshi animated movie, which was after all the best-known of all the earlier efforts and was the (low) standard against which his live-action films would be judged. And of course that earlier film had been among those adaptations that omitted these chapters.

Jackson's own justification for omitting Bombadil is that "the plot of ... our movie in its most simple form is Frodo carrying the Ring."[11] From this point of view, anything that falls outside Frodo's story as Ringbearer dilutes the focus of the film and thus could been considered extraneous. It's only fair to note, however, that if Frodo and the Ring are the main focus of Jackson's trilogy, Jackson devotes much more space than Tolkien's original to building up the secondary plot of Aragorn and Arwen's love story. Bombadil and other omitted material can be said to have been deleted more to make room for such new scenes than because there wasn't enough time to tell the whole story. That is, it was not entirely time pressure that led to the elisions and exclusions that distinguish Jackson's story from Tolkien's but deliberate choice on the filmmaker's part.

Shaun McKenna's London Stage Play (2006/2007): NO

Finally, we might make mention of the one major post–Jackson adaptation: the elaborate musical staged first in Toronto (2006) and then in London (2007–08) which attempted to tell the story of the entire *The Lord of the Rings* in just a little over three hours. Given the severe compression required to try to present such a complex story within such a brief span — in the London version Rohan and Gondor were blended into a single "Kingdom of Men" because there was no time for the Fellowship to visit both — it's no surprise that no hint of Bombadil made its way into this production, although again some space is devoted to the Arwen-Aragorn love story, demonstrating that Jackson's version is now exerting influence of its own on later adaptations.

To conclude, two observations suggest themselves from this survey of the eight major adaptations of Tolkien's story. First, the radio adaptations were on the whole more faithful to Tolkien's original than the film adaptations. This was partly no doubt because of medium — it's easier to describe unusual creatures, strange places, and magical events than to show or stage them (which is one of the reasons for Tolkien's disdain for stage plays). But probably it is due more to the audio adaptations being under somewhat less time pressure; even the Tiller ran for six hours, or roughly double what Boorman or McKenna had to work with. Second, the early adaptations were more inclined to include the Willow Man–Bombadil–Barrow-down sequence than those that came later: three of the first five included Bombadil in some form, while none have done so for the last three decades.[12] Here the major deciding factor is probably the influence by negative example of Sibley and Bakshi, both of whom excluded it.

The Omitted Elements

Having quickly looked at various adaptors' treatment of the Bombadil section in order to place Jackson's decisions in context, it's now time to focus on Jackson's own adaptation, and specifically on just how much Jackson omitted and how he dealt with the subsequent problems created by the deletion of such a large hunk from such a tightly woven story. In short, what effect do his omissions of these scenes have on his movie as a whole? And to what extent do his scriptwriters' claims to have created a film into which these missing scenes could be inserted hold up under scrutiny?

First, it should be pointed out that the Jackson/Boyens/Walsh omissions here are larger in scope than at first appears. It is not just the chapter devoted to Bombadil that has vanished (*The Fellowship of the Ring*, Chapter VII: "In the House of Tom Bombadil"), but the one preceding it (Chapter VI: "The Old Forest") and the one following (Chapter VIII: "Fog on the Barrow-Downs"), as well as the whole of the Crickhollow chapter preceding these three (Chapter V: "A Conspiracy Unmasked"). Furthermore, the two chapters that come before this block (Chapter III: "Three Is Company" and Chapter IV: "A Short Cut to Mushrooms") have been severely cut down to a highly effective montage of walking scenes (just as Tolkien had long ago suggested in another context; see note 3), bringing the total of chapters deleted or heavily abridged to six out of a total of twenty-two, or more than a quarter of the first volume. Replacing all of this is a relatively brief sequence of Frodo and Sam in the cornfield, Frodo and Sam meeting Merry and Pippin, the first encounter with the Black Rider, and the escape to Bucklebury Ferry. In the expanded edition of Jackson's film, which also adds a brief encounter with the Elves (where a sighting of Wood-Elves replaces the hobbits' rescue by, travel alongside, and conversation with Gildor and his people), all of this is compressed into about thirteen and a half minutes, of which a third is devoted to Gandalf and Saruman.[13]

Second, and equally important, we must acknowledge that Jackson and his writers do not simply skip over major parts of the story but instead employ a variety of strategies for dealing with material being left out of the film and the subsequent gaps this created in the story. In fact, it is the consequences of some of these solutions that call into question their claim that absent scenes could still have taken place. In the rest of this section we will examine the four major scenes that disappeared when this four-chapter block was omitted, identifying whether each could easily be part of the film world we just happen not to be shown (elided) or could not be part of the film world because that would create contradictions or paradoxes in the existing film (excluded). In some cases fragments from these absent scenes appear elsewhere in the film, transformed or displaced; these too will be noted when relevant. In addition, I offer a brief evaluation of that scene's importance and the impact its absence has upon the story as a whole — that is, whether its omission creates a significant divergence between Tolkien's story and the film's world.

Crickhollow (EXCLUDED)

This entire chapter represents a scene that could not take place within the world of Jackson's movie. Frodo's careful plan in the book for a gradual, unobtrusive withdrawal from the Shire is replaced by his throwing a few clothes and snacks in a bag and leaving at once upon hearing Gandalf's news. Hence Merry's equally careful conspiracy to help him must fall by the wayside, replaced instead by a chance meeting in Farmer Maggot's fields.

In addition, as a more subtle shift, the exclusion of the whole "Conspiracy Unmasked" episode required a transformation of Merry's character. The careful planner of the book who always looks ahead and prepares for contingencies[14] is replaced by an observant quick thinker: within seconds of learning that Frodo needs to leave the Shire, he's already thought of the best way, via Bucklebury Ferry. Similarly, near the end of the first film it is Merry, not Sam or Strider, who notices that Frodo is missing ("The Breaking of the Fellowship"). And when he and Pippin find Frodo amid the orc-raid it takes only a few wordless seconds for Merry to grasp Frodo's plan to leave the Fellowship and comes up with a (self-sacrificing) distraction to help him slip away.

The Old Forest (ELIDED)

This chapter forms the best example in support of Boyens' claim. Although we have no evidence that they did, so far as we know the hobbits could well have wandered into the Old Forest at some point between their escape from the Black Rider and their arrival in Bree, without any of it being shown in the film.[15] And in this context, it may be significant that on the map of Middle-earth shown somewhat earlier in the film Buckland, the Old Forest, and the Barrow-downs all appear, although none are labeled, proving that they do at least exist in the film's version of Middle-earth.[16]

By contrast, we can say with confidence that the scene with Old Man

Willow did *not* happen, because in the film that encounter takes place elsewhere and much later in the story, as part of the Fangorn Forest story line in the expanded edition of *The Two Towers*. Boyens specifically discusses moving the Old Man Willow scene to the second movie and giving Tom's lines to Treebeard.[17] It therefore follows that even if the film's hobbits did enter the Old Forest (for which we have no evidence one way or the other), their passage through it lacked the most iconic encounter from that chapter.

Tom and Goldberry (ELIDED)

As with the Old Forest, the encounter with Tom Bombadil falls into the realm of something that could have happened in the film world but, if it did, left no trace behind in the parts of the movie we do see. We have the example of Sibley to show that such an extended episode could exist outside the original production, and we have Jackson's expanded editions to show how many extra scenes could be added into his theatrical releases, to the great improvement of his films overall. But against this we must counter that out of no fewer than forty new and over sixty extended scenes in the expanded editions of the film trilogy there was still, in Jackson's judgment, no room for Tom in his films, indicating how nonessential he felt this character to be to the story as a whole. Furthermore, if Boyens is right and such scenes did occur for the four hobbits ("we just don't meet them"), we have to take into account clear evidence that Bombadil's absent scenes would not be quite the same as what appears in the book. We already know that Bombadil did not save the hobbits from Old Man Willow, since that role is reassigned to Treebeard in the film. And, to anticipate a bit, it is highly probable that in the film world Frodo and his friends did not encounter the barrow-wight (see the next section) and thus Tom would not have saved them from that peril either. Therefore the posited off stage encounter with Bombadil is shrunken in significance by having its links to other scenes cut. There is something of a catch-22 at work here: filling the gaps left by omitted scenes means that those absent scenes become detached from the whole, negating (or at least diminishing) their impact on the story. Thus, stripping Tom of part of his narrative function (the two rescues) makes it easier to argue that the self-contained bubble that remains is without relevance to the story being told.

This is a great pity, because of all the omitted material in *The Fellowship of the Ring*, the hobbits' time with Bombadil is the most important, as suggested by the fact that Boyens, Jackson, and Christopher Lee all feel obliged to comment upon its absence and defend the decision not to include him within the film.[18] As we have seen, Jackson essentially argues that Bombadil doesn't play a decisive role in helping Frodo carry and ultimately destroy the Ring. Tolkien himself, by contrast, felt that Bombadil was of great importance for precisely that reason, because "he represents certain things otherwise left out" (*Letters* 192). That is, he embodies a point of view Tolkien felt needed to be included, one bigger than the whole Quest of the Ring upon which the narrative is otherwise focused ("the Power of the Ring ... is not the whole picture,"; *Letters* 192). This larger perspective is elsewhere hinted at twice: in the "Star over Mordor" scene, in which Sam suddenly realizes that "in the end the Shadow was only a small and passing thing" (*The Return of the King*, Book VI, Chapter II: "The Land of Shadow," page 199) and in Gandalf's words to Denethor: "I shall not wholly fail ... if anything passes through this night that can still grow fair or bear fruit and flower again" (*The Return of the King*, Book V, Chapter I: "Minas Tirith," pages 30–31). Throughout *The Lord of the Rings* Tolkien is not just telling an exciting story but introducing the reader to Middle-earth itself as a character, and in the Bombadil chapters this literally becomes the case, for Tom is a *genus loci* ("the spirit of the ... countryside," *Letters* 26), or earth-spirit of a specific locale, just as Goldberry is a nymph ("river-daughter") of a particular river (either the Withywindle or one of its tributaries). As such, he has no interest in playing Sauron's game. For Sauron, everything is about power. By engaging him on his own terms both Denethor and Saruman are crushed, like lesser players with too few pieces inexorably checkmated by a master. Gandalf evades a similar feat by deciding to play by his own rules, as it were — opting to destroy the Ring rather than bringing it into play. But Bombadil is outside the game altogether; in a sense the Ring has no power over him because he's more real than it is.

All this, of course, would be difficult to convey in a film performance, if the prior adaptations by Tiller and Zimmerman and Mayes (and Sibley) are any guide, focusing as they do on Tom's merry antics rather than on the subtlety of the point Tolkien is making. I believe that, perhaps without intending it, Jackson did find an acceptable substitute in the many shots of New Zealand landscape he included in his film, from sweeping panoramas of snow-topped mountains to the aforementioned montage of woodland scenes in the Shire — a natural world full of beauty, vulnerable to the spreading taint from Mordor, and, in Sam's words, "worth fighting for."[19]

The Barrow-Wight (EXCLUDED)

In the journey over the Barrow-downs we have another absent but possible scene, like that in the Old Forest. But as with that earlier scene, the missing scene in the movie could not have followed that in the book at all closely because its most iconic encounter, that with the Barrow-wight, could *not* have happened. The proof of this is that the swords the four hobbits gain from the barrow in the book are instead worked in elsewhere in the movie, where Aragorn hands them out just before the fight with the Ringwraiths on Weathertop.[20] This latter inserted scene raises the rather awkward question as to why Aragorn should happen to be carrying four hobbit-sized swords. Even if we assume Aragorn had been on the lookout for Frodo and Sam in Bree at Gandalf's request, there is no way he could have known Merry and Pippin would have joined them, since in the film this is a chance encounter neither Gandalf nor anyone else could have foreseen. As it stands, the inserted scene does achieve its basic goal of arming the hobbits just in time for their first combat, but in such a way that it stands as an anomaly within the film (along the lines of, how did Gandalf regain his staff after escaping from Saruman?). It is a pity that Jackson did not bring to life the scene in the barrow, which would seem tailor-made for his talents; it's easy to picture the wight in terms of *The Frighteners'* grim reaper. As it is, unless greatly transformed by the addition of new material not in the book, the absent scene can perhaps best be imagined as a few glimpses of the hobbits passing among old standing stones littering a bleak landscape.

Conclusion: What Isn't There

In the end, we see that, while a comforting thought, the Jackson-Boyens-Walsh claim is ultimately of limited applicability. Certainly many minor scenes from the books could have occurred between the scenes shown in the films, and Jackson did a brilliant job of enriching his film by the inclusion of many such moments within the expanded editions of his trilogy. As a general explanation of the major cuts, such as the Old Forest–Bombadil–Barrow-downs sequence, however, it falters for the simple reason that Tolkien's story is too tightly woven and interlinked for whole episodes to be removed without consequences down the line. As Tolkien himself said, in the course of writing the book he incurred "narrative debts" (*Letters* 258), and the same proves true of Jackson's films. I have argued elsewhere[21] that, in such a closely woven web and interconnected story, deleting or changing even a small detail in one place has an impact elsewhere that can rarely be ignored. And when the deletion is of a whole scene or encounter, it has a cascading effect, as Jackson and his team discovered. Jackson wisely pulled back from most of his major departures from Tolkien's original story, sometimes even after he'd shot the scene in question — e.g., deciding not to have Arwen, Warrior Princess, fight at the Battle of Helm's Deep (a reversal executed at the cost of reducing her to a sort of Lady of Shallot languishing for most of the final two films) or transforming Aragorn's duel with Sauron before the Black Gate (which would have served as a bookend to the first film's opening scene of Sauron versus Elendil and Isildur) into a simple fight with a troll. Given those examples, the omission of the Bombadil scenes becomes relatively minor in perspective: regrettable, but hardly tragic. In the end, the absence of Tom Bombadil from Jackson's film might simply be an indication that just as there are some things film does better than prose, so too there are things prose does better than film, and portraying Tom Bombadil is one of them.

NOTES

1. Phillipa Boyens, "From Book to Script," in *The Fellowship of the Ring* DVD, Extended Edition, disk three: The Appendices. This comment occurs at the 11.20 minute mark.

2. Bob Verini, "Hobbit-Forming: Adapting *The Lord of the Rings*," interview with Fran Walsh and Philippa Boyens. *Scr(i)pt* 7, no. 6 (November/December 2001), 62. In this particular excerpt, the words within quotation marks are those of Boyens, with the bridging passages being paraphrased by Verini.

3. Tolkien's comment comes in his discussion of the Zimmerman script; see *Letters of J.R.R. Tolkien* 272. As an example of the sort of selection or reduction he meant, Tolkien considered the Fellowship's journey south from Rivendell to Moria a good candidate for abbreviation in the form of a montage: "It is well within the powers of pictures to suggest, relatively briefly, a long and arduous journey, *in secrecy*, on foot, with the three ominous mountains getting nearer" (*Letters* 274–275). We might note that Tolkien's proposed montage would have collapsed the greater part of two chapters (roughly two dozen pages) from the book, as opposed to the four chapters totaling some fifty pages deleted by Jackson's removal of the whole Crickhollow–Old Forest–Bombadil–Barrow-downs sequence.

4. Peter Jackson, "From Book to Script," in *The Fellowship of the Ring* DVD, Extended Edition, disk three: The Appendices. This comment occurs at the 11.04 minute mark.

5. This does not count the many minor or local stagings of Tolkien's story, primarily of *The Hobbit* but sometimes of all or part of *The Lord of the Rings* as well, which occur with fair frequency but leave little record behind.

6. The original Zimmerman script, with Tolkien's annotations, is now at Marquette University. For Tolkien's comments on Bombadil's role in this adaptation, see *Letters* 267 and 272.

7. Like the Zimmerman script, a copy of the Boorman script is now part of the Tolkien Collection at Marquette. For more on this little-known version, see Janet Croft's "Three Rings for Hollywood" (2004).

8. This exchange takes place starting at about the 11.55 minute mark in the film.

9. The other major adaptations of *The Hobbit* are the eight-part (four-hour) BBC radio play adapted by Michael Kilgariff (broadcast in 1968 but not released until 1988 as a four-cassette set), best known for its rather supercilious Gandalf; Rob Inglis' one man show; Nicol Williamson's tour-de-force reading (1974, unfortunately

abridged onto a four-album set and now long out of print); and the 1977 Rankin-Bass cartoon, which combined superior voice talent (John Huston as Gandalf, Hans Conried — best known from his work on the *Bullwinkle* show — as Thorin, and Richard Boone (his last performance) as Smaug), with a slightly facetious script and deliberately weird animation (though still superior to Bakshi's). A two-part live-action film produced by Peter Jackson is currently in the works.

    10. In addition to the Bombadil episode, the other contents that make up the BBC's *Tales from the Perilous Realms* are *Farmer Giles of Ham,* "Leaf by Niggle," and *Smith of Wootton Major.*

    11. For Jackson's remark, see "From Book to Script," in *The Fellowship of the Ring* DVD, Extended Edition, disk three: The Appendices. This comment occurs at the 10.55 minute mark, just before the passage quoted in note 4 above.

    12. Aside, that is, from the self-contained stand-alone episode by Sibley included in *Tales from the Perilous Realm,* which occupies an anomalous position, and the Bombadil section in the original Conklin screenplay for Bakshi's movie, which was removed in the course of Beagle's rewrites.

    13. The departure from Hobbiton takes place at the 43.45 minute mark, and their arrival in Bree at the 57.24 mark. Of this roughly thirteen and a half minutes, four and a half (46.38 to 51.15) is devoted to Gandalf and Saruman, a scene told later in flashback in the book (*The Fellowship of the Ring,* Book II, chapter 2, "The Council of Elrond") being brought forward in the movie into its chronological place. That leaves a bit over nine minutes for all the rest: their vision of the Elves' passing (45.10), Sam's sense of leaving home behind (51.18), their being joined by Merry and Pippin (51.50), the advent of the Black Rider (53.05), and their nighttime flight through the woods to the Ferry (55.07 to 57.23).

    14. After Merry and Pippin find themselves free but hundreds of miles, they think, from their friends after escaping the Uruk-hai, it is Merry who turns out to have studied maps back in Rivendell (*The Two Towers* Book III, 62) and thus has a good idea of where they are and where they should be going.

    15. It might even be possible to argue that the brief scene of them making their way among a tangle of trees at night immediately after the first encounter on the road is a displaced and much-transformed version of their journey through the Old Forest, moved forward a bit in the story so that it comes before the Bucklebury Ferry, not after it. If such should be the case, Jackson may perhaps have been influenced here by Zimmerman's version of events, in which the Hobbits plunge into the Old Forest under immediate pursuit by the Black Rider.

    16. For the best view of this portion of the map within the film, see the 7.46 minute mark of the extended edition of *The Fellowship of the Ring.* This same map appears on the inside left gatefold of the packaging holding the DVDs. Buckland and the Old Forest *are* labeled on a second map of Middle-earth created in connection with the films which appears as a front endpaper in ancillary film tie-in books such as Chris Smith's "*The Lord of the Rings": Weaponry and Warfare* (2003) and Brian Sibley's "*The Lord of the Rings" Official Movie Guide* (2001); the Barrow-downs, although clear to see on the map, remain unlabelled. The Bucklebury Ferry, unfortunately, does not appear on either of these maps. In fact, the route of Frodo's journey marked on the gatefold map shows him crossing the river by way of the Brandywine Bridge instead, though this is probably no more than a minor glitch on the mapmaker's part.

    17. Boyens' remark comes in a second documentary, "From Book to Script: Finishing the Story" (*The Two Towers,* extended edition, disk three: The Appendices),

68   I. Techniques of Story and Structure

beginning at the 7.52 mark. For Treebeard's charm to Old Man Willow — "Away with you! You should not be waking. Eat earth, dig deep. Drink water, go to sleep. Away with you!" (contrast Bombadil's words in *The Fellowship of the Ring*, Book I, chapter 6, "The Old Forest," 131) — see *The Two Towers*, extended edition. This brief scene can be found on disk one, starting at the 1 hr. 10.15 mark and running to the 11.04 mark, or about fifty seconds in all.

   18. Lee's comment comes in "From Book to Script" (*The Fellowship of the Ring*, extended edition. Disk Three: The Appendices), between the 10.47 and 10.55 marks.
   19. See *The Two Towers*, extended edition. Sam's words occur on disk two at the 1 hr. 37 minute mark.
   20. Hobbits gaining their swords in the movie world: in the extended edition of *The Fellowship of the Ring*, this occurs on disk one at the 1 hr. 10.55 minute mark.
   21. "A Kind of Elvish Craft: J.R.R. Tolkien as Literary Craftsman," *Tolkien Studies* 6 (2009). This essay was originally delivered as the 2007 Blackwelder Memorial Lecture at Marquette University on October 4, 2007.

WORKS CITED

Boorman, John, and Rospo Pallenberg. *J.R.R. Tolkien's "The Lord of the Rings."* Screenplay, unproduced film script c.1970. Marquette University Archives, Milwaukee. Tolkien Collection, Series 8, Box 2, Folder 1.
Conklin, Chris. *The Lord of the Rings, Part One: The Fellowship*. Unproduced film script. September 21, 1976. Marquette University Archives, Milwaukee. Tolkien Collection, Series 8, Box 2, Folder 2.
Croft, Janet Brennan. "Three Rings for Hollywood: Scripts for *The Lord of the Rings* by Zimmerman, Boorman, and Beagle." In *Fantasy Fiction into Film: Essays*. Edited by Leslie Stratyner and James R. Keller. Jefferson, NC: McFarland, 2007. Also available online at http://faculty-staff.ou.edu/C/Janet.B.Croft-1/three_rings_for_hollywood.htm (accessed May 22, 2009).
The Frighteners. Directed by Peter Jackson. Universal Pictures, 1996.
"From Book to Script: Finishing the Story" (documentary). *The Lord of the Rings: The Two Towers*. DVD set, disk three.
"From Book to Script" (documentary). *The Lord of the Rings: The Fellowship of the Ring*. DVD set, disk three.
Jackson, Peter, dir. *The Lord of the Rings: The Fellowship of the Ring*. New Line Cinema. Theatrical Release, 2001; Extended Edition, 2002. DVD.
_____. *The Lord of the Rings: The Return of the King*. New Line Cinema. Theatrical Release, 2003; Extended Edition, 2004. DVD.
_____. *The Lord of the Rings: The Two Towers*. New Line Cinema. Theatrical Release, 2002; Extended Edition, 2003. DVD.
Mayes, Bernard, adptr. *The Lord of the Rings*. Audio play. Petaluma, CA: The Mind's Eye, 1979. Boxed set, twelve cassettes.
McKenna, Shaun, with Matthew Warchus, adptrs. *The Lord of the Rings*. Original London Production. London stage musical, with music by A.R. Rahman. Kevin Wallace Music, 2007. CD.
Rateliff, John D. "'A Kind of Elvish Craft': Tolkien as Literary Craftsman." *Tolkien Studies* 6. Morgantown: University of West Virginia Press, 2009.
Russell, Gary. *"The Lord of the Rings": The Official Stage Companion*. London: HarperCollins, 2007.

Sibley, Brian, and Michael Bakewell, adptrs. *The Lord of the Rings*. Radio play. London: BBC Radio, 1981. Boxed set, thirteen cassettes
Sibley, Brian, adptr. "The Adventures of Tom Bombadil." Radio play, part of *Tales from the Perilous Realms*. London: BBC Radio, 1993. Two-cassette set.
Sibley, Brian. *"The Lord of the Rings": Official Movie Guide*. London: HarperCollins, 2001.
Smith, Chris. *"The Lord of the Rings": Weaponry and Warfare*. London: HarperCollins, 2003.
Tolkien, J.R.R. *The Letters of J.R.R. Tolkien*. Selected and edited by Humphrey Carpenter, with the assistance of Christopher Tolkien. Boston: Houghton Mifflin, 1981.
_____. *The Lord of the Rings*, Vol. I: *The Fellowship of the Ring*. 2nd ed.. Boston: Houghton Mifflin, 1965.
_____. *The Lord of the Rings*, Vol. III: *The Return of the King*. 2nd ed. Boston: Houghton Mifflin, 1965.
_____. *The Lord of the Rings*, Vol. II: *The Two Towers*. 2nd ed. Boston: Houghton Mifflin, 1965.
Verini, Bob. "Hobbit-Forming: Adapting *The Lord of the Rings*." Interview with Fran Walsh and Philippa Boyens. Scr*(i)pt* 7, no. 6 (November/December 2001), [1], 34–37, 62–63.
Zimmerman, Morton Grady. *"The Lord of the Rings": Story Line*. Unproduced film treatment c.1957. Marquette University Archives, Milwaukee. Tolkien Collection, Series 8, Box 1, Folder 1.

Tolkien's Resistance to Linearity
Narrating The Lord of the Rings *in Fiction and Film*

E.L. Risden

In interviews from around the time of the release of the film version of *The Fellowship of the Ring* (2001), Peter Jackson remarked that he found the first film of the series easiest to plot because the story in the first segment of the trilogy exhibits a greater inherent linearity. But even *FOTR* presented interesting problems, not merely with respect to cinematic method and expediency but also given the necessary consideration of the expectations (and demands?) of Tolkien fans. The essential story, Jackson observed, involves Frodo carrying the ring to Mordor. Though we enjoy them in the book, Old Man Willow and Tom Bombadil don't advance that story or provide information that we "need to know" (see "From Book to Script," in which actor Christopher Lee makes the same point). In Jackson's cutting of the material of Tolkien's plot (and occasionally adding to it) to suit the medium of film, we may observe also that he aimed to produce as nearly as he could a linear narrative throughout. Even where linearity becomes impossible — when Gandalf seeks Saruman's advice and the plot must follow parallel courses — Jackson sought to maintain compelling progress with as few asides as possible while remaining true to as much of Tolkien's story as he could. He avoided introducing plot elements or tangential characters that would slow the film or confuse the viewer, and he omitted where he thought he could those elements, however appealing (e.g., Tom Bombadil and the Barrow-Wight), that drove the narrative progress from its central movement, the disposition of the Ring. *TT* (2002), Jackson added later, conformed less easily to a linear pattern, exhibiting essential parallel stories: Frodo and Sam travel toward Mordor; Merry and Pippin get taken by Saruman's Uruk-Hai, and the others (minus Boromir, who has before his death contributed to the breakup of the linear narrative) follow them, meeting the Rohirrim; offscreen Gandalf is "reborn" following his battle with the Balrog. *The Return of the King* (2003), we may add, again necessarily follows parallel plots that ultimately dovetail in the destruction of the ring: Frodo and Sam progress to Mount Doom as the battle at Gondor concludes and the small army, led by Aragorn, waits outside the gates of Mordor to distract Sauron from the Ring's actual position. The aftermath of that apocalyptic event returns to linear narrative both in the book and in the film, though again Jackson leaves out what he must have considered inessential material (the "Scouring of the Shire" and the death of Saruman) to move a long and expensive trilogy toward a satisfying ending.

While few viewers would dispute the artistic success of *The Lord of the Rings* as film (I certainly do not), Jackson's choices — at least for fans of the text — to some degree undermine Tolkien's clear resistance to narrative linearity. *LOTR* itself (both text and film versions) takes the form of a ring, ending (like *The Hobbit*) where it begins: in the Shire. But from its seed in *The Silmarillion* to its root in *The Hobbit* to its completion in *The Return of the King*, the development of the narrative takes a form one may more accurately describe with other metaphors. For instance as *fractal* it moves episodically or incrementally, guided by one or more "strange attractors," unfolding, varying, gaining complexity. As *Gothic* it explores, cathedral-like, pacing, chiaroscuro, and artifice that expands and completes the world of the text. In the perspective of either metaphor, Tolkien's narrative constantly resists simple linearity, leaving Jackson as filmmaker with an essentially impossible task had he stayed slavishly with the original. By comparing the pattern of book-narrative to that of film-narrative, we uncover essential differences in media and throw particular relief on the exigencies of adaptation. We can also get a strong sense of what Tolkien accomplished by means of the more complex narrative pattern.

In this chapter I'll discuss some instances of where and why Tolkien strays from linearity to suggest, that though linear as well as incremental narrative could have supported his *theme*, a reliance on linearity would have neglected one of the great pleasures of reading *The Lord of the Rings*: the complexity and welcome redundancy of Tolkien's Middle-earth. Narrative asides also allow opportunities for the exploration of good and evil, joy and suffering. I'll also briefly examine Peter Jackson's film versions, working from the cinematic releases, for narrative structure to determine where he pursues and where he strays from linear progression so that I may reflect on those choices and how they affect the translation of Tolkien's ideas to a different medium and a different time.

Traditional scholarship provides us a number of ways of schematizing narrative. Episodic plots, for instance, such as those in Homer's *Iliad* or *The Odyssey* or Virgil's *Aeneid* appear commonly enough. *The Odyssey* and *The Quest of the Holy Grail*, while nominally linear (they pursue, as does *The Lord of the Rings*, a plot with a fixed goal), also have episodic elements much like Tolkien's. *The Odyssey* alone (unless one adds to the narrative the full background of Odysseus and his departure from Ithaka for Troy) lacks his ultimate circularity, ending far from where it begins. The *Quest*, like *The Lord of the Rings*, ends back in Arthur's court, though the hero has not changed, but apotheosized (Frodo's departure from the Grey Havens?). The story of which the *Quest of the Holy Grail* forms a part, the adventures associated with Lancelot, moves inexorably toward an end in which the world of the story is worse, not better, than it was. The death of Arthur and the fall of Camelot and its ideals (the fall of the Elves and the rise of humans in Tolkien?) and particularly the loss of Galahad, the perfect Christian knight, leave the world lacking the greatness that had for a brief time defined it. Their loss seems almost to diminish human potential rather than to encourage one to seek an ideal: neither the Grail nor any character worthy and able to attain it shall ever appear again. Middle-earth, is not better for the loss of the Elves and the dominion of humans. Wizards, too, have gone, leaving the now dominant people without their chief sources of magic, goodness, and guidance.

Tolkien's "episodes" and narrative asides allow for the expansion of character and for the exploration of alternative sources of power and goodness in the world, and like those of their classical and medieval counterparts they also deepen our sense of the romance of a world at the edge of our imagination but out of tangible reach, distanced from us by time and the inevitable changes of nature. In eliminating Sauron, the Ring, the Wraiths, Saruman, and Gollum they also remove the greatest sources of evil. Tom Bombadil and Old Man Willow remain, but they too will now fade into quietness. The remaining world, blander, has more narrowly circumscribed limits. Heroism becomes a more pedestrian experience: resisting no dragon, but the dragon-sickness within ourselves, no Dark Lord, but any evil man who seeks lordship over our lands and purse strings — hardly insignificant, but less grandly inspiring. Episodic structure provides clear items for narrative and thematic comparison: Hektor fighting Patroklos, Hektor fighting Achilles; Bilbo's birthday party in the Shire; the returning Hobbits' scouring of the Shire.

Geometric progressions also occur in narrative, such as in *Beowulf*, where the hero undergoes three increasingly difficult monster fights, though *Beowulf* also circles imagistically, beginning and ending with a funeral. *Sir Gawain and the Green Knight* we may also call circular: the hero begins and ends the story at Arthur's court. Gawain returns chastened, regardless of what Arthur's court learns or fails to learn. But *Sir Gawain* also uses geometric progression: the deer hunt, the boar hunt, and the fox hunt. The animals represent the increasing cunning that Morgan le Fay applies to ensnare Gawain in error and that he must employ to avoid failure in a world tainted by Original Sin. Anyone who has used allegory—including nearly all the writers of the Middle Ages and probably the majority during the Renaissance—employs embedding or layering, what people of the medieval period called the fourfold exegetical method. One reads on four levels at once — literal, historical, moral, and cosmological — but those layers don't represent simple parallels. For the Christian reader they increase in importance, ending with questions of Salvation. Gawain seeks to attain a perfection he can never reach, but he fails in the sole virtue that from the Christian point of view can get him nearest to it: faith. Faith can prepare him to accept God's mercy, but he turns from faith to a belief in the efficacy of the green sash. *Trawpe* can establish him as the best of knights, but he fails to keep complete honesty with his host. For additional examples we need look no further than Dante's *Commedia* or Spenser's *Faerie Queene* to see an "everyman" learning the implications of a plenipotentiary cosmology or a field of virtuous knights who provide a young male reader with models of the quest for life's virtues. A multiplicity of episodes in Spenser gradually unfolds the development and display of all the facets of gentility, whereas Dante moves from the *contrapasso* of damnation to that of purgation to that of salvation — episodes unveil the choice of evil, the desire for penance, the acceptance of mercy.

Parallel structures such as arise in both *The Two Towers* and *The Return of the King* also have medieval siblings that Tolkien knew thoroughly, such as "Pwyll, Prince of Dyfed" in the Cymric *Mabinogi*, where part of the plot takes place in the human world and part occurs alongside it in the realm of the Otherworld. *The Quest of the Holy Grail* also uses parallel plot — the early movements of the three Grail Knights — that then meld into one for the achievement of the Grail. With all those examples Tolkien would of course have had perfect familiarity; in fact, the early literatures he knew so thoroughly seldom exhibit simple linear plots. Even such a brief work as the Old English *Battle of Maldon* employs what we may term a wave-style plot, with rising and falling action punctuated by speeches leading to a crest and a catastrophe, but with the story never moving physically from a single spot. *Sir Gawain and the Green Knight* has perhaps the most linear plot of all, but even it briefly employs a parallel structure, as Gawain resists the Lady's advances and Bercilak hunts for game: the pairing in the structure urges the reader to compare the events directly in emotion and meaning.

So while contemporary literary theory gives us some new language with which to approach narratology, we need not look only to contemporary literature for narrative complexity or innovation: the Old World also offers many options. To consider Tolkien's method of plotting, I suggest we can find apt metaphors in diverse sources: first a model from contemporary science, then another from medieval architecture. While he wouldn't have known the first and would have known the second intimately, both can help us understand his plot structure and show how he used it to build his world and reinforce his ideas. These models also highlight — usefully but not exclusively — some of the particular difficulties in transferring Tolkien's narrative from fiction to film, which requires a remapping from literary to cinematic time and from imaginative to two-dimensionally visualized space.

In *The Road to Middle-Earth* Tom Shippey has called Tolkien's plot *cartographic*; that is, it not only exposes but is guided by the geography, topography, and *feel* of Middle-earth, with a built-in redundancy but with incremental variations that deepen our sensory experience of the world. "Frodo," Shippey observes, "has to be dug out of no less than *five* 'Homely Houses'": Bag End, Crickhollow, the house of Tom Bombadil, the Prancing Pony, and Rivendell (79). In *J.R.R. Tolkien: Author of the Century*, Shippey lauds the neat complexity of *LOTR*'s symmetrical design: three volumes divided into two books each, with the structure of each book paralleling that of the others as the journey begins, as the companions join forces, break up, pursue their separate adventures, then meet again in the end. Even the individual adventures have parallel sub-adventures, such as the "meeting with the helpful stranger": Aragorn, Legolas, and Gimli meet Éomer and the Riders of Rohan; Merry and Pippin meet Treebeard; and Frodo and Sam meet Faramir (50 ff.). In *Tree and Leaf* Tolkien says that fairy stories serve three functions: recovery (meaning regaining a clear view of the world), escape, consolation. We may say that the "map" of *Lord* follows a pattern derived from those functions: each member of the fellowship must (and does — even Boromir) locate a sense of what's going on in the world, find a way to escape or, ideally, eliminate its horrors, and then seek consolation. So in a sense Tolkien's book maps the range of fairy stories.

Derek Brewer has argued that *Lord* isn't really a novel, but a romance (Tolkien himself called it so), in the medieval sense of the word. Romances typically pursue one of two plots, each of which follows a character as they grows toward and cross some important barrier. One takes the protagonist from childhood to adulthood, the other from life to death, and both by means of heroism and often through love. As Brewer observes, "[i]n one sense the *whole* story is Frodo's dream of growing-up and dying" (262) and "we do not live our lives in a single linear sequence" (263). The "map" in this approach derives not from cartography but from the natural order of events in life. Such romances tend to follow either a linear pattern, from birth to death, or a circular one, journey and return (as in *The Hobbit*). Joseph Campbell's *monomyth*, another well-trodden model, has both linear and circular aspects: it moves toward a particular end, the completion of a quest, but as a journey it involves both movement away from home to search and a return home with a boon.

An alternative way to envision at the circular tendency of the narrative suggests that we consider "loops," a useful term that Nick Otty uses in an otherwise often derogatory and deconstructive essay. Increments of the *Lord* story proceed as the separate groups pursue their tasks — Frodo and Sam on the way to Mordor, Aragorn and the others ultimately toward Gondor — then we loop back to pick up the parallel plotlines and weave them back into the whole. But I think we can find a better descriptor yet than loops.

A more comprehensive model appears in chaos theory in the geometry of fractals, my first suggestion for a less-explored but interpretively useful structural metaphor. Though Tolkien wouldn't have known of chaos theory, the formalization of which came after his time, the idea of fractal movements — seemingly occurring by chance but directed by some potentially locatable factor — provides an apt means of following plot development for someone who worked on narratives in increments, often over many years. By definition a fractal is an open-ended geometric pattern with repeated divisions descending to smaller and smaller scales into greater and greater detail, directed by an initial force upon a medium with sufficient chaotic properties to produce a unique, growing, not entirely predictable shape. For example, if when you cook pasta you add some olive oil to your water before it boils, the oil will spread out over the surface in a way difficult if not impossible to predict but governed by the laws of physico-chemical interaction and determined by the amounts, forces, and surface qualities present for the interaction. The splashing of the oil on the water creates a dynamic, chaotic system, and the oil moves and spreads fractally, though the final result, because of the tendency of oil to bead, doesn't take a fractal shape. An example of a fractal shape is a snowflake: we know on a large scale the forces that create it, but the shape of each individual flake evolves fractally according to ambient conditions too variable on a small scale for one to predict the exact result. In either example, the system does its job: the oil helps create a better cooking environment for the pasta, and the shape of the snowflake gives it temporary stability as it falls. In *Author of the Century* Shippey notes that the "inching, small-scale progress of Frodo, Sam, and Gollum," as well as — with respect to the day-to-day chronologies of the movements of different groups — "that the effects created of variety, contrast, and irony are in major part responsible for the book's phenomenal ... success" (52).

Fractal variations allow the author to throw especial light on the contrasts between one group and another, each fragmented from an original fellowship. Shippey observes that even in *The Hobbit* the maps and the wide range of names "do their work by suggesting that there is a world outside the story, that the story is only a selection" (68). We attend to only a small swirl amidst the rapidly boiling whole. No surprise that such a narrative as *Lord* would develop fractally; in his letters Tolkien describes developing the plot sporadically over years, often with long periods of quiescence. Stop-and-start plotting means that incidents will arise that one must cut, while others that one *could* cut one will remain. Despite their turning from linearity, they add enough coloring or depth to the world that the author must keep them for aesthetic (or philological) if not philosophical reasons.

Now I will return to my own textual examples. In the first book of the trilogy alone, Crickhollow, the House of Tom Bombadil, Rivendell, and Lothlórien represent encircled, fractal microcosms that resist danger or change, deepen the creative, sustaining, and redemptive powers of Middle-earth, and offer necessary respite. The truth and power of *Lord* lies as much in those moments of respite as in the narrative climaxes, and they, as much as the pursuit and fulfillment of the great quest, attract readers to the text, giving it shape, completeness, clarity, a sense of "truth." The theoretical and aesthetic implications of those fractal narrative "asides" may establish Tolkien's greatest accomplishment as a storyteller because each represents, in its straying from the linear path, a setting into which the reader may expand his or her own imagination for additional and equally appealing story lines — what in the study of Shakespeare we might call offstage action. We could eliminate any one of those locations from the plot and still have an effective, moving story, but the loss of any one diminishes the *affective* quality of the text as a whole: repeating a motif with variation reinforces the feelings and themes associated with the motif. That capability accrues particularly to the best written fiction. Films, even the best films ever made, have yet to exhibit that power, not because of bad filmmaking, but because of the inherent limitations of the genre — just as written fiction lacks the incarnated physical, sensory properties of film. One may say that, for physical immediacy, a stage play surpasses film — not making it a better medium, but allowing it a different range of motion. What the book lacks in sensory immediacy it gains in imaginative potential — especially in the hands of a writer so expert in world-building. So let's consider the importance of some exemplary individual "fractal" elements of *Lord* with respect to what they accomplish as plot movements. An excellent example from which to work appears in Professor Shippey's "Homely Houses."

We begin *Lord* as we do *The Hobbit*, at Bag End, from the viewpoint of any hobbit the ideal homely house, because it is the ideal house and home. Well-situated, well-protected (except perhaps for the likes of Lobelia Sackville-Baggins), and well-pantried, it evolves fractally in *Lord* from Bilbo's perfect home to Frodo's perfect home. As was Bilbo, Frodo is rousted from its warmth by visitors so that he may undertake a quest, but a quest that has also evolved considerably, though it retains important connections to its narrative parent. With fractals one knows that new wrinkles will appear and that they will have connections to the old, but one can't know the exact direction or magnitude any wrinkle will undergo.

The house at Crickhollow of course represents little change from Bag Eng in terms of hobbit comfort, though in its stand-apart, above-ground structure it more particularly resembles human comfort — Frodo is migrating toward the bigger world with a greater variety of preferred accommodations — and it resituates him at the border of wilder lands, another significant wrinkle in his experience. It shows Frodo's remnant unwillingness to abandon the Shire and the life he has loved. Even the best of hobbits changes slowly, and even for him the burden of heroic action weighs heavily. Frodo's journey has astonishingly more significance than had Bilbo's, and he and we readily suspend it for a short holiday. Occurring too soon for a furlough, the Crickhollow episode gives one more free breath of Shire-air before the inevitable rush of the narrative events to come.

As we pass into the Old Forest and find trouble with Old Man Willow and other evil trees, we have moved, apparently, thoroughly beyond the world of hobbit comfort — until the appearance of Tom Bombadil as rescuer and protector. As the hobbits will further learn at Bree, they have actually had such protection at their borders all along, though they didn't know it. But Tom's help demonstrates that point and returns them briefly to comforts of "home," though those comforts arise in someone else's home. There we see a continuation of the fractal pattern of homely houses, but a much different incarnation in the individual branch of the larger fractal arch-pattern.

The Prancing Pony at Bree provides another homely respite familiar to hobbits, with its homey food and beer and comfortable rooms, but it adds additional twists and variations: a dispossessed warrior-king, different sorts of men with less than kind intentions toward the hobbits, and probably even mixed-breeds with the blood of orcs in them. The dangers that the hobbits risked in leaving the Shire have worsened, and Frodo sees a new, larger pattern emerging. Through subsequent iterations of this aspect of his adventure he gains a growing sense of the absolute seriousness of his quest. While Bilbo had to survive trolls, a dragon, and a great war, the fate of the world did not yet lie in the balance, as it does with Frodo's quest. And of course the Black Riders catch up to the hobbits at Bree. We may suspect that no more homely houses remain available to shield them from the Enemy, who have by the plot point of Weathertop gotten to Frodo physically.

Yet, with Aragorn's help, they reach Rivendell, the greatest if Last Homely House of all, with the possible exception of Lothlórien later (it serves the same function without taking the form of a house per se). Weathertop offers a parody or antithesis or mirror image of the pattern, something that was once to some a safe fortress but has now become a ruin and the site of a desperate and nearly disastrous battle. But the hobbits survive it, again with the intervention of as yet unknown friends, to reach the safety and healing of Elrond's home, the antitype of the homely house and the antithesis of fallen Weathertop, a retreat that has retained its power. We follow in the narrative possible directions that evolve into actual events, likely destinations that appear then as actual places, places that have differences but that conform to a pattern, that of the homely house, safe, if only for a time, from the dangers of the greater world.

What then does the fractal development of the homely house do for *Lord*? First, by repetition of the motif we find the range of possible havens, greater than even the hobbits suspect as their quest introduces them to evils beyond their imaginings. Friends, like enemies, come in many shapes and sizes, and their presence in the world holds at bay what might otherwise have already become deadly despair (or simply death). And along with the journeying hobbits we meet the charming and marvelous array of folk who dwell in the world. Aren't we willing to risk meeting orcs if we may also find a Bombadil? Who doesn't enjoy a basket of steaming mushrooms and a hot bath and a quaint inn with good beer, and who, as Sam says, would miss a chance to see and hear real Elves singing under the stars? The varied repetition expands the potentials of the world of Middle-earth; though it has great and horrible evils, perhaps worse than ours, it has great good and beauty, perhaps also greater than ours. The world of our romantic longing — in the medieval sense of romance — unfolds to our ever-increasing awe. That awe contributes to the grandeur of the world, to the "spiritual" feel of Middle-earth, so that despite a dearth of what we may call religion, the book leaves us with a strong sense that our actions and our stories *matter* on a stage grander than our daily quibbles and squabbles. The various havens also allow the hobbits incremental steps toward their goal at a stage of the journey when they would not likely have had the wherewithal to manage the full import and horror of its end.

A linear plot would limit if not disallow the repetitive retreat to the homely house: a linear plot does not need a Bombadil. But Middle-earth needs a Bombadil, a protector and an eldest, and thematically the character serves as an embodiment of love of woods and trees. And we need a Bombadil, a representative of the Old Forest so that the environment may speak for itself even as we destroy it. Tolkien persists in the pattern to ferret out as many as he can of the variable incarnations of a motif that appeals to our senses and also to our desire to believe that good may prosper in the world and that we may find and share in it, and that we may enjoy the daily pleasures of life — food, drink, companionship, sightseeing, restful sleep — without guilt and free, at least for a time, from the clutches of evil.

As an American reader I can hardly help comparing the arrival of the Ringwraiths to the 9/11/2001 disaster. I think Tolkien's notion of "applicability" allows for such a reading, non-allegorical and nonintrusive but useful as an analog. To the hobbits the wars of the past lay as distant as Pearl Harbor to us, and we may have thought, or wished, Sauron dead with the end of the Cold War. We dwelt comfortably in our homely houses only to be roused again; we have yet to find whether we may form a laudable fellowship or whether we have become Sarumans and Wormtongues.

One can trace fractal variations throughout *Lord*, even to open-ended allusions such as Aragorn's references to Queen Beruthiel's cats and the Forsaken Inn east of Bree. But I have another metaphor to apply as well, one unlike the fractal in that it would have had immediacy and significance to Tolkien himself. I think we may also compare the anti-linear structure of *Lord* to the architectural pattern of the Gothic cathedral. In his preface to Max Dvořák's *Idealism and Naturalism in Gothic Art*, Karl Maria Swoboda succinctly defines "the basic problem of Gothic art as the relationship between transcendental ideas and the finite world" (xxvii) — a good description also of Tolkien's Middle-earth. Both Romanesque and Gothic art would have influenced Tolkien's religious experience as well as his imagination. Henri Focillon observes that "Romanesque sculpture was the expression of faith ... [and] Gothic sculpture was the expression of piety.... Romanesque faith, shot through with visions and prodigies, accepted and cherished the mysterious; it moved among superhuman things; it trembled in anticipation of rewards and punishments ... [while] thirteenth century [Gothic art] brings us back to the paths of the Gospel; in God-made-man, it cherished humanity; it loved and respected God's creatures as He loved them" (71).

Please consider for a moment the environment surrounding, and also inside, the cathedral: entering the cathedral is like entering a separate, discrete world, much like opening a book and engaging the world of a text. The whole structure takes the shape of a Latin cross, indicating its purpose clearly were anyone in doubt. If one is nominally a Christian and absolved of sin or seeking sanctuary, one finds there a safe haven. But the medieval visitor not so aligned met the danger of a hierophany, of an encounter with God or Church hierarchy that would require a reckoning — perhaps atonement or sacrifice or even conversion or judgment. Thus the sanctuary presents, like the fairy story, potential consolation, escape, or recovery, or, if the protagonist fails, death.

But the Gothic cathedral unfolds not merely a single experience but a huge and varied world. Through the enormous, often elaborately decorated front door the Gothic world may open into a lobby, or narthex, or directly into the nave, or body, of the church, a long, open passage through which one moves forward underneath the great sky-like arch. Toward the far end appears the transept, the cross-arms that cut across the nave at right angles. The hemispherical dome sometimes arises above the point where nave and transept cross and sometimes above the apse, or choir, the enclosure opposite the entrance and usually at the east end of the building which houses the altar, the point at which the ritual "sacrifice" takes place and around which curls an ambulatory for access or egress. The variable movement of light through many high windows inflects the experience according to the time of year or of day or in response to weather.

But the cathedral has many other architecturally "episodic" facets. It has more than one aisle by which one may approach the altar. It has high walls and galleries above and stained-glass windows, often decorated with biblical, historical, or natural scenes, each fractally illuminating a story and individually or together aiming to evoke a theme or mood. It may house tombs or treasures. And along the outside a isles the visitor may filter off into any number of small specialty chapels with representations of saints, designed for small services or private prayer but aiming in the short or long run to accomplish the same goal — though with a different emotional path — as a visit to the altar. Depending on when or where one visits, the cathedral may offer silence, music, public or private services, or it may be closed entirely. It may serve as a seat for judgment or inquiry, but historically almost without exception it represented the centerpiece, both physically and psychically, of a city.

The astute reader will already have noticed metaphorical similarities between the cathedral and the world of Tolkien's romance: the discrete world waiting for one to enter, the decorative door (cover), the passageway with events and items of interest (plot), the play of chiaroscuro and its influence on one's course. Like the Gothic cathedral *Lord* visually exploits movements between light and dark (see particularly Verlyn Flieger's *Splintered Light* on this point). I think the metaphor applies especially well structurally to *Lord*, particularly in its similar resistance to simple linearity. A significant turn occurs, of course, in *Lord*'s climactic liminality: the destruction of the Ring occurs at the Crack of Doom, whereas the epiphany of the Eucharist occurs at the cathedral altar — infernal rather than celestial, yet eucatastrophic both.

A walk through cathedral and plot shows many connections. Frodo and Sam follow an aisle as directly as they can to Mordor, the place of their sacrifice, the altar in the apse. Along the way good fortune allows them respite at the "homely houses" we've discussed, which we may fashion here as sidechapels of spiritual rest, prayer, and preparation for the greater service at the head of the church. The hobbits also experience suffering, which we may parallel to Stations of the Cross, tombs (barrows!), representations of martyrs. They enter Mordor through an "ambulatory" and achieve their quest at the brink of death — accepting the Eucharist represents the movement through death to life again with concurrent cleansing of, but not yet final escape from — sin.

The other characters take different paths, but they also seek or even find epiphanal ends. Merry and Pippin visit the sexton or caretaker (Treebeard), while Aragorn and the others visit the underground crypt (Helm's Deep) and, through a side aisle, the attached chapter house (Gondor). Gandalf has entered a tomb and Galahad-like fought and exorcised a demon. By Grace he has returned, resurrected, to join with the others for the final ritual — in this case "good" battles to survive, to return from darkness to light, the experience that typifies the visual/tactile spirituality of the cathedral experience. The remaining members of the Fellowship face an infernal Dark Night, another "descent," at the battle before the gate of Mordor, but they also have ahead of them a return to the "altar" in the crowning of the king at Gondor.

When Frodo and Sam's ritual rebirth occurs, they are carried by a symbol of the spirit, the eagle (John the Evangelist!) out again, and their service has ended. They join the others for its culmination (or its recapitulation as holiday) at Aragorn's official ascent to kingship. Then they must leave the cathedral for home. All may meet afterwards for tea and cakes, but the spiritual struggle continues, not only in the Scouring of the Shire, but in its aftermath and in their suffering the effects of their adventures. One may find family, the Grey Havens, or death at the end of the journey.

I don't propose that Tolkien had in mind specifically such a Gothic structure as he composed *Lord*. I suggest only that the Gothic cathedral may have influenced his imagination in a productive way, as it must affect anyone who visits one and pays it the least attention. The structure provides a useful metaphorical means of envisioning his plot patterns; whether we call a plot linear, circular, or episodic, we are seeking a structural metaphor the better to grasp its movement. In visualizing its structure as we read, we may find another productive way to enjoy and appreciate Tolkien's work, its variety, artistic depth, and spirituality. Similarly, while the concept of fractals wouldn't have entered into Tolkien's world, our familiarity with them may increase our appreciation for the value of the apparent redundancies of the text: while they may not fit the cinematic medium, they beautifully enrich the fictional one. And that is the critic's job: as the Roman poet Horace would have said, to make our reading more *dulce et utile*— sweet and useful. Linearity may limit a reader's pleasure; Tolkien sought to make his work more complex and thus more satisfying and illuminating.

The difficulties of his own medium led Jackson to attempt to linearilize the plot, but given the structure of, especially, the final two volumes, he had no chance of avoiding parallel plots and frightening complications (Shelob!) in the second and third films if he was to stay at all true to the original. Scriptwriting wisdom has for more than a generation followed Syd Field's 1979 book *Screenplay* almost biblically: the idea of the three-act structure divided ¼, ½, ¼ deeply embedded both in lore and in practice. Kristin Thompson's clear and insightful *Storytelling in the New Hollywood* revises some old notions, reinforces others, and introduces some new ideas about cinematic narrative structure. She elucidates both theoretically and practically (with detailed discussion of ten successful films from the 1980s and 1990s) a four-part structure of often roughly equal-length sections comprising setup, complicating action, development, climax and epilogue. She begins with basic principles of filmmaking that apply, she argues, to both classic and recent Hollywood films: a preference for clear and unified narratives assembled through a "conglomeration of blocks" (shots and scenes), clearly to relate causes and effects, to assign characters a clear set of traits, to relate protagonists' goals or desires to the main lines of action (often two in number), to move forward with temporal and narrative clarity, to include romance, and to centralize a turning point (10–31).

Jackson sought, and in fact produced, that clear and unified narrative not only in each film individually, but also for the three as a whole — an incredible achievement given the inherent resistance of his source to that process, the enormous financial demands of film production, and the knowledge and expectations of a multigenerational fanbase. The three *LOTR* films neatly adhere to the four-part structure, with only a slight truncation in the epilogue — no surprise given the length of the series up to that point. I have wondered if including the Scouring of the Shire as an extension of the epilogue may not have provided both fuller balance to the plot and fuller expression of Tolkien's theme of the persistent evil effects of war, of the fact that war has not "ended" just because the soldier has got home. We have, of course, dispatched the Ring as physical object, and maybe even the most devoted fan would have grown weary with the addition of another fifteen-minute battle sequence well after the climactic war has ended. Fractals persist, and one may always take another turn around the ambulatory or pause over another tomb or artifact. Film scripts, though, must attract producers who see them as "makeable," and they must finally end, allowing even the most stalwart of hobbits a drink and a well-earned rest.

Works Cited

Bal, Mieke. *Narratology: Introduction to the Theory of Narrative*. 2nd ed. Toronto: University of Toronto Press, 1997.
Brewer, Derek S. "*The Lord of the Rings* as Romance." In *J.R.R. Tolkien, Scholar and Storyteller: Essays in Memoriam*. Edited by Mary Salu and Robert T. Farrell. Ithaca: Cornell University Press, 1979.
Field, Syd. *Screenplay: The Foundations of Screenwriting*. New York: Delta, 1979.
Flieger, Verlyn. *Splintered Light: Logos and Language in Tolkien's World*. Grand Rapids: Eerdmans, 1983.
Focillon, Henri. *The Art of the West in the Middle Ages*. Vol. 2, *Gothic Art*. Translated by Donald King. Greenwich, CT: Phaidon, 1963.
"From Book to Script." *The Lord of the Rings: The Fellowship of the Ring*. Extended Edition. Disk 3. New Line Cinema, 2001.
Otty, Nick. "The Structuralist's Guide to Middle-earth." In *J.R.R. Tolkien: This Far Land*. Edited by Robert Giddings. London: Vision; Totowa, NJ: Barnes & Noble, 1983.
Shippey, Tom. *J.R.R. Tolkien: Author of the Century*. Boston: Houghton Mifflin, 2000.
_____ [T.A.]. *The Road to Middle-earth*. Boston: Houghton Mifflin, 1983.
Swoboda, Karl Maria. Preface. In *Idealism and Naturalism in Gothic Art*. Max Dvorák. Notre Dame, IN: University of Notre Dame Press, 1967.
Thompson, Kristin. *Storytelling in the New Hollywood: Understanding Classical Narrative Technique*. Cambridge, MA: Harvard University Press, 1999.

Filming Folklore
Adapting Fantasy for the Big Screen through Peter Jackson's The Lord of the Rings

DIMITRA FIMI

Film, Folklore and Fantasy

In the last few years the interdisciplinary study of folklore and film has produced a series of important articles and monographs which have mutually illuminated both fields. In his 2003 article Mikel Koven presented a critical survey of folklore studies in relation to popular film and television. He distinguished between two main types of folkloric approaches to these media. The first approach is folklore *in* film and television, something akin to the paradigm of "folklore in literature," consisting mainly of what Koven calls "motif spotting," that is, the use of myth, tale types, legend and any other expression of folklore in films and television. The second approach is folklore *about* film and television, including popular legends and stories about these media, as well as fan ethnography or "the folklore of audiences." Since then, more publications have contributed new insights and analytical categories to the study of popular film and folklore, including a special issue of the journal *Western Folklore* (2005) and a collection of new articles (Sherman and Koven 2007).

Although distinguishing between folklore *in* film and folklore *about* film is a good starting point and certainly a very useful methodological tool in the study of folklore on screen, when it comes to film adaptations of fantasy literature the terrain becomes much more intricate and complicated. Fantasy literature often betrays the influence of what one could term "folklore proper": motifs, characters and plotlines deriving from material originally known from myths, legends and fairy tales. Pre-Tolkienian fantasy bears the marks of such sources more clearly, but even in the post–Tolkienian fantasy world, however original or derivative, the presence of magic in writings of the fantastic guarantees the ever-powerful inspiration of folklore. In the best works of fantasy this folkloric inspiration is taken into a new creative route, generating memorable new characters, plots, and themes. As a result, in the case of the cinematic adaptation of J.R.R. Tolkien's three-volume novel, *The Lord of the Rings*, the dichotomy between folklore *in* film and folklore *about* film is further complicated by the fact that the three films are based on a literary work which is itself not only inspired by folklore but is also a source of generating folklore.

Tolkien's work is deeply rooted in Northern European myth, legend and fairy tale, from the Old Norse material to Celtic myth and the Arthurian legend, and from the Finnish *Kalevala* to Victorian popular culture. Indeed, tracing Tolkien's sources in such folkloric material and identifying their creative uses is one of the most fruitful approaches in Tolkien studies. However, Tolkien's own mythology has also generated its own folklore. *The Hobbit* proved immediately popular with readers. But after the publication of *Lord* and its huge success, especially following the "Tolkien cult" of the mid–1960s, a dedicated and enthusiastic fan readership emerged who not only read and talked about the book but also formed numerous Tolkien groups and societies around the world and published a plethora of fanzines with articles and other fan activity on Tolkien's fiction.

Lord influenced numerous fantasy writers as well as the RPG industry, while it also played an important role in standardizing the image of key characters of the fantasy genre, like Elves, wizards, and even Halflings, in twentieth-century popular culture. When Tolkien started writing *The Book of Lost Tales*, the first version of his mythology, he used the terms "Elf" and "fairy" interchangeably, like many of his predecessors had. In the post–Tolkien world this equation seems untenable, even absurd. Elves spelt with a capital "E," following Tolkien, are respected characters in the realm of fantasy literature, while fairies are only associated with Victorian whimsy.[1] Tolkien's work generated a tradition, an authoritative but still dynamic folklore of the fantastic. It is significant that Richard Taylor, the creative supervisor of Weta Workshop (the company that undertook the task of creating Middle-earth for the films) said that for him Peter Jackson's film adaptation of *Lord* was an "opportunity to bring a piece of modern English folklore to the screen."[2]

Peter Jackson's films managed to exploit both the folklore that arose from Tolkien's books and the role of fans and fandom in Tolkien's popularity. The film consolidated a few much-debated points of Tolkien folklore, which future generations of readers — given the cultural influence of the film industry and the power of visual representation — will be taking for granted. The question of whether Balrogs have wings and the ability to fly was the topic of debate among Tolkien fans for years, important enough to figure in the FAQ Webpage of the Tolkien Society, which contains a brief but detailed treatise of the matter and still concludes that the answer is "yes and no" (Tolkien Society).

The visualization of the Balrog in Moria in Jackson's adaptation will probably mean that a younger generation of readers will not find it necessary to debate this fine point any longer: the Balrog's bat-like wings in the film are an expression of the creature's satanic, demonic nature. Similarly, the Elves' pointed ears and Legolas' fair hair — both equally debated issues among Tolkien readers — have undergone the same process of standardization. Interestingly, Bakshi's animated adaptation of *Lord* had already presented a Balrog with such satanic wings and also included a fair-haired Legolas and other Elves with pointed ears, but its cultural influence cannot rival that of Jackson's blockbuster. Before Jackson's films, Tolkien-inspired artists had fluctuated between presenting Balrogs with or without wings in their illustrations (compare for example John Howe's *Gandalf Falls with the Balrog* and Ted Nasmith's *The Balrog*). Jackson's adaptations have, therefore, played the role often begrudged by folklorists, especially when it comes to Disney versions of popular fairytales (Koven 2003, 177): it has imposed a definitive, solidified version of Tolkien folklore.

Apart from folklore arising from Tolkien's novel, Peter Jackson's team also realized very quickly the importance of fans and fan activity in Tolkien's popularity. While the film was still being created, Peter Jackson and his team launched an official *The Lord of the Rings* fan club, the members of which would receive a monthly publication on the progress of the film, together with other perks, such as discounts on film merchandise. It was also announced that the names of these fans would be acknowledged in the film credits. This really radical innovation not only made sure that the interest in the films would remain enormous and build up until the release of the films, but it also safeguarded the fact that the film would be generally well received by fans all over the world since deviations from the book were "sanctioned" by the fan club and thus more easily accepted. The names of the fan club members finally found their way into the credits of the extended DVD editions of the film trilogy, together with several hours of commentaries and insights into the process of making the three films.

Having access to two different versions of each of the three films (a "theatrical" version and an "extended" one) as well as hours upon hours of commentary on the films by its creators, plus all other printed and online material on Peter Jackson's awfully big adventure of bringing Middle-earth to the screen, an essay on folklore and *Lord* films has endless possibilities of scope and range. What I have chosen to concentrate on in this essay are three main issues that I consider central to how folklore relates to film, and especially to a film adaptation of a work of fantasy literature. The first is how folklore "external" to Tolkien's novel found its way into the film and influenced it; second, how "global" folklore originating in the cinematic world itself entered the *Lord of the Rings* adaptation, contrary to the imagery of the book; and third, how fandom folklore shaped parts of the film. I will examine one main example for each of these three categories.

"External" Folklore: Jackson's "Celtic" Elves

A good instance of how "external" and "internal" folklore work in Jackson's trilogy is the case of the Elves and their "Celtic" imagery. In this essay, by "external" folklore I mean material from myth, legends and fairy tales, as well as any other expression of folklore, that exist independently of Tolkien's Middle-earth mythology. I use "internal folklore" to signify Tolkien's creative use of such material, especially in the cases where a clear source can be identified. For example, I would consider "external" folklore the stories of Kullervo in the *Kalevala* and Sigurd of the Volsungs in the *Volsunga Saga*, but Tolkien's creative reworking of these two mythical characters in the doomed hero Túrin Turambar would qualify as "internal" folklore.[3]

In the case of Tolkien's Elves, "internal" folklore points to a variety of sources. Tolkien's Elves are probably the most venerated characters in his mythos. They stand higher than all the other Middle-earth creatures and are right at the heart of Tolkien's legendarium. They are portrayed as a higher race of beings, immortal, with exceeding beauty, wisdom and a strange grief. It has been pointed out that their image has been influenced by Tolkien's interpretations of the Anglo-Saxon, Middle-English and Norse Elves (Shippey 2005, 65–74; 2004), and also by the fairies of Celtic sources, especially the Irish Tuatha Dé Danann (Fimi 2006). The Celtic inspiration for the Elves, however, is not as pronounced in *Lord* as it is in Tolkien's mythology of the First Age, as recorded in *The Silmarillion*. Lady Galadriel is much closer to the Anglo-Saxon notion of *ælfsciene*, "Elf-beautiful" but also perilous. The Elf-guards of Lothlórien are armed mainly with bows and arrows, a creative use of the Anglo-Saxon belief in "Elf-shot," the ability of the Elves to cause illness and nightmares by shooting arrows. The reference to High Elves and Grey Elves points to the Old Norse distinction of Elves into *ljósálfar* (light–Elves) and *dökkálfar* (dark–Elves). Burns has recently written that Tolkien's Elves "*feel* Celtic" (2006, 25), and she points to Tolkien's uses of ideas and beliefs of the Celtic otherworld as a land in the West (c.f. Valinor) and a place you enter by passing a water barrier in an enchanted forest where time passes in a different way (c.f. Lothlórien). However, these elements of Anglo-Saxon, Old Norse and Celtic folklore and tradition have been merged in Middle-earth and have created a blended new tradition, already evident in how Elves are portrayed in Middle-English sources such as *Sir Gawain and the Green Knight* and *Sir Orfeo* (see Fimi 2007).

However, Peter Jackson's film version of *The Lord of the Rings* brings in "external" folklore to enhance the "Celtic" attributes of Tolkien's Elves. I am using Celtic in quotation marks here to denote the popular, romanticized idea of "Celticity," which is prevalent in modern folklore and not necessarily true for the original medieval texts in Celtic languages, mainly Irish and Welsh. Tolkien himself was very much aware of this use of the term "Celtic," talking about the "romantic misapplication" of the terms "Celts" and "Teutons" in his essay "English and Welsh."[4] This modern reinterpretation of Celtic folklore derives mainly from the Irish Twilight, or Celtic Revival, of the end of the nineteenth and the beginning of the twentieth century, which made the term "Celtic" an all-inclusive "magic bag" (as Tolkien called it) into which all sorts of mixed traditions could fit. Tolkien mocked the stereotyping of "the wild incalculable poetic Celt, full of vague and misty imaginations, and the Saxon, solid and practical when not under the influence of beer" (Tolkien 1983, 171–2). It is exactly this romanticized, popular folkloric notion of the spiritual, visionary and melancholic quality of all things "Celtic" that has been introduced in Jackson's adaptation of *Lord*, in the visualization and portrayal of Tolkien's Elves. I would argue that the reason is not the film creators' awareness of Tolkien's real Celtic sources, but that in popular culture and folklore Elves and fairies would bring "Celtic" connotations to mind.

The first point where such associations can be made is one of the early scenes in the extended edition of *The Fellowship of the Ring*, in which Frodo and Sam have left the Shire and come across a group of travelling Elves on their way to the West (scene 11). This scene corresponds chronologically to the first time that Elves appear in *Lord* in the chapter "Three Is a Company" in Book I of *Fellowship*. In this chapter Frodo and his company encounter a host of Elves led by Gildor. The first impressions of this scene are evocative of the more lighthearted Elves present in *The Hobbit*. There is a playful tone at the beginning of the conversation between the hobbits and the Elves, with the same kind of slightly rude comments by the Elves' that is very reminiscent of the first encounter of the Dwarves' company with Elves in Rivendell in *The Hobbit*, where the latter are teasing the Dwarves for their long beards. The tone of the whole scene soon becomes more serious when the Black Riders are mentioned.

In Jackson's film, though, the scene is quite different. Instead of the levelheaded Gildor and his companions, we see an otherworldly procession of Elves, some on foot and others on horseback, moving slowly and gracefully towards the West, accompanied by ethereal music. The scene might bring to mind references in the very first chapter of *Lord* to Elves "passing westward through the woods in the evening, passing and not returning" (Tolkien 1993a, 68). Nevertheless, the atmosphere of the scene in Jackson's film has a significant visual analogue: John Duncan's 1911 painting *The Riders of the Sidhe* (see The McManus: Dundee's Art Gallery and Museum).[5] Duncan's painting is very much in the vein of the Celtic Revival movement and it seems to illustrate the procession of the Sidhe (the Irish term for the fairies) as described in Fiona Macleod's "The March of the Faërie Host" (Sharp 1896: 12) and as discussed by Lady Wilde in *Ancient Legends of Ireland* (1888). The Sidhe ride proudly on horseback, dressed in magnificent clothes and jewels, and Duncan's painting succeeds in depicting both the power of their supernatural presence and an implied melancholy for past splendor. I would argue that this was a conscious borrowing in Jackson's film, albeit via mediation. Alan Lee, who was responsible for the conceptual design of the Elvish realms of Rivendell and Lothlórien, had already been inspired by Duncan's painting when illustrating the "Faerie Rades" for the book *Faeries* (1978).

In this book, Lee and Brian Froud wrote the texts and illustrated fairy folklore from the British Isles as well as more literary fairylore. In the entry for "Faerie Rades"[6] Lee quotes Lady Wilde's *Ancient Legends of Ireland* for the "cavalcade" of the Irish fairies. His illustration is very much after Duncan, with splendidly dressed men and women in medieval style, most of them riding decorated horses and one of them holding an unfolding banner. The only noticeable difference is that the fairy procession in Lee's illustration is heading from the left to the right of the page, while in Duncan's painting the Sidhe are riding from the right to the left of the canvass.

If one looks at scene 11, "The Passing of the Elves," in the extended DVD of *Fellowship*, one can clearly see the continuity of visual intertextuality between Duncan's Celtic Revival representation of the Irish fairies and Jackson's solemn procession of Elves, via the mediation of Alan Lee's illustration.

The same visual borrowing appears once more in Jackson's trilogy — becoming even more pronounced if certain stills are isolated — in scene 9, "Arwen's Vision," in the extended DVD of *ROTK*. Again, the procession of Elves, some riding, some walking, and some holding banners, is even closer to Duncan's painting, as this time the scene is shot in brighter light and the different colors of the Elves' clothes are visible more clearly.

The portrayal of both processions of Elves on their last voyage to the West in Jackson's trilogy evokes the same kind of atmosphere as Duncan's painting: an alluring otherworldliness and an implied sadness for a legend that is no more. This melancholic sentiment for a lost tradition, often blamed on the domination of English imperialism, is another important strand of modern "Celtic" folklore. Tolkien's Elves in *Lord* are indeed surrounded by a strange grief, related to their weariness of the world and their realization that they will have to leave Middle-earth, which in the Fourth Age will become the dominion of Men. The melancholy of the popular notion of "Celticity," although of a different source and quality, is introduced as "external" folklore to enhance the Elves' portrayal.

But what reinforces this initial impression of a "Celtic" air and ambience of the Elves in the film is their material culture, and here the creators of the film are very specific. In the commentaries included in the extended DVD version of *FOTR*,[7] when talking about how the setting of Rivendell was created, the Tolkien illustrator John Howe refers to an "eternal culture, that could be forever perfecting itself." He talks about searching for "some form of simplicity which can allow you to stop evolving and find that perfect line." Alan Lee, however, who finally was given the task of creating the conceptual design of Rivendell, talks about "the use of natural forms ... the use of flowing graceful lines" and of the use of "elements of Art Nouveau and Celtic design." Even the jewelry, and especially the headgear, that the important Elf-characters wear in the films immediately brings to mind modern examples of "Celtic" design jeweler, full of curving lines and interlacing patterns, often advertised and sold in suitable venues.

The use of the term "Celtic" for interlacing design is, again, at best a romantic misapplication. The curvilinear design patterns of the Iron-Age La Tène culture are not considered Celtic by most archaeologists today.[8] Interlace design in medieval art was never a particularly Celtic feature, as it was very much present in Anglo-Saxon material culture as well as in other Germanic cultures; but it gained prominence during the period of the Celtic revival and has been popularly associated with Celtic art since then (see Laing 1975, 239–40; Collis 2003, 80–4). The design team of Jackson's adaptation not only embrace the spirit of the Celtic revival by adopting this romanticized "Celtic" design for the Elves but also seem to acknowledge its relation to Art Nouveau, which in late 19th- and early 20th-century Britain was very much influenced by the new vogue for all things "Celtic." Alan Lee's comments further on in the commentary show the influence of how "Celtic" art has been popularly interpreted in such a way as to romanticize ideas of "Celtic" aesthetics and spirituality. He talks of the setting of Lothlórien, describing it as a "slightly more unworldly ... otherworldly ... and more mysterious and probably a more kind of spiritual place...."[9] Indeed, the interlacing patterns of Iron Age La Tène artifacts and medieval Celtic manuscripts and decorative objects have been often used to claim that "Celtic" art was "natural" and "spiritual." Chapman has summarized this tradition (in very similar terms to Tolkien's mocking of stereotyping Celts and Teutons, quoted above) thus:

> Many of the high-flown metaphysical and moral conclusions drawn from "Celtic" art by its admiring critics are suspiciously like an elaboration of the idea that curves are more natural than corners. With a curve, like with a Celt, you might be anywhere and one thing flows into another; with a corner, like with an Anglo-Saxon, you know where you are: nature makes curves, humanity makes corners [Chapman 1993: 226].

The same "Celtic" feel is also intended in the music associated with the Elves of Rivendell. As the composer of the film music, Howard Shore mentions in one of the film commentaries Enya, the Irish folk–cum–New Age singer, was approached and was asked to write and perform a vocal piece for one of the Rivendell scenes. Enya's music has been variously described as "Celtic," "Irish," or "Celtic fusion." Her music belongs to a new wave of "ethereal voices and mournful cadences of so-called 'Celtic' music" (O'Shea 2005, 132) which internalizes the discourse of "Celticity" as melancholy over a lost tradition.[10] In addition, Viggo Mortensen, who plays Aragorn in the film, sings a little piece based on Tolkien's Lay of Lúthien in the extended DVD of *FOTR* (scene 17, "The Midgewater Marshes"). He made up the tune himself, and he claims in the film commentary that he intentionally gave it a "Celtic feel."[11] Mortensen's tune reminded me of nothing particularly Celtic at all (not even in the romanticized tradition of "Celtic" music), but he intended it to be "Celtic" and this is what counts.

Global Cinematic Folklore: The Paths of the Dead

The Army of the Dead are men who had sworn allegiance to Isildur during the Second Age of Middle-earth, but when they were called to fight with the Last Alliance of Elves and Men against Sauron they refused. Isildur cursed them never to rest until their oath was fulfilled. In *Lord* Aragorn is reminded by Elrond that he can call upon this forgotten army as the heir of Isildur and command them to fight against Sauron's threat in the Third Age of Middle-earth. Thus they will fulfill their oath and redeem themselves. Aragorn, together with Legolas, Gimli, and a few more Elves and rangers, has to face the Paths of the Dead, a subterranean passage through Dwimorberg, the Haunted Mountain, where the Dead abide. This is one of the most powerful scenes in the book: the Dead remain unseen by most of Aragorn's company, and only a chilling feeling of dread and slight echoes of whispering betrays their presence. Aragorn summons them to the Stone of Erech, where their original oath had been sworn, and the Dead follow him and his company through the underground passage and out in the open air. Legolas, who seems to be the only one able to see them, describes them thus: "I see shapes of Men and of horses, and pale banners like shreds of cloud, and spears like winter-thickets on a misty night. The Dead are following" (Tolkien 1993b, 67–8). At the Stone of Erech, Aragorn addresses the Oathbreakers and they answer him. This is the only time the Dead speak in *Lord*, and their voice is "heard out of the night ... as if from far away" (Tolkien 1993b, 69).

In Peter Jackson's adaptation, however, there is a complete departure from the scene as described in the book, both in terms of dialogue and, most important, in terms of feel and atmosphere. Tolkien's Dead Men invoke fear and terror but it is their mere presence, or rather their shadowy non-presence, that makes them effective. In Jackson's film, however, the ghosts of the Dead are visible in a misty greenish light, partly skeletons, partly ghosts and partly rotten-fleshed zombies. The King of the Dead — whose existence in *Lord* is only glimpsed much later in the book, when Aragorn releases the Dead as having fulfilled their oath after defeating the Corsairs of Umbar — is in Jackson's version a speaking, interacting character, worthy of casting a real actor to impersonate him. Moreover, he is not the hauntingly awe-inspiring character one would expect from reading the book: he laughs sardonically and mocks Aragorn and his companions (only Legolas and Gimli in the film). His Army of the Dead reinforces this threatening and challenging attitude by encircling Aragorn, Legolas and Gimli and there is a sense that they might be attacked. The King of the Dead does not realize who Aragorn is until the latter unsheaths Anduril, the reforged sword of Isildur. Even after Aragorn has revealed himself, he seems to be unable to command the Dead and to be begging for their allegiance. The King of the Dead releases another round of sardonic laughter, and then all the ghosts disappear. In the extended DVD version of the scene, Aragorn and his companions have to run out of the subterranean realm of the dead to avoid being buried under an enormous avalanche of thousands of skulls.

If one considers "internal" folklore in the case of the Paths of the Dead, Tolkien's sources point to medieval Latin traditions of the *exercitus mortuorum* (the army of the dead), a band of armed ghosts who traveled in the air inspiring terror, or wandered in penitence begging for forgiveness for their sins (see Sinex 2003). Also, Old Norse literature features many instances in which the dead fight again, such as the fallen heroes in the *Prose Edda* who spend their days in Valhalla fighting each other and being resurrected every morning to continue the battle (see Burns 2006). On the contrary, the "external folklore" used in Jackson's film is one of a very particular type: "global folklore," originating in cinema itself.[12]

What is initially intriguing about the cinematic scene of the Paths of the Dead is the reaction of different groups of the filmmakers in the extended DVD commentaries. In his commentary, Peter Jackson seems very apologetic about the Army of the Dead. He says, "I found that ghost stuff quite tricky because you don't quite know what to do.... [Y]ou don't want to get too haunted mansion kind of ... you know, generic ghost stuff, and yet you have to have something."[13] Later on, he refers to the design team and how they worked out how the "ghosts" would look, as well as how the team ended up using a design that looked not that dissimilar to the ghosts in the film *Pirates of the Caribbean*, which raised concerns of accusations of copying their idea.

Interestingly, the commentary of the same scene by the design team has a totally different tone — that of excitement for the opportunity to design and film "zombies"! Richard Taylor, the Weta Workshop creative supervisor, initially sets the problem very well by saying that "we didn't want these characters to be zombies living in a ghost world but rather the spirits of fallen soldiers that have been captured in this almost lining tomb under the ground."[14] This sounds like a sensible approach for a team assigned to visualize Tolkien's own portrayal of the Dead Men, who are never referred to as "zombies" anywhere in *Lord*.[15] However, the term "zombies" keeps on coming up continuously in extended DVD commentaries. Peter Jackson himself, commenting on the design of the Army of the Dead, notes that "we had this idea of having a scull underneath the fleshy, sort of zombie make up, so that you morph between the two."[16] Richard Taylor adds this: "We didn't want them to be zombies as such but the feeling that they were emaciated away because their spirits had been corrupted by their shame."[17] In the appendices of *ROTK*, Jason Docherty, one of the Weta Workshop supervisors, commented that "the army of the Dead was something that we got very excited about early on; I mean all make-up fix guys want to do zombies at some point."[18] The most telling element of the entire design team commentary is the fact that towards the end of the scene the design team's voices become mock-frightening and mock-zombie-like, and they seem to be having great fun with the zombies who are their own creation.[19]

What is happening here is that the filmmaking team is dealing in a cinematic way with a problematic category of beings I will call the "undead." Traditional European folklore has always dealt with the concept of the undead by elaborating the idea of the ghost, and later on the figure of the vampire. Tolkien's Dead Men are rooted in traditional material on ghostly warriors that goes back to the Middle Ages; but Jackson's team seem to be drawing from a different "tradition," from a new, global vernacular culture created by popular film and specifically the modes and motifs of the horror film.

The popular horror film has been a successful genre since the birth of cinema. Ghosts have figured prominently in horror films, by utilizing and transforming traditional folklore. The zombie is a different kettle of fish. It originates in Haitian ethnography and folk belief; but it was misinterpreted and appropriated by Hollywood in the earliest period of cinema and mutated into a new stock character of global folklore: the "cinematic zombie."[20] The main difference between the portrayal of cinematic ghosts and of cinematic zombies is that the former are usually spectral and ethereal while the later are corporeal and visceral (Koven 2008: 41). Bearing in mind this well-established cinematic global folklore on the visualization of the undead, it is not that surprising to find out that Jackson's team had to make a decision as to which of these two models to follow. Warren Mahy, a Weta designer and sculptor, gives us a good idea of the initial dilemma:

> The Army of the Dead.... At that time we weren't sure whether [this] was going to be done physical or digital or a combination of the two.... Pete and Richard wanted to see everything that we could think of ... our thoughts on the Army of the Dead ... whether there were corpses, you know, like rotting people, or were they the spirits of people that were still physically solid, they were still transparent, like a ghost, but they were normal-human-being-looking, rather than a corpse....

The more corporeal visual image of the zombie seems to have prevailed, I suspect, because these Dead Men were expected to fight in battle and thus had to appear slightly more solid than the traditional, spectral ghosts in films.

It is important to note that Peter Jackson is a director well versed in the genre of the horror film, as his first successes came with such horror/comedy films as *Bad Taste* (1987) and *Meet the Feebles* (1989) and his major Hollywood production before *LOTR* was the splatter film *The Frighteners* (1996).

A number of scholars who have recently examined Jackson's *Lord of the Rings* trilogy have noted the extensive use of horror film conventions (Thompson 2008, 54–61; McLarty 2006; Hall 2007), and one could argue that Jackson and his team were bound to be inspired by his previous film projects. Indeed, the dialogue and general ambience of the scene at the Paths of the Dead are very reminiscent of Jackson's previous comical horror parodies. However, I would argue that the design and visualization of the Army of the Dead posed a problem of a different sort: that of deciding what type of characters these Dead Men would be and where they would fit into the stereotypical categories of global, cinematic folklore. The Jackson team decided to go for the "cinematic zombie" and this conscious decision is reflected in Richard Taylor's words at the conclusion of his commentary on this scene: "I thought they had certain overtones to some of the Italian zombie movies of the 1970s, and that's a good thing in my book!"[21]

Folklore of the Audiences: The Case of Figwit

As briefly discussed above, Peter Jackson's *Lord of the Rings* trilogy was quick to exploit the wide range of fan activity that Tolkien's literature had been generating since its publication. The involvement of the fans was sought not only through the Official *Lord of the Rings* fan club and New Line's official film site but also through "endorsing" and communicating frequently with other Websites like theonering.net and waroftherring.net (see Thompson 2008, 133–164). The "folklore of the audiences," or "audience ethnography," has long been one of the most fruitful approaches in interdisciplinary studies of film and folklore. As Bird has noted, "If audience members are seen as active in helping to shape the way popular culture is created, they become much more comparable with folk 'audiences'" (1996, 345). In 1989 Bruce Jackson had already defined the first of three subdivisions of the "folklore of audiences" as "the information the audience brings to the experience of a film" (389). In Jackson's *LOTR* trilogy the fan community had the chance to shape, name and fully develop a new character that had initially started life as an extra. Through the fans, this extra acquired a name and a specific role, and a whole folklore evolved around him. I am referring to the Figwit phenomenon.

In the first film of the trilogy, *FOTR*, among a group of other extras, is an Elf featured in the scene "The Council of Elrond" (extended DVD, scene 27). In the book, the Council is attended by a few unnamed Elves, and this is also true for the film. However, one of the extras caught the attention of some of the film's fans, who promptly christened him "Figwit" and thus spawned a whole new cult specifically about him. The name Figwit is the acronym of "Frodo Is Great.... Who Is That?" and came about because this particular extra appears in the shot directly after Frodo has offered to take the ring to Mordor with the memorable line "I will take it." The following is a quote from the fan Website "Figwit Lives!," "When Frodo says 'I will take it!,' we are so impressed we start to think 'Frodo is great!' But before we finish, the camera pans and we see Figwit, smoldering enigmatically in the background. All other thoughts are whisked away by that Elf—who is THAT?! He's gorgeous!" It is remarkable that this playful acronymic name does fit phonetically with Tolkien's Sindarin nomenclature of many Elves in his mythology (for example, Finarfin, Finduilas, Fingolfin, Fingon, Finrod, Finwë), so the fans seem to be making fun—perhaps unintentionally—of Tolkien's linguistic obsession too.

This example of how fan folklore can affect the film industry via the creation of a character out of an extra would not seem so remarkable if the story ended here, but it does not. Precisely because of the fans' fascination with him, Figwit eventually managed to become an established character in the trilogy by appearing in the third film, *ROTK*. In the scene "Arwen's Vision," also discussed above, Arwen is about to leave Middle-earth for Valinor when she has a vision about her future and decides to turn back and stay in Middle-earth. In that scene (which is another deviation from the book) the screenwriters needed just one anonymous Elf to address Arwen to ask her where she is going, but Peter Jackson decided to acknowledge the Figwit fan base and used the same extra to play the anonymous Elf.

In the extended DVD commentary, Jackson admits that he used that specific actor for this scene "for the fans," although he is a little confused with how his name is supposed to be pronounced and the acronym it comes from. However, most of the other members of the filmmaking team are well aware of the Figwit cult, and they refer to it as a "legendary internet phenomenon." While they do not provide any specific detail, they are clearly aware of a number of other stories that evolved around this character during the filmmaking.[22]

Of course, as expected, the fans themselves made sure that the Figwit phenomenon and every story associated with it was related and archived. They created a Website, figwitlives.net, which serves as a meeting point for all Figwit fans. It provides updated information on Figwit the character as well as on the actor who played him and even includes galleries with fan art. The Figwit phenomenon was also taken up by the press and was covered in articles in *USA Today*, *Big Issue*, *Guardian*, and *Toronto Star*. Even the film merchandise industry has recognized Figwit's place in the film folklore: in Decipher's *The Lord of the Rings* Trading Card Game there is a card dedicated to Figwit. He is given the name Aegnor, a marginal character from Tolkien's legendarium,[23] but the card notes also that he is "affectionately referred to as Figwit by his contemporaries in Rivendell."

The case of Figwit shows clearly the power of the "folklore of audiences" over films and filmmaking. In the case of *LOTR* this process was even more effective, as Figwit was spotted in the first film and by the time the third film appeared two years later, Peter Jackson had enough time to be made aware of him and to give him extra lines. But, as mentioned before, Jackson did the revolutionary thing of acknowledging the importance of fans right from the beginning, by promising to name them in the film's credits. Internet film communities played an important role in the making and promoting of the film, and it is worth noting that Jackson stayed only for a little while at the official after–Oscars party and quickly headed to the party of theonering.net, one of the most important Web meeting places for the book and film fans.

Conclusion: Filming Fantasy, Filming Folklore

As mentioned earlier, an exhaustive discussion of the interaction of film and folklore in Jackson's *The Lord of the Rings* trilogy is beyond the scope and range of one essay only. The three films attempted to adapt a three-volume novel rooted in folklore and producing its own vibrant and influential folklore. Scholars now have in their possession 11 hours and 22 minutes of film that was shaped and molded over at least five years. Its creators, most of whom were long-term and enthusiastic Tolkien fans, were in touch with other Tolkien fans, old and new alike. The three main topics I have examined in this essay are, in my opinion, of especial importance in discussing folklore and its relation to film adaptations of fantasy literature. Fantasy is often inspired by folklore, and locating instances of where "external" folklore has been brought in to enhance (as in the case of the Elves) the "internal" folklore of the work of fantasy adapted shows us how concepts of folklore change in time and in different cultural concepts. Tolkien was a scholar of medieval studies and his concept of "Celticity" is very much dependent upon material that is authentically (which for him meant linguistically) Celtic. On the contrary, the filmmaking team relied on much more romanticized "Celtic" folklore which has dominated popular culture since the late 19th and early 20th centuries. Fantasy is also a genre akin to fairy tales and myths, full of monsters and traditional "baddies." Examining the stock characters of horror film (either meant to be scary or meant to be funny and satirical) in relation to how evil or terrifying fantasy characters are portrayed in film adaptations shows the importance of "global" cinematic folklore, either enhancing the imagery of such characters as they appear in the literary work or contradicting it, like the half-zombie realization of the Army of the Dead in Jackson's trilogy. Finally, the "folklore of the audiences," which seems to be a natural phenomenon when a film reaches cult status, has an even better chance to emerge in adaptations of fantasy literature, as fantasy is one of the best-selling genres in the publishing world and habitually generates fan activity from a dedicated readership. The leap from fan activity based on the books to fan activity based on a film adaptation is a very small one. Folklore in film and television seems to create daily a new vernacular culture, and the position of film adaptations of fantasy literature in this process is bound to remain of paramount importance.

NOTES

1. For a detailed discussion of the development of Tolkien's Elves from the tiny elves and fairies of his early poems to his latest writings see Fimi 2008, 13–27.
2. *The Fellowship of the Rings*, Extended DVD edition, The Appendices, Part One: From Book to Vision > Designing and Building Middle-earth > Weta Workshop.
3. For a discussion of the creative uses of these two sources in the character of Túrin Turambar see Helms 1981 and St. Claire 1995.
4. See Fimi 2006 for a full discussion of Tolkien's own conceptions of these terms.
5. "Sidhe," pronounced "Shee," is the Irish name for the fairies.
6. The book is not paginated. The entry and illustration is found in pages 34–5 counting from the frontispiece.
7. In this paragraph all quotations are from *The Fellowship of the Ring*, Extended DVD edition, The Appendices, Part One: From Book to Vision > Designing and Building Middle-earth > Designing Middle-earth.
8. Nowadays, the concept of a homogeneous "Celtic" people that formed the main population of Britain before the Anglo-Saxon "invasion" or "migration" has been vigorously challenged. Indeed, the validity of the terms "Celt" and "Celtic" itself in archaeology has been called into question, triggering a heated debate which started in the 1980s and is still going on today. As Hale and Payton have shown, Hobsbawm's notion of the "invention of tradition" (1983) "shook the foundation upon which the Celts were constructed" (2000, 5). The first all-encompassing critique of the notion of "the Celts" was Chapman's *The Celts: the Construction of a Myth* (1992). The response of archaeology to this criticism has been mainly supportive. Many archaeologists like Champion (1996), James (1999), and Collis (2003) have questioned the use of the term "Celtic" for the La Tène and Hallstatt "cultures." Indeed, as Collis has shown, the equation of the La Tène/Hallstatt cultures with the Celtic peoples originated in the mid nineteenth-century, and was mainly based on a simplistic ethnic interpretation of burial rites, as well as on an urge to provide the archaeological evidence for historical sources which were taken for granted (1997, 196–8; see also Champion 1996 and Cunliffe 1997). In terms of the culture and population of the British Isles, Simon James

has even proposed the elimination of the term "Celtic," in favor of the more faithful "Iron Age peoples of Britain and Ireland" (1999).

9. *The Fellowship of the Ring*, Extended DVD edition, The Appendices, Part One: From Book to Vision > Designing and Building Middle-earth > Designing Middle-earth.

10. For an overview of "Celtic" music, its characteristics and its invented tradition, see Smyth 2002.

11. *The Fellowship of the Ring*, Extended DVD edition, The Appendices, Part Two: From Vision to Reality > Sound and Music: Music for Middle-earth.

12. I am using the term "global folklore" here after Peterson 2007 who discusses the transformation of the Jinn of Middle Eastern and Islamic lore into the "Genie," a new "global" folklore character created by Hollywood.

13. *The Return of the King*, Extended DVD edition, Special Features — Audio Commentaries > The Director and Writers.

14. *The Return of the King*, Extended DVD edition, Special Features — Audio Commentaries > The Design Team.

15. They are referred to only once as "ghosts of Men" and later on we find out that when they gathered at the Stone of Erech "a chill wind like the breath of ghosts came down from the mountains" (Tolkien 1993b, 69).

16. *The Return of the King*, Extended DVD edition, Part One > Special Features–Audio Commentaries > The Director and Writers.

17. *The Return of the King*, Extended DVD edition, Part One > Special Features–Audio Commentaries > The Design Team.

18. *The Return of the King*, Extended DVD edition, The Appendices, Part Five: The War of the Ring > Designing and Building Middle-earth > Designing Middle-earth.

19. *The Return of the King*, Extended DVD edition, Part One > Special Features–Audio Commentaries > The Design Team.

20. See Koven 2008 (chapter 3, "Searching for Tale-Types and Motifs in the Zombie Film") for an overview of the challenges of discussing the zombie film via the methodology of folklore.

21. *The Return of the King*, Extended DVD edition, Part One > Special Features–Audio Commentaries > The Design Team.

22. See *The Return of the King*, Extended DVD edition, Special Features — Audio Commentaries > The Director and Writers and The Design Team.

23. Aegnor was the fourth son of Finarfin and brother to Finrod Felagund and Galadriel. He was slain in the Siege of Angband (Tolkien 1977, 61, 151).

WORKS CITED

Bakshi, Ralph, dir. *The Lord of the Rings*. USA: Warner Home Video, 2001.

Bird, S. Elizabeth. "Cultural Studies as Confluence: The Convergence of Folklore and Media Studies." In *Popular Culture Theory and Methodology*. Edited by Harold E. Hinds. Bowling Green, Ohio: Bowling Green University Popular Press, 1996.

Burns, Marjorie. "Old Norse Literature." In *The J.R.R. Tolkien Encyclopedia: Scholarship and Critical Assessment*. Edited by Michael D.C. Drout. New York: Routledge, 2006.

_____. *Perilous Realms: Celtic and Norse in Tolkien's Middle-earth*. Toronto: University of Toronto Press, 2005.

Champion, T. "The Celts in Archaeology." In *Celticism*. Edited by Terence Brown. Amsterdam and Atlanta: Rodopi, 1996.
Chapman, Malcolm. *The Celts: The Construction of a Myth*. London: Macmillan, 1992.
Collis, John. "Celtic Myths." *Antiquity* 71, no. 271 (1997), 195–201.
_____. *The Celts: Origins, Myths & Inventions*. Stroud: Tempus, 2003.
Cunliffe, Barry W. *The Ancient Celts*. Oxford; New York: Oxford University Press, 1997.
Figwit Lives! "F.A.Q." http://www.figwitlives.net/faq.htm (accessed June 2009).
Fimi, Dimitra. "'Mad Elves' and 'Elusive Beauty': Some Celtic Strands of Tolkien's Mythology." *Folklore* 117, no. 2 (2006): 156–170.
_____. *Tolkien, Race and Cultural History: From Fairies to Hobbits*. Basingstoke, UK: Palgrave Macmillan, 2008.
_____. "Tolkien's 'Celtic' Type of Legends: Merging Traditions." *Tolkien Studies* 4 (2007): 51–71.
Froud, Brian, and Alan Lee. *Faeries*. Edited by David Larkin. New York: Abrams, 1978.
Hale, Amy, and Philip Payton. Introduction to *New Directions in Celtic Studies*. Edited by Amy Hale and Philip Payton. Exeter: University of Exeter Press, 2000.
Hall, R.D. "Through a Dark Lens: Jackson's *Lord of the Rings* as Abject Horror." *Mythlore*, 25, no. ¾ (2007): 55–9.
Helms, Randel. *Tolkien and the Silmarils*. Suffolk: Thames and Hudson, 1981.
Hobsbawm, E. (Introduction) "Inventing Traditions." In *The Invention of Tradition*. Edited by E. Hobsbawm and T. Ranger. Cambridge: Cambridge University Press, 1983.
Howe, John. *Gandalf Falls with the Balrog*. Iron Crown Enterprises, 1997.
Jackson, Bruce. "A Film Note." *Journal of American Folklore* 102 (1989): 388–89.
Jackson, Peter, dir. *The Lord of the Rings: The Fellowship of the Ring*. Special extended DVD edition. USA: New Line Home Entertainment, 2004.
_____. *The Lord of the Rings: The Return of the King*. Special extended DVD edition. USA: New Line Home Entertainment, 2004.
James, Simon. *The Atlantic Celts: Ancient People or Modern Invention?* Madison: University of Wisconsin Press, 1999.
Koven, Mikel J. *Film, Folklore, and Urban Legends*. Lanham, MD, and Plymouth: Scarecrow, 2008.
_____. "Folklore Studies and Popular Film and Television: A Necessary Critical Survey." *Journal of American Folklore* 116 (2003): 176–195.
Laing, Lloyd Robert. *The Archaeology of Late Celtic Britain and Ireland, c. 400–1200 AD*. London: Methuen, 1975.
McLarty, Lianne. "Masculinity, Whiteness, and Social Class in *The Lord of the Rings*." In *From Hobbits to Hollywood: Essays on Peter Jackson's Lord of the Rings*. Edited by Ernest Mathijs and Murray Pomerance. Amsterdam: Rodopi, 2006.
The McManus: Dundee's Art Gallery and Museum. "The Riders of the Sidhe." http://www.mcmanus.co.uk/content/collections/database/riders-sidhe (accessed May 2010).
Nasmith, Ted. *The Balrog*. 1987 Tolkien Calendar. Unwin, 1987.
O'Shea, Helen. "Nation, Gender and Musical Stereotypes in Irish Music." In *Popular Music: Commemoration, Commodification and Communication*. Proceedings of the 2004 IASPM Australia New Zealand Conference, held in conjunction with the Symposium of the International Musicological Society, 11–16 July 2004.

Edited by Denis Crowdy. Melbourne: International Association for the Study of Popular Music, Australia New Zealand Branch, 2005.

Peterson, Mark Allen. "From Jinn to Genies: Intertextuality, Media, and the Making of a Global Folklore." In *Folklore/Cinema: Popular Film as Vernacular Culture.* Edited by Sharon R. Sherman and Mikel J. Koven. Logan: Utah State University Press, 2007.

St. Claire, Gloriana. "Volsunga Saga and Narn: Some Analogies." In *Proceedings of the J.R.R. Tolkien Centenary Conference, 1992: Proceedings of the Conference Held at Keble College, Oxford, England, 17th–24th August 1992, to Celebrate the Centenary of the Birth of Professor J.R.R. Tolkien, Incorporating the 23rd Mythopoeic Conference (Mythcon XXIII) and Oxonmoot 1992.* Edited by Patricia Reynolds and Glen GoodKnight. Milton Keynes: Tolkien Society, 1995.

Sharp, Elizabeth A., ed. *Lyra Celtica: An Anthology of Representative Celtic Poetry.* Edinburgh: P. Geddes and colleagues, 1896.

Sherman, Sharon R., and Mikel J. Koven, eds. *Folklore/Cinema: Popular Film as Vernacular Culture.* Logan: Utah State University Press, 2007.

Shippey, T.A. *The Road to Middle-earth.* Rev. ed. London: HarperCollins, 2005.

Shippey, Tom. "Light-Elves, Dark-Elves, and Others: Tolkien's Elvish Problem." *Tolkien Studies* 1 (2004): 1–15.

Sinex, Margaret A. "'Oathbreakers, why have ye come?' Tolkien's 'Passing of the Grey Company' and the Twelfth-century Exercitus mortuorum." In *Tolkien the Medievalist.* Edited by Jane Chance. London and New York: Routledge, 2003.

Smyth, Gerry. "Review of *The Complete Guide to Celtic Music: From the Highland Bagpipe and Riverdance to U2 and Enya* by June Skinner Sawyers." *Popular Music* 21, no. 2 (2002), 242–4.

Thompson, Kristin. *The Frodo Franchise: "The Lord of the Rings" and Modern Hollywood.* Berkeley and London: University of California Press, 2008.

Tolkien, J. R.R. *The Lord of the Rings.* Vol. 1, *The Fellowship of the Ring.* Paperback ed. London: HarperCollins, 1993a.

———. *The Lord of the Rings.* Vol. 3, *The Return of the King.* paperback ed. London: HarperCollins, 1993b.

———. *The Monsters and the Critics and Other Essays.* Edited by Christopher Tolkien. London: Allen and Unwin, 1983.

———. *The Silmarillion.* Edited by Christopher Tolkien. London: Allen and Unwin, 1977.

Tolkien Society. "Frequently Asked Questions." http://www.tolkiensociety.org/faq 01.html (accessed May 2010).

Lady Wilde. *Ancient Legends, Mystic Charms and Superstitions of Ireland: With Sketches of the Irish Past.* London: Ward and Downey, 1888.

Making the Connection on Page and Screen in Tolkien's and Jackson's *The Lord of the Rings*[1]

Yvette Kisor

The basic structural method of Tolkien's *The Lord of the Rings* has been identified as that of *entrelacement*, or interlace. This refers to the narrative pattern typified by the interlace romances of the thirteenth century, particularly the great prose Arthurian Vulgate cycle, as well as glancing at the somewhat different use of interlace evident in *Beowulf*.[2] Indeed, Tolkien's use of interlace partakes of characteristics of the rather sprawling *entrelacement* of the cyclic romances, weaving together the various narrative strands, particularly after the breaking of the Fellowship at the end of *The Fellowship of the Ring*. In bringing different strands of the story together, Tolkien utilizes a variety of techniques, only one of which entails characters involved in separate adventures actually meeting (as happens, for example, when Aragorn, Legolas, and Gimli finally meet up with Merry and Pippin at Isengard [III:8]). As well as this kind of physical interaction, Tolkien weaves strands of story together through the recurrence of physical phenomena, the use of objects, the resonance of place, the echoing of language, the use of song and poetry, and direct narrative connections made by the authorial voice, and in so doing makes use of several techniques prominent in *Beowulf*. The importance of connection is evident in Peter Jackson's films as well, where different techniques, such as intercutting, visual doubling, and voice-over, are possible. These connective nodes, whether visual or literary, work to underline the links between strands of story that exist both on the level of plot and of theme, ultimately connecting not only the separate adventures of the members of the Fellowship, but also joining the story of the Ring to the entire history of Middle-earth.

The interlace pattern Tolkien uses is, as Shippey notes, not a neat and tidy one. As the narration follows first one group of characters and then another, the different strands of the story follow different chronologies. This is in part due to the narration following one group farther forward in time before it returns to another group (and an earlier point in time). But it is also due to the use of flashback as some segments of the action are narrated by individual characters, such as Pippin and Merry relating the storming of Isengard (III: 9) or Legolas and Gimli recounting Aragorn's journey on the Paths of the Dead (V: 9). Shippey refers to this as "a 'leapfrog' pattern, the strands of story overtaking one another and then backtracking" ("From Page" 70). Shippey characterizes this "chronological 'leapfrogging'" as deliberate on Tolkien's part and stresses the importance of his inclusion of both maps and a chronology to prevent the "meaningless confusion" so typical of the thirteenth-century romances featuring *entrelacement* (*Road* 161). Among the advantages of this tightly controlled "leapfrogging" are the possibilities it creates for suspense, but the primary import is much more significant and goes to the thematic heart of the novel. Because the characters in different strands of story generally cannot see what is happening elsewhere, they experience confusion, even despair, and must make choices in the face of that feeling of uncertainty. The bravest characters do not give in to despair but continue to choose and keep moving forward. According to Shippey their metaphysical situation reflects the human condition: "The whole structure of *Lord* indicates that decision and perseverance may be rewarded beyond hope. This, I would suggest, is Tolkien's philosophic core. He believes in the workings of Providence" ("Another Road" 251–2).[3]

Jackson, however, has largely abandoned Tolkien's "leapfrogging" narration in preference of following a stricter chronology in which actions taking place in different strands of story are shown simultaneously through intercutting. As Shippey notes, "[t]his makes excellent sense in narrative terms and shows what competent and imaginative professionals can do" ("From Page" 71). However, while Shippey acknowledges the sensibleness of this streamlining of the narrative, he does feel something has been lost. That something is important, in Shippey's estimation, because it is the philosophic message of the novel, the idea that dogged perseverance in the absence of knowledge or assurance has value. The loss of this message, embedded in the narrative structure Tolkien uses, may not be accidental: "This somber awareness of likely defeat, *very far removed from the mode of commercial cinema*, may explain why

Tolkien took some of the narrative turns he did" ("From Page" 72, italics added). Here Shippey suggests the possibility that the elimination of Tolkien's narrative method of staggered chronologies is not simply due to a preference for a "neater" narration that simplifies chronology, but to a fundamental discomfort with the narrative message contained therein: "Tolkien's narrative structures, I would suggest, are a part of his worldview. That is why they cannot be imitated on screen" ("From Page" 71).

While Shippey's emphasis on the thematic importance of Tolkien's narrative method is perhaps unique,[4] he is not alone in observing the difference, and the ramifications of the difference, between Tolkien's and Jackson's narrative techniques. Some critics focus on the more immediate effects of the changes. Janet Brennan Croft, for example, discusses Jackson's decision to intercut the narrative strands of the last two films at some length, pointing out the loss of dramatic irony that results and stressing Tolkien's own insistence on treating the different branches of the story in sequence rather than simultaneously (*Letters* 275, quoted in Croft 70–1). Others, while less outwardly negative in their assessment, suggest perhaps more significant losses to the core meaning of the novel. One critic notes that "this format [Tolkien's use of interlace] allows plot threads to dangle for prolonged periods and forces readers to make connections between events on their own. The film trilogy makes several narrative choices that substantially alter the structure and tone of the story. One of the most important is the depiction of simultaneous action through editing, with cuts back and forth between Sam and Frodo and the other adventurers. Additionally, dividing events between three films involves some radical shifts from novel to film in the sequencing of the plot" (Lane 68). This is on the surface an essentially neutral assessment, observing the changes Jackson makes and noting that they are significant without elaborating on the specifics. However, the invoking of the activity of the reader in making connections is suggestive of Iser's characterization of readers as cocreators of texts and suggests how, if Shippey's sense of the novel's message is accepted, that message is conveyed, for "[t]he advantage of his non-chronological explanations in *Fellowship*, of the recurrent flashbacks and crosscuttings in *The Two Towers*, is that the reader is forced to share the characters' repeated bewilderments" (Shippey, "From Page" 72). It is through sharing the characters' state — confusion, with only incomplete knowledge at best — that the reader becomes cognizant of an important theme of the novel.

Many of these critical commentaries on Jackson's restructuring of the narrative on the whole favor Tolkien's technique, though not all.[5] I would like to suggest here that through intercutting Jackson develops a method of making connections that, while different from Tolkien's, is capable of suggesting similar thematic resonances, at least in some instances. At least one critic has suggested that, rather than simplifying Tolkien's narrative technique, "Jackson develops a still more intricate interlace structure [than Tolkien's], reshaping and intercutting scenes and revising characters' actions and motivations while casting each of his three films as a dramatically satisfying experience on its own terms" (Leitch 138). In order to examine Jackson's narrative technique, I would like to look at a few scenes in some detail. It may be, as Shippey suggests, that Tolkien's emphasis on the workings of Providence is obscured by Jackson's changes to the narrative structure. I will return to this relationship between narrative technique and core message in due course. Yet in order to approach this larger question I would like to consider whether, at least sometimes, even when the method is radically different, Jackson appears able to achieve an effect consonant with the impact, and perhaps even the message, of elements of Tolkien's work. Perhaps this can be best appreciated by taking a look at two scenes: the encounter with Shelob and Éowyn's slaying of the Witch-king.[6]

Both of these scenes are featured in the third film of Jackson's movie trilogy, and on the surface, it may seem that with each Jackson has taken liberties with Tolkien's conception. From the encounter with Shelob, Jackson has eliminated Sam in perhaps the biggest departure from Tolkien's epic, and Frodo therefore faces Shelob alone; further, Jackson has moved this encounter from the end of *TT* to the middle of *ROTK* and added a physical fight between Frodo and Gollum (or rather, has given Gollum's surprise attack and subsequent battle with Sam to Frodo) that includes Frodo's telling Gollum that he is going to destroy the Ring. In the scene between Éowyn and the Witch-king Jackson has minimized Merry's role, though he allows him the telling stroke against the Witch-king, and rearranged the sequence of events in the scene itself. But when one considers the emotional and thematic content and focuses on the way each scene is put together and how other aspects of the larger narrative are interwoven in it, it becomes clear that by using the techniques of film Jackson can render a similar effect.

In Tolkien's narrative, Éowyn's challenge of the Witch-king takes place in the space of less than two pages, and is related primarily from Merry's perspective (822–4; V:6). The account of the attack of the Lord of the Nazgûl upon Théoden and Dernhelm's standing forth alone is given from an omniscient perspective, followed by the transition to Merry's perspective as the dialogue between Éowyn and the Witch-king is narrated from his sightless point of view. Merry's own thoughts and reactions are also shown. Éowyn's laugh and revelation of her identity mark the lifting of Merry's fear and the opening of his eyes, and from that point the scene is related visually as well as aurally. The rest of the scene is recounted from Merry's perspective and includes not only what he sees but also what he thinks, remembers, and does as he becomes an actor in, as well as an observer of, the scene. The narrative itself is largely uninterrupted — with the single exception of Merry's vision of Dernhelm's face as he rode from Dunharrow, which flashes into Merry's memory as he determines to come to Éowyn's aid. No reference to events outside the encounter intrudes upon its narration; and its conclusion, a description of the defeated cry of the Witch-king, is marked by white space in Tolkien's chapter.

By contrast, the same scene in Jackson's film is cut into two pieces.[7] The first features Éowyn's challenge of the Witch-king, her decapitation of the Fell Beast, and her battle with the Witch-king as he swings his mace at her, finally shattering her shield (and arm) and standing over her, looking victorious. The scene is then broken, and the film cuts to a scene depicting the landing of the corsair ships, the disembarking of Aragorn, Legolas, and Gimli, and the Hosts of the Dead surging onto the land.[8] The return to the scene of Éowyn and the Witch-king is signaled by a shot of Merry coughing and scrambling out from beneath a fallen mûmak[9] and extends from the Witch-king's seizing Éowyn by the throat and raising her from the ground through Merry's stroke, Éowyn's stabbing of the Witch-king, and his disintegration as Éowyn collapses.[10]

Jackson's version has reshaped the scene into two climaxes and in so doing has reordered the scene into something rather different from Tolkien's version. In Tolkien's conception, the continuous scene has two essential movements and two moments of climax, but they are noticeably different from Jackson's. The first movement, Éowyn's verbal challenge of the Witch-king, reaches its climax in Éowyn's revealing of her identity and the lifting of the blackness from Merry's eyes. The second movement, the physical battle, reaches its climax in the rapid sequence of events as the Witch-king's apparent victory over Éowyn is suddenly reversed through Merry's unseen and unexpected stroke (narrated only after it is accomplished) and Éowyn's seizing of victory as she stabs the Witch-king. This moment of sudden reversal is Tolkien's great moment of eucatastrophe writ small; it will be repeated at the Cracks of Doom and at the Black Gate of Mordor.

Tolkien uses imagery of light and dark to emphasize these reversals. As Éowyn fells the Fell Beast and victory seems within her grasp we are told that "with its fall the shadow passed away. A light fell about her, and her hair shone in the sunrise" (824; V: 6). Yet as the Witch-king, referred to here for the only time in the scene as "the Black Rider," rises "[o]ut of the wreck" and strikes her with his mace, reversing the dynamic of victory, he is described as "ben[ding] over her like a cloud" (824; V:6), obscuring her light. When the dynamic of victory shifts for the final time and Éowyn drives her sword into her enemy, the sword's breaking is described as "sparkling" as the shift is accomplished and light is renewed. The dynamics of the scene's first movement too, Éowyn's verbal challenge of the Witch-king climaxing in Éowyn's revelation of her identity, are also expressed through images of light and dark. As the Witch-king descends on Théoden, the king's "golden shield was dimmed. The new morning was blotted from the sky. Dark fell about him" (822; V: 6). This darkness is literally figured in the darkness before Merry's eyes, which is lifted as Éowyn reveals herself and he sees her "her bright hair ... gleam[ing] with pale gold," facing her enemy, who looms "like a shadow of despair" where "all seemed dark about it" (823; V:6).

These two movements of Tolkien's scene, each expressing a parallel movement from light to dark to light again, are rearranged in Jackson's film. He too structures the scene into two movements but they are different both in narrative and emotional structure. He has shifted the revelation of Éowyn's identity to after the physical battle, which is extended, and made it continuous with her victory over the Witch-king. Further, Éowyn's line "I am no man" in response to the Witch-king's "You fool — no man can kill me. Die now" is emphasized through a break in the musical score of the scene — though the rest of the scene is accompanied by music, which builds until the moment Éowyn pulls off her helmet, allowing her long hair to fall free. The music breaks off at that point and her line is delivered into silence; the music begins again almost immediately as she drives her sword into the Witch-king's masked face.[11] Rather than two parallel movements of light to dark to light again, Jackson has structured two opposing movements, the first downward toward defeat, and the second upward toward victory. Thus Tolkien's two moments of climax, Éowyn's revelation of her identity and her slaying of the Witch-king, are united and moved to the end of the second scene. The moment of apparent defeat, when things seem darkest, becomes the climactic moment of the first scene.

The basic structure, then, is not wholly different; what appears as two parallel movements from light to dark to light again in Tolkien's conception becomes a single movement cut in two in Jackson's film. Jackson's version emphasizes the moment of darkness by cutting the scene at the point when things seem darkest. And his "doubling" of the structure comes into play not in the scene itself but in the scene that he places between the two halves: the scenes depicting Éowyn's encounter with the Witch-king are intercut with a scene depicting Aragorn's arrival at the Pelennor Fields. This scene exemplifies the same thematic and emotional content as the scene it bisects — the idea of sudden reversal. Just as Éowyn's apparent defeat will be turned to unexpected victory, the arrival of the corsair ships — which should bring aid to the forces of Mordor and presage the defeat of the forces of Gondor — becomes, in an unexpected reversal (at least as far as the Enemy is concerned), the arrival of Aragorn and the Armies of the Dead.

While Jackson has chosen to intercut the scene between Éowyn and the Witch-king with another scene of the battle of the Pelennor Fields, thus highlighting the connection between them and emphasizing the sudden reversal implicit in both, he achieves a different effect through a similar method in the Shelob scene. Tolkien's narration of the encounter with Shelob is remarkable for the presence of Galadriel. In considering how Tolkien has interlaced her person into the scene in Shelob's lair, it is useful to consider how differently he treats the scene of Éowyn's encounter with the Lord of the Nazgûl. While the battle between Éowyn and the Witch-king is largely continuous, the sole intrusion of ancillary material is the image of Dernhelm's face that flashes upon Merry's memory: "For into Merry's mind flashed the memory of the face that he saw at the riding from Dunharrow: the face of one that goes seeking death, having no hope" (823; V:6). The phrasing itself is almost an exact repetition of the thought expressed then: "the face of one without hope who goes in search of death" (785; V: 3). Yet the intrusion is brief and wholly sensible, the workings of memory as Merry hears Éowyn identify herself and he realizes that Dernhelm and Éowyn are one and the same.

The presence of Galadriel in Shelob's lair is of a different order. Rather than an act of memory, her presence seems to come unbidden. In fact, the memory that Sam recalls when he and Frodo hear the first stirrings of Shelob as they grope through the oppressive dark of Shelob's lair is of the barrow and Tom Bombadil, a memory called to mind by the feel of his sword and his recollection that his sword came from the barrow. As he stands, feeling the "blackness of despair and anger in his heart," the image of Galadriel comes as if in response to his wish for Bombadil's rescue: "It seemed to him that he saw a light: a light in his mind, almost unbearably bright at first, as a sun-ray to the eyes of one long hidden in a windowless pit. Then the light became colour: green, gold, silver, white. Far off, as in a little picture drawn by elven fingers, he saw the Lady Galadriel standing on the grass in Lórien and gifts were in her hands:" And you, Ring-bearer, he heard her say, remote but clear, for you I have prepared this" (703–4; IV:9). Everything about the narration of this scene suggests that it is something more than simple memory. Even the description of the image as "a little picture *drawn by elven fingers*" (italics added) suggests that Galadriel is actively present in the scene, creating the image in Sam's mind, as does the characterization of Sam hearing her voice, "remote but clear." Sam is not remembering the gift of the star-glass, or at least not *just* remembering it. The image is sent to him. Compare the way the workings of memory are described as Merry realizes the truth of Dernhelm's revelation that he is Éowyn: "For into Merry's mind flashed the memory" (823; V:6). The point is emphasized a few lines later as Frodo draws out the glass and it shines forth from his hand: "*Aiya Eärendil Elenion Ancalima!* he cried, and knew not what he had spoken; for it seemed that another voice spoke through his, clear, untroubled by the foul air of the pit" (704; IV:9).

The indication that he does not know what he has said and the phrasing "for it seemed that another voice spoke through his" suggests the active presence of Galadriel, just as for Sam "it seemed to him that he saw a light." We have been prepared for Galadriel to have this kind of presence and power throughout Book Four, from the effect of her elven rope on the darkness that overcomes Frodo's sight with the cry of the Black Rider in the Emyn Muil ("the silken-grey rope made by the folk of Lórien" (594; IV:1), "made by Galadriel herself, too, maybe" [597; IV:1]) to the dreams that bless Frodo's sleep on the journey towards Mordor (620; IV:2, 641; IV:4). The figure of Gandalf has a similar power to impose his presence upon them (601; IV:1), as he did for Frodo upon Amon Hen (630; IV:3).

Whatever other changes Jackson has made to this scene he has preserved Galadriel's presence and used voice-over and intercutting, techniques of film, to create her presence. Galadriel is first felt in the scene through voice-over. Her voice becomes the impetus to use the star-glass, just as it does in Tolkien's conception, though because Frodo is alone it is he, and not Sam, who hears her voice. The scene in Shelob's lair is a long one, extending in Jackson's version from Gollum's insistence that Frodo enter the tunnel, all the way through Frodo's discovery of Shelob, their brief battle, his escape out of the tunnel through the web, his subsequent fight with Gollum/Sméagol, his collapse, his vision of Galadriel, and his resulting determination to go on.[12] It is broken at only one point, as a brief scene of Sam falling down the stairs of Cirith Ungol, spotting the lembas, and turning to look back up the stairs is placed into the larger scene of Frodo in Shelob's lair. The point at which the scene intrudes is right before Galadriel's voice is heard: Frodo realizes he has been abandoned by Sméagol and utters Sam's name in a tone of obvious regret. When the scene resumes, Frodo is running through the tunnel and falls into a web, at which point he hears Galadriel's voice and he responds, as in the book, by drawing out the phial and crying out in Elvish. Jackson has, through this brief inserted scene and Frodo's uttering Sam's name, injected Sam into the scene right before Galadriel's presence is felt. Thus Sam's presence is felt at exactly the right moment (and, it could be argued, at the moment Frodo obviously realizes he was wrong to send Sam away and Sam determines to rejoin Frodo).

Galadriel's presence is felt a second time, much more strongly, in a scene created by Jackson, but, I would argue, very much in the spirit of Tolkien's concept of Galadriel's effect on Frodo.[13] As Frodo struggles on after the fight with Gollum/Sméagol, he collapses. As he falls, the setting suddenly becomes that of Lórien, though Frodo's figure remains the same dirt-stained, cobweb-covered form. As he lifts his head, Frodo sees a light that seems to emanate from the figure of Galadriel as she appeared in Lórien, and in a voice-over words similar to those she spoke to him before her fountain are heard: "This task was appointed to you, Frodo of the Shire. If you do not find a way ... no one will." She reaches down, extending her hand. With renewed determination Frodo takes it, and she smiles as she pulls him up. At that moment the scene switches abruptly back to Mordor and Frodo struggles on, renewed by his vision. It is clearly a vision and not a memory, for the voice-over heard here is not an exact repetition of Galadriel's words spoken before her fountain (the address "Frodo of the Shire" is new) and that scene took place at night. This scene takes place in the bright sun and corresponds to no specific scene from Frodo's time in Lórien. In terms of content this vision of Lórien corresponds to no specific creation of Tolkien's, either; but it does encapsulate, in a visual way, the effect of Galadriel's presence on Frodo. For an audience, the visual image of Frodo's unchanged figure moving with surprising suddenness between Mordor and Lórien has a memorable effect.

For that portion of Jackson's audience who are also lovers of Tolkien's original conception, the changes Jackson makes may finally be too great.[14] However, this essay has tried to explore the ways in which Jackson has succeeded in translating Tolkien's conception to the screen. By using the techniques of film, Jackson has been able in these two scenes to realize a visual counterpart to Tolkien's conception and to emphasize two themes crucial to Tolkien: the concept of eucatastrophe and the idea of the web of story. Through his structuring of the scene in which Éowyn defeats the Witch-king, and primarily his intercutting of that scene, Jackson has emphasized the eucatastrophe, the "sudden joyous 'turn,'" as Tolkien defined it ("On Fairy-stories" 68). Through the creation of Frodo's vision of Galadriel and his use of voice-over and intercutting in the Shelob scene, he has found a visual way of expressing Galadriel's action on Frodo and of emphasizing the interconnectedness of all things, joined in the web of story. In acknowledging the way these two scenes, through different techniques, succeed in conveying ideas important to the source text, we are back to the importance of theme and perhaps approaching the way in which a film can succeed in remaining "faithful" to the thematic core of a novel.

André Bazin has averred that "faithfulness to a form, literary or otherwise, is illusory: what matters is the *equivalence in meaning of the forms*" (20). If Jackson can use the techniques of film to convey ideas so central to Tolkien's ethos, as I suggest he does in these two particular scenes, then we are perhaps getting closer to equivalence of meaning in some form. By abandoning Tolkien's narrative technique of "leapfrogging" narration in favor of a more streamlined chronology in which simultaneous action is depicted through intercutting, Jackson has drawn near the kind of fidelity Bazin suggests is the more important. In other words, by being unfaithful to Tolkien's narrative technique he has achieved a fidelity to Tolkien's message, or theme — or at least some of his themes.

Shippey reached a very different conclusion in discussing just this issue of narrative technique, averring that by jettisoning Tolkien's technique, Jackson jettisons his emphasis on the value of determination in the face of incomplete knowledge as well. He also suggests that Tolkien's narrative technique reveals his faith in the workings of Providence: the idea that there is an overarching plan or purpose, even if the individual participants in the action cannot see it. "The world is a Persian carpet," he wrote, "and we are ants lumbering from one thread to the other and observing that there is no pattern in the colours" (*Road* 165). Yet the author of *Lord*, and the careful reader, Shippey goes on to say, has a larger view, and "[i]n this contrast between half and full perception lies the point of interlacings" (*Road* 163). In Jackson's technique of portraying simultaneous action through intercutting he has not wholly abandoned this thematic emphasis on Providence, I would argue, though he connects it with Tolkien's idea of eucatastrophe and the interconnectedness of all things rather than emphasizing the value of perseverance or the connection between the uncertain knowledge of the characters and the human condition.

This nexus of themes — Providence, eucatastrophe, interconnectedness — gains force when Jackson presents Éowyn's unexpected defeat of the Witch-king along with Aragorn's unexpected arrival in the corsair ships and both as part of the unexpected victory over the forces of Mordor at the Pelennor Fields. It attains prominence again when at the close of *The Two Towers* he shows us the unexpected arrival of Éomer with Gandalf at Helm's Deep turning that defeat into a victory, along with the Ents' destruction of Isengard (an unexpected reversal of the Entmoot's decision to stay out of the conflict) and Faramir's unexpected release of Frodo and Sam at Osgiliath.[15] Many more examples could be given.

By intercutting the events occurring in different strands of story Jackson suggests they are connected, and by presenting them in parallel moments,[16] whether it looks like defeat or victory is suddenly and unexpectedly achieved, he stresses not only their interconnectedness but repeats the moment of eucatastrophe in smaller and larger guises and through both of these tendencies suggests, ultimately, that there is a larger plan at work — a rather different method than Tolkien's narrative "leapfrogging," but perhaps Jackson attains thereby a thematic relevance not wholly inconsonant with Tolkien. Thus perhaps, as one critic has suggested, "[t]he screenplay's unusually free reshuffling of incidents from Tolkien in the interest of simplified chronology, economy, and drama underlines Jackson's often repeated determination to remain faithful to Tolkien's epic as a whole rather than to any of its component parts — perhaps the only goal that remained consistent over the trilogy's production" (Leitch 136–7). By allowing himself to be unfaithful to specific aspects of Tolkien's work, such as his narrative technique, or his character development and motivation, or particular incidents, Jackson is striving for a faithfulness to the totality of Tolkien's epic — its impact, its look and feel, and, perhaps, some of its themes.

NOTES

 1. Elements of this essay were first presented at the Second Annual Tolkien Conference, University of Vermont, April 2005.
 2. Shippey makes this identification in *The Road to Middle-earth* 160; it is earlier discussed at some length by West, who credits Thomson with being the first to identify Tolkien's structural technique as that of medieval interlace. Shippey's discussion of Tolkien's use of interlace expands significantly on these, in part by including not only the *entrelacement* of the medieval romances but also the interlace technique found in the epic poem *Beowulf*, as identified by Leyerle.
 3. Shippey has summarized these views in multiple writings; the fullest exposition is found in *Road* 160–7, "The Ethics of Interlace."
 4. Though West suggests something like this when he observes that "the technique of interlace ... may also show purpose or pattern behind change" (89).
 5. Paxson, for example, discusses the increased use of authorial omniscient commentary that explicitly connects the various narrative threads in time, characterizing this as evidence of Tolkien's increased concern "with clarifying the chronological relationship between the various story lines" and noting that "Jackson's solution was to intercut the action of all three story lines" (89). While I do not wholly agree with her assessment, it does characterize Jackson's changes as a solution to a problem evidenced in the literary text.
 6. The comparative method I employ here perhaps needs some defense. The recent trend in adaptation studies is away from so-called fidelity criticism that utilizes a comparative approach and toward a methodology grounded in postmodern theory that situates adaptations in an intertextual continuum, one which seeks to de-privilege the source text (the literary work). Stam is perhaps the best-known proponent of this "dialogic" approach; an example of how *The Lord of the Rings* can benefit from this kind of analysis, though not specifically following Stam's ideas, might be Flieger's "A Distant Mirror" in *Postmodern Medievalisms*. Other critics, such as Andrew, urge greater attention to the social and historical contexts of adaptations. However, dis-

senting voices, especially Kranz, have critiqued some of these stances, urging instead that critics take seriously the criticisms of a comparative approach and, rather than "throwing the baby out with the bathwater," seek to reform comparative methodologies. I would add further, along with Leitch, that when a film adaptation sets fidelity to the literary source text as a goal, however conceptualized, then comparative criticism is both called for and potentially fruitful.

7. In the EE, Scene 50 "The Nazgûl and His Prey" and Scene 52 "Shieldmaiden of Rohan"; in the TR these are Scenes 39 and 41 respectively. The first of these includes shots of Théoden pinned under his horse Snowmane as he watches the scene, suggesting his perspective rather than Merry's, as in Tolkien's rendering of this scene.

8. In the extended edition, scene 51, "The Black Ships," and scene 40 in the theatrical release.

9. In the theatrical release only; in the extended edition this brief shot is used earlier and the scene opens with a close-up on Éowyn's frightened face as the Witch-king reaches for her and grasps her by the throat.

10. In the extended edition this is scene 52, "Shieldmaiden of Rohan," and scene 41 in the theatrical release.

11. Though he does not note the way the musical score highlights this line, Høgset observes that the adaptation alters both "the original dialogue and sequence of events," turning Éowyn into a "modern action heroine" and her dialogue into "a catch phrase" (176).

12. "Shelob's Lair," scene 38 in the extended edition and scene 29 in the theatrical release, clocks in at 9 minutes and 8 seconds. Only one scene is longer: the final scene, "The Grey Havens" (scene 76 in the extended edition and scene 59 in the theatrical release) is ten seconds longer.

13. Timmons has called this "a most curious scene" (144); while he posits that Frodo's calling out Galadriel's name might have served as inspiration he does not observe the close associations that I point out here, though his focus is not on the structure of the scene nor on the role of Galadriel but on Jackson's portrayal of Frodo.

14. The reality of a Frodo who rejects Sam, for example, or a Faramir who falls to the lure of the Ring, may be too jarring for some to accept. Jackson and his cowriters have argued that they have taken moments latent in Tolkien's work and explored them — there *is* a certain distance that grows between Frodo and Sam once Sméagol becomes their guide, and there *is* a moment, albeit a very brief one, when Faramir appears capable of taking the Ring (665; IV:5). Of course, some might respond to this argument by pointing out that there is a vast difference between the idea that Sméagol's presence engenders a distance between Frodo and Sam and Sméagol's actually creating a real rift between the two (and through a false accusation of theft, no less!), or that Faramir's character is seriously compromised by making him a weaker version of Boromir.

15. Scenes 58–60 in the extended release and 48–50 in the theatrical release: "Forth Eorlingas," "The Flooding of Isengard," and "The Tales That Really Mattered."

16. Leitch has commented on the screenwriters' "concern for chronology, counterpoint, and dramatic effectiveness" (136) and though he does not pursue this idea his suggestion that Jackson has concerns beyond just simplifying the narrative chronology is an important one.

Works Cited

Andrew, Dudley. "Adaptation." In *Concepts in Film Theory*. Oxford: Oxford University Press, 1984.

Bazin, André. "Adaptation, or the Cinema as Digest." In *Film Adaptation*. Edited by James Naremore. New Brunswick, NJ: Rutgers University Press, 2000; Rpt. of chapter 3, *Bazin at Work: Major Essays and Reviews from the Forties and Fifties*. Translated by Alain Piette and Burt Cardullo. New York: Routledge, 1997; Translation of "L'*Adaptation* ou le cinéma comme digeste," *Esprit* 16, no. 146 (July 1948): 32–40.

Croft, Janet Brennan. "Mithril Coats and Tin Ears: 'Anticipation' and 'Flattening' in Peter Jackson's *The Lord of the Rings* Trilogy." In *Tolkien on Film: Essays on Peter Jackson's "The Lord of the Rings."* Edited by Janet Brennan Croft. Altadena, CA: Mythopoeic, 2004.

Flieger, Verlyn. "A Distant Mirror: Tolkien and Jackson in the Looking-glass." In *Postmodern Medievalisms*. Edited by Richard Utz and Jesse G. Swan. Cambridge: D.S. Brewer, 2004

Høgset, Øystein. "The Adaptation of *The Lord of the Rings*—A Critical Comment." In *Translating Tolkien: Text and Film*. Edited by Thomas Honegger. Zurich and Berne: Walking Tree, 2004.

Iser, Wolfgang. "The Reading Process: A Phenomenological Approach." *New Literary History* 3 (1972): 279–99.

Kranz, David L. "Trying Harder: Probability, Objectivity, and Rationality in Adaptation Studies." In *The Literature/Film Reader: Issues of Adaptation*. Edited by James M. Welsh and Peter Lev. Lanham, MD: Scarecrow, 2007.

Lane, Cara. "The Ring Returns: Adaptation and the Trilogy." *Film & History* 35, no. 1 (2005): 67–9.

Leitch, Thomas. "Exceptional Fidelity." In *Film Adaptation and Its Discontents: From "Gone with the Wind" to "The Passion of the Christ."* Baltimore: Johns Hopkins University Press, 2007.

Leyerle, John. "The Interlace Structure of *Beowulf*." *University of Toronto Quarterly* 37 (1967): 1–17.

The Lord of the Rings: The Return of the King. Screenplay by Peter Jackson, Fran Walsh, and Philippa Boyens. Directed by Peter Jackson. Performed by Elijah Wood et al. New Line Home Entertainment, 2004. Special Extended DVD Edition.

The Lord of the Rings: The Return of the King. Screenplay by Peter Jackson, Fran Walsh, and Philippa Boyens. Directed by Peter Jackson. Performed by Elijah Wood et al. New Line Home Entertainment, 2004. Theatrical Release DVD.

Paxson, Diana. "Re-vision: *The Lord of the Rings* in Print and on Screen." In *Tolkien on Film: Essays on Peter Jackson's "The Lord of the Rings."* Edited by Janet Brennan Croft. Altadena, CA: Mythopoeic, 2004.

Shippey, Tom. "Another Road to Middle-earth: Jackson's Movie Trilogy." In *Understanding "The Lord of the Rings": The Best of Tolkien Criticism*. Edited by Rose A. Zimbardo and Neil D. Isaacs. Boston: Houghton Mifflin, 2004.

_____. "From Page to Screen: J. R. R. Tolkien and Peter Jackson." *World Literature Today* 77, no. 2 (2003): 69–72.

_____. *The Road to Middle-earth: How J. R. R. Tolkien Created a New Mythology*. 1982. Rev. ed. Boston and New York: Houghton Mifflin, 2003.

Stam, Robert. "Beyond Fidelity: The Dialogics of Adaptation." In *Film Adaptation*. Edited by James Naremore. New Brunswick, NJ: Rutgers University Press, 2000.
Thomson, George H. "*The Lord of the Rings*: The Novel as Traditional Romance." *Wisconsin Studies in Contemporary Literature* 8, no. 1 (Winter 1967): 43–59.
Timmons, Daniel. "Frodo on Film: Peter Jackson's Problematic Portrayal." In *Tolkien on Film: Essays on Peter Jackson's "The Lord of the Rings."* Edited by Janet Brennan Croft. Altadena, CA: Mythopoeic, 2004.
Tolkien, J.R.R. *The Letters of J.R.R. Tolkien: A Selection*. Edited by Christopher Tolkien. Boston and New York: Houghton Mifflin, 2000.
_____. "On Fairy-stories." 1947. *The Tolkien Reader*. New York: Ballantine, 1966.
_____. *The Return of the King*. 1955. Boston and New York: Houghton Mifflin, 1999.
_____. *The Two Towers*. 1954. Boston and New York: Houghton Mifflin, 1999.
West, Richard C. "The Interlace Structure of *The Lord of the Rings*." In *A Tolkien Compass*. Edited by Jared Lobdell. LaSalle, IL: Open Court, 1975.

"It's Alive!"
Tolkien's Monster on the Screen

SHARIN SCHROEDER

> ...*I wanted to become a filmmaker the moment I saw [the original King Kong at age nine].... Actually, I wanted to become a monster-maker first,"* Jackson corrects himself, *"because I didn't really know what directing was.*
> *Evening Standard*, December 8, 2005

Peter Jackson's *The Lord of the Rings* shows a fascination with monsters, unsurprisingly for a director who began his career making monsters in splatter science fiction and horror films such as *Bad Taste* (1987) and *Brain Dead* (1992). In the director's commentary to the extended DVDs of *LOTR*, Jackson shows that his portrayal of monsters was an integral part of his vision of Middle-earth. He consistently argued on behalf of giving the monsters important roles in *LOTR*, even when New Line would have preferred to cut the Watcher in the Water and initially asked for as little Gollum as possible.[1] Jackson not only fought to keep as many monster sequences in the film as he could, he also often notes that his conception of the monsters was developed quite early in his planning. He began developing the Moria cave troll two years before he began shooting the scene in Balin's tomb, and he claims that his goal was to create a monster that felt "real" (*FOTR* Scene 35). Jackson's attempts to create "real" monsters, though not always following J.R.R. Tolkien's vision for his monsters, do take a similar approach to sub-creation, the term Tolkien uses to describe the artist's shaping of believable secondary worlds.[2] This approach to sub-creation has not been adequately linked to another monster story, Mary Shelley's Frankenstein myth.

To mention Peter Jackson's trilogy alongside *Frankenstein* has by now become a commonplace in critical studies. However, most scholars who make the connection have examined *Frankenstein* and *Lord* as studies in film adaptation. They describe how the reincarnation of a book into a film can change the way the story is received and evolves — and, keeping in mind how James Whale's 1931 *Frankenstein* and Terence Fisher's 1957 *Curse of Frankenstein* transformed the cultural memory of Shelley's text — they prophesy as to how Jackson's work will change or replace aspects of Tolkien's text.[3] I wish to show the implications of a different parallel between *Frankenstein* and *Lord* by demonstrating that Tolkienian sub-creation is Frankensteinian. The retellings of the *Frankenstein* myth inform both Tolkien and Jackson's methods of sub-creation and their portrayal of their monsters by raising the ethical questions of monster creation that were inherent to Shelley's myth. Indeed, Jackson's portrayal of monsters has instigated or renewed criticisms of both his and Tolkien's portrayal of the "other."[4] Why are some monsters irredeemable? Are the monsters like us or not like us? What role do we play in making and redeeming monsters?

Tolkien had been interested in monsters long before he wrote *Lord*. In "Beowulf: The Monsters and the Critics" (1936), Tolkien diverged with previous *Beowulf* scholars by defending the central place of the monsters in the poem: "[I]t is an enhancement and not a detraction, in fact it is necessary, that [Beowulf's] final foe should be not some Swedish prince, or treacherous friend, but a dragon: a thing made by imagination for such a purpose.... If the dragon is the right end for Beowulf, and I agree with the author that it is, then Grendel is an eminently suitable beginning" (32). As Tolkien claims in his notes on W.H. Auden's 1956 *New York Times* review of *The Return of the King*, a monstrous enemy makes Beowulf "something quite different and more horrible than a 'political' invasion of equals ... such as Ingeld's later assault upon Heorot":

> The overthrow of Grendel makes a good wonder-tale, because he is too strong and dangerous for any ordinary man to defeat, but it is a victory in which all men can rejoice because he was a monster, hostile to all men and to all humane fellowship and joy. Compared with him even the long politically hostile Danes and Geats were Friends, on the same side [*Letters* 242].

Tolkien's and Jackson's work shows us that the appeal of wonder-tales like *Beowulf* remains: human audiences still understand community by reading and watching marvelous tales of monster defeat. But conceptions of the monster have evolved from *Beowulf* to *Frankenstein* to Tolkien to Jackson. Even the horrific Grendel, with whom the audience is never supposed to sympathize, is described in terms that save him from being an exclusively nonhuman monster.[5] By the time Tolkien and Jackson created their monsters, both artists could not help but think of their monsters in Frankensteinian terms. Just as Mary Shelley created a monster whose actions the reader can both pity and reject, Tolkien and Jackson both have alternatively sympathized with and condemned their monsters.

Despite Tolkien's acceptance of even irredeemable monsters in *Beowulf*, Tolkien ultimately found his created monsters much more problematic than Jackson does. Jackson's easy appropriation of Tolkien's monsters may stem in part from the fact that Jackson made his monsters using Tolkien's published text (Tolkien's finished creation), sometimes raiding specific parts of that text in order to create his own monsters. Jackson was less focused on Tolkien's later doubts about his monsters. But Jackson's work also places his creation within a long tradition of literary and movie monsters. Since Frankenstein's monster has so frequently been reappropriated in films, Jackson can borrow the Frankensteinian monster without conflict. He easily accepts the Frankensteinian monster in its own right and often sees his monster and adventure sequences as paying homage to filmmakers who have gone before him. In his commentary to *FOTR*, Jackson cites his admiration of aspects of the Hammer Horror series, Ray Harryhausen movies, and Spielberg's *Indiana Jones*. Jackson's visions of his monsters clearly come out of a long history of monster films. Consider Jackson's lighthearted commentary on the Moria cave troll's death scene and how he tries to separate his cave troll from the monsters that have come before it:

> JACKSON: I always loved the idea of a monster that sort of felt real. I wanted to not make it an over-the-top movie monster but a creature that you could sort of believe in, so we wanted to make him a little stupid—you know, like he's not really evil, but he's just fallen into bad company; he's like a big simple kid who has just got bad friends ... he comes in waving his hammer around, but I wanted there to be sympathy for the troll 'cause I always imagined that the troll has a mother, you know, and she's probably got his bed turned down and a glass of warm milk [a laugh] by his bed and he's just not going to come home....
> WALSH: Ah!
> JACKSON: And I always felt quite sad really but a...
> WALSH: He is quite empathetic when he dies.
> JACKSON: Yeah, yeah.
> WALSH: ... which is, I think is...
> BOYENS: It is in the book [*FOTR* Scene 35]

Of course, the empathetic nature of the Moria cave troll's death is not in the book at all. When the cave troll arrives, the Fellowship is trapped and terrified, seeing only a few body parts of the approaching horror. The door of the chamber opens: "A huge arm and shoulder, with a dark skin of greenish scales, was thrust through the widening gap. Then a great, flat, toeless foot was forced through below. There was dead silence outside" (*Fellowship* 316). Boromir attempts to cut off the troll's arm, but his blade is notched and falls from his hand:

> Suddenly, and to his own surprise, Frodo felt a hot wrath blaze up in his heart. "The Shire!" he cried, and springing beside Boromir, he stooped, and stabbed with Sting at the hideous foot. There was a bellow, and the foot jerked back, nearly wrenching Sting from Frodo's arm. Black drops dripped from the blade and smoked on the floor. Boromir hurled himself against the door and slammed it again [316].

After fighting a battle with oncoming Orcs, not trolls, Gandalf calls out, "Now is the time.... Let us go before the troll returns!" It is at this point that "a huge orc-chieftan" leaps into the chamber and pins Frodo to the wall. The orc-chieftain is killed. We never see the cave troll again.

Jackson, Walsh, and Boyens may not have represented the troll as it appeared in the book, but Jackson's films are participating in the sub-creation of Frankensteinian monsters, creatures who are both vile and empathy-inducing. This Frankensteinian approach to sub-creation is, indeed, "in the book." In Tolkien's essay, "On Fairy-stories," Tolkien, like the scientists in Whale's 1931 *Frankenstein* and Fisher's 1957 *Curse of Frankenstein*, claims his right to create monsters. However, once the monster has been created, Tolkien frequently shows the doubt more apparent in Victor's musings in Mary Shelley's *Frankenstein*. Even though Tolkien's crime, if any, is far lesser than Victor Frankenstein's abandonment of his soon-to-become-murdering creature, like Victor, Tolkien has second thoughts about the moral implications of his creation.

Jackson's film is much less self-conscious about its monster creation. Monster creation is the film's raison d'être, and the *Frankenstein* monster movies are so well known to Jackson that their conventions are appropriated in an almost celebratory manner. Nonetheless, Jackson's wholehearted embrace of the Frankensteinian monster is extremely effective at presenting the moral questions that plague both Shelley and Tolkien's work. How much responsibility does the creator have towards its creature? Is it fair to identify the monsters we create as uniformly evil? What is our relation to the monster? How do we become monsters? Looking at how Jackson appropriated both Tolkien's Frankensteinian methods of sub-creation and the conventions of Frankenstein monster films helps us to understand the unsettling debates about monsterhood that the film has fueled, including debates about race.

Tolkien's Monster-Making

Tolkien's method of sub-creation is always caught between two conceptions of origin: the biblical account of the earth's genesis with its theological formulations of Lucifer, the fallen angel, and Shelley's *Frankenstein* myth. Of course, the *Frankenstein* story consciously links itself to biblical accounts of Adam and Satan by way of *Paradise Lost*. But Tolkien's creation mythology shows a Frankensteinian twist that is not present in the Bible or *Paradise Lost*. In Tolkien's mythology, evil is linked to the desire to create things for the wrong motives.

Tolkien's "The Music of the Ainur" represents a Genesis-like creator's ability to bring objects into being by envisioning them. His own fallen angel, Melkor, is fallen because of his Frankensteinian aspirations to create, a desire the biblical Satan never evinces. Unlike the Morning Star (translated "Lucifer" in the Vulgate), who, in Isaiah 14, is represented as saying "I will ascend to heaven; I will raise my throne above the stars of God," Melkor's sin is not about dethroning Ilúvatar. Although Melkor does wish to receive personal glory, this glory is linked to his desire to participate in individual acts of creation: "[I]t came into the heart of Melkor to interweave matters of his own imaginings that were not in accord with the theme of Ilúvatar; for he sought therein to increase the power and glory of the part assigned to himself.... [D]esire grew hot within him to bring into Being things of his own" (*The Silmarillion* 4).

Tolkien's myth stresses that Melkor was able only to corrupt, never to make original creations. As is stressed numerous times throughout the trilogy, the shadow can only mock, not make, and Melkor's desire led to the enslavement of Ilúvatar's creation (*Return of the King* 893, *Morgoth's Ring* 417). Given that Melkor's desires to create went so far awry, it is interesting that Tolkien claims a very similar desire for himself.

In "On Fairy-stories," Tolkien quotes a poem he had written to C.S. Lewis to defend sub-creation and to contest Lewis's early view that myths and fairy stories were lies breathed through silver (65).[6] In his poem, Tolkien not only shows that "Fantasy is a natural human activity," he also seems to defend monster creators. Even if humans fill the world with "Elves and Goblins" or "dared to build/Gods and their houses out of dark and light, / and sowed the seed of dragons," Tolkien claims these as their rights:

> Man, Sub-creator, the refracted Light
> through whom is splintered from a single White
> to many hues, and endlessly combined
> in living shapes that move from mind to mind.
> Though all the crannies of the world we filled
> with Elves and Goblins, though we dared to build
> Gods and their houses out of dark and light,
> and sowed the seed of dragons — 'twas our right
> (used or misused) [65].

Tolkien's defiant defense of sub-creation in this poem seems counter both to published elements in *Lord* and *The Silmarillion* and Tolkien's later creation anxiety. Should we read this splintered light as positive, as Tolkien here appears to, or should it be seen as a loss of purity? Saruman, we remember, was another light splinterer (*Fellowship* 252). Is the human sub-creative power important enough to make monster-creation a human right? Tolkien here demands a free will for human creatures — they must be allowed to sub-create creatures of their own.

Tolkien is aware of the dangers of this desire, but in "On Fairy-stories," he passes over them by falling back on his theological defense of sub-creation: "Fantasy remains a human right: we make in our measure and in our derivative mode, because we are made: and not only made, but made in the image and likeness of a Maker" (66). Tolkien acknowledges that "Fantasy can ... be put to evil uses. It may even delude the minds out of which it came. But of what human thing in this fallen world is that not true?" (65–66).

Tolkien gives his theological reasons for creating, but he has not adequately defended fantasy-making against the Frankensteinian crime of overreaching. The Frankenstein in James Whale's 1931 film, after all, is also creating in imitation of God; when he brings his monster to life, he ecstatically exclaims: "[N]ow I know what it feels like to be God!" The way Tolkien writes his characters, however, shows his critique of irresponsible creators. Tolkien is therefore not justifying monster creation, but only fantastic monster sub-creation. It is this distinction that proves so problematic.[7] Tolkien's defense does not quite take responsibility for the implications of his sub-creation — effects that would later bother him when he puzzled over the Uruk-hai and Orcs' irredeemability. He had made them. He had watched them fall. Could they not be redeemed? Tolkien's defense of sub-creation does, however, reject the option of looking at the dangers of sub-creation and despairing as a result. If we return to Tolkien's characters in *The Silmarillion* rather than to Tolkien the writer, we see that when a creator creates with humility rather than with a desire for power, the creation can be redeemed.

In his texts, Tolkien demonstrates several attempts at creation, including Melkor's, Aulë's, and Saruman's. In *The Silmarillion*, Melkor's creative ambition is contrasted to Aulë's. In making the Dwarves, Aulë also creates without the permission of Ilúvatar. Like Melkor, Sauron, Saruman, and Victor Frankenstein, Aulë creates his creatures is isolation and in secret. However, Aulë creates not out of a desire for glory or for slaves but out of impatience for the fulfillment of the theme of Ilúvatar: "I desired things other than I am, to love and to teach them" (38). Aulë makes a defense of his own creativity by comparing himself to a child who imitates his father, not out of "mockery, but because he is the son of his father" (38). Aulë is repeating Tolkien's Judeo-Christian defense of sub-creation. We create because we are in God's image. However, Aulë's defense quickly takes a Frankensteinian turn. After offering his work to Ilúvatar, to do what seems best to Ilúvator, Aulë asks, "But should I not rather destroy the work of my presumption?" (38). Tolkien's use of the word "presumption" links Aulë's work to Frankenstein's desire not merely to be in the image of God but to play God. Richard Brinsley Peake's *Presumption, or the Fate of Frankenstein* (1823) was the first play adaptation of Shelley's 1818 novel.

Peake's adaptation was responsible for many of the plot twists that have appeared in later *Frankenstein* adaptations, including the nonspeaking monster. Susan Wolfson's Longman edition of the novel, which includes Peake's play, states that Shelley's "memory of Peake's elaborate title prompted her to add" the new sentence in the 1831 edition where Victor called his monster "the living monument of presumption and rash ignorance" (Hitchcock 83, Wolfson 326). As was the case in Shelley's novel, the ethical decision as to whether or not Aulë should destroy his work hinges on the creator's responsibility towards the beings he has brought into existence. When Aulë raised the hammer to destroy his Dwarves, "the Dwarves shrank from the hammer and were afraid, and they bowed down their heads and begged for mercy" (38). Ilúvatar says to Aulë, "Does thou not see that these things have now a life of their own, and speak with their own voices? Else they would not have flinched from thy blow, nor from any command of thy will" (38). In an unfinished essay on Orcs, printed in *Morgoth's Ring*, Tolkien contrasted Aulë's desire with Melkor's, but he noted that both types of creation lead to a control that is evil: "*Aulë* wanted love. But of course had no thought of dispersing his power. Only Eru [Ilúvatar] can give *love and independence*. If a finite sub-creator tries to do this he really wants absolute loving obedience, but it turns into robotic servitude and becomes evil" (411).

What is the difference then, between Ilúvatar's desire, Melkor's desire, and the creative desires of Tolkien and Jackson? Sub-creating monsters raises the question as to whether we are new Frankensteins. Have we created a creature we accept? Should we kill our creation as soon as we meet it? Like Shelley's original monster, Jackson's monsters present themselves to the viewer and then must suffer our judgment. Are they like us, or not like us? Do we, as Jackson did with his Uruk character, Lurtz, and his Orc captain at the battle of Pellenor Fields, Gothmog (played by the same actor, Lawrence Makaore), create monsters with the set purpose of destroying them? Or do we recognize ourselves in the monsters — using the same language, falling into the same tricks of speech, so that the distinction between the creator and creature, hobbit and monster is less clear to the eye? When we watch Jackson's film, do we see and hear it from the monster's point of view, or do we see only our own?

Peter Jackson's Frankenstein: Saruman and Lurtz

Jackson's method of creation is Frankensteinian not only because his film, like all films, involved patching scenes together — often using shots that were originally intended for another part of the film entirely — but also because Jackson found himself reading (and raiding) Tolkien's text in a Frankensteinian manner, searching for the parts he needed but losing, as he and Boyens noted in their commentary to *Return of the King*, "the experience of the book as a whole" (*Return* Scene 62). By the time Peter Jackson filmed *LOTR*, Shelley's story of the monster's origins had become so much a part of our cultural heritage that Jackson can casually call an early scene in *FOTR* "a bit of a *Frankenstein* number" and, with his fellow screenwriters, condemn Saruman in another for his Frankenstein-like tendencies (*FOTR* Scenes 10, 40).

Because Jackson, Fisher, Whale, Tolkien, and Shelley all implicitly condemn the "real" creation of monsters by the characters in their works, their fascination with monster-creation becomes an important part of understanding sub-creation. Again, Jackson's commentary on his monsters shows him to be much less worried about the morality of his own creation than Tolkien became. Jackson relies upon Tolkien's published works and a long history of film monsters in order to create monsters that felt "real," without necessarily considering the implication of his creation. Jackson's understanding of the origin of Orcs is Tolkienian, but it follows Tolkien's earlier beliefs on the Orcs rather than his later doubts about his monsters.[8] The account of the Orcs' creation that Jackson drew on is described in *The Silmarillion*:

> But of those unhappy [Elves] who were ensnared by Melkor little is known of a certainty.... Yet this is held true by the wise of Eressëa, that all those of the Quendi who came into the hands of Melkor, ere Utumno was broken, were put there in prison, and by slow arts of cruelty were corrupted and enslaved; and thus did Melkor breed the hideous race of the Orcs in envy and mockery of the Elves, of whom they were afterwards the bitterest foes. For the Orcs had life and multiplied after the manner of the children of Ilúvatar; and naught that had life of its own, nor the semblance of life, could ever Melkor make since his rebellion in the Ainulindalë before the Beginning: so say the wise. And deep in their dark hearts the Orcs loathed the Master whom they served in fear, the maker only of their misery [*Silmarillion* 47].

Although this legend of the Orcs' origin is not the one Tolkien ultimately accepted, it was his vision when *Lord* was written, and it makes several important points about monster creation — corruption is not creation, and even corrupted races are not automata — they have life and free will of their own.[9] They speak and are not puppets.[10] Note that in this account the Orcs "multiplied after the manner of the children of Ilúvatar." Neither Tolkien nor Jackson portrays Orc women, Orc children, nor even the imagined mother of Jackson's cave troll. Jackson limits sympathy for his Uruk-hai, the only monsters whose physical creation the audience witnesses, by making their births inhuman.[11] As Saruman watches, Orcs in the Orthanc dig the motherless Uruk-hai out of mud and slime. When Lurtz, a character invented by Jackson, is born, Saruman's creation is still more unnatural than Frankenstein's monster. No grin wrinkles Lurtz's cheek as he seeks his creator. Lurtz's first action is to strangle the Orc who pulled him from the mud. The other Orcs look on horrified. Saruman watches with an almost expressionless face; he has just the hint of a proud smile as he holds back the shocked Orcs who appear desirous of saving their dying comrade (*FOTR* Scene 20).

By creating this murderous monster in such an unnatural way, Jackson limits audience questions as to how evil is passed down generationally, a missing piece in both Tolkien and Jackson's work. We do not like to see the generation of these creatures — it is safer to see the Uruk, Lurtz, torn full-grown from a pulpy mass than to have him born from a mother's womb. We can envision the original story of the Elves being corrupted because we have seen the corruption of Gollum and near fall of Boromir and Frodo. But the Orcs and Uruk-hai seem without the choice that even Gollum has. By showing a full-grown, motherless, and never innocent Lurtz, Jackson is able to create a creature only to kill it without raising Frankenstein's creature's question: "How dare you sport thus with life?" (72).

What film viewers may not realize is that in the scene of Lurtz's creation, Jackson's vision has gone in a full Frankensteinian circle. In the *FOTR*, Christopher Lee, who played Frankenstein's creature in 1957, gets a chance to create his own monster. Jackson cast Lee as his Saruman, noting in his audio commentary to *FOTR* that "it was a great thrill working with Christopher because I'd always been a fan of the old Hammer horror movies" (*FOTR* Scene 12).[12] The first of these Hammer horror movies was, of course, *The Curse of Frankenstein* (1957). The monster creation sequences mirror each other: Lee plays a monster born to kill in *The Curse of Frankenstein*; he welcomes another such monster into the world in *FOTR*.[13]

The Curse of Frankenstein's particularly cold and heartless Baron Frankenstein (Peter Cushing) has the scientific capability of bringing whole bodies back to life, but he insists on "creating" a being of his own. This creation is, of course, a corruption. Frankenstein patches together a body from a hanged criminal and from mutilated bits of corpses he buys from suppliers. To add the final touch of perfection to his creature, the brain of a genius, Frankenstein murders a famous scientist whom he has invited to his home.

When a chance lightning strike powers his machine and brings his creature to life unexpectedly, Frankenstein is away from his laboratory. Hearing crashing glass, he reenters the laboratory quickly, his look of confusion turning to surprise and joy at the sight of his living creature. The creature (Lee) rips away his bandages, revealing a hideous face. His eyes turn to and fro, uncertain where to look. The monster's gaze then zeroes in on his creator. He grabs Frankenstein with his left hand, whirls him round by the collar, and begins to strangle him. Frankenstein survives only because his tutor, Paul Krempe (Robert Urquhart), enters the room and is able to stop and knock out the monster. Frankenstein, when revived, is pleased with his violent and unspeaking creation and refuses Krempe's demands that he destroy what he has made.

Jackson and Lee were both certainly influenced by this earlier conception of the heartless creator and the monster that kills. Unlike Mary Shelley's Frankenstein, Saruman, though evincing a guarded disgust upon Lurtz's creation, does not turn from his creature. Like Peter Cushing's character in *The Curse of Frankenstein*, he educates Lurtz instead. Saruman explains the Orcs' history to the newly created Lurtz in *The Fellowship of the Ring*. The camera closes in on Isengard and then moves to a shot of Saruman talking with a low-growling, naked, and still somewhat slimy Lurtz:

> SARUMAN: Do you know how the Orcs first came into being? They were Elves once, taken by the Dark Powers, tortured and mutilated [Lurtz roars]. A ruined and terrible form of life. [Lurtz's eyes look down.] And now ... perfected. My fighting Uruk-hai! Whom do you serve?
> LURTZ: Saruman! [*FOTR* Scene 40].

Without mentioning Frankenstein by name, Philippa Boyens links Saruman's creation of the Uruk, Lurtz, to that of the mad scientist who attempts to play God, the Frankenstein from Whale's film who cries, "It's alive. It's moving. It's alive. Oh, it's alive.... In the name of God, now I know what it feels like to be God!" The screen writers discuss the scene as follows:

> BOYENS: The whole thing we were constantly trying to show is one of the reasons why Saruman has fallen is just as Melkor fell, the original spirit of evil within the world fell, is because of the jealousy of the power of life, the power of creation, and he's playing God, and that's what I love about the look in his eye in that scene between Saruman and Lurtz is he says "and now perfected," meaning that he is, he has that power, that power is now in him.
> WALSH: Genetic engineering.
> BOYENS: Genetic engineering. Exactly. And of course Tolkien is saying, sorry, within the greater ... within his own faith ... there is only one source of that power [*FOTR* Scene 40].

Even as they condemn Saruman's actions, the screenwriters note that they created Lurtz to be expendable. According to Jackson, Lurtz was created in order to give a focal point for an audience who needed a physical villain, not a distant disembodied eye or an absent wizard. In the fight scene between members of the Fellowship and the Orcs at the end of *FOTR*, Jackson noted that "a character like Lurtz comes in handy because we could now make it personal, that it wasn't just an anonymous Uruk that was shooting Boromir with the arrows, it was this creature called Lurtz that we sort of knew, and we hated him already."[14] Two minutes later, Jackson adds, "Having created our villain in Lurtz, we obviously have to finish him off" (*FOTR* Scene 44).

Lurtz was created to be killed; he is perhaps most representative of the monster that we want to maintain is not like us. Jackson relies on Lurtz's violence and his lack of history in order to make him disposable. If audience members can pity Lurtz at all, it is only in their anger at Sauron or Saruman for creating debased creatures as an expendable commodity, with the creatures' inherent evil serving as a justification for their rapid destruction. However, Jackson has to do a lot of work to keep us from sympathizing with Lurtz. Jackson needs to provide this violence, lack of history, and lack of language in order to turn Lurtz into a monster. Visually, Lurtz is one of the creatures who is most like us — more human in looks than Shelob, the Balrog, the cave troll, or even Gollum. Because Lurtz is anthropomorphic, he is the most troubling of Jackson's monsters. Lurtz's very humanness leads audiences to wonder where the difference is, and, as is discussed in detail by other critics and film reviewers, some viewers feel that their discomfort derives from something to do with race. Lurtz is tall and muscular, with black skin and long, dark hair. He does not creep on all fours like Jackson's Gollum (actor Andy Serkis) or lumber about like the cave troll. Indeed, unlike these CGI monsters, Lurtz is made of flesh and blood (and prosthetic). Uruk-hai look like men — indeed, they are bred from men. Because audience members recognize Lurtz as looking so similar to themselves, they may feel uncomfortable.[15] The Orc is no longer a demon who has nothing to do with us.[16] Tolkien's discomfort with his Orcs and the negative response in some quarters to Jackson's Lurtz may result from the fact that our culture cannot always comfortably kill our Grendels.

Monster Identity Crises: The Intersection Between Form and Speech

Tolkien and his characters, particularly Melkor, Aulë, and Saruman, raise the Frankensteinian question of whether the creator has overreached permissible boundaries. In this final section of my essay on Tolkien and Jackson's

Frankensteinian creations, I wish to examine how Shelley's *Frankenstein* presents an artistic model in which language intersects with form in order to create a monster—or humanize a creature. How did Jackson succeed in making Lurtz, his most anthropomorphic monster, so unlike us that cinematic audiences cheer at his death scene?[17] And why do the critics in the wings blame Jackson for such a portrayal? We blame Victor Frankenstein, not Mary Shelley, for creating a monster. So why should the guilt go to Tolkien and Jackson instead of to Melkor, Sauron, and Saruman?

Here, again, Shelley's work forms a useful point of comparison. All three sub-creators, Shelley, Tolkien, and Jackson, raise the question of creator responsibility, and all three sub-creators invite us to examine our own monstrosity in detail. However, Shelley limits her investigation of monstrosity to one relationship, that between Victor and his creature, two rational, speaking beings. Because in *Frankenstein* there is (as yet) only one created monster, Shelley can focus the novel on the question of creator responsibility. The creature's aloneness makes the question of race and culture less important in Shelley's work than the distinction (or lack thereof) between the human and the monster.[18] Tolkien, by showing us a greater variety of monsters—monsters who live in groups and maintain cultures of Tolkien's invention—is faced with a greater difficulty with consistency. Jackson's work is the most complex of all; he builds upon Tolkien's text (and thereby upon Tolkien's inconsistencies), but he also builds upon the cinematic history of nonspeaking Frankensteinian monsters.[19] Tolkien's Uruk-hai make long speeches (*Towers* ch. 3); Lurtz growls and roars.[20] While raising many of the same questions as Tolkien and Shelley about the spectrum of monstrosity, Jackson yet provides us with the most troubling monster of all—cruelty that appears in anthropomorphic form and yet will not explain its motives, a creature invented to embody the film's disembodied evil.

In both tales, it is language—that power that allowed Tolkien, Jackson, and Shelley to sub-create their monsters—which ultimately decides whether the sub-creator is an irresponsible Frankensteinian god or, on the other hand, an Incarnate who recognizes the inherent creatureliness of the monsters and humans within the story. The ability of language to serve as monster-maker or monster-redeemer is especially evident in the contrasts among Jackson's non-demonic monsters.[21]

Jackson has many means of creating sympathy for his monsters, and he makes conscious choices about where he wants his audience's sympathies to fall. In the case of the non-anthropomorphic monsters, Tolkien, Jackson, Walsh, and Boyens show that they do not feel any need to separate themselves from the monsters. Indeed, they are likely to try to find a way to portray these monsters sympathetically. Since these monsters don't look like us, they are less of a threat. Peter Jackson and his cowriters, clearly fascinated with all the monsters they portray, at least laughingly find some point of commonality between themselves and the monster. When the audience watches Frodo from various angles in Shelob's lair, Philippa Boyens wants to know from whose point of view we're watching. Is this Gollum's point-of-view? she asks. "I've always imagined it a Shelob POV in actual fact," Jackson responds, "it kind of, could be anything of course" (*ROTK* Scene 38). At this point, the audience takes the viewpoint of the monster. Fran Walsh and Philippa Boyens then go on to comment on their own supposed identification with this female monster.

> WALSH: We've always seen Shelob as Tolkien's non-idealized view of womanhood.
> BOYENS: Yeah, we related to her; she's a little bit overweight.
> WALSH: She's got hairy legs.
> BOYENS: Hasn't shaved her legs for a while [pent-up laughter]. Men flee from her, and she's having a bit of trouble squeezing through places she could get through before! [laughter] So we had some sympathy for her [*ROTK* Scene 38].

Walsh and Boyens's comments are similar to Jackson's remarks on the cave troll: they use the language of their audio commentary to make the monster less monstrous — to identify with a monster who could otherwise get no sympathy in the film. Shelob, not even being in anthropomorphic form, requires language to make her pitiable. Jackson cannot even rely on the facial expressions that he can give to Orcs, Uruk-hai, and cave trolls. Interestingly, Tolkien also gives Shelob this sympathetic commentary in *The Two Towers*. Like Jackson, Tolkien gives us a Shelob point of view. When Shelob impales herself upon Sam's sword in her haste to crush him, Tolkien tells us, "No such anguish had Shelob ever known, or dreamed of knowing, in all her long world or wickedness" (712). Tolkien describes the "unbearable pain" of the light of Galadriel's starglass and how Shelob's sight was "blasted by inner lightnings, her mind in agony" (713). The reader is always on Sam and Frodo's side, but Tolkien's language makes Shelob understandable.

But Jackson does everything he can to show us that Lurtz, despite his looks, is really not like us. He places him in a long line of Frankensteinian movie monsters by restricting the creature's access to language, thereby limiting Lurtz's ability to move the audience with his "powers of eloquence and persuasion" (Shelley 176). Jackson, like other playwrights and filmmakers who reenvisioned Frankenstein's monster, removes not only the monster's language but also his original innocence and his lonely history. Jackson and his cowriters will defend the monsters who cannot speak for themselves, but Lurtz is a creature who can speak and chooses not to speak.[22] It is evident that Lurtz can understand every word Saruman tells him, though his answering snarls to

Saruman seem to belie the loyalty to his creator that Lurtz's actions prove. Lurtz says only four different words in the entire film: "Saruman," when asked whom he serves, and "Find the halflings!" when he and the other Uruk-hai are doing their best to literally destroy the Fellowship. All of Lurtz's other communications consist of snarls, growls, and roars. Although Lurtz looks more like a man than the Orcs, he speaks less. Since Lurtz is also absent from Tolkien's original creation, none of Tolkien's language, no memory from the book, can make him more sympathetic.[23] Lurtz, who never makes a sympathetic speech nor is given a sympathetic commentary, is a clear contrast to Tolkien and Jackson's other most anthropomorphic monster, the highly verbal Gollum.

In Mary Shelley's *Frankenstein* and both the film and book version of *Lord*, language can be used as effectively as visual cues to draw the reader's or viewer's sympathy — a fact that is particularly impressive for Jackson as it would seem that he is working outside of his medium. Tolkien's use of language is expected: as a philologist, he made careful word choices and developed Gollum's psychology through linguistic signs: As Frodo notes in *The Two Towers*, whenever Gollum speaks of himself using the first-person singular pronoun, rather than as "we" or "he," it is a sign that "some remnants of old truth and sincerity were for the moment on top" (629). Tolkien goes further, claiming in an essay in *The Peoples of Middle-earth* that the type of language a creature speaks is evidence of that creature's level of corruption. Orcs are so corrupt that their language is continually degenerating; trolls are even worse off (*Peoples* 21). In his letters and in *Morgoth's Ring*, Tolkien toys with the idea of whether the power of speech indicates the possession of a soul. In a draft of a 1954 letter to Peter Hastings, Tolkien writes of Trolls that "when you make Trolls *speak* you are giving them a power, which in our world (probably) connotes the possession of a 'soul'" (191).[24] In his later note about Auden's 1956 *Return of the King* review, Tolkien distinguishes the "humane" from the monster based solely on the creatures' ability to speak (rather than on what side they choose). Tolkien calls the object of Frodo's quest "the liberation from an evil tyranny of all the 'humane'"— including those, such as "Easterlings" and Haradrim, that were still servants of the tyranny. In a footnote, Tolkien wrote that, "humane: this [being in a fairy-story] includes of course Elves, and indeed all 'speaking creatures'" (241).[25]

Although Jackson does not stress languages or speech as a part of Middle-earth's good-and-evil hierarchy, he is stronger than Tolkien in showing how language functions to turn Frodo into Gollum.[26] Like Mary Shelley, when it comes to Gollum, Jackson is not interested in showing the distinction between monster and man, as he was with Lurtz. Just as Mary Shelley does, he shows their exchangeabilty by making Frodo's and Gollum's language match up. Mary Shelley uses similar patterns of speech for the creator and created, linking both embodied creatures to fiends and evil spirits. Victor Frankenstein informs his hearer that "anguish and despair had penetrated into the core of my heart; I bore a hell within me, which nothing could extinguish" (64). A few chapters later, his creature informs Victor that "I, like the arch fiend, bore a hell within me" (104). Frankenstein compares himself to "an evil spirit, for I had committed deeds of mischief beyond description horrible" but protests that he "had begun life with benevolent intentions" (65). A few pages later, Frankenstein's creature says, "I ought to be thy Adam; but I am rather the fallen angel.... I was benevolent and good; misery makes me a fiend" (73). In Jackson's version, when Frodo snaps at Sam in the forests of Ithlien with "The Ring was entrusted to me. It's my task! My own!" Sam counters back with "Can't you hear yourself? Don't you know who you sound like?" (*TT* Scene 28).

Peter Jackson's *TT* stressed the risk that Frodo would transform into Gollum. The screenwriters note that they were trying to set up a special relationship between Gollum and Frodo, Jackson says that the scene in the Dead Marshes was shot in a way that would "start to mirror that Gollum has shared knowledge with Frodo about what it's like to carry this ring, information that Sam can never know" (*TT* Scene 14). Peter Jackson sets the two up as visual doubles. In a pick-up scene, Frodo fingers the Ring while Gollum is simultaneously fingering an imaginary ring. The screen-writers note that Frodo disarms Gollum and shows he has knowledge too, calling Sméagol by his name. At this point, language and visual cues work together. Frodo's use of "Sméagol" in *TT* is not Frodo's casual "Gollum, or Sméagol if you wish" as pictured in Tolkien's text (*TT* Scene 14, 626). It is a defining moment in assigning Gollum a level of humanity. By naming Sméagol, Frodo calls him out of the nameless monsterhood to which Frankenstein's creature had been consigned. Frodo explicitly explains the doubling to Sam. Realizing that he is becoming more and more under the power of the Ring, Frodo says, "I have to believe Gollum can come back" (Scene 28). In Middle-earth, we always know that there is the potential that we may turn into a monster — and it is not even clear which sort of monster we will become. Under the influence of the Ring, Frodo may turn into a Gollum of flesh and blood, or he may turn into a disembodied wraith. The point of no return for the monstrous comes when the monsters can neither be defended by language nor defend themselves with their own language.

In the Frodo and Gollum relationship and in the Lurtz and Fellowship relationship, Jackson is really dealing with the same question: How do you portray the monstrous when it comes too close to home—when we are too like the monsters? And Tolkien's work provides him with two very different options: the option of exterminating the monstrous, as Tolkien's Fellowship does in their battles against Orcs, or the option Tolkien's characters quite as frequently take—that of realizing their own commonality with the monster, their own creatureliness. The monsters that Tolkien's text exterminates are Frankensteinian monsters, monsters that their creators/corrupters saw from the beginning as expendable. Melkor and Saruman do not mind when their Orcs die. Tolkien's other characters have difficulty identifying with these Frankensteinian creations. In Jackson's film, the threat is heightened because, despite Jackson's portrayal of Lurtz as a true Frankenstein movie monster, Lurtz looks too much like us. Jackson does his best to keep us from identifying with his violent Frankensteinian monster. That, combined with Tolkien's textual portrayal of Orcs, who "are not easy to work into the theory and system," provides a problematic picture of the monstrous.

Only through identifying with the creature can Tolkien and Jackson's characters (and perhaps even Tolkien and Jackson themselves) be saved from the charge of playing Frankenstein, playing God. At some points in his writings, Tolkien seemed to recognize the affinity between his evil and good characters. Seldom does he do so with the Orcs.[27] However, in the essay in *Morgoth's Ring* that Christopher Tolkien identified as Tolkien's "final view" on the subject, Tolkien does make a connection between Orcs and the other creatures of Middle-earth, whom he calls Incarnates, a word which links even Orcs to the Incarnation, that central tenet of Christian theology in which Christians see themselves as not only created in God's image but also sympathized with by a God of flesh. "[Orcs] had other characteristics of the Incarnates also," he wrote before listing their similarities (418).

The relation between Tolkien's Fellowship and non–Frankensteinian monsters like Gollum more clearly shows that Tolkien's characters can come to understand the monstrous in themselves. When Frodo reacts in horror to the story of Gollum's murder of Déagol in *Fellowship*, Gandalf stresses Gollum's hobbitlikeness: "I think it is a sad story," said the wizard, "and it might have happened to others, even to some hobbits that I have known" (*Fellowship* 53). Indeed, in both the text and the film, Frodo does become Gollum, slave to the Ring, saved finally by the monstrous in Gollum himself: "But for him, Sam," Frodo says, "I could not have destroyed the Ring" (926).

NOTES

1. Listen to the "Audio Commentary: The Directors and Writers" for Scene thirty-three of *FOTR*, "Moria," and scene three of *TT*, "The Taming of Sméagol."

In "Moria," Jackson notes that the studio thought the Watcher in the Water sequence was "unnecessary ... but I ... loved the notion of the scene. I thought the film needed a good monster sequence at this point in time. And so, I kind of fought for it." Regarding Gollum, Jackson notes that the problem was that originally the people from New Line could neither see nor understand Gollum: "I remember for a long time New Line were listening to a voice they couldn't understand and they were looking at a guy in leotard on the screen instead of the CG [computer generated] creature, and we were just getting strong feedback from them saying, 'Less Gollum, Less Gollum, Less Gollum, Less Gollum.' I remember them saying 'Yeah, this guy's okay in a very small dose, but you wouldn't want too much of him,' and it was because they just were not seeing him; they were not hearing what he was going to sound like."

2. Tolkien's term *sub-creation*, which describes the primary-world artist's creation of imaginary secondary worlds, is rooted in his view of humans as created image-bearers. The successful sub-creator "makes a Secondary World which your mind can enter. Inside it, what he relates is 'true': it accords with the laws of that world. You therefore believe it, while you are, as it were, inside. The moment disbelief arises, the spell is broken; the magic, or rather, the art, has failed" ("On Fairy-stories" 52).

3. Because viewers of the Jackson film far outnumber readers of the book, Bratman fears that *Lord* will become another example of the "colonized" book: "Films have colonized books before. The general public has no idea that the monster in Shelley's *Frankenstein* is nothing like the one in the 1931 Universal film. Almost anyone reading Shelley's novel for the first time is in for a big surprise" (42). Rosebury entertains the possibility that Jackson's work could force Tolkien's to "recede to an unambiguously 'literary' status, rather like 'Mary Shelley's' *Frankenstein*" or, given the fact that *Frankenstein* has been embraced by the literary canon while *The Lord of the Rings* has not, to "be read very much less" (220). However, Rosebury rejects the possibility he has entertained and takes a more positive view of film adaptation than Bratman does. Rosebury claims that "many people will agree that Whale's *Frankenstein* (Universal Pictures, 1931) is a great film, even though it does not even attempt the dramatic adaptation of many powerful elements of Shelley's novel, and moreover assimilates the story shamelessly to other post–Shelley traditions, including nineteenth-century melodrama and the Gothic aspects of 1920s German expressionism" (206). Hopkins also treats connections between *Frankenstein* and *FOTR* in her book, *Screening the Gothic*; however, her reading of Jackson's film too hastily maintains that the film is more Frankensteinian than the book, which, based on the evidence of one or two scenes referencing Gollum, she claims is closer to *Dracula* (141).

4. There are now many essays and book chapters dealing with Tolkien and race, but see in particular Fimi's detailed study in *Tolkien, Race and Cultural History: From Fairies to Hobbits*, especially chapter nine, "A Hierarchical World," pp. 131–159. See also Rearick's "Why Is the Only Good Orc a Dead Orc?: The Dark Face of Racism Examined in Tolkien's World" and Kim's "Beyond Black and White: Race and Postmodernism in *The Lord of the Rings* Films." For a spoof of critical readings of race in Middle-earth, see Alexander and Bissell's "Unused Audio Commentary by Howard Zinn and Noam Chomsky, Recorded Summer 2002, For *LOTR:* (Platinum Series Extended Edition) DVD."

5. Although the *Beowulf*-poet never takes Grendel's side, Grendel's descriptors vary from words such as *scynscaþa* (demonic foe, line 707), *mānscaða* (wicked enemy, line 712, 737), *gǣst* or *ellengǣst* (spirit and powerful spirit, lines 102 and 86), to the

less monstrous *féond* (enemy, line 101), or even to *wonsǣlī wer* (unblest or miserable man, lines 105). As we know Grendel is also a descendant of Cain's clan (and thus of human origin), it becomes clear that monstrosity has long been difficult to define.

6. Tolkien's entire poem, *Mythopoeia*, is published in the 1988 HarperCollins edition of *Tree and Leaf*. The portion I quote from "On Fairy-stories" appears in lines 61–69 of *Mythopoeia*, with slight variations in punctuation and capitalization.

7. Tolkien frequently contrasted "real life" with his fantasy, continuing his comments on Beowulf and Grendel in his response to Auden's 1956 review with the following: "Of course in 'real life' causes are not clear cut — if only because human tyrants are seldom utterly corrupted into pure manifestations of evil will" (242). Tolkien had shown this same belief in earlier letters to Christopher, in which he found the orc-like among the English as well as among England's enemies. In letter seventy-one Tolkien writes, "In real (exterior) life men are on both sides: which means a motley alliance of Orcs, beasts, demons, plain naturally honest men, and angels. But it does make some difference who are your captains and whether they are orc-like per se!" (82). See also letter 78: "Urukhai is only a figure of speech. There are no genuine Uruks, that is folk made bad by the intention of their maker; and not many who are so corrupted as to be irredeemable (though I fear it must be admitted that there are human creatures that seem irredeemable short of a special miracle, and that there are probably abnormally many of such creatures in Deutschland and Nippon — but certainly these unhappy countries have no monopoly: I have met them, or thought so, in England's green and pleasant land)" (90).

8. Many members of the cast of *FOTR* aren't quite clear on the origin of Orcs and Uruk-hai. Listen particularly to the cast commentaries for chapters twenty and forty. In the first, Astin and Boyd maintain that the Uruk-hai are a cross between Moria-goblins and Orcs. In the second, Wood maintains, "I believe he just said Elves, so I think that they are Orcs and Elves, Billy." Boyd: "I think, um, well, Orcs actually came from Elves who had been captured by Saruman and tortured to the point that they became Orcs, and then he's mixed Orcs and Goblins ... to become Uruk-hai." Wood: "Oh, I see." (The actual cast commentary contains many more injections of understanding and agreement from Wood.)

9. Tolkien never worked out his doubts about Orcs. See Dmitra Fimi's *Tolkien, Race and Cultural History*, pp. 154–155, and Tolkien's partially finished essays on Orcs on pages 408–424 of *Morgoth's Ring*. In the first of these, dated by Christopher to the mid-to-late 1950s, Tolkien begins thus: "[Orcs'] nature and origin require more thought. They are not easy to work into the theory and system" (409). He then works his way through several possibilities about the origin of Orcs and tries to better fit them into his mythology. In a later essay, Tolkien writes that "the Wise" taught that mercy should be granted to Orcs who surrender and ask for it, "though in the horror of the War [this teaching] was not always heeded" (419). Tolkien tries to make the division between good and evil clearer, blaming Morgoth for Orc deaths, instead of the Orcs' adversaries: "Morgoth [had convinced] the Orcs beyond refutation that the Elves were crueler than themselves" (419). Tolkien's actual storytelling in *Towers*, however, does not even appear to consider mercy for Orcs (ch. 8, 532). For more on Tolkien's doubts about Orcs, see Tolkien's 1965 letter to Auden where Tolkien "cannot claim to be a sufficient theologian to say whether my notion of orcs is heretical or not" (355).

10. See *Morgoth's Ring* where Tolkien stresses the free will of the Orcs, even though he had previously considered the option of making them creatures who "had just as much independence as have, say, dogs or horses of their human masters" and

who "had little or no *will* when not actually 'attended to' by the mind of Sauron" (416–422, 410, 413).

11. In the novel, this breeding also occurs "offscreen." However, Tolkien is somewhat more graphic about the process in his unfinished essay about Orcs printed in *Morgoth's Ring*: "Finally, there is a cogent point, though horrible to relate. It became clear in time that undoubted Men could under the domination of Morgoth or his agents in a few generations be reduced almost to the Orc-level of mind and habits; and then they would or could be made to mate with Orcs, producing new breeds, often larger and more cunning. There is no doubt that long afterwards, in the Third Age, Saruman rediscovered this, or learned of it in lore, and in his lust for mastery committed this, his wickedest deed: the interbreeding of Orcs and Men, producing both Men-orcs large and cunning, and Orc-men treacherous and vile" (418). In this same essay, which Christopher Tolkien called his "father's final view of the question," Tolkien posits that Orcs have their origin not in Elves but in Men. Although he finds some difficulties in chronology, Tolkien writes, "though Men may take comfort in [the chronological difficulties], the theory remains nonetheless the most probable. It accords with all that is known of Melkor, and of the nature and behavior of Orcs — and of Men" (417).

12. Besides being the most well-versed in on-screen monsters, Lee is also the actor most conversant with Tolkien's text. Not only did he read *The Lord of the Rings* as soon as it was published, he has read the books yearly ever since ("Wloszczyna 6E"). Lee was also the only cast member to have met Tolkien. "I met him in a pub," Lee says. "He used to always go to this pub in Oxford and I was having a beer with friends and he walked in. One of the people I was with knew him and he very kindly came over to us" (Sherlock 72).

13. Lee is clearly thinking about Lurtz in Frankensteinian terms. In his reflections on his experience filming, Lee discusses what very hard work the film was for him, particularly with its 3:30 A.M. call time: "But that's nothing to what my monster Lurtz ... went through, spending 11 hours in make-up" ("The Real Saruman").

14. Jackson uses his creation of an embodied and expendable monster as a cinematic tool. But Tolkien's fantasy also embodies its evils. See letter 157 where Tolkien describes the difference between his world, "in which Evil is largely incarnate," and later ages. "Of course the Shadow will arise again in a sense ... but never again (unless it be before the great End) will an evil daemon be incarnate as a physical enemy" (207).

15. See Rearick, 864.

16. As Tom Shippey notes in *Road to Middle-earth*, the word "orc" first appears in the English language alongside the word "Elf." In *Beowulf* the two creatures are listed among "the descendants of Cain ... *eotenas ond ylfe onde orcnéas*, 'ettens [giants] and Elves and demon-corpses'" (57, *Beowulf* line 112). It is interesting to note that *both* Elves and orcs in *Beowulf* are, like Grendel, irredeemably bad (being the descendants of kin-killer), despite their inherent similarities to many of the kin-killing Danes and Geats who, after the wergild is paid, are welcomed into Hrothgar's hall. (Unferth is a case in point.) Tolkien did not claim any relation between the Old English *orc* and his Orcs, apparently because in his final conception, Orcs were embodied. (See *Letters* 177–178 and page 410 of *Morgoth's Ring* for evidence that Tolkien did not always represent Orcs as embodied.) However, as Rearick points out in his essay, Tolkien's evil Orcs are more palatable if they are seen as a part of the religious imagery of light and dark, angels and demons in the Bible. Rearick separates such imagery from race. Rearick writes, "Why is 'the only good Orc a dead Orc?' One might just

as likely ask Tolkien, 'Why is the only good demon an exorcised demon?' In Christian thought the elimination of evil is the only way to respond to it. There is no parley in the battle between heaven and hell" (See *Morgoth's Ring* 422). The problem of the Orc in Tolkien and Jackson is that it comes across as too human.

17. In the cast commentary, Bloom discusses Lurtz's decapitation by Aragorn: "Every time I've seen this in the cinema, like with all the audiences, there's a cheer." (Two other cast members say "there's a cheer" simultaneously with Bloom.) Audiences who cheer at the death of film villains have coded those villains as monsters, whether the villains are genetically human or not. But whether it is artistically pleasing, ethical, or useful for creators and audiences to code characters as monsters varies from work of art to work of art (and perhaps also from audience member to audience member). Depending on the context, the cheering at a film death scene could be an example of the monstrous in us; it would certainly be monstrous if we cheered at the death of another in life rather than at the movies. On the other hand, if we believe that monsters deserve a place in literature, the defeat of the fantastic monster can function as a reassertion of our own humanity. For Boromir, fighting Orcs saves him from the monstrous in himself—his betrayal of Frodo and of the fellowship. In Jackson's *FOTR*, Lurtz's death in particular leads Aragorn and Boromir to reconciliation and recognition of their mutual goals. Aragorn affirms his commitment to protect "our people" in Gondor, and Boromir dies stating, "Our people ... our people ... I would have followed you, my brother, my captain, my king!" (*FOTR* Scene 45).

18. In Shelley's *Frankenstein*, the creature curses his creator for their very similarities: "Cursed creator! Why did you form a monster so hideous that even you turned from me in disgust? God in pity made man beautiful and alluring, after his own image, but my form is a filthy type of yours, more horrid from its very resemblance" (Shelley 99).

19. As is clear from Whale's *Frankenstein*, it is possible to portray a nonspeaking but sympathetic monster.

20. Lurtz's limited speech contrasts strongly to the many speeches of Tolkien's Uruk-hai leader, Uglúk. Uglúk, in the orc Grisnákh's words, has "spoken more than enough" (436). (Uglúk insults Orcs from the north and from Mordor while praising his Uruk-hai comrades and Saruman the White.) The speeches by Tolkien's Uruk-hai and Orcs make them no less cruel, but they do naturalize the creatures. They demonstrate that, while quick to mistrust those from outside their own tribe, the Orcs and Uruk-hai do have at least a limited sense of loyalty to their leaders and to one another (*Towers* 436, 441).

21. I exclude, for example, the Ringwraiths and the Balrog.

22. Every audio commentary about the Moria cave troll is sympathetic. Hopkins, the supervising sound editor, stresses the "amazing job" Farmer did "with getting emotion into the cave troll's vocals" because they really wanted to give "some sort of character" to the "not too bright" cave troll (Production/Post-Production Team Commentary). McKellen also stressed the importance of humanizing the cave troll *because* the cave troll does not have access to language of his own: "The cave troll doesn't have any language to express his situation. We don't know where he's come from, or what he's fighting for, except survival, and so I think it's appropriate that there should be something pathetic and melancholy about his death" (Scene 35).

23. There are few areas of Tolkien's text where Orcs are sympathetic. However, those who look to sympathize often point out Shagrat and Gorbag's conversation in *Towers*, where the two war-weary Orcs debate whether the Nazgûl or Shelob are

worse company and wish for a chance to "slip off and set up somewhere on our own with a few trusty lads, somewhere where there's good loot nice and handy, and no big bosses" (*Towers* 721). Even though these Orcs are clearly planning on a life as bandits, and even though Shagrat and Gorbag will stab each other over Frodo's mithril shirt by *Return*, their conversation does show that they are on Sauron's side out of fear rather than out of desire. Tom Shippey in "Orcs, Wraiths, Wights: Tolkien's Images of Evil" calls attention to the fact that Shagrat and Gorbag live within a moral world. Shippey notes that when the two Orcs discover Frodo alive, they think poorly of his comrade's having abandoned him, calling it a "regular Elvish trick" (722). Shippey writes, "There is no mistaking the disapproval in Gorbag's last three words…. It is clear that he regards abandoning one's comrades as contemptible, and also characteristic of the other side. And yet only a page later it is exactly what characterizes his own side [when Shagrat recounts how he did not interfere upon discovering a fellow Orc trussed up by Shelob]" (183). Shippey writes, "orcs are moral beings, with an underlying morality much the same as ours. But if that is true, it seems that an underlying morality has no effect at all on actual behavior…. If one starts from a sound moral basis, how can things go so disastrously wrong?" Shippey notes that this question has been "raised with particular force during the twentieth century, in which the worst atrocities have often been committed by the most civilized people" (184).

24. Tolkien steps back from this view in an essay on Orcs in *Morgoth's Ring*. At that time, he was experimenting with the idea of Orcs as ant-like, parrot-like beings without free will (410). In a later essay, Tolkien returns to his earlier idea that Sauron's slaves had free will, noting as part of his evidence that the Orcs "had languages of their own." Here, however, he refused them immortality. In this version, Orcs had free will and language, but no soul (*Morgoth's Ring* 418). As Tolkien wrote in the draft to Hastings above, "inevitably my world is highly imperfect even on its own plane nor made wholly coherent — our Real World does not *appear* to be wholly coherent either" (*Letters* 191).

25. Tolkien's claim is inconsistent with his world, of course. If this rule were strictly followed, even dragons would be among the "humane."

26. Intriguingly, Tolkien is perhaps more successful at portraying the visual similarity between his monsters and his heroes; that is to say, Jackson relies on setting up the scenes so that Gollum and Frodo act in similar ways. But although Jackson effectively demonstrated Bilbo's earlier transformation upon seeing the Ring in Rivendell, Jackson avoids making a repeated visual parallel. In the book, Gollum looks like a Hobbit when he is acting nobly, and Frodo can see only the Orc-like characteristics of Sam when his desire for the Ring overmasters his loyalty to his friend. It is Tolkien and not Jackson who shows Gollum's moment of regret after returning from his mission to find Shelob: "very cautiously he touched Frodo's knee — but almost the touch was a caress. For a fleeting moment, could one of the sleepers have seen him, they would have thought that they beheld an old weary hobbit, shrunken by the years that had carried him far beyond his time" (699). In *Return*, when Frodo grabs the Ring from Sam in the Tower of Cirith Ungol, he sees Sam "changed before his very eyes into an orc again, leering and pawing at his treasure, a foul little creature with greedy eyes and a slobbering mouth" (891).

27. Gandalf does rebuke Denethor for thinking of Gondor only: "Yet there are other men and other lives, and time still to be. And for me, I pity even his slaves" (*Return* 795). It appears that Orcs would also be included in this pity.

Works Cited

Alexander, Jeff, and Tom Bissell. "Unused Audio Commentary by Howard Zinn and Noam Chomsky, Recorded Summer 2002, for *The Fellowship of the Ring* (Platinum Series Extended Edition) DVD." ("Parts One and Two." *McSweeney's Internet Tendency.* 22–23 Apr. 2003).

"Audio Commentary: The Cast." *The Lord of the Rings: The Fellowship of the Ring.* Narrated by Elijah Wood, Ian McKellen, Liv Tyler, Sean Astin, John Rhys-Davies, Billy Boyd, Dominic Monaghan, Orlando Bloom, Christopher Lee, and Sean Bean. Directed by Peter Jackson. 2001. Special Extended DVD. New Line, 2002.

"Audio Commentary: The Director and Writers." *The Lord of the Rings: The Fellowship of the Ring.* Narrated by Phillipa Boyens, Peter Jackson, and Fran Walsh.

"Audio Commentary: The Director and Writers." *The Lord of the Rings: The Return of the King.* Narrated by Phillipa Boyens, Peter Jackson, and Fran Walsh. Directed by Peter Jackson. 2003. Special Extended DVD. New Line, 2004.

"Audio Commentary: The Director and Writers." *The Lord of the Rings: The Two Towers.* Narrated by Phillipa Boyens, Peter Jackson, and Fran Walsh. Directed by Peter Jackson. 2002. Special Extended DVD. New Line, 2003.

"Audio Commentary: The Production/Post Production Team." *The Lord of the Rings: The Fellowship of the Ring.* Narrated by Barrie Osborne, Mark Ordesky, Andrew Lesnie, John Gilbert, Rick Porras, Howard Shore, Jim Rygiel, Erhan Van der Ryn, Mike Hopkins, Randy Cook, Christian Rivers, Brian Van'T Hul, Alex Funke.

Bratman, David. "Summa Jacksonica: A Reply to Defenses of Peter Jackson's *The Lord of the Rings* Films, after St. Thomas Aquinas." In *Tolkien on Film: Essays on Peter Jackson's "The Lord of the Rings."* Edited by Janet Croft. Altadena, CA: Mythopoeic, 2004.

Colley, Ed. "Remaking King Kong? It's the reason I'm in the film business." *London Evening Standard,* 8 December 2005, p. A SPR 34.

The Curse of Frankenstein. Directed by Terence Fisher. Performed by Peter Cushing, Hazel Court, Robert Urquhart, and Christopher Lee. Warner Brothers, 1957. DVD. Warner Home Video, 2002.

Fimi, Dimitra. *Tolkien, Race and Cultural History: From Fairies to Hobbits.* New York: Palgrave Macmillan, 2009.

Frankenstein. Directed by James Whale. Performed by Colin Clive, May Clarke, John Boles, and Boris Karloff. 1931. DVD. Universal Studios, 2004.

Fulk, R.D., Robert E. Bjork, and John D. Niles, ed. *Klaeber's Beowulf.* 4th ed. Toronto: University of Toronto Press, 2008.

Hitchcock, Susan. *Frankenstein: A Cultural History.* New York: Norton, 2007.

Hopkins, Lisa. *Screening the Gothic.* Austin: University of Texas Press, 2005.

Isaiah, Book of. *The New Oxford Annotated Bible.* New Revised Standard Version. Edited by Bruce M. Metzger and Roland E. Murphy. New York: Oxford University Press, 1991.

Kim, Sue. "Beyond Black and White: Race and Postmodernism in *The Lord of the Rings* Films." *Modern Fiction Studies.* 50.4 (2004): 875–907.

Lee, Christopher. "The Real Saruman." *Queensland (Australia) Courier Mail* 20 December 2003, p. M03.

Rearick, Anderson, III. "Why Is the Only Good Orc a Dead Orc?: The Dark Face of Racism Examined in Tolkien's World." *Modern Fiction Studies* 50, no. 4 (2004): 861–874. Project Muse. Web. 23 Apr. 2001.

Rosebury, Brian. *Tolkien: A Cultural Phenomenon.* New York: Palgrave Macmillan, 2003.
Shelley, Mary. *Frankenstein.* 1818. 2nd ed. Edited by Susan Wolfson. New York: Pearson Longman, 2007.
Sherlock, Jim. "Count me out." *Melbourne (Australia) Herald Sun,* 23 February 2004, p. 72. Lexis Nexis. Web. 23 Apr. 2009.
Shippey, Tom. "Orcs, Wraiths, Wights: Tolkien's Images of Evil." In *J.R.R. Tolkien and His Literary Resonances: Views of Middle-earth.* Edited by George Clark and Daniel Timmons. Westport, CT: Greenwood, 2000.
_____. *The Road to Middle-earth: How J.R.R. Tolkien Created a New Mythology.* Revised and expanded ed. Boston: Houghton Mifflin, 2003.
Tolkien, J.R.R. "Beowulf: The Monsters and the Critics." In *The Monsters and the Critics and Other Essays.* London: HarperCollins, 2006.
_____. *The Fellowship of the Ring.* (1954) Boston: Houghton Mifflin, 1999.
_____. Letter to Christopher Tolkien. 6 May 1944. Letter 66 of *The Letters of J.R.R. Tolkien.* Edited by Humphrey Carpenter with the assistance of Christopher Tolkien. Boston: Houghton Mifflin, 1981.
_____. Letter to Christopher Tolkien. 25 May 1944. Letter 71 of *The Letters of J.R.R. Tolkien.* _____. Letter to Christopher Tolkien. 12 August 1944. Letter 78 of *The Letters of J.R.R. Tolkien.* 173–181
_____. Letter to Miss J. Burn (draft). 26 July 1956. Letter 191 of *The Letters of J.R.R. Tolkien.*
_____. Letter to Naomi Mitchison. 25 Apr. 1954. Letter 144 of *The Letters of J.R.R. Tolkien.*
_____. Letter to Peter Hastings (draft). September 1954. Letter 153 of *The Letters of J.R.R. Tolkien.*
_____. Letter to W.H. Auden. 12 May 1965. Letter 269 of *The Letters of J.R.R. Tolkien.*
_____. *Morgoth's Ring.* Edited by Christopher Tolkien. Boston: Houghton Mifflin, 1993.
_____. "Notes on W.H. Auden's Review of *The Return of the King.*" [1956?]. Letter 183 of *The Letters of J.R.R. Tolkien.*
_____. "On Fairy-stories." *Tolkien on Fairy-stories.* Expanded ed. with commentary and notes. Edited by Verlyn Flieger and Douglas A. Anderson. London: HarperCollins, 2008.
_____. *The Peoples of Middle-earth.* Edited by Christopher Tolkien. Boston: Houghton Mifflin, 1996.
_____. *The Return of the King.* 1955. Boston: Houghton Mifflin, 1999.
_____. *The Silmarillion.* Edited by Christopher Tolkien. 2nd ed. (1977) New York: Del Rey, 2002.
_____. *Tree and Leaf, Including Mythopoeia and the Homecoming of Beorthnoth.* London: HarperCollins, 1988.
_____. *The Two Towers.* (1954) Boston: Houghton Mifflin, 1999.
Wloszczyna, Susan, Stephen Schaefer, and Claudia Puig. "Return with us now ... to the land of Tolkien." *USA Today,* Final ed., 14 December 2001, P. 6E.

The *Matériel* of Middle-Earth
Arms and Armor in Peter Jackson's The Lord of the Rings *Motion Picture Trilogy*

ROBERT C. WOOSNAM-SAVAGE

Introduction

"Build me an army worthy of Mordor" Sauron commands Saruman in The Lord of the Rings: The Fellowship of the Ring.[1] His Orcs then proceed to turn the mines and caverns beneath Isengard into a vast munitions factory, churning out thousands of pieces of arms and armor, as well as his "fighting Uruk-hai." In the real world and New Zealand in particular, however, things were different. No Orcs were available to arm the armies of Mordor and the other armies of Middle-earth; just a team of enthusiastic and skilled human artisans, all with a rather humble and humbling approach to the task. Peter Lyon, the senior swordsmith, put it simply, "Great! Steady work, and on a feature film too."[2]

This overview looks at some of the craft and artistry that was essential in creating the arms and armor of Jackson's *The Lord of the Rings* (hereafter *LOTR*). It examines the designing, manufacturing and logistics of such work as well as giving a brief overview of the creation of the battle scenes. Perhaps most importantly, also discussed is how and why the designers of the arms and armor of this Middle-earth took the major and decisive step to deliberately eschew the literally "fantastic" pieces found in most "sword and sorcery" (and previous Tolkien) movies and create "real" arms and armor for the "reel" world Jackson envisioned. It is arguably this "reality," treating the *matériel* of the War of the Ring as part of a real, grounded, history that helped give a greater strength and heart to the Middle-earth that Jackson and Weta created. This last point, without doubt, is one of the reasons that Jackson's motion picture trilogy has been so successful and became a deserved classic almost instantaneously. The material culture created for the films is an area that has been comparatively overlooked in previous studies, possibly a reflection of the literary criticism background of many of the commentators.³ Rather than examine what was made and used in the movies, other essays have often been more concerned about the way the movies deviate from Tolkien's writings or depictions.⁴

Antipodean Armorers: The Making of Arms and the Building of Armor at Weta Workshop

Over the seven years of production, 1996–2003, Weta Workshop undertook the design, fabrication and on-set operation of all the arms and armor required for *The Lord of the Rings* motion picture trilogy (2001–2003). The

Weta Workshop Entrance Sculpture. The company was named after the weta, a large flightless insect, which can weigh up to 2½ ounces (70g) and grow to 4 inches (10cm) in length. Weta is a shortened form of the Maori word *Wetapunga*, which can be translated as "God of ugly things." The sculpture of a weta that adorns the entrance to Weta Workshop is made from No. 8 fencing wire, a type of wire originally used to fence homesteads and farms. Even this is significant, as there is a New Zealand phrase which sums up Kiwi ingenuity and enterprise. "Putting it together with No. 8 fencing wire," meaning that anything can be fixed by twisting this wire together (Image © Weta Workshop Ltd.).

fact that all the material, both physical and virtual, was made under one roof at Weta brought about a "singular 'Tolkienesque' brush-stroke" to Jackson's epic "so that the armor looked like it was worn by the creature who designed it that looked like it came from the land it grew up in."[5] Richard Taylor has said he "chose to take on an insane amount of work because .... I was convinced that if things like armor and weaponry were farmed out to other companies, we'd lose the integrity of the design aesthetic. The issue was making it feel as if the orcs, for example, had built their armor and weapons. The honest way to do that was to design it all under one roof."[6] Key actors also appreciated and responded positively to this grand scheme. Sean Astin (Sam Gamgee) commented that "the armor worn during battle scenes was not simply the product of a designer's imagination. The amount of intelligence and sophistication applied during the research phase of the project, coupled with the money that was invested, allowed everyone to do their jobs at a level I had never seen on a movie set."[7]

The necessary creation of this *matériel* helped Jackson forge a "real" cinematic world. As he has stated "I like doing things that are pure to film, that have no actual existence outside of cinema. That's what I find the challenging thing—making these little daydreams look convincing and real."[8] The latter he has indeed done and he recognizes this: "All movies are artificial, all movies are pretence, and we worked really hard to make our pretence as real as possible."[9] In fact, to make these live-action films "convincing and real" Jackson and his team created physical artifacts that, although primarily used to make these "daydreams" a reality, do have an "existence" both in cinema and outside of it. Many of these objects have been the centerpieces of the well-received exhibition *LOTR* Motion Picture Trilogy: The Exhibition in national museums around the world, including Te Papa Tongarewa, which conceived the exhibition (2002–2003 and 2006) in Wellington, New Zealand, and the Science Museum, London (2003–2004), in the UK, thus fulfilling the prophecy of one of the film's producer's, Barrie M. Osborne: "You pick up one of these hero swords and you realize you are holding a real weapon in your hands. Incredible craftsmanship and many of these pieces belong in museums."[10] Alan Lee had no doubts as to the quality of the work being created "Weta made a lot of very finely crafted armor and weapons that will last and be admired for hundreds of years."[11] The museum-quality nature of many of the pieces was recognized by others as well. Karl Urban (Éomer) noted, "It was just incredible. Individually handcrafted rivets in my armor ... no two rivets were the same. They are like museum pieces."[12]

Many of the pieces temporarily became actual museum objects when the present author became cocurator, along with Richard Taylor, of the exhibition

Arms & Armor from the Movies: The Wonderful World of Weta. Held between 12 July and 16 November 2008 at the Royal Armouries in Leeds, England, this was the first exhibition ever held at the national museum of arms and armor that dealt with arms and armor made for the movies. The exhibition included over 200 iconic pieces created by Weta for *The Lord of the Rings* trilogy, *Chronicles of Narnia—The Lion, the Witch and the Wardrobe, The Last Samurai, Hellboy* and *King Kong*. Over 120 pieces of arms and armor from *The Lord of the Rings* motion picture trilogy formed the core of the exhibition and included pieces such as a hero version of Frodo's sword Sting and the helmet of the King of the Dead. Twelve fully armored figures included a spectrum of "good" and "evil" characters, and illustrated a range of arms and armor being worn, from that of the Orcs of Moria and the Uruk-hai to that of the Royal Guard of the Rohirrim and the spectacular panoply of Théoden himself (which alone weighed about 48 ½ lbs; or 22kg). All were specially selected by this author during a research trip to Weta in March 2008 (following a personal visit in 2006) to show the incredible levels of craftsmanship that had gone into their creation (the exhibition was created within 11 months which, for a project of this scale, was an impressive achievement by the exhibition team). With so much CGI (computer-generated imagery) in movies today the curators felt it was crucial to show that much filmmaking still involves the actual making and building of physical props, weapons and armor and so "The exhibition would be a celebration of the craft and skills of the modern day men and women who work at Weta Workshop and who create these wonderful works of art."[13]

It was obvious that even four years after the release of the final film in the trilogy interest had not diminished. This was proved by over 160,000 visitors who saw the exhibition, to which admission was free, unlike the major Te Papa Tongarewa touring exhibition. Unlike that exhibition, this one concentrated solely on the arms and armor. There were no elements of costume or any other type of props. It might have been thought rather strange to present the *matériel* of Middle-earth alongside the historical and recent arms and armor of conflict, sport and pageant; but because of its nature, it is one of only a few museums in the world that can show arms and armor from the "real" world alongside those from the "reel" world. A similar exhibition held at a museum of the moving image or similar institution could simply not have this verisimilitude. The exhibition enabled us to make this new and direct link between the Royal Armouries' collection and the arms and armor seen in the movies. After visiting the exhibition, visitors could immediately explore the museum and see "real" arms and armor, some of which were of types and styles that had inspired the "fantasy" arms and armor created by

Weta conceptual artists and designers: "As George MacDonald Fraser, the author of 'Flashman' wrote: 'the costume picture ... by providing splendid entertainment, has sent people to the history shelves in their millions.'"[14] "We [the Royal Armouries] are one of only a few museums in the world that has a collection of such material to use in this way"[15] The exhibition's focus on the creation and visualization of such pieces was "an ideal pathway into our collection that would widen intellectual and emotional access and engage our diverse audiences regardless of background, gender, age or culture."[16] It is known from the exhibition comment books that new visitors were indeed brought into the museum who had previously been put off visiting a museum of arms and armor.

It was also noted at the time that "the theme of the exhibition is to see and enjoy the objects for what they are; the result of skilled craftsmen and women. These are used as props in movies but have an artistic value in themselves as examples of the use of crafts such as blade-making and armor building. The exhibition is not about what is historically incorrect or correct in a movie."[17] In fact, the relationship between the movies and the Royal Armouries is an interesting and old one. Film companies and designers have often turned to the Royal Armouries and its staff for help in researching the accuracy of arms and armor seen in many historical films and TV series, from Olivier's *Henry V* (1944) to more recent movies such as Branagh's *Henry V* (1989), Zeffirelli's *Hamlet* (1991), Gibson's *Braveheart* (1995), Caton-Jones' *Rob Roy* (1995), and the BBC TV series *Ivanhoe* (1997). More recently the Royal Armouries has worked with the costume designer Janty Yates and her teams on Scott's *Kingdom of Heaven* (2005) and *Robin Hood* (2010). Whether such advice is followed is of course a matter for the filmmakers.

The exhibition was a unique collection of material and it is unlikely that this collection will ever be exhibited in this form again. Pieces selected included some that had never before been displayed in any previous public exhibition, such as Arwen's quiver from a time when she was to have had a, literally, more combative role in the film's stories. It allowed the rare chance to spend time close up to these pieces from Weta, examining the craft and artistry essential to the creation of these beautiful objects, which may have been on screen for only a fleeting few moments. For the visitor it did give a chance of "grasping a 'reality' that is essentially ungraspable, the desire for Middle-earth to exist, even though we know it does not."[18] Again visitor response certainly confirmed "the immense pride of artisans in a job well done. That pride too becomes part of our fascination — there is almost as much pleasure to be had with identifying with the crew as with the heroes of the quest."[19]

It was decided to treat each piece as primarily a "real" object from the world that *The Lord of the Rings* movies depicted and for which it was created but then simultaneously (on an accompanying and differently colored label) to give facts regarding its existence in the "reel" world as an artifact made as a prop for a motion picture. This notion was an important decision and one made comparatively early on: "The idea being that although the material is used in the make-believe worlds of the cinema ... the pieces have a duality co-existing in this world as 'real' movie props yet being 'real' weapons brought to life on the screen.... The accompanying labels throughout the exhibition ... will also reflect this dual reality."[20] For example, the information regarding some of the arms and armor of Boromir was given as follows:

[Middle-earth: Case A.6]

The Sword, Scabbard and Shield of Boromir

Boromir, the eldest son of Denethor, Ruling Steward of Gondor, and brother of Faramir, was one of the Fellowship of the Ring until seduced by the power of the One Ring. He fell at the battle of Amon Hen, slain by the Uruk-hai of Saruman, while protecting Frodo. The edge of the central iron boss of his shield bears an embossed design, which, with its use of feathers and stars, reflects the devices of Gondor.

Reel facts: The hero sword has a steel blade and the stunt "fighting" sword has an aluminum blade:

> Boromir's sword is a big sword for a big man — not overly long, but with a very wide blade and heavy pommel. Luckily Sean Bean is a strong man to wield it! The scale version of Boromir's sword is one of several made for the scene where Boromir's body goes over the waterfall — everything (boat, Boromir, clothes, weapons) were made to exacting detail, to make the falls appear twice as high as they were. In the end the boat appeared almost as a speck as it went over the falls — but the detail was there if needed! The hero shield had a brightly polished steel and bronze boss; on set it was called "The Hubcap" and had to be dulled down, as it would reflect the camera and crew perfectly!—Peter Lyon, Swordsmith[21]

Another example is that of the equipment of one of the Uruks:

[Middle-earth: Case B.11]

The Helmet and Sword of an Uruk-hai "Berserker"

The helmets of the Berserkers, a special breed of Uruk, were filled with human blood and then rammed down onto their heads, creating a blood lust for killing humans with their massive two-handed cleavers which were swung in huge, lethal arcs, cutting down whomever it met.

Reel facts:

The Berserker sword was one of the first weapons I worked on.... When Richard [Taylor] said he wanted it "real" I still didn't understand filmic "real" vs. real-world "real" and so I made it out of 16mm thick spring steel and forged the blade — splitting, spreading and shaping the two prongs while the steel was orange-hot! The blade was massively heavy and the [lighter] urethane versions were molded from this hero version.—Peter Lyon, Swordsmith[22]

Without a doubt the arms and armor painstakingly built for *The Lord of the Rings* were obviously a major part of the "worldbuilding" process that was conceived to create a coherent and *"rich, fully furnished ambience for the action."*[23] The creating of such *"richly realized"*[24] worlds is crucial to the sustaining of disbelief in historical and, in particular, fantasy-orientated movies, and it is clear that Jackson and Weta applied this concept to *The Lord of the Rings*.

The design of every piece of arms and armor, like everything else in the movies, had first to be approved personally by Peter Jackson and, although the first film was released in 2001, design began in 1996. Weta set up its own smithy to manufacture the arms and armor, which included over 100 hero swords, 1,200 suits of hand-built armor (including 169 Orc armors, 110 Gondorian armors and 110 suits of Uruk-hai armor), 2,500 weapons (including 500 injection molded rubber bows), 10,000 arrows (2,000 for the Rohirrim alone) — in all, 48,000 individual pieces of armor. Some of the bows were built with varieties of poundage, enabling a few to be used in close-up and for-real shooting (although see below regarding Legolas and arrows). The workshop was originally crewed with 28 people, but at the film production's height 148 crew were employed with between 38 and 45 staff on the set. It is perhaps not surprising to discover that "The largest department at Weta [was that] making the armor and weapons ... 50–70 people."[25]

The number of objects created and staff employed reflects a unique feature of these films and that is the creation of the illusion of the height difference between humans (5' 9"—1.8 m) and Hobbits (4' 2"—1.3 m). One way was to use small "scale-double" actors who were filmed with full-size actors. However, this also required that all props, including swords, be made in two scales — one "normal scale" and the other "smaller-scale," for use by the "scale-doubles" (the scale was 1:38 larger or smaller).[26] Peter Lyon said he would "basically, take the sword and scale it up or scale it down as needed.... It was just a matter of making sure I kept the proportions correct."[27] In some scenes a third scale was used which was larger than normal, such as the gauntlet of the Ringwraith that almost discovers the Hobbits,[28] to again to show the difference in scale between the inhabitants of Middle-earth.

As in a real military operation, a number of logistics support teams were created to ensure the required arms and armor were at the correct shoot each day — in all, "five armory trucks that had every piece of equipment that you would need for servicing, repairing or rebuilding weapons, or building weapons from scratch ... five mobile workshops on location around New Zealand at any one time, servicing the five shooting units."[29] The largest use of practical arms and armor elements was for the six week shoot of the Rohirrim and Orcs during the Pelennor Fields sequence which involved some 350 horses and 500 extras.[30] The battle of Pelennor Fields even necessitated the construction of "three working full-scale catapults ... [which] could throw missiles about 25 meters, which was enough to get them out of shot."[31] (However, the working range of these full-size prop catapults is disputed, as it is also recorded that they "only threw 3–4 metres,"[32] a point confirmed elsewhere: "The Orc catapults looked great but didn't throw that far"[33]).

Crucial to the success of creating Middle-earth was the team Jackson surrounded himself with. At the heart of this was Richard Taylor, the inspirational director of Weta. On *LOTR* trilogy Taylor was "Creature, Miniature, Armor, Weapons and Special Makeup Effects Supervisor." According to Jackson:

> Richard Taylor and his Weta team were the group that really made it all happen, All the designs that came from Alan [Lee], John [Howe] and Grant [Major], if they involved weapons or armor ... anything at all, got channeled into Richard's department. He ran a huge operation in an incredibly smooth way. If we wanted 100 archers, we'd have no doubt they'd be there with all the support and backup they required. Just giving the filmmakers a bunch of swords ... wasn't really the limit of Richard's job. He also had to provide technicians on set who could dress these people and make running repairs. When someone's sword broke during a take, there'd always be a Weta technician there with tools ready to go.... I can't imagine anyone else in the world being able to pull it off as well as Richard did.[34]

Other important team members included senior leather master Michael Grealish, who brought all his expertise and craftsmanship together to create suits of armor and other accoutrements. The comprehensive leatherworking facility employed a crew of 35 at its height: "People [were] just detailing the stamping into the leather — that's all they were doing. There was so much involved. It was like a chain gang of cutting, stamping, coloring, and then aging back. It wasn't just one person doing one specific thing; it would be a huge team. It was a team effort."[35]

Another person who played an integral part in bringing this story to the screen was Peter Lyon. Lyon, a self-taught swordsmith and armorer, first began making swords in 1986, and his strong personal interest in medieval history ensured great authenticity. In April 1998 Lyon joined Weta Workshop as senior swordsmith for *LOTR*, the first film he had ever worked on. His extraordinary craftsmanship can be seen in the hero weapons, of which he made over 100 and the 300–400 aluminum blades he produced for the stunt swords used in the trilogy (see below). Taylor has said that "No person was more important to the weapons than Peter Lyon,"[36] and that he "made weapons that were so exquisite and rich in culture and subtlety of use that the actors grew to find it a complete delight using these weapons."[37] Howe has also described the swords made by Lyon as being "absolutely exquisite ... he was actually making real swords," and Lyon himself as "A cross between a librarian and a wrestler!"[38]

Much of the arms and armor was based upon the work of two famed Tolkien illustrators, John Howe and Alan Lee, who were both employed as conceptual designers. As Taylor said, "Then John stepped into our lives — like a living emissary from the Middle-Ages!"[39] Howe's arrival, with Lee in early 1998, proved inspirational for the armorers, as he brought with him a practical knowledge of European medieval arms and armor due to his involvement with a Swiss medieval reenactment group, Company of Saynte George, and he had also coauthored a splendid book on the medieval soldier.[40] Taylor also added that "he was able to let us know what worked and what didn't. Why things were built in a certain way."[41] As Howe has stated, for example, "Armor is the most impossible thing to understand ... because all these static shapes interact with each other."[42]

Other designers, such as Daniel Falconer, have confirmed this practical approach and shown how influential he was: "John was able to actually sit down with us and explain how things work. Good design always follows function."[43] Howe also worked in other areas. He "spent a lot of time in the [leather] workshop.... He had a lot of input in the development of the products. One of his favorite sayings was — if you'd make something — he would just look at it and say 'They wouldn't have done it that way; they wouldn't have made it that way.' He was very specific about what the look was or how functional it was of that time."[44] His contribution to the look of the *matériel* in the film cannot be overestimated. Howe was heavily involved with arms and armor designs, particularly of those of the forces of evil, such as "some of the Nazgûl blades, the Moria orc weapons and armor."[45] He was impressed by the work of Weta swordsmith Peter Lyon and armorers Warren Green and Stu Johnson, and "Howe could occasionally be spotted jousting with a crew member in front of the Weta headquarters in Miramar, making sure that the swords were up to the combat readiness required."[46] As Howe has said, "Fencing in the afternoons was one of the big enjoyments.... After work, we would go out in the parking lot and try to give each other a few nicks and scrapes."[47]

Armor

The armor-making department, with its own armorer's smithy, makes up an important part of Weta Workshop and is able to produce fully articulated plate and mail armor. There was "Always a frenzied feeling in the armor department.... [T]here was armor being created out of leather ... then the area where the steel armor was made."[48] Astin, on his arrival in New Zealand in 1999, was taken "through Weta [where I] ... saw ironsmiths working on swords and shields.... I was struck by the array of techniques being applied to bring Tolkien's world to life: some of it was clearly on the technological forefront, but some of it was decidedly low-tech. I would learn, over the course of the production, that anything was worth trying."[49]

The process of making plate armor begins with the hand-forging of a mock-up in steel plate to see if the form and proportions, as well as any fine detailing, look good, and if it all works mechanically. Once approved, silicon molds are made of these pieces and then the armor can be mass-produced in their hundreds. These are all cast in urethane, painted, and then aged. By

Weta Armor Workshop. Not a cavern beneath Isengard! An unusually empty and quiet interior view of the normally bustling armor workroom where much of the armor for *The Lord of the Rings* motion picture trilogy was built. It illustrates well how age-old skills, such as those of working metal on an anvil, were used alongside modern machining tools (Steve Unwin, Image © Weta Workshop Ltd.).

beginning with authentic materials and processes Weta has ended up producing some of the most realistic and effective armor for use on the silver screen: "The feeling, that you used to have when you were standing surrounded by all this armor, felt that it had been discovered on an archaeological dig. It had that sort of realism about it. What was so deceptive about it was that it wasn't. It was made out of plastic, urethane, all those sorts of materials that are so modern today, but in actual fact the look of it had that detail and realism so well captured it really did deceive people."[50]

The other major form of armor is mail (popularly and incorrectly known as "chain mail").[51] Mail armor is constructed from interlinking rings of metal. The realistic depiction of cinematic mail armor has always been problematic due to a difficult and time-consuming production technique allied to the fact that if made of metal it is perhaps too heavy for the actor to perform in. The most common solution to this was the use of "knitted mail" (often knit by hand), which was then coated with a metallic paint. This method has been used since the earliest days of cinema, from Méliès' *Jeanne d'Arc* (1899) through *The Adventures of Robin Hood* (1938), *El Cid* (1961) and *The Warlord* (1965) to such recent productions as *Henry V* (1989) and *Braveheart* (1995). As Howe has so rightly commented, "Chainmail [sic] is a problem. Chainmail is a cinema nightmare and there is no convincing way to make any approximation of chainmail without a stroke of genius and most chainmail in movies is just awful. It's terrifyingly bad; it's either knitted mail sprayed with aluminum paint or it's made of whatever. It always looks crappy."[52]

It was Weta Workshop that had that stroke of genius. They developed an extremely lightweight, strong and "much more real looking"[53] mail armor for *LOTR* which was used throughout the motion picture trilogy, with only a very limited amount of knitted mail being used in the background. The amount of time and effort put into creating the mail shirts and other pieces of mail armor by Carl Payne, senior mail maker (a friend of Peter Lyon who had begun making mail as a medieval reenactor in the 1990s), and his team of up to seven were simply staggering.[54] The mail for *LOTR* was laboriously made, the small team working ten hours a day over a period of up to three-and-a-half years by slicing black PVC alkathene pipe into tiny rings, each one looking like a single ring of mail.

A total of 12,500,000 individual links from almost 9 miles (12km) of pipe were used to make the mail for the movies. Although the links were originally cut by hand, the team "devised a machine which could chop [the pipe] into tiny slices."[55] The rings were then linked together by hand, like real mail armor, to build up mail shirts, caps and leggings: "it would generally take five to eight days ... to complete a ... mail vest for a character."[56] Some of the team even wore off the fingerprints on their thumbs and forefingers in the process: "They ... [were] just worn flat, like shiny smooth fingers."[57] The mail was then zinc-coated or colored to give a metallic finish. Because of the construction technique the mail looks and "hangs" just like real mail armor.

Being only a third of the weight of real mail, Weta mail is easily the most realistic and successful mail substitute used in the movies today. It was easy to repair on set and was worn by both lead and background actors. Even so, its manufacture is still a very labor intensive process. For the *Kingdom of Heaven* (2005) a new process was used, in which each link was cast individually using an injection molding system and the links snap-fitted together. This process, in partnership with Taylor's long time friend Fred Tang, resulted in the product bearing the trade name *Weta Tenzan Chainmaille* and was also used to build the mail armor seen in more recent productions such as *The Chronicles of Narnia* movies, *The Lion, the Witch and the Wardrobe* (2005) and *Prince Caspian* (2008), and *Robin Hood* (2010).

Disappointingly for the craftsmen and the fans the ultimate mail armor, the shirt of Dwarven Mithril, was seemingly made out of something other than silver. It has been stated that the Mithril vest was "made ... out of tiny, tiny rings of chain mail ... and we had it silver coated, sort of a platinum color — and it took somebody weeks and weeks to put all this chain mail together ... assembled by hand."[58] However Taylor has explained that the "The Mithril vest is a big cheat.... We did consider it, we did ponder it, and we were stumped by it ... we failed to do something special.... We were hoping that we could weave titanium twine or something like that. But it was not to be."[59] The Mithril shirt was actually made up of the same "light weight stainless steel chain mail used for butchers' gloves. That mail was finer than the movie's craftsmen would have been able to produce ... and looked appropriate when sprayed with a pearlescent paint."[60] The differing recollections may be due to there having been "hero" and "stunt" vest versions, but this is not at all clear.

Weapons

Working with a team of craftspeople, Weta's in-house master swordsmith, Peter Lyon, and the senior model maker, John Harvey, produced all sorts of weapons, from one-off hero swords to large numbers of bows, quivers, spears, axes and shields. The weapons not only had to look the part but also be fought with realistically on the set or on location. Blade manufacturing is now slightly more automated at Weta to allow more efficient mass production, as in the milling of weapons such as the aluminum swords from the more recent *The Lion, the Witch and the Wardrobe* (2005). Each of those swords took anywhere from 3

Peter Lyon at Work. If only Orcs had machines like these! Peter Lyon at work in the Weta armory where many swords were made. The ancient skills of hand-crafting weapons is now supplemented by the use of modern labor-saving tools and materials, but many edged weapons for *The Lord of the Rings* motion picture trilogy were made using traditional techniques (Steve Unwin, Image © Weta Workshop Ltd.).

to 6 days to make. Narsil, for example, took "about a week,"[61] but the number of designs of swords that were made before locking down was variable. For some central pieces, such as Sting, "they 'probably went through 20 or 30 different drawings' before Peter [Jackson] got one that he actually said 'That's the one.'"[62]

Kirk Maxwell, assistant sword master on the movies, has stated that "the craftsmanship that went into the weapons by the folk at Weta is mind-boggling."[63] This is repeated in comments made by sword master Bob Anderson: "Weta made better swords than anybody I've ever worked with." He was also surprised that despite "being used to fifteen to twenty blades getting broken during a film. On *LOTR*, we made *three* films and only broke *one* sword. And that was only because it got so battered and bent that it finally fell apart!"[64] The actors themselves were equally impressed with the quality of the swords: "When you get your sword that becomes quite personal to you and you get familiar with it, but you feel as though it is part of your body, it's an extension of your arm and we all took great pride in that."[65]

Weapons made at Weta are of three types:

Hero weapons were made from the finest materials. All the main characters in the movies have a variety of weapons — but the most important was always the hero version, for so-called "beauty" shots, such as when a sword is held for tight close-ups or is being drawn from its scabbard. Hero weapons have hilts of cast bronze or forged and ground steel, and the grips are usually of wood and the blades of heat-treated spring steel with a tang which continues into the grip. This use of the same materials and techniques that were used in the manufacturing of real swords was for a reason. Taylor "was adamant that we would do them in spring steel ... because you can't get aluminum to take on that subtle blue hue of forged spring steel. And in close-ups ... it's imperative that the metal gives off the correct color hue."[66] Although the blades have no edge many are as well balanced as real swords and made as they would have been in the medieval period, the only difference being that power tools are used to grind away the metal. Usually at least two hero weapons were made, providing a contingency for emergencies or for simultaneous use on multiple sets. "Over 200 hero/foreground weapons" were built in the end.[67]

Stunt weapons were for combat scenes. Not necessarily seen in close-up, they could be so if necessary. As such, they have to look both real and in every way identical to their hero counterparts, especially regarding any decoration. The main difference is in the materials of manufacture, stunt weapons usually having soft aluminum blades and urethane grips. Aluminum is very light and replicates steel very well, so it is used for most swords in most films. Edged weapons of aluminum are easy to use and don't tend to carry as much force when swung, making them safer to use in on-screen battles. Taylor has made an interesting observation regarding the use of these weapons: "The physics of stunt weapons is a very interesting thing.... To make something soft enough that it won't injure someone.... We've always found that ... if you give [an actor] a real hero sword with a sharp edge they'll respect it with great care and respect their fellow actors. You give them a slightly rubber sword and they will beat the living daylights out of the person next to them!"[68] For any given character's signature sword around five stunt copies were produced.[69]

A different type of stunt weapon was the stunt arrow used in sequences, such as the battle of Helm's Deep. Although the arrow storms were further augmented with digital arrows[70] the physical effects team of special effects coordinator Stephen Ingram kept the air full of arrows by shooting "volleys of arrows across the battlefield, using wire-flown effects for close-ups and pneumatic arrow-launching rigs for criss-crossing showers of up to 320 arrows per shot. We made plastic-shafted arrows and put rubber heads on them," explained Ingram, "then slid them over finely machined brass tubes attached to an air machine. With one burst of air we'd fire all the arrows. They were used against people ... [and] even if these arrows hit them, they would not be hurt."[71] Jackson obviously enjoyed the artistic freedom and safety aspects that using computer generated arrows, as well as the physical effect arrows, gave him during the huge arrow storms at Helm's Deep: "All the arrows that are flying through the air are all CG arrows. In the old days you used to have to fire them down wires, but now you can just put them in with the computer."[72]

Incidentally, not one bow in the trilogy was made from wood. The bows give the appearance of wood but are all made from urethane molded around a spring steel rod armature. Although Elven "magic" was not used to enhance the archery skills of Legolas, computing "magic" was, and the arrows that he shoots from his bows are all-digital arrows:

> Even Errol Flynn had experienced difficulty in smoothly "nocking" his arrows ... so Peter [Jackson] and I figured that if Errol Flynn couldn't do it, whoever wound up playing Legolas wouldn't be able to do it, either. So we decided pretty early on to give it some digital help and have the actor just pantomiming the action, without really shooting arrows. He'd just reach for an invisible arrow, pull the string back, snap it and go for the next one. That way, he could shoot a perfect arrow every time."[73]

The bow used by Legolas (Orlando Bloom) has acquired almost iconic status for some fans of the films. Weta still receives: "Many requests by people who are big fans of Legolas to see if they can acquire the actual Legolas bow and arrow and quiver. It's the most popular item that people request to see whether they can own."[74]

"Extras" Weapons had urethane (similar to the material used to manufacture skateboard wheels) blades and hilts cast in one piece. They were pulled from silicon molds and painted to match the original steel masters. This allowed such weapons to be made speedily and in vast quantities. "Stunt safe" edged weapons can also be made with a harder internal core and a flexible outer skin. These background weapons, developed by John Harvey, were made and painted so convincingly they are almost indistinguishable from the hero versions.[75] They do not appear thicker than the "real" sword and a blow from one will do less damage, as they are made as safe as possible to use. They were also used when an actor was running or riding, so if the actor fell they would not be injured by a solid hilt or blade. As Taylor explained, "Although it would bruise them, it wouldn't puncture their skin, and so these weapons became an absolutely essential part of the repertoire of the armorer on set."[76]

Weta Weapons at Work

Although it is clear that Howe's arrival and input was crucial in forging a new "reality," Taylor himself has also pointed out that while Howe designed "or heavily influenced, specific designs ... for the most part, that design work fell on the shoulders of Ben Wootten, Warren Mahy and Daniel Falconer, who are the three specific weapon designers at Weta."[77] Collectively they understood that the armor and weapons in the film, although belonging to the fantastic, had to be rooted in reality. "We focused," says Howe, "on trying to design weapons with the unambiguous purpose of being used to ram into someone's guts and building armor that is intended to protect your own guts from being rammed into by somebody else!"[78]

It was equally important that although the weapons should look as though they would work they should not look like any particular historical counterpart. Taylor has stated how he "was very insistent upon ... not [letting] the armor and the weapons and the props of Middle-earth look as though they had come from a 1990's art department.... The idea was to invest the props with a high level of richness and heraldry and realism."[79] The story would be treated as an authentic history:

> We were determined that our work would never have the predictable "fantasy" look used in dozens of movies designed by the art departments of Hollywood. This was never going to be a *Conan the Barbarian*-style film: we wanted audiences to feel that when it came to warfare, life in Middle-earth was real and earnest. A sword, first and foremost, is something with which to defend oneself against a foe; so, regardless of any decoration and embellishment, it had to be totally functional.[80]

Taylor had to contend with some design input from some unexpected quarters as well: "At all times, the overriding design ethic was to never approach *The Lord of the Rings* as if it was a fantasy. So, no spikes bursting out of the sides of the shields, as some of the actors requested."[81] As Howe has said, "A great deal of effort went into making convincing fantasy armor.... We tried very hard while maintaining a happy fantasy element to it, that it actually be functional, that it actually work, that it actually be able to be worn by real people."[82] He also thought "it was very important to create something that would function as armor believably, but still represent something that would be worn by this culture, that we can barely imagine."[83]

Another design paradigm was the need for identifiability: "We set out to create the iconographic look of each of these cultures so when you looked at the film, you immediately would be able to tell the difference between them. A Dwarf, for example, is short and stout; so the geometry of Dwarf armor was square and boxy and geometric. The motifs of the elven armor, in contrast, were very nature-driven and spiritual looking."[84] But this was not all, for "Not only did the designers differentiate the various cultures and races of Middle-earth from each other, but they also tried to reflect their historical backgrounds.... The Weta designers studied the change in historical armors of various real cultures and tried to make the style of Elvish armor evolve in a similar fashion. The helmets in the prologue have been altered noticeably in the three thousand years between that era and the Helm's Deep battle."[85]

Jackson was clearly the driving force behind this historical/archaeological approach, for he was clearly aware that "Tolkien thought of [Middle-earth] ... as being our world in a historical period that predates ancient history."[86] He has even said this: "Imagine this: 7,000 years has gone by.... Rohan heraldry is studied and faithfully reproduced. Théoden's original saddle is in a museum — far too valuable to use in the movie, but an exact copy is made ... the battle of Helm's Deep is about to be captured on film."[87] To reflect this, as Taylor has stated, "At every stage ... we tried to step outside what we've seen in our own world and create armor not of our world. We've drawn on some of the best design-elements from armor and weapons throughout our own times whilst avoiding the trap of producing what fits people's perceptions of 'classic historic armor.'"[88] To see a film whose design elements fall well and truly into the type of trap Taylor is describing, one has only to look at the terrible mélange of *matériel* to be found in Ron Howard's film — also coincidentally involving "small people"— *Willow* (1988).

Many pieces of the arms and armor bore relevant inscriptions, in either Elvish or Rohirric, for example, and these had been duly designed. Again, these helped to give the weapons a subtle place and time in a "real" history (the inscription on Sting, for instance, refers to when Bilbo used it against the giant spiders of Mirkwood, in *The Hobbit*). These translations were created by David Salo, an academic who had been studying the languages of Tolkien since about 1995; his first work for the movies involved the inscriptions on swords, and Sting in particular.[89]

When asked about this almost obsessive attention to detail there are inevitably two answers. The first is that, because of Jackson's shooting style, one was never quite certain what might be required as a foreground object and so any piece had to be able to withstand the utmost scrutiny. Taylor was adamant that he "could provide Peter Jackson with background weapons that — if he pushed the camera through the crowd till he reached actors in the deep background — the armor and weapons would stand up to tight close-ups and not give away the fact that they were only manufactured out of rubber!"[90] The best example of this is perhaps the sword and scabbard built for Denethor, which was never intended to be drawn or used by the actor who played him (John Noble). Lyon "ended up making that as a complete sword, just in case of the day they decided that he was going to draw the sword. So he had a blade there, but you never see that."[91] As the film turned out, it is almost unnoticeable, but (and perhaps most important), as Taylor has stated, although the detail may appear invisible the detail "is seen, because it is important, because without visual clutter, you can't create historical reference. Our world is all about clutter."[92] It is this attention to detail and "clutter" that makes Jackson's *LOTR* as visually dense and coherent as any other cinematic world ever created, such as those by Kubrick in *2001: A Space Odyssey* (1968) and *Barry Lyndon* (1975).

But behind the "historicity" there also lurks humor. On a number of occasions, such as at Helm's Deep, we see a version of the now almost obligatory cinematic "suiting up moment," as Jackson aptly calls it: "The 'classic' strapping on the weapons. You always see it in Science Fiction films don't you when they pull their armor and their kind of gadgets on, but we sort of do that in a medieval kind of way."[93] One only has to think of films such as *Commando* (1985) and the opening sequences of *Batman Forever* (1995) and *Batman & Robin* (1997).

More fun is seen in the weapons and armor of the spectral zombie-like Army of the Dead that were, like the army, decayed and rotten. Many of the breastplates of the army were designed by Warren Mahy to deliberately be rib-cage-like in appearance. The source for the general appearance of the Army of the Dead is an interesting one as it eschews any possible "classic" source and goes for a much more recent and popular image: "I thought they [the Army of the Dead] had certain overtones toward some of the Italian zombie movies of the 1970s and that's a good thing in my book"[94] In fact, I would suggest that the movies their appearance actually recalls are the (in)famous series of four Spanish films by Amando de Ossorio known collectively as *The Blind Dead* (1971–1975). They tell of the return of another group of long-dead, reanimated, sword-wielding warriors, Templar knights.

Just as the arms and armor were uniquely related to the various inhabitants of Middle-earth so too were their combat styles. These were created on both an individual basis and cultural levels and were devised (by sword master Bob Anderson, his assistant, Kirk Maxwell and Tony Wolf, "cultural fighting styles" designer) for both human and CG actors: "The different races have their distinct fighting styles.... Those different styles ... were an integral part of Peter Jackson's vision from the time *LOTR* began to take shape. The idea of contrasting fighting techniques ripples throughout the films, from the different 'hero swords' forged by swordsmith Peter Lyon ... to the work of sword master Bob Anderson."[95] One even finds historical antecedents here in, for example, the Riders of Rohan attack on the Uruks and Orcs. One of the horse archers turns around in his saddle and, facing back, looses his bow, a wonderful interpretation of the classic "Parthian Shot."[96]

The Matériel of Middle-earth (Woosnam-Savage) 157

In fact, some eight major styles were created[97] including, for instance (and perhaps most strikingly), that of the Elves, seen in the opening battle scene of the prologue sequence in *FOTR*.[98] Tony Wolf recalls that "the image of the Elvish warriors performing a synchronized upward slash was partly to demonstrate the total contrast between the Elves and the Orcs — the former being magical, ultra-disciplined warriors and the latter being basically an insane rabble."[99] The fighting style of the Elves is depicted as one of elegance and beauty: "as warriors, they would be superbly balanced.... Their style ... [was] based on spiraling action — circular, gliding footwork patterns."[100] This elegance was also a key factor in the design of Elven fighting kit: "While the armor and weapons were functional, there was never any doubt that the Elves should look at least as stylish wielding a sword as they would lounging on a flet, reciting *The Lay of the Leithian*."[101]

Middle-earth at War

The huge armies in *The Lord of the Rings* were made using the revolutionary and Academy Award winning software program Massive (Multiple Agent Simulation System In Virtual Environment), developed at Weta by Stephen Regulous between 1996 and 1998.[102] This allowed huge crowd scenes to be created using various individual characters called Agents which, in Massive, have their own "brain," allowing them to see, hear and touch, and therefore respond to these various stimuli autonomously with any one of up to 350 actions.[103] The result is that they can react accordingly using a series of actions captured by motion capture techniques from stunt-men, horses, etc. Thus they can engage in combat with the enemy. This what makes Massive different from any previous "crowd replication system.... It's a very effective and realistic presentation for creating vast armies on screen."[104]

The numbers speak for themselves: 12,000 Uruk-hai agents at Helm's Deep and over 200,000 Orcs for the battle of the Pelennor Fields.[105] Jackson stated: "Now, we're able to ride horses around and do things with them that are captured by the computer. We can do stunts that you could never do with real horses safely. It creates very exciting looking sequences, where, obviously, no animal is in danger. We also did a lot of the battle with real horses; we mustered together our own army of about 250 horses, which is a huge number of horses to see in one place."[106] Jackson is also aware that "Filmmakers are in a great position of being able to really show battle scenes of a size and scale and complexity ... you could never ever do. You know even the biggest battle scenes to date [had] 4–5,000 extras, but because you have these computers and all these little CG soldiers there's no problem putting 10,000–20,000 soldiers on screen now. You can finally show the size and scale."[107] The subsequent visualizations of epic battle scenes in movies following the successful use and development of the Massive program happened with astonishing rapidity and illustrate how influential the work of Jackson, Regulous and Weta has been in this area of mainstream cinema alone. Films such as *Troy* (2004), *I, Robot* (2004), *The Lion, the Witch and the Wardrobe* (2005), *The Promise* (2005), *Jet Li's Fearless* (2006), *X-Men: The Last Stand* (2006), *300* (2007) and *Red Cliff* (2008) — which used Massive to create 70,000 soldiers and 2,500 ships — show that the armies originally spawned for Middle-earth continue to dominate the cinematic battlefield and the mise-en-scéne of such films.

Perhaps curiously, though, despite the high-tech means of producing the trilogy's amazing battle sequences, their inspiration lay in the older art of oil painting:

> [Jackson was] inspired ... by a ... Renaissance artist named Albrecht Altdorfer at the very beginning of planning in 1997. There was one painting, in particular [*The Battle of Alexander at Issus*, that depicts] this ... battle [with] people holding all of these pikes and spears [all against an] incredibly stormy landscape. It has incredible light and shade ... huge armies battling, and they have these enormous long pikes that are clashing together and waving like a wheat field in the wind. That painting was really the inspiration for the pikes at Helm's Deep. When I saw it, I thought, "Why don't we give the Uruks these incredible long pikes?!" ... It has also, to some degree, influenced what the Pelennor Fields look like too. It is wonderfully evocative and moody.[108]

Altdorfer (c. 1480–1538) was an early landscape artist and part of the Danube School of southern Germany. His painting of 1529, probably his most famous (now held by the Alte Pinakothek, Munich) is one of the most delirious and wonderful images of war captured on canvas (or panel, in this case). Thousands of infantry and cavalry jostle for victory in a blaze of heraldry and violence beneath brooding skies and Alpine mountains, upon which castellated cities sit, all visual precursors of Minas Tirith. The painting has worked its magic on many, including Napoleon, who took it back to Paris and in whose bathroom (at the Château de Saint-Cloud) it was hanging when the Prussians took it in 1814. This awareness of the work of Altdorfer has been picked up by at least one critic: "Miraculously, the films seem more painterly than digitized. To see the great armored hosts clashing at Helm's Deep in *The Two Towers* and at the Pelennor Fields in *ROTK* is to see Albrecht Altdorfer's *The Battle of Issus* (1528–29) come tumultuously to life."[109]

The battle scenes in the movies, their grandeur, color and scale have been compared with those of Kurosawa[110] and "the battle of Helm's Deep ... is staged as a satisfying bit of spectacle including intricate medieval-style siege warfare and Gandalf showing up like the Seventh Cavalry at the end of *Stagecoach* (1939)."[111] They would also appear to owe something to films such as Bondarchuk's *Waterloo* (1970), which Jackson saw when a teenager and which obviously made an enormous impact on him, leading him to think: "God! What would it be like to see the *real* battle? That's why I wanted to create these formidable-looking armies in *The Lord of the Rings* which, with the aid of computers we were able to achieve."[112]

The computers and their programmers transformed a small army of "orc extras and 350 Rohan riders clad in Weta Workshop armor"[113] into the largest army seen on screen at that time and orchestrated the magnificent charge of the 6,000 Rohirrim colliding with 22,000 Orcs.[114] Jackson has also enthusiastically described the scenes of Pelennor Fields:

> From a purely cinematic point of view it shows the scale of these horse charges. This is 6,000 horses, which is exactly what Tolkien describes in the book. And interestingly you see 6,000 horses in those one or two wide shots that we have here and interestingly enough in Napoleonic battles, the battle of Waterloo, the French Heavy Cavalry that charged the English [*sic*], was 6,000 horses, exactly the same size, so this is historically ... what those battles used to be like; I mean unbelievable seeing 6,000 horses on one spot![115]

Jackson's interest in things Napoleonic is shown in his looking at making a production of Naomi Novik's Tremeraire series of novels, which, although including dragons, are set during the Napoleonic Wars. Alternatively, maybe it will be Jackson's destiny to film Kubrick's unfilmed *Napoleon* now that he has the technology to create the vast battlefields of the era, Bondarchuk's fine achievements notwithstanding. The charge of the Rohirrim against the forces of Sauron in *The Lord of the Rings: The Return of the King* successfully conveys, for the first time in cinema, the full impression of what a large-scale cavalry charge looked like and what it might be capable of. The full mass shock of impact between horse and infantry is depicted without the worry or concern of injuring horse and rider, as CG was integrated so successfully and on such a convincing scale.[116]

At Pelennor Fields the city of Minas Tirith is shown besieged by 200,000 of Sauron's Orcs. It is not surprising to learn that "before preparing to shoot the battle scene, cinematographer Andrew Lesnie reviewed combat footage from such past spectaculars as *Ben-Hur*, *War and Peace*, *Braveheart* and *Spartacus*: "Sometimes you just look at those references and pick things up you like,'" explained Lesnie "...the nature of the battle itself, and the nature of the movement of vast numbers of people."[117]

Strangely the movies have been criticized for being "highly militarist, spending tremendous amounts of time, energy, and money on creating the great battle scenes that were highly acclaimed by fans and uncritical critics.... Indeed there are few films that have shown more bodies stabbed, shot with arrows.... The trilogy is one of the bloodiest epics in contemporary cinema."[118] This view must be regarded as both perverse and patronizing. The films are taken from a tale written about a period of Tolkien's "pre-history" also known as the War of the Ring. Given this, it is not at all surprising that there is concentration on war-like activities, just as there is in films such as *War and Peace* (1968), *The Battle of Britain* (1969) and *Waterloo* (1970). To acknowledge the spectacle, as well as the horror, of war (even as Altdorfer does) does not mean one has lost one's critical faculties, be it a fan or otherwise. The film does describe in a number of scenes the destructive nature of warfare, probably most memorably in the scenes where Faramir sees the face of a slain enemy and poignantly states, "War will make corpses of us all,"[119] and of course in the terrible and futile charge of Faramir and his horsemen at Osgiliath.[120] In fact, even at the risk of over-simplifying the depth of the movie trilogy, the films very easily slot into the "war film" genre, a fact reflected even in the opening paragraph of Jackson's original 92-page treatment from 1997: "We suddenly take in a Breathtaking Vista of Battle ... [M]ighty armies of Men and Elves battle Sauron's army of Orcs—loathsome ape-like humanoids.... With nearly 150,000 soldiers on screen this is prob-ably the single most spectacular shot ever committed to film ... a seething mass of sword and spear."[121] This is what became the opening scene four years later.

One may be forgiven for thinking that the following quote was written about *LOTR* in particular, but it was in fact written about war movies in general. "Many of the war films that have made their mark on the imaginations of the viewer have been stories of characters moving from innocence to experience ... [and] war is frequently used in cinema as a means by which to dramatize the enduring issues that all of us face—mortality, frailty (physical and emotional), community and courage."[122] This is a perfect synopsis of Jackson's (and Tolkien's) "Ring Cycle." The same author also makes the point that "In many instances the war film is a subset of the action genre, but the war film has also been able to graft onto it a range of other generic devices so that it can be ... a fantasy such as *Lord of the Rings: The Two Towers*."[123]

Arms and armor of the past had a number of functions and was made for display as well as for combat. Much of it was made for the spectacular theatre and entertainment of tournament, pageant or parade. The finely crafted and authentic looking arms and armor made for *LOTR*, taken with the creation of new CG technology, allowed Jackson and his team at Weta to convincingly create some of the most visually audacious and amazing battle sequences ever committed to celluloid. In the process, they have created a worthy successor to this "spectacular theatre and entertainment" of the past. For what are the movie blockbusters of today if not just that?

Acknowledgements: The author would like to thank the following, without whose help this chapter could not have been written. *At Weta:* Matt Appleton, Rob Gillies, Mike Grealish, John Harvey, John Howe, Sir Peter Jackson, Stu Johnson, Tris McCallum, Tracey Morgan, Dallas Poll, Tania Rodger, Ri Streeter, Emily-Jane Sturrock, Steve Unwin and, in particular, Peter Lyon and Sir Richard Taylor. *Elsewhere:* Janice Bogstad, Kelly DeVries, Antonia Lovelace, Axel E.W. Müller, Alison Watson and Edward Woosnam-Savage.

NOTES

1. Sauron in *FOTR-EE*, Sc. 18, *The Spoiling of Isengard*. For works which include details and illustrations of the arms and armor of Middle-earth see Fisher, 2004, and Smith, 2003. Also see http://www.wetaworkshop.co.nz/.
2. Hellqvist, 2002.
3. Even in such a comprehensive book, such as Cubitt, King & Jutel (eds.), 2008 (which includes a whole section on "Making a film trilogy," 133–192), little time is actually spared discussing this act of making even while simultaneously admitting that "the technical labor involved in creating the films could easily generate further analysis on the scale of a three-volume book of its own" (Cubitt & King, 135).
4. For example Bratman, 2004, 42, where there is much concern over Arwen's depiction with a sword. (A much more generous and rewarding interpretation of Arwen and her sword can be found in Akers-Jordan, 2004, 200.)
5. Taylor in Russell, 2004, 140.
6. Duncan, 2002, 83.
7. Astin, 2004, 137.
8. Sibley & Jackson, 2006, 190.
9. Jackson in Nathan, 2004, 7.
10. Osborne in *FOTR-EE*, The Appendices Part 1: 'From Book to Vision, Designing and Building Middle-earth: Weta Workshop," chapter 6. It should perhaps be noted that pieces of arms and armor made by Weta are now being acquired by museums. For example the Royal Armouries purchased the Artists Proof editions of the first two swords of "The Master Swordsmith's Collection," a copy of the sword Andúril built by Peter Lyon in 2009 (Acq. No. IX.5619) and a copy of Strider's sword built by Peter Lyon in 2010 (Acq. No. IX.5620).
11. Lee, 2005, 186.
12. Urban in Thompson, 2007, 93.
13. Woosnam-Savage, 2007.
14. MacDonald Fraser, 1988, xvii.
15. Woosnam-Savage, 2007.
16. Ibid.
17. Woosnam-Savage, February 26, 2008.
18. Cubitt, 2008, 191.
19. Ibid.
20. Woosnam-Savage, November 4, 2008.

21. Lyon, personal comment.
22. Lyon, personal comment.
23. Bordwell, 2006, 58–9, quoted in Thompson, 2007, 84.
24. Thompson, 2007, 84.
25. Taylor in *ROTK-EE*, Design Team Commentary, Sc.20, "Théoden's Decision."
26. Taylor in Snyder, 2002, 67.
27. Lyon in Fry & Burns, 2004, 45.
28. *FOTE-EE* Sc.13, "A Short Cut to Mushrooms."
29. Taylor in Snyder, 2002, 66–7.
30. Fordham, 2004, 113. Most sources, including Jackson (see French, 2005, 157 for example), usually put the actual number of horse at 250.
31. Ingram in Fordham, 2004, 92.
32. Major in *ROTK-EE*, Design Team Commentary, 2004, Sc. 36, "The Siege of Gondor."
33. Lee in *ROTK-EE*, Design Team Commentary, 2004, Sc. 36, "The Siege of Gondor."
34. Helms in Woods, ed., 2005, 126.
35. Grealish in Lobred, 2004, 46 (and see this article for a more detailed appreciation of Grealish and his work).
36. Taylor in *FOTR-EE*, The Appendices Part 1: "From Book to Vision, Designing and Building Middle-earth: Weta Workshop," chapter 6.
37. Taylor in Byko, 2002 .
38. Howe in *TT-EE*, The Appendices Part 3: "The Journey Continues," chapter 3.
39. Sibley, 2002, 100.
40. Embleton & Howe, 1994.
41. Taylor in *FOTR-EE*, The Appendices Part 1: "From Book to Vision, Designing and Building Middle-earth: Weta Workshop," chapter 5.
42. Howe in *FOTR-EE*, The Appendices Part 1: "From Book to Vision, Designing and Building Middle-earth: Weta Workshop," chapter 5.
43. Falconer in *TT-EE*, The Appendices Part 3: "The Journey Continues," chapter 1.
44. Grealish in Lobred, 2004, 46.
45. Hellqvist, 2002.
46. Pryor, 2003, 244. Peter Lyon said, "In fact it was not 'jousting' at all, rather it was sword combat practice; we probably only had about six practice sessions like this, but they have entered into myth!"
47. Lalumière, 2002, 53.
48. Rodger in *FOTR-EE*, "The Appendices Part 1: From Book to Vision, Designing and Building Middle-earth: Weta Workshop," chapter 5.
49. Astin, 2004, 131.
50. Rodger in *FOTR-EE*, The Appendices Part 1: "From Book to Vision, Designing and Building Middle-earth: Weta Workshop," chapter 5.
51. See Blair, 1979, 20, for a short discussion on the correct use of "mail."
52. Howe in *FOTR-EE*, The Appendices Part 1: "From Book to Vision, Designing and Building Middle-earth: Weta Workshop," chapter 5.
53. Osborne in *FOTR-EE*, The Appendices Part 1: "From Book to Vision, Designing and Building Middle-earth: Weta Workshop," chapter 5.
54. Matthews & Burns, 2004, 44.

55. Howe in *FOTR-EE*, The Appendices Part 1: "From Book to Vision, Designing and Building Middle-earth: Weta Workshop," chapter 5.
56. Matthews & Burns, 2004, 44.
57. Jackson in *TT-EE*, Director and Writers Commentary, Sc. 48, "The Host of the Eldar."
58. Jackson in *FOTR-EE*, Director and Writers Commentary, Sc. 35, "Balin's Tomb."
59. Taylor in Byko, 2002.
60. Ibid. Of course Jackson's previous comment may reflect his wry sense of humor.
61. Taylor in *FOTR-EE,* The Appendices Part 1: "From Book to Vision, Designing and Building Middle-earth: Weta Workshop," chapter 6.
62. Fry & Burns, 2004, 44.
63. Fry, 2004, 56.
64. Sibley, 2002, 103.
65. Bean in *FOTR-EE*, The Appendices Part 1: "From Book to Vision, Designing and Building Middle-earth: Weta Workshop," chapter 6.
66. Taylor in Snyder, 2002, 63.
67. Ibid.
68. Taylor in *TT-EE*, Design Team Commentary, Sc. 58, "Forth Eorlingas."
69. See Snyder, 2002, 64, and Byko, 2002, 20–23.
70. Fordham, 2003, 129, and Fordham, 2004, 82.
71. Fordham, 2003, 125.
72. Jackson in *TT-EE*, Director and Writers Commentary, Sc. 49, "The Battle of the Hornburg."
73. Cook in Duncan, 2002, 129.
74. Rodger in *TT-EE*, Design Team Commentary, Sc. 46, "The Three Hunters."
75. Taylor in Snyder, 2002, 62.
76. Ibid., 66.
77. Snyder, 2002, 62.
78. Sibley, 2002, 101.
79. Duncan, 2002, 82.
80. Sibley, 2002, 99.
81. Snyder, 2002, 62.
82. Howe in *FOTR-EE*, Design Team commentary, Sc. 33, "Moria."
83. Howe in *TT-EE*, The Appendices Part 3: "The Journey Continues," chapter 1.
84. Taylor in Duncan, 2002, 81.
85. Thompson, 2007, 90.
86. Jackson in Sibley & Jackson, 2006, 423–4.
87. Sibley & Jackson, 2006, 413.
88. Sibley, 2001, 99.
89. Nathan, ed., 47, and Thompson, 2007, 95–6. Regarding inscriptions see Derdzinski, "Sword Inscriptions," *Falconer* (April–May 2002), 18–19, and *Falconer* (June–July 2002), 20–21
90. Sibley, 2001, 86.
91. Lyon in Fry & Burns, 2004, 45.
92. Thompson, 2007, 96.
93. Jackson in *TT-EE*, Director and Writers Commentary, Sc. 48, "The Host of the Eldar." This is of course paralleled by a similar sequence depicting the arming

of the Witch-king before joining battle (see *ROTK-EE*, Sc. 50, "The Nazgûl and His Prey").
   94. Taylor in *ROTK-EE*, Design Team Commentary, Sc. 35, "The Paths of the Dead."
   95. Fry, 2004, 53–54.
   96. *TT-EE*, Sc. 10, "Night Camp at Fangorn."
   97. Ko, 2002, 4.
   98. *FOTR-EE*, Sc. 1, "Prologue: One Ring to Rule Them All..."
   99. Ko, 2002, 1.
   100. Ibid., 2.
   101. Lee, 2005, 72. For Elves see Atkinson, 2003, 48–57.
   102. For short but useful summaries of Massive and its achievements see Thompson, 2006, 292–9, and Koeppel, 2002, 44, as well as Sibley, 2002, 167–8, Duncan, 2002, 84–89, 117, and Fordham, 2004, 113–16.
   103. Koeppel, 2002, 42.
   104. Osborne in French, 2005, 157.
   105. Thompson, 2006, 296–7.
   106. French, 2005, 157.
   107. Peter Jackson in *TT*, Director and Writers Commentary, Sc. 53, "Retreat to the Hornburg." However, Bondarchuk's *Waterloo* (1970) claims to have used a total of 18,000 soldiers of the Red Army as extras. See Reeves, 1970.
   108. Madsen, 2003, 26–7.
   109. Fuller, 2005, 165–172.
   110. O'Hehir, 2005, 135 and Newman, 2005, 154.
   111. Newman, 2005, 152.
   112. Sibley & Jackson, 2006, 31–2.
   113. Fordham, 2004, 108.
   114. *ROTK-EE*, Sc. 46, "The Ride of the Rohirrim"; Fordham, 2004, 117 (see note 30 regarding the numbers of horse).
   115. Jackson in *ROTK-EE*, Director and Writers Commentary, Sc. 46, "The Ride of the Rohirrim."
   116. Ibid.
   117. French, 2005, 156. Indeed a scene in Sergei Bondarchuk's *War and Peace* would seem to have directly inspired a shot in *FOTR*. In *War and Peace: 1812* cinematographers Anatoly Petritsky and Aleksandr Shelenkov devised a primitive "cable-cam" rig on a suspension track, with two cables running down from a 15-meter (49.2 feet) high tower. The camera rapidly descended along these cables to create a spectacular 12-second scene in which the camera sweeps down over Rayevsky's battery and the Russian soldiers during the Battle of Borodino. For *FOTR-EE*, Sc. 44, "The Breaking of the Fellowship," a similar rig (nicknamed "The Flying Fox") was created. An attached camera rolled down a cable, almost half a mile long, which allowed the camera to create the same effect, but this time flying through the trees over the head of the running Uruk-hai at the battle at Amon Hen.
   118. Kellner in Mathijs and Pomerance, 2006, 31–2.
   119. Faramir in *TT-EE*, Sc. 30, "Of Herbs and Stewed Rabbit."
   120. *ROTK-EE*, Sc. 28, "The Sacrifice of Faramir."
   121. Sibley & Jackson, 2006, 343–4.
   122. Clarke, 2006, 1.
   123. Ibid., 11.

WORKS CITED

Akers-Jordan, Cathy. "Fairy Princess or Tragic Heroine? The Metamorphosis of Arwen Undómiel in Peter Jackson's *The Lord of the Rings* Films." In *Tolkien on Film: Essays on Peter Jackson's "The Lord of the Rings."* Edited by Janet Brennan Croft. Altadena, CA: Mythopoeic, 2004.
Atkinson, Carla. "Elven Armor & Weaponry." *"The Lord of the Rings" Fan Club Official Movie Magazine* 8 (April–May 2003): 48–57.
Astin, Sean. *There and Back Again: An Actor's Tale, A Behind-the-Scenes Look at "The Lord of the Rings."* London: Virgin, 2004.
Blair, Claude. *European Armor circa 1066 to circa 1700.* London: BT Batsford, 1979.
Bordwell, David. *The Way Hollywood Tells It.* Berkeley: University of California Press, 2006.
Bratman, David. "Summa Jacksonia: A Reply to Defenses of Peter Jackson's *The Lord of the Rings* Films, after St. Thomas Aquinas." In Janet Brennan Croft, ed. *Tolkien on Film: Essays on Peter Jackson's "The Lord of the Rings."* Altadena, CA: Mythopoeic, 2004: 27–62.
Byko, Maureen. "Fabricating the Weapons and Armor of *The Lord of the Rings." JOM: A Publication of the Minerals, Metals & Materials Society*, Vol. 54, 11, Nov. 2002: 20–23 (http://www.tms.org/pubs/journals/JOM/0211/Byko-0211.html, accessed 26 February 2008).
Clarke, James. *Virgin Films: War Films.* London: Virgin, 2006.
Croft, Janet Brennan, ed. *Tolkien on Film: Essays on Peter Jackson's "The Lord of the Rings."* Altadena, CA: Mythopoeic, 2004.
Cubitt, Sean. "Realising Middle-earth: production design and film technology." In Harriet Margolis, Sean Cubitt, Barry King and Thierry Jutel, eds. *Studying the Event Film: "The Lord of the Rings."* Manchester and New York: Manchester University Press, 2008. 185–91.
Cubitt, Sean, and Barry King. "Dossier: production and post-production." In *Studying the Event Film: "The Lord of the Rings."* Edited by Harriet Margolis, Sean Cubitt, Barry King and Thierry Jutel. Manchester and New York: Manchester University Press, 2008.
Duncan, Jody. "Ring Masters." *Cinefex*, 89, Apr. 2002: 64–131.
Derdzinski, Ryszard. *Sword Inscriptions: A Linguistic Survey*, The One Ring.net. http://www.elvish.org/gwaith/movie_inscriptions.htm (accessed 29 May 2008): 35–68.
Embleton, Gerry, and John Howe. *The Medieval Soldier: 15th Century Campaign Life Recreated in Colour Photographs.* London: Windrow & Greene, 1994.
Falconer, Daniel. "The Languages of Middle-earth: Weapons." *"The Lord of the Rings" Fan Club Official Movie Magazine*, 2, April–May 2002: 18–19.
———. "The Languages of Middle-earth: Weapons: Elven Weapons." *"The Lord of the Rings" Fan Club Official Movie Magazine* 3 (June–July 2002): 20–21.
Fisher, Jude. *"The Lord of the Rings": Complete Visual Companion.* Boston: Houghton Mifflin, 2004.
Fordham, Joe. *"The Lord of the Rings: The Return of the King,* Journey's End." *Cinefex* 96 (January 2004): 66–142.
———. *"The Lord of the Rings: The Two Towers,* Middle-earth Strikes Back." *Cinefex* 92 (January 2003): 70–142.
French, Lawrence. "All Hail the King." In *Peter Jackson: From Gore to Mordor.* Edited by Paul A. Woods. London: Plexus, 2005. 154–61.

166   I. Techniques of Story and Structure

Fry, Jason. "Forging a Fellowship." *"The Lord of the Rings" Fan Club Official Movie Magazine* 17 (October–November 2004): 40–47.
Fry, Jason, and Dan Burns. "Fighting the good fight." *The Lord of the Rings Fan Club Official Movie Magazine*, 12, Dec.–Jan. 2004: 52–57.
Fuller, Graham. "Kingdom Come." In Paul A Woods, ed. *Peter Jackson: From Gore to Mordor*, London: Plexus, 2005. 165–172.
Hellqvist, Björn. "The Men Behind the Swords in *The Lord of the Rings*: An Interview with Peter Lyon and John Howe." *Sword Forum International.* 8 Aug. 2002. http://lotr.swordforum.com/lyon-and-howe.php/ (accessed 5 October 2009).
Helms, Richard. "*Rings* Bearer." In *Peter Jackson: From Gore to Mordor.* Edited by Paul A. Woods. London: Plexus, 2005. 121–7.
Kellner, Douglas. "*The Lord of the Rings* as Allegory: A Multiperspectivist Reading." In *From Hobbits to Hollywood: Essays on Peter Jackson's "Lord of the Rings."* Edited by Ernest Mathijs and Murray Pomerance. Amsterdam and New York: Rodopi BV, 2006.
Ko, Adrian. "The Martial Arts of Middle Earth: An Interview with Tony Wolf, Fighting Styles Designer for *The Lord of the Rings* Motion Picture Trilogy." *Sword Forum International* 8 (August 2002): 1–4. http://swordforum.com/articles/ent/tonywolf.php (accessed 31 March 2010).
Koeppel, Dan. "Massive Attack." *Popular Science* 261, no. 6 (December 2002): 38–42, 44.
Lalumière, Francis K. "Master of High Drama: An Interview with *The Lord of the Rings* Conceptual Artist John Howe." *"The Lord of the Rings" Fan Club Official Movie Magazine* 3 (June–July 2002): 48–57.
Lee, Alan. *"The Lord of the Rings" Sketchbook,* London: HarperCollins, 2005.
Lobred, Peter. "Aged to Perfection." *"The Lord of the Rings" Fan Club Official Movie Magazine* 15 (June–July 2004): 42–49.
MacDonald Fraser, George. *The Hollywood History of the World.* London: Michael Joseph, 1988.
Madsen, Dan. "Update with Peter Jackson." *"The Lord of the Rings" Fan Club Official Movie Magazine* 8 (April–May 2003): 22–31.
Margolis, Harriet, Sean Cubitt, Barry King and Thierry Jutel, eds. *Studying the Event Film: "The Lord of the Rings."* Manchester: Manchester University Press, 2008.
Mathijs, Ernest, and Murray Pomerance, eds. *From Hobbits to Hollywood: Essays on Peter Jackson's "Lord of the Rings."* Amsterdam and New York: Rodopi BV, 2006.
Matthews, Julie, and Dan Burns. "The Other Lord of the Rings." *"The Lord of the Rings" Fan Club Official Movie Magazine* 16 (August–September 2004): 40–47.
Nathan, Ian, ed. *The Lord of the Rings: A Celebration by Empire.* London: Emap Consumer Media, 2004.
Newman, Kim. "The Two Towers." In *Peter Jackson: From Gore to Mordor.* Edited by Paul A. Woods. London: Plexus, 2005.
O'Hehir, Andrew. "The Fellowship of the Ring." In *Peter Jackson: From Gore to Mordor.* Edited by Paul A Woods. London: Plexus, 2005.
Pryor, Ian. *Peter Jackson: From Prince of Splatter to Lord of the Rings.* Auckland: Random House, 2003.
Reeves, Leonard. *Waterloo,* London: Sackville, 1970.
Russell, Gary. *The Art of "The Lord of the Rings."* HarperCollins, 2004.
Sibley, Brian. *"The Lord of the Rings": Official Movie Guide,* HarperCollins, 2001.

_____. "*The Lord of the Rings*": *The Making of the Movie Trilogy.* HarperCollins, 2002.
Sibley, Brian, and Peter Jackson. *Peter Jackson: A Film-maker's Journey.* London: HarperCollins Entertainment, 2006.
Smith, Chris. "*The Lord of the Rings*": *Weapons and Warfare. An Illustrated Guide to the Battles, Arms and Armor of Middle-earth.* London: HarperCollins, 2003.
Snyder, Jon B. "Forging Swords for *The Lord of the Rings* with Richard Taylor." "*The Lord of the Rings*" *Fan Club Official Movie Magazine* 1 (February–March 2002): 60–67.
Thompson, Kirsten Moana. "Scale, Spectacle and Movement: Massive Software and Digital Special Effects in *The Lord of the Rings.*" In *From Hobbits to Hollywood: Essays on Peter Jackson's "Lord of the Rings."* Edited by Ernest Mathijs and Murray Pomerance. Amsterdam and New York: Editions Rodopi BV, 2006. 283–99.
Thompson, Kristin. *The Frodo Franchise: "The Lord of the Rings" and Modern Hollywood.* Berkeley and Los Angeles: University of California Press, 2007.
Weta Workshop. http://www.wetaworkshop.co.nz/.
Woods, Paul A., ed. *Peter Jackson: From Gore to Mordor.* London: Plexus, 2005.
Woosnam-Savage, Robert. "Design Brief." Unpublished, November 4, 2008.
_____. "Discussion Document." Unpublished, February 26, 2008.
_____. "Exhibition Synopsis." Unpublished, September 19, 2007.

II. TECHNIQUES OF CHARACTER AND CULTURE

Into the West
Far Green Country or Shadow on the Waters?

JUDY ANN FORD AND ROBIN ANNE REID

And then it seemed to him that as in his dream in the house of Bombadil, the grey rain-curtain turned all to silver glass and was rolled back, and he beheld white shores and beyond them a far green country under a swift sunrise. But to Sam the evening deepened to darkness as he stood at the Haven; and as he looked at the grey sea he saw only a shadow on the waters that was soon lost in the West.[1]

This departure into the West from the Grey Havens in chapter 9, "The Grey Havens," in *The Return of the King* is one of many endings belonging to different narrative threads in J.R.R. Tolkien's *The Lord of the Rings*. It is one of the few that occur in the present of the story rather than reported as written or spoken about some time in the future; and it is confirmed by the witness of two characters, Frodo and Sam. Despite its location in the present, the passage communicates an uncertainty about what is taking place, both in the choice of the word "seemed" for Frodo's experience and in Sam's view through darkness to shadows. This uncertainty about Frodo's journey into the West goes to the heart of the religious themes of Tolkien's novel. In a real sense, the story of *Lord* is eschatological; that is, it is about the end of the world, or the narrow averting of that ending, in a final battle between good and evil. An understanding of Frodo's journey into the West must encompass Tolkien's presentation of Valinor and its history, the history of the Men of Númenor, Aragorn's family, the White Tree of Gondor, and thus the religious and spiritual themes that pervade his story.[2]

Peter Jackson's film, in subtle but unmistakable ways, changes Frodo's journey into the West and related story elements to suggest both greater certainty about the afterlife and greater optimism about the future of the world. That ultimate end, the end of all things, is presented quite differently in Jackson's film than in Tolkien's novel. Jackson's presentation is more historical than mythic. The analysis of these changes found in this essay rejects the premise that the primary criterion for evaluating a film adaptation of a novel is faithfulness to the book: each story will be judged on its own merit. Novels and films must tell stories in different ways, and each text, novel and film, emerges from a specific historical context. This essay addresses the question of how Jackson's film treatment of Frodo's future after he leaves Middle-earth and, more broadly, the future of Middle-earth, differs in tone from Tolkien's. It explores the ways in which those differences shape the religious and spiritual message of each story.

Tolkien's *Lord*, a complex work that operates on many levels, is, in one sense, a mock-history of the Third Age of Middle-earth. The historical quality is obvious in Tolkien's framing of the novel. *Lord* does not follow a simple linear narrative format. Prior to the opening of Book One, the "Prologue" offers a history book-like introduction to the topography of the Shire, its customs, and its architecture. The "Note on the Shire Records" offers a fictional manuscript history of the sort with which medieval scholars are all too familiar: the careful description of a record, its archival location, its scribal history, and the almost invariable loss of the original on which surviving copies are presumed to be based. The "Prologue" and the "Note on Shire Records" provide the reader with a sense of historic verisimilitude. Umberto Eco does much the same thing in his introduction to *The Name of the Rose* (Eco 1–5). Tolkien follows the conclusion of Book Six with six appendices containing genealogies, chronologies, and notes on language, all suggesting that the narrative of *Lord* is just one sequence of events in a much larger history of a real place. The suggestion and hints in the appendices are amply fulfilled by the posthumous publications of the multiple volumes of the *History of Middle-earth*, edited by Christopher Tolkien.

Peter Jackson does a superb job of suggesting this larger sense of history to his audience, both by weaving parts of Tolkien's framing introductions and appendices into the narrative of the film, but also by downplaying imagery associated with "fantasy" in the minds of a modern audience in favor of more historically based costumes, weapons, architecture, and props. Jackson's decision to attempt to convey a sense of being in a real, historic place is something he discusses in the commentary included in the extended edition of *The Fellowship of the Ring* (Appendices Part I, "From Book to Vision: Designing and

Building Middle-earth: Designing Middle-earth," *FOTR-EE*). While the historical tone of the film is quite "Tolkienian," being grounded in an easily justified reading of the book, it nevertheless serves to obscure other aspects of Tolkien's work. For Tolkien's *Lord* is not just historical, it is also mythic. The term "myth" is being used here in the dictionary sense of a "story, typically involving supernatural beings or forces, which embodies and provides an explanation or justification for something such as the early history of a society, a religious belief or ritual, or a natural phenomenon" (OED). The mythic character of the work is best seen in the context of the larger mythic cycle, a legendarium, that Tolkien hoped to create for England, contained not only in *Lord* but also in *The Hobbit* and in posthumously published works such as *The Silmarillion*.

The myths Tolkien tapped to provide a legendarium for England are those of the pre–Christian Germanic peoples, such as the Anglo-Saxons— best, although imperfectly, preserved in medieval Scandinavian literature. Tolkien was, of course, a professor in the English department at Oxford University specializing in historical philology, which today might be called comparative linguistics, particularly the literature and languages of medieval northwestern Europe. Tolkien was one of the world's foremost experts of his day on Anglo-Saxon and early Scandinavian texts, and he was keenly aware of how little of them survived. He expressed in his letters a deep regret for the loss of much of the early literature of these cultures, which leaves us with a paucity of knowledge about their mythologies in comparison to those of the Greco-Roman culture, for example.[3] Tolkien's fiction was, in part, his attempt to fill in the gaps, to imaginatively recreate such early medieval northern European myths and epics as once may have existed (Shippey xv).

The surviving Scandinavian myths have a pessimistic outlook in regard to their eschatology. These stories contain the expectation that good will ultimately lose to evil, that the gods will lose a final battle to the giants, the enemies of mankind. In other words, evil triumphs. Eschatological pessimism survived, in Anglo-Saxon culture, the transition from paganism to Christianity (Boenig 29–46). The Christianity of Tolkien's times, while certainly less eschatological in outlook, nevertheless had a theology which taught that prior to the sacrifice of Christ there was no hope of human salvation. According to that theology, only Christianity would permit humanity to look forward to the end times and expect good to triumph over evil; and only Christianity would allow individuals to look forward to life after death with any certainty about the existence of heaven.

Tolkien, a devout Catholic who loved the pre–Christian cultures and languages he studied as a philologist, does not include any aspect of organized religion in *Lord*, yet he saw the work as fundamentally religious, specifically Catholic (Carpenter 172). Tolkien's Middle-earth is a world in a pre–Christian state. Certainly no one would deny the Christological symbolism present in the work; nevertheless, Middle-earth is a world without knowledge of Christ and without any priesthood or church. Tolkien infuses this non–Christian world with pessimism grounded in an acceptance of the idea that evil can never really be defeated and with an uncertainty about the afterlife, in accord both with what is known of Anglo-Saxon beliefs and with what a devout Christian such as Tolkien might have expected.

The spiritual pessimism of Tolkien's work can be seen in two aspects of Middle-earth: spiritual decay and the persistence of evil. The text of *Lord* is permeated with the idea that the world is in spiritual decay. The end of the Third Age will be the end of the Elves in Middle-earth. In Tolkien's mythology, Elves are a higher spiritual order than men. In Tolkien's work the departure of Elves from Middle-earth means the loss of a grace, a spiritual presence which men cannot provide. Moreover, in Tolkien's text, the men of the Third Age are not as noble or morally elevated as they were in previous ages. The best praise that can be given to Aragorn is that he resembles men of the Second Age more than he does men of his own time and that under his rule for a time Gondor, specifically Minas Tirith, preserves something of the Second Age (*Return* 980).

The changes Jackson makes in regard to the decay of the world are subtle but consistent. Jackson does make explicit the departure of the Elves, yet he undercuts the consequent spiritual diminishment by emphasizing the dawn of the world of men. For example, in Galadriel's speech as she says farewell to the Hobbits at the Grey Havens in *Return of the King*, she states that the age of the Elves is over but also that the time has come for the dominion of men ("The Grey Havens," *Return* 76). These are her final words, and so the import of her speech is to stress the rise of men. It is never really made clear in the films that the Elves are supposed to be superior to men in any but the most physical ways — their eyesight, for example, or their balance or their aim. Their replacement by men is presented as a change rather than a diminution. Moreover, there is little sense that men in the Third or Fourth Age are not as good as their predecessors. In the film, Aragorn at his coronation speaks not only of the world renewed but also of sharing in the days of peace — implying that the days ahead will be better than the days past ("The Return of the King," *Return* 74).

The suggestion in the coronation sequence of Jackson's film that the new age of men will be as good as or better than the past is underscored by his treatment of evil, which can be overcome and defeated. In Tolkien's works, evil can never be permanently eradicated from the world. *The Silmarillion* recounts attempt after attempt to remove evil from Middle-earth, each one succeeding incompletely. The seeds of evil always remain to sprout again. The Dark Lord Morgoth is destroyed in the First Age, but his lieutenant Sauron remains. In the Second Age, Sauron is defeated, but his spirit remains, as do the rings he caused to be created, allowing evil to rise to power again. Morgoths's helper in the corruption of Valinor, the first Eden of the world, is a giant spider, Ungoliant. Although she is forced from the world, she leaves behind offspring who will ultimately include Shelob. Evil endures. Indeed, in Tolkien's attempt to write about the Fourth Age, he was certain of one thing: evil had returned (Carpenter 338). This return is foreshadowed in *Return*. Consider the death of the Lord of the Nazgûl: the text reads that his voice "was never heard again in that age of this world" (*Return* 852). The clear implication is that it might be heard again in future ages.

In Jackson's Middle-earth, evil can be permanently destroyed if human and other agents make the right choices. In Galadriel's prologue in *The Fellowship of the Ring* she s.tates that when Isildur cut the ring from Sauron's hand, he had "this one chance to destroy evil forever, but the hearts of men are easily corrupted" ("Prologue: One Ring to Rule Them All," *FOTR-TR* 1). Again, the clear implication is that if Isildur had not been corrupted, and had not kept the ring, evil would have been destroyed. Later in *FOTR-TR*, when Frodo looks in Galadriel's mirror and sees the Shire over-run by orcs and the Hobbits forced into slavery, she tells him, "It is what will come to pass if you should fail" ("Galadriel's Mirror," *FOTR-TR* 39). Of course, Frodo succeeds, the ring is destroyed, and in the film, the Shire is saved. In Tolkien's novel, in contrast, even though Frodo and others make the same basic choices and submit to the same sacrifices to destroy the ring, the Shire is nevertheless corrupted by Saruman, as is shown in "The Scouring of the Shire." In spite of the sacrifices of Frodo and the others, evil endures. Jackson's film seems to be expressing a kind of modern faith in historical progress largely absent from Tolkien's work.

The degree of certainty that one may have about the afterlife is also very different in Jackson's Middle-earth from Tolkien's Middle-earth. Knowledge of the afterlife is an issue Tolkien addresses explicitly in *The Silmarillion*. The Elves know that while the world endures, although they may leave Middle-earth, the land of the mortals, they will never really die (Carpenter, 147). Elves that leave Middle-earth dwell on Valinor, where they may wait in the Halls of Mandos until the world's ending. The Elves are nevertheless uncertain about their ultimate fate: they do not know if they will survive the end of the world.

In Tolkien's mythology, Valinor is the land of the Valar, the gods or Powers of Middle-earth created, along with all else in the cosmology of Tolkien's world, by the one god, Ilùvator. The Valar were the small group among the Ainur, equivalent to angelic powers, who chose to enter into Middle-earth. The servants of the Valar, the Maiar, the wizards, are who are given bodily form and sent by the Valar into Middle-earth. The Valar and the Maiar have a long and complex history, as do Elves and Men, before the time of the events of *Lord*. As a result of warfare with one of their own, Melkor, the other Valar retreated to Valinor, a protected island, distant from Middle-earth. Later conflict in the Second Age leads to the decision to make Valinor unreachable by any save the Valar and Elves. Valinor was removed from the sight of men as a punishment for hubris during the Second Age.[4] No man or mortal can journey there. Because of Bilbo's and Frodo's service and self-sacrifice in the novel, they are rewarded by being allowed to sail with the Elves and Gandalf to this far country. For all other mortals, knowledge of the lesser gods, the Valar, and their home, Valinor, comes only from legends and visions. In Tolkien's work, mortal men who die move beyond the Outer Sea to the unknown and never return.[5]

The name of the far green land glimpsed by Frodo is not mentioned in *Lord* in either the passages set in the house of Bombadil or those in the Grey Havens. Readers of the wider body of Tolkien's fiction recognize the destination as Valinor. Otherwise, Valinor is described mainly in other works edited and published by Christopher Tolkien after his father's death. *The Silmarillion* was published in 1977, so readers, general and expert, would not have had this information in 1955 when *Fellowship* was first published. The question of how much a contemporary reader's knowledge of the later work affects their sense of Tolkien's novel, as well as their evaluation of Jackson's film, is one that bears consideration.

There is little information about Valinor in Jackson's film, but there are references an alert viewer can catch. Throughout the film, in various scenes, some only in the Extended Editions, there are references to the Elves leaving Middle-earth, but the only information given about their destination is that it is a place of safety and a refuge from the dangers of the war. There is only one verbal and one visual reference to Valinor, both in the same scene of the extended version of *ROTK*. When Elrond encourages Arwen to leave Middle-earth, he uses "Valinor" as the name of the land to which the Elven ships sail ("Arwen's Fate," *TT-TR* 38). At that point, he is speaking to her in Elvish with English subtitles.

In her room, during that same scene, it is possible to see a wall hanging which has the image of the Two Trees of Valinor created by the Valar to give light before the sun and moon. The story of the trees is an important part of *The Silmarillion*; the White Tree of Gondor ultimately derives from the Two Trees of Valinor, and represents, among other things, a link between Gondor and Valinor. In the director's commentary on the Extended Edition of *ROTK*, as Pippin and Gandalf walk past the dead White Tree in the courtyard of the Citadel of Minas Tirith on their way to their first meeting with Denethor, Steward of Gondor, Peter Jackson observes that it was difficult to get the White Tree into the film and he does not think that they managed to convey what it stood for properly although they did the best they could. He says that he believes it is one of those details that show how a film cannot sustain all of that information that Tolkien put into the books (Special Features Audio Commentaries: Director and Writers, 11 "Minas Tirith," *ROTK*). Much of the information in the novel about the history, legends, and mythology of the earlier ages of Middle-earth comes from Gandalf and Elrond, who are millennia old, and from Aragorn, whose line descends from the legendary kings of Númenor. The information is often conveyed in speeches, often lengthy, explaining the background to the Hobbits, a method of exposition difficult to incorporate in film. Although Jackson acknowledges that the White Tree is important to Tolkien's Middle-earth, he determined that it was not as important to the film they were making.

And yet, as we have noted above, Tolkien himself provides little specific information about Valinor in his novel, as opposed to Númenor, for example, an island given by the Valar to the men who fought with the Elves against Morgoth (*Return* 1045–50). Originally, Tolkien wanted to publish parts of what became *The Silmarillion* with *Lord*, but his publisher refused; the appendices are the unhappy compromise (Carpenter 144). Within the text of the novel itself are some references to that wider mythological history. In *Fellowship*, Bilbo sings a song he made up based on an Elvish poem about the legendary mariner Eärendil and which speaks of Valinor, also known as Eldamar, where Eärendil sought help for Middle-earth (234–7). Later, in Lórien, Galadriel sings a farewell song to the Company in Quenya, the High Elvish language, and that song also refers to Valinor ("Valimar" in the text) (380).

In *The Two Towers*, Gandalf tells Pippin about the history of the Palantiri, the Seeing Stones, and mentions Eldamar as a possible origin for the stones (600). The songs and Gandalf's story contain some seeds of the mythology contained in works outside *Lord*. In other works, much of which was composed in part prior to *Lord*, Tolkien constructs a creation myth, relates various legends and tales, and in some versions translates them to poetry or lays covering the creation of Elves and Men, how evil comes in to the world, the long ages of conflict and war which can never completely end evil, the reasons for the Elves leaving Valinor. All of these elements have bearing on the events of the novel and lend greater significance to some of those events. Readers of Tolkien, and Tolkien scholars, since 1977 have had access to the mythology of Tolkien's Middle-earth to a greater degree than readers of the novel as it was originally published. Although Tolkien wanted that information to be published with the novel, in a sense, he and Peter Jackson made similar choices in omitting the majority of the mythological substrata from the main narrative arc of the story of the War of the Ring.

In *The Lord of the Rings*, both book and film, the main narrative ends when the spiritually damaged Frodo sails into the West and Sam returns alone to the Shire; but the similarity in the events of these endings belies a great difference in interpretation. In Tolkien's novel, Frodo's journey is prefigured by a dream. In chapter 8 of *Fellowship*, "Fog on the Barrow Downs," the narrator relates an experience that Frodo has in Tom Bombadil's house: "But **either in his dreams or out of them, he could not tell which**, Frodo heard a sweet singing running in his mind: a song that **seemed** to come like a pale light behind a grey rain-curtain, and growing stronger to turn the veil all to glass and silver, until at last it was rolled back, and a far green country opened before him under a swift sunrise" (*Fellowship* 135, emphasis added).

In both this incident and in the description of the actual journey in *Return*, which closely echoes the wording of the incident in Bombadil's house, the narrative persona, that is, the perspective from which readers experience the story, carefully constructs Frodo's and Sam's experiences in such a way as to deny a clear statement of the unnamed land's existence for the characters and thus for the readers. Frodo is not sure whether his experience in Bombadil's house is a dream or something else — for example, a vision. The reader cannot be sure at the end of the novel whether or not Frodo is actually reaching the land he seemed to dream about earlier because of the shading of the phrasing: "And then **it seemed to him that as in his dream** in the house of Bombadil, the grey rain-curtain turned all to silver glass and was rolled back, and he beheld white shores and beyond them a far green country under a swift sunrise" (*Return* 1042, emphasis added). Seeming is not being. And Sam, standing on the shore, sees only that the ship sails into greyness and shadows, an image that recalls Saruman's mockery of the Elves he meets after being cast out of Isengard. Saruman knows, as does Galadriel and the others of the Wise, that the defeat of Sauron in the War of the Ring will bring about the death of many fair things, as well as lead to the final departure of the Elves. Saruman takes comfort in the Elves' doom as he says, "You pulled down your own house when you destroyed mine. And now, what ship will bear you back across so wide a sea?... It will be a grey ship, and full of ghosts" (*Return* 995).

Tolkien leaves his reader hopeful, perhaps, that what Frodo sees is the far green country of Valinor, but without clear certainty whether what Frodo sees might not be a shadow on the waters, a mockery, or a delusion.

In Jackson's film, in contrast, the knowledge of survival in the afterlife has nothing dreamlike or uncertain about it. During the battle of the Pelennor Fields, as Osgiliath waits for the army of Mordor to break through the City Gates, Pippin fears that all will come to an end. Gandalf reassures him: "No, the journey doesn't end here. Death is just another path.... One that we all must take. The grey rain-curtain of this world rolls back, and all will change to silver glass.... And then you see it: white shores ... and beyond, the far green country under a swift sunrise" ("A Far Green Country," *ROTK-TR* 49). During the latter part of Gandalf's speech, the melody "Into the West" is played in the background. Pippin appears comforted. These words are spoken by Gandalf as a certainty, not something that he might have seen in a dream or out of it. Gandalf is in a unique position to speak authoritatively about the afterlife. Not only is he a wizard, one of the Wise; but also, by this point in the story, he has returned from the dead himself. It is hard to think of a more authoritative source for the afterlife than Gandalf. Although the language used borrows heavily from Tolkien's words, the transfer of this set of images from Frodo's dreaming and seeming to Gandalf's confident reassurances changes their meaning. Additionally, Gandalf's speech presents this far green land as a place that all souls will reach after death, in the journey that continues beyond our physical or material life, clearly a more inclusive goal than the hidden land of Tolkien's Elves.

Certainty that the afterlife includes a journey to a pleasant, far green country is repeated and reinforced in Jackson's scene of the departure from the Grey Havens, a harbor controlled by a powerful Elf, Círdan the Shipwright. In the wake of the controversy over "The Scouring of the Shire," deleted entirely from the film except for images glimpsed in Galadriel's mirror as potential events that might be avoided, few critics have analyzed the Grey Havens scene. Some might argue that little was changed in the film from the novel, especially compared to some of the other more overt and controversial changes made in the film: the cutting of sections of the novel, the absence of characters such as Tom Bombadil, and the major changes in characters, such as Faramir. The events of the Grey Havens scene are more or less drawn from the novel with the exception of who travels with whom and in what order. In the novel, Frodo and Sam leave alone for the Grey Havens; later on their journey they are joined by Elrond, Galadriel, other Elves, and Bilbo. Gandalf meets the group at the Grey Havens. Merry and Pippin also join Frodo and Sam at the last minute, having been warned by Gandalf that Frodo would be leaving. The Elves take Bilbo and Frodo along with them on a ship which sails into the West, into a shadow on the water, leaving Sam and the others on the shore. The Hobbits return to the Shire, and the book closes with Sam rejoining his family and announcing his return. In the film, Gandalf brings Bilbo to the Shire; and Frodo, Merry, and Pippin travel with them to the Grey Havens, where they meet Elrond and Galadriel. After farewells, Bilbo and Frodo board the ship with Gandalf and the Elves, and the ship sails out into the harbor, into the bright light of a setting sun. Sam and the others return to the Shire, and Sam is seen rejoining his family and announcing that he has returned ("The Grey Havens," *ROTK-TR* 76).

In spite of the similarities, there are important differences in the film's presentation of the Grey Havens scene that significantly change its tone. In the film, Bilbo hurries towards the ship from the dock, cheerfully exclaiming that he is ready for another adventure. There is no direct description of Bilbo boarding the ship in the novel and nothing to indicate his hurrying in eagerness. Moreover, Bilbo's words in the film are taken from another part of the novel and altered. In the novel, when Frodo and Sam encounter Bilbo and the Elves on the way to the Grey Havens, an elderly Bilbo wakes up, greets Frodo, announces that he is now older than the longest-living Hobbit known and says that he is quite ready for another journey. He then asks Frodo if he is coming. When Frodo replies in the affirmative, an anxious Sam asks where they are going. Frodo tells him that they are going to the Havens (*Return* 1041). Given that, in the novel, Bilbo says that he is ready for another journey while en route to the Grey Havens, it is quite possible for the reader to understand him to mean the actual journey in which he is engaged: the ride to the Grey Havens. Sam's question and Frodo's reply support that interpretation. Even if a reader chooses to interpret Bilbo as meaning the journey into the West beyond the Havens, the term "journey" is far more neutral than "adventure." An eager Bilbo hurrying to board a ship sailing into the West and declaring that he views that voyage as an adventure indicates a far greater confidence about what that voyage will bring than an elderly, sleepy Bilbo declaring himself ready for a journey which might be understood to terminate before he ever boards the ship.

More significantly, in the film, Frodo's good-bye to the tearful Merry, Pippen and Sam is followed with a shot of Frodo boarding the ship and turning to face his fellows with a beaming, cheerful smile. The scene then shows the Hobbits returning the smile. There are no such reassuring smiles in Tolkien's version. In the novel, the narrative voice relates that, after the farewell, Frodo boarded the ship, the sails were drawn up, the wind blew, and the ship slipped out of port until the light of the glass of Galadriel carried by

Frodo could no longer be seen on shore. Sam watches far into the night, seeing only shadows and deepening darkness. Jackson reverses the light imagery: instead of a light being lost, the ship leaving port merges into a bright white light that first illuminates and then fills the screen so that nothing can be seen but a blindingly intense light.

Both types of light imagery — increasing darkness and a blinding white light — might symbolize death, but only Jackson's suggests entry into a heaven-like afterlife. White light in a myriad of forms, natural and mystical, serves the same purpose in novel and film: it is a sign of the good powers, of the Valar. Gandalf tells Frodo in the novel that his perception of Glorfindel as a white shining figure shows that the Elf is one of the Firstborn, who have power in both realms, material and spiritual (*ROTR-TR* 223). Gandalf as both the Grey and as the reincarnated White is a figure whose power is shown through light. Saruman loses his status as the White when he turns to evil. In the film, Arwen's first appearance in a blaze of the light, Gandalf's use of white light, and of the light of the sun, moon, and stars mirror Tolkien's novel. Viewers of the film, even those who do not know the book, may well associate the light that the ship sails into in the end with more than a literal sunset, a metaphorical death, or an entrance into that spiritual realm. The perception of the white light for all in the film and the viewers makes Frodo's vision concrete rather than "seeming." The image of Sam, left behind on the dock, peering into the darkness and seeing shadows, is not presented visually in the film. Sam's viewpoint is nonetheless represented in the song played as the film concludes.

Arguably, the final ending of this film that has many endings is Annie Lennox's performance of "Into the West," a song with lyrics by Fran Walsh and music by Howard Shore. "Into the West" presents an intriguing modulation of the ending of the film to a tone closer to that of the novel. This song embodies the ambiguities of Tolkien's novel in a way that the light at the end of the film does not. In this song, which, according to the filmmakers, was written in memory of a friend, Cameron Duncan, who died of cancer before the final film was released, the question of what lies beyond the sea after the passage from Middle-earth is complex (Special Features Audio Commentaries: Director and Writers, "The End Credits," *ROTK:EE* 76). The language of dreaming, of the pale moon, of the grey ship passing into the west is moved from the description of Sam's perceptions at the end of the novel to the lyrics at the end of the film. The subject addressed by the narrative voice of the song is told to dream. Color imagery (silver, grey) is associated with water, and even though there is light, references to weeping, shadows, and fading are woven into the lyrics. The song brings back into the film some of the ambiguity, pessimism, and doubt of Tolkien's novel that its visual elements obscure or contradict.

On one level, the dichotomy between the visual components and the song in the film's Grey Haven's scene — between the cheerful confidence of smiling Hobbits boarding the ship for another adventure then merging into a pure, white light and the weeping listener in the song whose hope is fading in a vision of darkness and shadows — mirrors the two perspectives that Tolkien wrote into this scene in his novel. The journey into the West is one of the few endings of *Lord* for which the perspective of two witnesses is offered, and Frodo's experience is quite different from that of Sam's. As this essay has argued, the certainty implied by the visual elements of Jackson's Grey Haven's scene is far stronger than what may be found in Tolkien's narrative description of Frodo's experience. As well, the belief that human actions can lead to the triumph of good over evil is far stronger in Jackson's Middle-earth than in Tolkien's, reflecting in the film a modern secular notion of historical progress, and in the book a Christian belief that a world that has not experienced Christ cannot be certain of the afterlife or of any eventually defeat of evil. Nevertheless, the contrast between the relative optimism of the perspective of the one who experiences the journey beyond Middle-earth and the relative sadness and doubt of the perspective of one who is left behind is similar in both the film and the novel. The contrast between those perspectives, in both Tolkien's and Jackson's work, makes this ending more complex, muted, perhaps more sorrowful.

Every film based on a book is an interpretation of the book, and Peter Jackson's *LOTR* is no exception. Different readers and viewers will judge the interpretation differently. Jackson's choice of stressing the historical aspects of the book and introducing a theme of historical progress achieved through human action cannot be judged to be more or less valid than a film that might have stressed more mythic and pessimistic themes. Indeed, it may be the case that a visual medium such as film might be better suited to provide a more historical, event-based emphasis. There were many tears among the audience of Jackson's Grey Havens scene in spite of the film's relatively greater optimism, so it may have inspired an emotional response among its audience as effectively as Tolkien's novel. An analogy might be made to another film of the same year, Mel Gibson's *The Passion of the Christ*. Some viewers praised its accuracy to the narrative of the Bible, while others felt that this very accuracy ignored the spiritual message of the Bible: in other words, that Gibson's literal rendering of the story left out Christ's spiritual message. Yet there were Christian viewers moved to tears by Gibson's presentation. Although, as Tom Shippey notes, different paths may be taken, Jackson's audience and Tolkien's may have found themselves in the same emotional location when the stories ended.

Notes

1. J.R.R. Tolkien, *Return of the King* (2002), 1042. Pagination for subsequent quotes will be indicated in parenthetical notes in text.

2. Scholarship on the religious and spiritual themes in Tolkien's work is rich and varied, drawing on multiple traditions. Birzer, Curry, and Wood focus primarily on Christian elements in the Legendarium; Burns, Drout, Fimi, Flieger, and Jones are among the best known scholars working on the Celtic and Norse elements. Vaccaro and Cunningham have written on the Christian, Norse, and Celtic roots of Tolkien's White Tree of Gondor. However, work on the religious and spiritual elements of the film is less developed. The 2002 article "A Potion Too Strong?: Challenges in Translating the Religious Significance of Tolkien's *Lord of the Rings* to Film," by Mallinson, and the 2004 "Life as a Journey: The Spiritual Dimension in Peter Jackson's *Lord of the Rings*," by Garbowski, are the only existing works so far as we can determine. Both articles contain strong arguments: neither privileges the book over the film, giving both equal standing as texts while making useful comparisons. Mallinson focuses on the varying strength of Jackson's use of archetypes, eucatastrope, and a consistent secondary world. Garbowski, arguing that the spiritual elements are more successfully developed than specifically Christian elements, focuses on the existential nature of life as a journey in film and novel, considering along the way several elements that we cover here (the element of historicity in creating realistic fantasies, Gandalf's speech to Pippin in the film, the end sequence although not the closing song by Annie Lennox) but also including a wider range of examples of spiritual elements.

3. Tolkien, "Letter 131: To Milton Waldman" (in Carpenter 144). A similar sentiment is expressed in an unsent draft, "Letter 180 To 'Mr. Thompson' [draft]," 230–1.

4. "The Downfall of Númenor" is the subtitle of the Akallabêth (*Silmarillion* 267–291).

5. "Of Beren and Lúthien," chapter 19 of *The Silmarillion*, contains one of the clearest statements of the different natures of existence after death for Elves and Men, in the choice offered Lúthien (Christopher Tolkien, *Silmarillion* 1993, 186–7). Also, a discussion between an Elf, Finrod, and a human woman, Andreth, about immortality and mortality may be found in "Athrabeth Finrod Ah Andreth," in J.R.R. Tolkien (Christopher Tolkien, ed.), *Morgoth's Ring* (1993), 301–366.

Works Cited

Birzer, Bradley J. *J. R. R. Tolkien's Sanctifying Myth: Understanding Middle-earth.* Wilmington, DE: ISI, 2003.

Boenig, Robert. "Introduction." In *Anglo-Saxon Spirituality: Selected Writings*. Edited and translated by Robert Boenig, 1–57. "The Classics of Western Spirituality." Series editor Bernard McGinn. New York: Paulist, 2000.

Burns, Marjorie. *Perilous Realms: Celtic and Norse in Tolkien's Middle-earth*. Toronto: University of Toronto Press, 2005.

Carpenter, Humphrey, ed. *The Letters of J. R. R. Tolkien*. New York: Houghton Mifflin, 2000.

Croft, Janet Brennan. *Tolkien on Film: Essays on Peter Jackson's "The Lord of the Rings."* Altadena: Mythopoeic, 2004.

Cunningham, Michael. "In the Shadow of the Tree: A Study of the Motif of the White Tree in the Context of J. R. R. Tolkien's Middle-earth." *Mallorn* 44 (2006): 3–8.

Curry, Patrick. *Defending Middle-earth*. New York: Houghton Mifflin, 2004.

Drout, Michael D.C. "J.R.R. Tolkien's Medieval Scholarship and Its Significance." *Tolkien Studies* 4 (2007): 113–176.
Eco, Umberto. *The Name of the Rose*. Translated by William Weaver. 1st Harvest ed. San Diego: Harcourt Brace, 1994.
Fimi, Dimitra. "Tolkien's 'Celtic' Type of Legends': Merging Traditions." *Tolkien Studies* 4 (2007): 51–71.
Flieger, Verlyn. *Interrupted Music: The Making of Tolkien's Mythology*. Kent, OH: Kent State University Press, 2005.
Garbowski, Christopher. "Life as a Journey: The Spiritual Dimension in Peter Jackson's *Lord of the Rings*." *Journal of Religion and Popular Culture* 6 (Spring 2004). http://www.usask.ca/relst/jrpc/art6-lifejourney.html (accessed March 27, 2009).
Jones, Leslie Ellen. *Myth and Middle-earth: Exploring the Legends behind J.R.R. Tolkien's "The Hobbit" and "The Lord of the Rings."* Spring Harbor, NY: Cold Spring, 2002.
The Lord of the Rings. Theatrical and Extended Film Editions. Directed by Peter Jackson. New Line, 2001, 2002, 2003, 2004.
Mallinson, Jeffrey. "A Potion Too Strong?: Challenges in Translating the Religious Significance of Tolkien's *The Lord of the Rings* to Film." *Journal of Religion and Popular Culture* 1 (2002). http://www.usask.ca/relst/jrpc/article-tolkien.html (accessed March 27, 2009).
Shippey, Tom. "Another Road to Middle-earth: Jackson's Movie Trilogy." In *Understanding "The Lord of the Rings."* Edited by Rose A. Zimbardo and Neil D. Isaacs, 233–254. Boson: Houghton Mifflin, 2004.
_____. *J.R.R. Tolkien: Author of the Century*. New York: Houghton Mifflin, 2000.
Tolkien, J.R.R. *The Fellowship of the Ring*. New York: Houghton Mifflin, 2002.
_____. *The History of Middle Earth*. Edited by Christopher Tolkien. New York: Houghton Mifflin, 1984–1996.
_____. *Morgoth's Ring: The Later Silmarillion*. Part One. Edited by Christopher Tolkien. New York: Houghton Mifflin, 1993.
_____. *The Return of the King*. New York: Houghton Mifflin, 2002.
_____. *The Silmarillion*. Edited by Christopher Tolkien. New York: Houghton Mifflin, 1977.
_____. *The Two Towers*. New York: Houghton Mifflin, 2002.
Vaccaro, Christopher T. "'And One White Tree': The Cosmological Cross and the *Arbor Vitae* in J.R.R. Tolkien's *The Lord of the Rings* and *The Silmarillion*." *Mallorn* 42 (2004): 23–28.
Wood, Ralph. *The Gospel According to Tolkien: Visions of the Kingdom in Middle-earth*. London: Westminster John Knox, 2003.

Frodo Lives but Gollum Redeems the Blood of Kings

PHILIP E. KAVENY

Gollum won the only battle that really mattered and the battle upon whose outcome all future victories depended. He did so by destroying the "One Ring" and in the process making the supreme personal sacrifice of his miserable life. Thus J.R.R. Tolkien's literary Sméagol/Gollum and Peter Jackson's cinematic Sméagol/Gollum should be granted posthumous inclusion in the Fellowship of the Ring.[1]

Of course the destruction which completes the task of the ring bearer is accomplished only as Gollum falls into annihilation clutching his "Precious." This matter of Gollum's death, destruction and redemption of the quest where all others failed raises a number of theological questions which we will get to later. However, I would like to note that this proposition knocked the socks off my dear friend, the prominent Tolkien scholar Shaun Hughes, who has inspired me all my creative life and whose contribution will be sorely missed in this volume.

In *The Lord of the Rings* books and *LOTR* films, sometimes the naïve reader or viewer may hesitate when facing the daunting scope of Tolkien's secondary world. They must remember what Gandalf told Bilbo, in the specially revised edition of *The Hobbit*, which was done for a better fit with *Lord*, when on the last page Gandalf the wizard tells Bilbo his role in the great scheme. Gandalf tells Bilbo that he is really quite a little fellow in a very big world.

The vastness of the time scale in Middle-earth becomes manifest in the Peter Jackson films when Gandalf rides off on his great steed, Shadowfax, to seek aid for Helm's Deep, after his return from his defeat of the Balrog. He is no longer Gandalf the Grey, but Gandalf the White, as he says, "I have lived three hundred lifetimes and now I have not enough time to do what I must."

This, I think gives us some idea as readers and viewers as to what is at stake for both J.R.R Tolkien in the *Lord* books and Peter Jackson in the LOTR films; for both of them the task is to articulate a life and death struggle, between not so much good and evil, but between that which lies beneath the two. The struggle is between the creative and the perverse reaching back to the almost timeless prehistory alluded to but not expressed obliquely in published form in Tolkien's lifetime. The question is whether or not his secondary world will become like our own or descend into darkness — as our primary world, the one which we inhabit, still could do. Peter Jackson says as much through Strider's words and actions at the siege of Helm's Deep, the last refuge of the Riders of Rohan. The siege is not a military battle for a normal military objective, but rather genocidal warfare against humanity.

The shout that the world should descend into darkness is the battle cry of the Uruk-hai and Orcs, who were conceived by Sauron and empowered with modern methods of industrial production and self reproduction and who engage in not only a genocidal but also an ecocidal warfare against all that is green and living in Middle-earth, as they seek to bring in their own new world order once the One Ring is back in Sauron's hands.

A great deal of very fine work has been done concerning what is come to be known as "the book into film problem." However, though I am acutely aware of a number of issues raised in turning a book into film, particularly one as monumental as J.R.R. Tolkien's *Lord,* I have chosen to foreground a few of the similarities and some astounding overlaps in the challenges that both J.R.R. Tolkien and Peter Jackson in *LOTR* confronted in realizing the works as author and producer respectively, even though their creative lifetimes were separated by a half century and, of course, they never met.[2]

It is interesting to examine some of the challenges Tolkien and Jackson both faced through the lens of economic reality, which includes (but is not limited to) budget, production-time constraints, and lost opportunity costs, since what can be done in both a book and a film are molded, formed, crafted, and sometimes improved by market forces which are beyond the ability of the artist or creator, or even a production company, to control.

The vast scale of this undertaking is practically self-evident in the case of the Peter Jackson films. Tom Shippey, J.R.R. Tolkien's philological heir-apparent at both Leeds and Oxford University, told me the entire production cost of the first edition of Tolkien's *Lord* would have paid for three seconds of the opening credits of the film *FOTR*. However, the Tolkien books, including *The Hobbit*, were not culturally autonomous creations existing somehow outside harsh economic realities like the Great Depression, World War II, postimperial and, finally, Cold War Great Britain, which Tolkien so often refers to in his correspondence as limiting his creative choices and his publishing options, not the least of which was UK wartime and postwar paper rationing. This made his project as he originally intended it — of which *Lord* and *The Hobbit* are only offshoots, or side-branches, of the immense chronicle, or mythology/legendarium, which is *The Silmarillion* — an impossibility for any English language publisher.[3]

Yet Tolkien wished for nothing less than publication of that immense chronicle or mythology which is *The Silmarillion*. It was after all only the economic reality of the paucity of an Oxford professor's pension which would force him into his most dreaded occupation of examination grading, that then forced him to accept something rather than nothing in the publication of *Lord*.

On some level Tolkien seemed to sense that, in order to make the book sell — something his publishers were quite dubious of — he had to give the naïve readers, the ones who would pay the (then) exorbitant price necessary for the book to make the print run a success and who would not thumb back and forth between text and appendix — the backstory: the three thousand year history of the One Ring, which ruled all the others and held them all together, that made it critical to the readers' understanding of Tolkien's project. They had to be given the backstory so that they knew the Ring was a ring of power, because otherwise *Lord* is just another travel novel, as sadly, it is taught in some English departments.

Tolkien, and Peter Jackson, respectively, utilized the characterization of Gollum to address these naïve[4] readers and viewers and to incorporate essential elements of the backstory in both books and films. Of course, this was not Sméagol/Gollum's only literary and cinematic function. Gollum introduces an added moral or ethical dimension to both the books and the films, through his actions and interactions not only with the members of the Fellowship of the Ring, but also with those who humiliated and tortured and terrorized him from the forces of both good and evil as he bore the burden of his Precious even when it was not in his possession.[5] It must be remembered that this was a burden which imposed itself upon him and drove him into five hundred years of solitude and luminescent darkness.

There is something singular about *Lord* books, as was pointed out by professional linguist David Salo, who functioned as advisor and translator to Peter Jackson's New Line Cinema productions. Salo reminds us to not too quickly assume that many more people have seen the Tolkien movies than have read the books, suggesting that, in seven decades and in scores of various translations, Tolkien readership (simply in terms of copies sold) numbers in the hundreds of millions, as we have now easily moved into the third generation of worldwide Tolkien readership. This is very important because, through this reading and myriad artistic renderings of Tolkien's work by himself and others, this range of images exists in the popular consciousness for the skillful producer to draw upon and, in some cases, actualize. These images then serve as a kind of iconographic portal on three levels to create connections between film and text.

Therefore, for purposes of this discussion I would like to think of J.R.R. Tolkien's *Lord* novels and the Jackson films as similarly culturally situated artistic products accessible in an ever expanding myriad of formats and having simultaneous existence in both — what I will refer to as the literary and cinematic universe. These two universes exist in parallel yet semipermeable realities; that is to say the same narrative exists in both but in a different form depending on whether it exists in cinematic or literary medium or also mediating graphic art format, which will be important from my standpoint. It might be useful at least as a metaphor to think of this approach as a being a bit like the way multidimensional string theory is used to address certain physics problems which might otherwise be unsolvable. I would add that my approach shares something that a colleague of mine in physics was kind enough to point out — that though string theory is currently unverifiable in any empirical sense, yet it is nevertheless annoyingly useful.

Gollum as a Narrative Carrier and Abridger[6] Through Iconographic Portals Between Text and Cinema

Here I will define just what I mean by iconographic portals. I would start by addressing two things I am less concerned about. The first is that, at least on an artistic level, the illustrator definitely produces illustrations on the level of fine gallery art. The second is mimesis. Throughout his work Tolkien is forced to operate on several complexly intertwined time scales, some of which transcend and stand outside of time, and others lasting no longer than the physiological persistence of vision.[7]

I want say just a bit more about the universality of illustration, drawing from my own experience and memory. I recall an adorable six-year-old girl poking me with her rolled coloring book to interrupt my rather long-winded summary of a Tolkien (Mythopoeic Society) conference presentation I was preparing for during a flight from Minneapolis to San Francisco in 1996. I was sharing my insights with a very nice Jewish lady and her brother, a rabbi.[8] The little girl's question was quite direct. She wondered if she was right in that Gollum's actual color was green, because she wanted me to settle the argument between her and her father, who was reading *Lord* out loud to her.[9] Of course I agreed with her. (I will always hold dear the image of her frolicking off with her father towards the luggage carrousel, when she turned and waved good-bye to me with her coloring book.) So what I mean by iconographic portals is this: they are an access point into a larger reality, or perhaps the backstory of Tolkien's mythology/legendarium, which for mostly technical reasons can only be indirectly represented. Perhaps it is best to go back to the original Greek meaning or εικών, "image," and γράφειν, "writing," and take this to mean the image stands for something larger than what it represents. The key idea is that we are interested in the content, not the form, of the image.

The character Gollum in *The Hobbit* and *Lord* books and *LOTR* films carries the burden of the One Ring, the ring of power to rule all others, hundreds of years longer than any of the other characters. Along with carrying the One Ring he carries the narrative and makes connections in both the books and films. Briefly I would like to look at what I would argue is the most obvious function, first as it is shared by both the *Lord* books and the *LOTR* films. It is something that must be continually reiterated so that the reader or viewer gets the concept that no victory is possible if the One Ring is not destroyed and all the great victories are hollow since the One Ring really functions as an unlimited force-multiplier for the forces of darkness, as each force destroyed is replaced by one ten times as large. Also, the narrative progresses from the battles of Helm's Deep to the Battle of Pelennor Fields to the preemptive battle before the gates of Mordor fought in ROTK only give the Ring's bearers more time if they are still alive.

Aragorn flying into battle against impossible odds — with Merry and Pippin at his side and the cry for Frodo on their lips and brandishing his forebearer Isildur's reforged sword, Narsil, after the blood of men failed three thousand years ago — though it chills our souls is really only a diversionary action if Frodo does not live. Yet Frodo cannot destroy the One Ring alone. So in a very real sense grand narrative and individual action are inexecrably linked through the action of the Ring bearers.

Yet the grand narrative of both the books and the films is expressed in an individual sense in the effect of the One Ring on all who bear it. This is most horrific in Gollum's characterization in the Jackson films, particularly *ROTK* which visually teaches us the cautionary lessons about the overriding power of the One Ring to prolong and distort the life of a Hobbit. After all, as Gandalf points out, Gollum was once a Stoor Hobbit, much like Bilbo,

Frodo, Sam, Pippin, and Merry, and Hobbits are more like humans than anything else in Middle-earth.

In a sense, Gollum is more visually chilling than the Nazgûl, or, as they are referred to in Black Speech, Ringwraiths, sometimes written Ring-wraiths, the black riders who in Aragorn's words were "once men, great kings." True, their spectral essence is bone-chilling, yet there is, to our minds, nothing left of what they once were, only the terror of their Morgul Blades and the empty cowl behind the Iron Mask of the Witch-king. This is what Frodo will become if the wound he received from the Morgul Blade on Weathertop is not ameliorated.

The importance of the multidimensional characterization of Gollum in both the books and the films gives added information to the reader or viewer about the Tolkien legendarium as it existed in Tolkien's mind and unpublished works — nearly six decades ago as it appeared in the first published version of *Lord* and the revised edition of *The Hobbit*, which was necessary to connect it to *Lord*. It is important to note that Peter Jackson's film rights applied only to *The Hobbit* and *Lord* as they appeared when the rights were sold, in Tolkien's lifetime, in 1969. At a time when there was no Tolkien legendarium, which really did not assume its final form until Tolkien's death in 1973 when it was taken over by his son Christopher and at least some of Tolkien's fans became Tolkien scholars. One of them, Guy Gavriel Kay, worked extensively with Christopher Tolkien and ended up leaving the History of Middle-earth project as a result of profound differences with the Tolkien Estate over the final form of Tolkien's posthumous work. Kay went on to become a famous author in his own right and is still an important force in the high fantasy genre which Tolkien defined.[10]

Interestingly enough, Tolkien seems acutely aware of this problem as we turn to page 64 of the 1991 Houghton Mifflin edition of *Lord*, illustrated by none other than Allan Lee, the visual advisor to the New Line Cinema production of *LOTR*. In chapter 2, "The Shadow of the Past," Gandalf explains to Frodo about the history of the rings, or, said another way, he covers three thousand years of the history of Middle-earth before it appears as a discrete literary entity. Frodo asks, "This Ring! ... How on earth did it come to be." Gandalf answers: "Ah! ... That is a very long story. The beginnings lie back in the Black Years which only a lore-master now remembers. If I were to tell you that tale, we should be sitting here when spring passes into winter."

Tolkien is self referentially speaking of himself as that lore-master, who, if he were dealing with actual events in the history of the West, would find them extending back to Homer and *The Iliad*, a task which even as great a lore-master as himself cannot keep the listener/reader sitting until spring passes into winter. I think the following classic Tolkien quotation is really a very clever misdirection by the author to mask his work as the clever loremaster who tells his tale in its oft-repeated form and thus holds the reader's gaze to the embers of the text, which bursts, in a kind of transformational magic, into the full flame of the tale: "As for the inner meaning or message it has in the intention of the author it has none.... But I cordially dislike allegory in all of its manifestations and I have always done so since I grew old and wary enough to detect its presence. I much prefer history, true or feigned, with its varied applicability to the thoughts and experiences of readers" (Tolkien, *Letters*, Second Letter, 3–4, foreword). This often-cited paragraph in which Tolkien claims that his intention as a narrator is to have no intention is perhaps the most successful case of literary misdirection in the two thousand years since Marc Anthony claimed in Julius Caesar's funeral narration that he came not to praise Caesar but to bury him.

I would like to turn to another function for Gollum. I would contend Gollum functions as an abridger, integrating the big picture of what is at stake on a moral ethical and spiritual level. Gollum is really a kind of conduit drawing the reader or viewer into Tolkien's legendarium, which exists mostly by inference, *Lord* starts the events of Isildur's doom and continues to Gollum's seemingly unintentional destruction of the One Ring in the Cracks of Doom, where it was forged.

Of course, the destruction which completes the task of the ring bearer is accomplished only as Gollum falls into annihilation clutching his Precious. For many readers and viewers, this matter of Gollum's death and destruction and redemption of the quest where all others failed raises a number of theological issues, at least from the standpoint of two of the three great Abrahamic religions in the Hebrew Bible. Gollum might be thought of as the sheep provided to replace Abraham's son as a burnt offering on the mountain. The New Testament reading of Gollum's sacrifice of himself (intentional or not) redeems the weakness of Isildur's blood, which makes in Christian terms the perfect redemptive sacrifice that all of the, seemingly good, great, or powerful turn away from in fear.[11]

It is common knowledge among Tolkien scholars that extensive modifications were made by J.R.R Tolkien, perhaps a bit reluctantly, to the 1951 edition of *The Hobbit* (originally published in 1937) to make it less incongruent with the forthcoming publication of the three-volumes UK publishing launch of *Lord* (1952–1954). Noted Tolkien scholar Douglas Anderson[12] has pointed to the extensive revisions made in chapter four, "A Riddle in the Dark," in which Tolkien goes much farther to establish a stronger compassionate link between Bilbo and Gollum as sentient creatures and even moral agents, since they were after all from related Hobbit families — Bilbo, a Took and Brandybuck, and Gollum — five hundred years before, Sméagol of the Stoor Hobbit line. That was before Gollum had committed murder to claim the "One Ring to rule them all" and was driven into the depths of darkness to live an unnaturally long life of isolation and suffering with his Precious. That same ring was that which Isildur lost two and a half millenniums after the strength of men failed and he failed to cast it into the Cracks of Doom.

Image as Icon in The Lord of the Rings Books and Films: Frodo Lives but Gollum Redeems the Blood of Kings (or How to Read an Icon)

While working on a final project in the University of Wisconsin-Eau Claire Religious Studies Department on the role of art in healing the horrific, something occurred to me about a different kind of reading we do every time we see another human face. We read its emotional content almost as if it were written across a page. Dr. Harry Harlow did pioneer research in this area of primate psychology at UW-Madison in the 1960s dealing with the relationship of empathetic bonding between primates and their social development. Of course, now we have an ancestral primate (recently discovered in Indonesia) in the real world called a Hobbit. (Tolkien said that the little folk were still around, after all.)

Here is what we are seeing, then, in several scenes featuring Gollum in *LOTR* films: Tolkien's words and concern (shown by the majesty of Jackson's seemingly transparent direction, which really conceals hundreds of thousands of human hours of labor) written across Gollum's face. These expressions are Tolkien's words embodied, not as we would read a page in a book but as we have read each other's faces and looked into each other's hearts for thousands of generations, since we became empathetic and able to feel one another's pain. Deborah Roger wrote many years ago in her groundbreaking UW-Madison study of J.R.R. Tolkien, where among issues, she makes us aware of the compassionate link first between Gollum and Bilbo and then between Frodo and Gollum.

Film is more than just moving pictures or great romps and battle scenes, as essential as these are to the box office. It is also a way of allowing us to "read" and experience the subtlety and nuance of an 1193-page literary text in one volume — complete with illustrations, maps, and appendixes, genealogy table — in the faces and spoken words of the characters. Of course this is not just limited to Gollum. I think of the death of the West man who was as fair as any who fought for Middle-earth; his death is as moving as the victory of the great battle.

Similar Challenges for Jackson and Tolkien but Different Mediums Lead to Different Solutions

What the above meant was that both Jackson and Tolkien had to make what they considered the best choices in regard to production time and cost. But each of these preclude other choices. We can see examples of this as we again return to the lens of budget production time constraints and lost opportunity costs. An example may be drawn from Tolkien's *Lord*: "The Council of Elrond," which provides us with 3000 years of the history of Middle-earth and the War of the Ring, establishing that the Ring must be destroyed by being thrown into the Cracks of Doom and that only Frodo can do this. There are over 15,487 words in this text. Jackson's film presents this same information in a few minutes of screen time, establishing the weight that was on Gollum's skinny shoulders: the weight of the One Ring, which he carried longer than anyone else in the story. And Jackson's "Council" advances the narrative in compressed form here, thus allowing time for the Battle of Pellenor Fields to be expanded in the film, when, Frodo says, the council breaks in two.

Economic reality is expressed in a positive iteration through Moore's Law, which added dimension to the Peter Jackson films that nobody, not even the film production team, expected, since the principal shots, the non–special-effects shots, were completed in the first fourteen months of production, between September 1999 and November 2000. Rather than go into a technical explanation of the operation of Moore's Law it is sufficient to say that in the last forty-five years since it its inception the cost of raw computing power has been cut in half (in constant dollars) every eighteen to twenty-four months, thus making at least some aspects of special effects shot in the following two years progressively more affordable. This allowed for the creation of a Gollum that is "more human than human" through the relentless advance of computer generation of special effects.[12]

An example of Moore's Law follows: Jackson comments on how two hundred shots is a lot for a film, but they go from four hundred to eight hundred to fourteen hundred shots as they progress through the production and release of the three films. To say it another way, Sauron's army at the siege of Helm's Deep is represented as ten thousand, but at the gates of Mordor it is four hundred thousand. Moving that grand scale back to the Hobbit scale of the Ring bearers means that in the last shot of *ROTK* Jackson could do both live action and motion capture in the scene in which the One Ring and Gollum are destroyed, a scene is played with a reverential sadness. True, that is not the end of the film but as Jack Nicholson said, maybe it should have been. This is because everything after the death of Gollum is just pomp and circumstance, a great big tailgate party, and thus in a sense almost trivial.

Notes

1. As we summarize Gandalf's narrative in the chapter "The Shadow of the Past" it becomes a bit more complex and theologically interesting as Gandalf explains to Frodo that Isildur's will — and by extension his blood — was never an adequate match for the will of the Ring. Neither is the will of any of the great and powerful nor the knowledge of the "wise." Indeed the fact is that, until this point in the narrative, Hobbits are below Sauron's notice, since only Gandalf among the wise has any interest.
2. J.R.R Tolkien (1892–1973) was English and was born in South Africa where he lived till age three. Peter Jackson (1961–) was born in New Zealand, where he grew up.
3. Tom Shippey expressed the challenges facing Tolkien best on page 226 of *J.R.R. Tolkien: Author of the Century.* "*The Hobbit* and *Lord* are only offshoots, or side-branches, of the immense chronicle or mythology/legendarium that is *The Silmarillion* and that we have in the first form in which it was published as a connected narrative in 1977 and then in many of the twelve volumes of the "History of Middle Earth."
4. I am using the term naïve reader in the sense that Umberto Eco might in his *The Role of the Reader:* That is a nonpejorative way of thinking about what the reader takes to the text.
5. Even the beloved Gandalf at his darkest seems to cross the line in the chapter 4, "Shadow of The Past,"62–64, *Fellowship of the Ring*, when he speaks of terrorizing Gollum with the threat of fire to learn his secrets.
6. Etymology: Middle English *abregen*, from Anglo-French *abreger,* from Late Latin *abbreviare,* from Latin ad- + brevis short — more at brief. Date: 14th century (http://www.merriam-webster.com/dictionary/abridger).
7. Which, of course incidentally, must metaphysically ground Peter Jackson's cinematic universe, since this illusive physiological process turns a series of discrete images into the continuous flow of cinematic narrative.
8. My Topic was a comparative study of J.R.R Tolkien's and H.P Lovecraft's concept of evil through the lens of the theologian Martin Buber.
9. I was flying out to give a presentation at "Mythcon" (on Tolkien's concept of evil) at the 1996 annual conference of the American Mythopoeic Society, which is dedicated to the study of work of The Inklings — that is to say, the Oxford Fantasists, including Tolkien and his colleagues C.S Lewis and Charles Williams — and the study of the entire emergent field of high fantasy and its mythic multicultural substructure.
10. When Guy Gavriel Kay was the guest of honor in Vancouver B.C., he spoke fondly about his experience being that of just another nineteen-year-old going from waiting for *The Silmarillion* to six months later editing Tolkien's work.
11. Anderson describes the various versions of *The Hobbit*, including the revisions done after *Lord* appeared, in his introduction and documents them throughout the text, passim.

12. Moore's Law: The observation made in 1965 by Gordon Moore, cofounder of Intel, that the number of transistors per square inch on integrated circuits had doubled every year since the integrated circuit was invented. Moore predicted that this trend would continue for the foreseeable future. In subsequent years, the pace slowed down a bit, but data density has doubled approximately every 18 months, and this is the current definition of Moore's Law, which Moore himself has blessed. Most experts, including Moore himself, expect Moore's Law to hold for at least another two decades (*Wikipedia*, July 2, 2010).

WORKS CITED

Wikipedia. Revised July 2, 2010. http://en.wikipedia.org/wiki/Moore's_law (accessed July 5, 2010).
Bradbury, Ray. *Fahrenheit 451*. New York: Simon & Schuster, 1967.
Carpenter, Humphrey. *The Letters of J.R.R. Tolkien*. Boston: Houghton Mifflin, 1981.
Eco, Umberto. *The Role of the Reader: Explorations in the Seminotics of Texts*. Bloomington: Indiana University Press, 1984 (1979).
Hammond, Wayne, and Christina Scull. *J.R.R. Tolkien: Artist and Illustrator*. Boston: Houghton Mifflin, 2000.
Jackson, Peter, Fran Walsh and Philippa Boyens. *The Lord of the Rings: The Fellowship of the Ring*. DVD. Directed by Peter Jackson. Produced by Barry Osborne. New Line Cinema, 2004.
_____. *The Lord of the Rings: The Fellowship of the Ring*. DVD. Directed by Peter Jackson. Produced by Barry Osborne. New Line Cinema, 2001.
_____. *The Lord of the Rings: The Return of the King*. DVD. Directed by Peter Jackson. Produced by Barry Osborne. New Line Cinema, 2004.
_____. *The Lord of the Rings: The Return of the King*. Directed by Peter Jackson. Produced by Barry Osborne. New Line Cinema, 2003.
_____. *The Lord of the Rings: The Two Towers*. DVD. Directed by Peter Jackson. Produced by Barry Osborne. New Line Cinema, 2004.
_____. *The Lord of the Rings: The Two Towers*. DVD. Directed by Peter Jackson. Produced by Barry Osborne. New Line Cinema, 2002.
Shippey, T.A. *J.R.R. Tolkien: Author of the Century*. London: HarperCollins, 2000.
_____. *The Road to Middle Earth*. Boston: Houghton Mifflin, 1982.
Tolkien, J.R.R. *The Annotated Hobbit*. Revised ed. Edited by Douglas Anderson. Boston: Houghton Mifflin, 2002.
_____. *The Fellowship of the Rings*. Boston: Houghton Mifflin, 11994 (1955).
_____. *The History of Middle Earth*. Edited by Christopher Tolkien. Boston: Houghton Mifflin, 1985.
_____. *The Hobbit, or There and Back Again*. London: Unwin Paperbacks, 1981.
_____. *The Return of the King*. Boston: Houghton Mifflin, 1994 (1955).
_____. *The Silmarillion*. Edited by Christopher Tolkien. Boston: Houghton Mifflin, 2001.
_____. *The Two Towers*. Boston: Houghton Mifflin, 1994 (1955).

The Grey Pilgrim
Gandalf and the Challenges of Characterization in Middle-earth

BRIAN D. WALTER

> But G[andalf] is not, of course, a human being (Man or Hobbit). There are naturally no precise modern terms to say what he was. I [would] venture to say he was an incarnate "angel"—strictly an ἄγγελος: that is, with the other Istari, wizards, "those who know," an emissary from the Lords of the West, sent to Middle-earth, as the great crisis of Sauron loomed on the horizon.
> — J.R.R. Tolkien[1]

Early in Peter Jackson's third installment in the *Lord of the Rings* film trilogy, Gandalf the White appears briefly in a telling single shot in Meduseld, unobtrusively applauding the caperings of Merry and Pippin as they perform, in rousing fashion on top of a table, a Shire drinking song for the appreciative Rohirrim. As the white wizard returned from death, Gandalf is much more powerful than his earlier, grey incarnation; but he is also, necessarily, noticeably more distant and magisterial. This simple image of the joy he takes in the Hobbits' revelry subtly contributes to this sense of his transformation; for in the first movie, when Gandalf appears in Hobbiton for Bilbo's great birthday party, he eagerly joins in the festivities, eating and drinking and dancing along gaily with the much smaller Hobbits, every bit as much a partying guest as any of the Shire residents. The later scene, then, creates a continuity of sensibility in the wizard, still delighting in the innocently adaptable and congenitally joyful Hobbits he so loves; but it also, appropriately, registers a greater physical detachment from the proceedings. Gandalf is no longer one of the

Hobbits, no longer, in fact, really a resident of Middle-earth at all but sent back in this most powerful form only briefly, until the contest with Sauron has ended.

This brief image of a pleased but more remote Gandalf comprises one of many touches in the films that connect the screen character subtly to his counterpart in Tolkien's written narrative, honoring and invoking central aspects of Tolkien's conception of his "Odinic wanderer."[2] But Jackson's wizard is, without question, a much more screen-friendly version; in particular, the films find it necessary to reduce or limit Gandalf's almost universal and unquestioned authority in the books, frequently and tellingly doling out lines and decisions to other characters in the films that actually belong to the wizard in Tolkien's original treatments. The fine line that the films seek to walk, then, is to make Gandalf as memorable and compelling in his self-righteous wisdom as he is on the page without letting him dominate the strategy and action in a series of cinematic interpretations whose vast scale and ensemble structure requires the development, often in relatively brief screen time, of dozens of speaking parts to a semblance of plausibility and fullness.

Tolkien clearly found Gandalf's authority and power a challenge too, for in both *The Hobbit* and *The Lord of the Rings*, he repeatedly sends Gandalf away from the main quest, where his presence seems simply too dominant, even inhibitive, at least with respect to the kind of dramatic tension that the author instinctively sought. Tolkien wrote, for instance, that during the drafting of the chapters that would become *Fellowship* he did not know any better than Frodo or Strider what it could be that keeps Gandalf from meeting Frodo by his birthday to leave the Shire for Rivendell together.[3] The crucial element of this admission is Tolkien's instinctive sense as a storyteller that Gandalf must be absent to heighten the narrative tension and dramatic possibilities.[4] Drafts of these early chapters even show Tolkien considering the idea of using the Black Riders to detain the wizard in a tower.[5] It was only much later that the author began to develop the figure of Saruman, the first white wizard whom Gandalf later supplants, to explain his otherwise inexplicable absence.[6] As with many other details of characterization and plot, the figure of Gandalf emerged slowly, even haltingly for the author, generally guided by external narrative need rather than an internally consistent, organic conception of the character.

On the page as much as on the screen, then, Gandalf remains an oddly ambivalent presence, extraordinarily powerful and authoritative among his companions (especially the Hobbits), a "great mover of the deeds that are done in our time" (*Towers* 353), as Faramir describes him, but also a stranger, the only one of the Istari who never settles down at any fixed abode,[7] whose literal restlessness bespeaks his spiritual restlessness within a material body. He is, as Tolkien's description of him to a correspondent suggests,[8] an enigma, one whose core nature marks him out from all the other characters in the books (or the films). In his necessary elusiveness, he offers a revealing object lesson in several of the core strategies that governed the approach Jackson took to adapting Tolkien's story for the screen, for film, in the inevitably more sensual and visceral nature of the experience it offers its audience, both requires and galvanizes a tangibility in its characterization that no solely written character achieves. In other words, while Gandalf the White does seem more rarefied and remote in certain ways than Gandalf the Grey on screen, both of the wizard's incarnations seem less remote, less liminal, more bodily present, literally engaged, and physically formidable than in Tolkien's purely written treatment. Gandalf the angelic spirit shrinks in telling ways on screen, but with substantial benefits to the dramatic tension of numerous scenes and to the fuller, richer depiction of numerous other characters.

Privileged Information

In the films as in the books, Gandalf serves as a locus of privileged, even secret information, but even so, he is notably less knowing than in the books. For example, in the written original, Gandalf has clearly been in contact with Bilbo before he arrives and is privy to his full plans for the party and for passing on the Ring to Frodo,[9] whereas the movie takes great pains to show him making unpleasant discoveries about Bilbo's actions and motives all along the way, emphasizing a comparative state of innocence in the wizard to make the revelation of the Ring and its corrupting power all the more dramatic. In other words, as is usually the case, the films manage to convey elements of Gandalf's special status and quasi-omniscience while crucially limiting these aspects of the character to enhance the tension of the story for the more compressed form of film.

The scene that presents Bilbo's farewell speech at the long-expected party nicely conveys both Gandalf's special authority and the subtle limits that the films place on that authority, limits that the books' wizard does not suffer. The party scenes preceding the speech emphasize his combination of love for and sternness toward the Hobbits — the way he lifts his grey robes for freer movement to dance merrily with a couple of Hobbit partners and detonates various special fireworks to the delight of the Hobbit-children on the one hand, but punishes Merry and Pippin for stealing and igniting his special red dragon explosive on the other. Apart from his status as the master of the fireworks, then, Gandalf is little more than an unusually large guest, not really involved in the proceedings; he plays no significant part in advancing the key developments in this scene. But if he contributes little to the plot, he contributes much to the story,[10] his special know-it-all status put to important use in a series of special reaction shots during Bilbo's speech. Along with Frodo, Gandalf is the character present at the party who knows Bilbo best and has the most at stake (although Gandalf does not seem to realize it, at least initially, in the film) in Bilbo's actions. But the differences between the images of the wizard and the younger Hobbit are telling, subtly and appropriately emphasizing Gandalf's special marginal status. Gandalf first appears in a kind of three-shot with Merry and Pippin, their faces still begrimed with soot, washing dishes in atonement for their illicit detonation of Gandalf's special dragon firework.

As Bilbo makes his way up to the stump for his speech, the camera cuts to views of several of the party guests, including Frodo, but tellingly excludes Gandalf until Bilbo reaches the difficult compliment, "I don't know half of you half as well as I should like, and I like less than half of you half as well as you deserve." The first subsequent reaction shot shows a Hobbit couple in near profile turning to each other in unhappy, almost frightened confusion, setting up the first full reaction shot of the wizard, drawing on his pipe in single shallow focus close-up, but with the CinemaScope frame extending out far enough to the side of his head to show no one else. It is, in other words, a pure single, Gandalf alone in his confident understanding of Bilbo's challenging compliment (smiling, he glances sideways to verify the helplessness of the Hobbits to untangle Bilbo's joke). For the reaction shot of Frodo that soon follows, the camera sets itself at a similar distance and angle. This reaction is also shot in single; but even with the shallow focus and tight framing, the viewer recognizes the presence of other guests in the frame. The pairing of these similar perspectives — but with the wizard subtly alone in the frame — effectively underscores his marginal status based on the superiority of his perception. Frodo's reaction is of similarly intense interest, but Gandalf's conveys an authority unique to him. For this image of his special knowledge, he manages to be alone among the crowd of party attendees.

But when Bilbo places the Ring on his finger and disappears, the reaction shot of Gandalf tells a different tale. Most clearly, he is quite surprised too, even alarmed. He knows of the existence of the Ring, but apparently has not anticipated the Ring gambit (as he does in the books, "spoiling" Bilbo's surprise by adding a quasi-explanatory light flash).[11] He surprises Bilbo in the films as in the books by beating him back to Bag End for the tense conversation that ensues. But the reaction shot of his alarm has already delimited Gandalf's authority in crucial ways in the films, showing the limits of his knowledge. Of course, the benefits of this change are clear also in the way it heightens the fearful capacity of Bilbo's actions under the influence of the Ring, setting the stage for a confrontation that will seem even more disturbing on screen than in the books, Bilbo actually petting the Ring with his back to the wizard, lust gleaming in his eye.

Other reaction shots of Gandalf convey similar impressions of his unique authority. In scenes involving more than two characters in which Gandalf is present, the camera often cuts to him in single at crux moments, to register the extra significance of what has just transpired. For example, the scene of Wormtongue's expulsion from Edoras seeks out Gandalf's reaction only at the moment when Wormtongue turns to flee. The three principals in the drama of this scene are Théoden, Aragorn, and Wormtongue himself, flung down the stone steps in the opening shot. Having cast Saruman out of Théoden and effectively exposed Wormtongue, Gandalf does not contribute to the action of the scene. Subsequent images show Théoden stalking slowly down the stairs after his treacherous counselor, Aragorn intervening to stay the king's hand and offering his own to Wormtongue, which the shamed Wormtongue spits upon before fleeing down the hill, taking horse, and riding off through the gates in haste. Gandalf has appeared recognizably in the background of a wide shot of Théoden as the king descends the stairs menacingly early in the scene, but he has taken no part in the proceedings themselves. So it is striking that the camera nevertheless seeks out Gandalf at the moment when Wormtongue breaks away completely, to flee to Saruman. The shot, in other words, subtly underscores the special rivalry between Gandalf and Saruman, for only Gandalf apparently divines Wormtongue's destination. Aragorn continues to work to turn the king away from his killing rage, but Gandalf is anticipating consequences, and his sudden appearance in the midst of a scene that otherwise finds no use for him signals viewers to recognize meanings that might escape the other characters. Several other important characters stand by during Wormtongue's expulsion — notably Legolas, Gimli, and Éowyn — but it is only Gandalf whom the camera seeks out for the extra meaning his knowing glance will convey to the audience.

The authority Gandalf exerts in such reaction shots serves as something of a subtle antidote for the modification of many of Gandalf's key decisions and initiatives or their outright transfer to other characters. And the wizard's quasi-omniscience clearly results from direct authorial intention. As Gandalf says to an unhappy Bilbo early in Tolkien's narrative, the wizard indeed does always know best — when "[he] know[s] anything" (*Fellowship* 58). Such is not at all the case with Jackson's cinematic counterpart, who is humbled both literally and metaphorically in comparison to his original on the page.

Several notable differences between the book's and the first film's handling of the Moria detour offer a clear example of the films' careful and usually humbling modification of Gandalf for the sake of a more dramatically personal and intense treatment of the storyline. In the books, the three chapters covering the Fellowship's departure from Rivendell through Gandalf's fall from the bridge comprise a notable rarity: Gandalf is present throughout the main narrative and therefore dominates the action quite literally in a way that never happens for any other stretch of *Lord* (or *The Hobbit*, for that matter). The two chapters covering the actual journey through Moria particularly emphasize Gandalf's elevated status, the Company relying solely on his vast personal resources to survive a series of trials that would have proved literally insurmountable without their specially empowered guide. They also represent the peak of Gandalf's heroism by emphasizing his willingness to sacrifice himself to convey the Ring bearer safely through.

It is clear to Frodo from early on in the chapter called "The Ring Goes South" that Gandalf is contemplating some fearful secret move that Aragorn seeks desperately to forestall.[12] Nevertheless, Gandalf shows no concern over his ability to lead the Company through the mines, and in fact sees it as the safer route once the *crebain* and the company of wolves (the latter group of pursuers entirely absent from the films) have spotted their trail (*Fellowship* 386–7). He takes counsel with Aragorn and allows the Ranger to persuade him to attempt the pass of the Redhorn Gate on Caradhras first. But he uses even this delay as further evidence of his more or less infallible foresight, telling Sam, when the time comes to part with the Hobbit's beloved pony, Bill, that he had "feared all along" that the Company would need to resort to the path under the Misty Mountains through Moria (*Fellowship* 394). Moreover, Tolkien's narrative emphasizes the extraordinary authority that Gandalf wields in leading the Nine Walkers into, and then finding them (if not himself) safe passage through, the long and absolute dark of the abandoned Dwarf-colony. The Moria chapters serve up Gandalf in his most magnificent, even heroic capacity in the books, the environment in which his powers and authority are at their peak, the rest of the Fellowship depending utterly upon him, helpless otherwise to survive the trials they encounter there.

Several aspects of the Moria chapters underscore the heroic heights that Gandalf's authority and powers achieve in the build-up to his fall from the bridge of Khazad-dum. Apart from his deciding to lead the company into the mines in the first place, Tolkien's Gandalf also discovers on his own the password that opens the magic gate (albeit with an unknowing hint from Merry, who lights on the clue when he innocently asks about the inscription directing the visitor to "Speak, friend, and enter").[13] Similarly, the narrator informs the reader that the entire Company would soon have come to grief without its specially empowered guide, who holds his staff aloft to give off enough light to allow for reasonably safe passage.[14] And when the Company reaches the set of three passageways that temporarily halts their progress, Gandalf takes the watch by himself to let all the others sleep and comes to a decision after extensive counsel with himself, staking his reputation as a guide on what turns out to be the right one (*Fellowship* 409). When the Orc attack on the Company in the Chamber of Mazarbul is imminent, Gandalf likens the situation to the entrapment of the Dwarves as recorded in the record-book but immediately favors the Company's chances of survival simply because of his presence.[15] And even though the closing-spell he sets on the door does not hold proof against the Balrog's counter-spell, the encounter destroys the ability of the Orcs to pursue the Company directly, buying the Fellowship more time to traverse the bridge by forcing the pursuers to find an alternative route to the hall (*Fellowship* 427). In short, while Gandalf upbraids himself for delaying in the Chamber of Mazarbul, his special powers and heroism shine through all the more brightly as a result.

But even with his powers and heroism at their peak in the Moria chapters, Gandalf remains distinct from the others in the nature of his feats; in particular, Gandalf's heroism takes a more magical than literal form. This difference obtains first in the battle with the wolves in Hollin, during which the narrator picks out Aragorn, Boromir, Legolas, and Gimli for fighting valiantly with their various weapons, but in which Gandalf eschews the use of his sword, Glamdring, in favor of imposing the terrifying prospect of his holy anger and magical fire, looming up in the darkness, striding forth with a firebrand, dismissing his attacker as a "hound of Sauron," and apparently forcing the wolves back with the announcement that "Gandalf is here!"[16] Similarly, in the attack on the Chamber of Mazarbul, the narrator records a total of thirteen Orcs killed by the Fellowship, a tally that would apparently leave hardly any for the wizard when Legolas dispatches two, Gimli and Sam one each, and Aragorn and Boromir "many" (*Fellowship* 422). Most tellingly, Gandalf sends the Company flying from the chamber — especially a reluctant Aragorn, who wants to stay and help him — by declaring that swords "are no more use here!" (*Fellowship,* 423). This declaration underscores the special nature of Gandalf's presence and power, making it all the less material.

The first film's treatment of the same plot developments retains some of Gandalf's special authority but also dilutes it for the sake of building up other characters and rendering Gandalf's fall and loss more personally painful, the result of errors on the parts especially of Frodo and Pippin. The changes begin with the transferal of the idea of going through Moria from Gandalf to Gimli and Frodo and continue through the subtly despairing tone of the revelation of and confrontation with the Balrog.[17] While Gandalf almost always appears, in group shots, noticeably ahead of the rest of the Fellowship (especially in Moria), marking him out clearly as their leader, he is, on the whole, much more another member of the Fellowship in the film than in the books.

The arrival at the decision to attempt Moria differs substantially in the films, in the end serving to emphasize Gandalf's limitations by once again pointing out his inability to effectively counteract Saruman. Gimli first broaches the idea of Moria to Gandalf shortly before the attack of the *crebain*, and it is clear that the idea has not previously occurred to the film's Gandalf (in sharp contrast to Tolkien's original). The wizard sits apart from and above the other members of the Company in this scene, his hat off and his hair pulled back as he draws on his pipe. When Gimli suggests that Moria would make a useful shortcut, the camera cuts to a tight medium single of Gandalf gently but firmly rejecting the idea, noting that *he* would attempt Moria only if they had no other choice. Everything about the scene relaxes the tone considerably from the books, in which Tolkien consistently emphasizes the need for secrecy, the Company even hiding out during the day to the eyes of strangers.[18] Gandalf's relaxation and his decisive but calm rejection of Moria sap the character and situation of their original urgency, suggesting among other things the lower level of control and foresight that Gandalf exercises in the films.

Moreover, the final decision to attempt Moria actually and subtly imputes fear to the wizard that is clearly not present in the books. As soon as the *crebain* pass, Gandalf makes the Fellowship attempt Caradhras, but the decision seems immediately ill-fated, jeopardizing any impression of the wizard's full authority. Frodo falls in the snow and loses the Ring, nearly leading to a fight between Aragorn and Boromir when the latter returns the Ring to the Hobbit only reluctantly. The camera cuts immediately from the shot of Aragorn loosening his ominous grip on his sword to a long high-angle establishing shot of the company approaching a sharp corner high on a peak almost completely covered in snow — an impossible path that the wizard nevertheless continues to insist the Company take.

It is only when Legolas, comparatively unaffected by the blizzard, detects fell voices on the air that Gandalf apparently realizes Saruman's shaping hand in the impassable conditions. He stands forward to chant a counter-incantation, but Saruman clearly has the last word, the storm not only continuing but unleashing lightning to strike at the mountain above the Company's heads and loose an avalanche on them. Boromir urges the Gap of Rohan as an alternative, eliciting Aragorn's stern rejection; but when Gimli again suggests Moria, Gandalf is clearly at a loss, helpless to lead the company further up

Caradhras but apparently equally helpless to make a decision. He turns the decision over to the Ring bearer, who hesitates only a moment before choosing the mines, leaving a foreboding, even fearful Gandalf to appear in single in the final shot from the mountain, declaring, "So be it." The next shot shows Saruman paging through a book and taunting his inferior rival from afar, identifying Gandalf's fear of what he knows the Dwarves have awakened in Moria. The result of these arrangements is to make the detour to Moria embody Gandalf's failure and the unquestioned superiority of Saruman in the film—almost the exact opposite of the firmness, foresight, and fearlessness in Gandalf that the decision bespeaks in the books.

The developments before the walls of Moria continue subtly to reduce Gandalf's stature. The extended edition adds a scene in which Gandalf pulls Frodo aside for an ominous warning of the wizard's possible insufficiency to the task and of threats to the Ring within the Company. Gandalf looks furtively at the other members of the Fellowship who pass by during his conversation with Frodo and opens his eyes wide to emphasize the danger of powers greater than his. Following immediately on his failure at Caradhras, this scene only furthers the impression of the wizard's extra vulnerability and relative fecklessness in the films. It is perhaps no surprise, then, that Gimli announces their arrival at the walls of Moria, whereas Gandalf does so in the books, explaining also that the lack of sound from the choked stream is the reason it takes him longer to locate their destination (*Fellowship* 392–3). In the film, it is almost as if Gandalf is abdicating some leadership responsibility in accepting the Moria alternative, becoming Frodo's co-conspirator as much as the company's guide and captain.

The door-opening scene retains most of the key elements from the book's description—including even Gandalf's peevish rejoinder to Pippin that he will open the doors by banging the Hobbit's head against them if nothing else will serve—but a couple of key differences once again diminish the wizard's stature. The most obvious change is the granting of the solution to Frodo, who suddenly divines in a way the wizard has not that the inscription constitutes a riddle. But even before that point, Gandalf is more at a loss than Tolkien ever has him in the books, and he not only throws down his staff as he does in the book (*Fellowship* 401), but also declares the enterprise useless before sitting down in helpless befuddlement off to the side. When Frodo asks Gandalf to tell him the Elvish word for friend, Gandalf replies with wide eyes, apparently not yet perceiving the reason Frodo is asking. What this change does is to render Gandalf—the most infamously knowing character in Tolkien's Middle-earth, a self-congratulatory know-it-all—into a surprisingly helpless source of information, a vault to be opened and mined by others rather than a quasi-omniscient guide who always has the last word. This exchange, brief as it is, manifests an inversion of authority—with Frodo clearly ascendant over Gandalf—that simply would never happen in the books.

But what the film forfeits in Gandalf's authority with these changes in the Moria scenes it gains in the drama of the characters' relationships with each other. In particular, Gandalf's diminishment enhances the emotional weight of Frodo's personal journey, isolating him further from the rest of the Company in preparation for his decisive break at the end of the first film. Moreover, the shifts add to Frodo's guilt and sense of failure, for he has decided on the route in which Gandalf falls and is apparently lost forever. The aftermath of the bridge scene finds all the company grieving; but it singles out Frodo for the image of climactic loss, withholding the image of his grief until all the other characters have appeared, literally separating him from the group (Aragorn has to track him down) to emphasize the horrible betrayal that Frodo feels he has committed in choosing the Moria route. Much of Frodo's journey constitutes a gradual wearing away of his sense of his own security and belonging. In making Gandalf's loss so much the devastating result of Frodo's personal decision, the filmmakers take a sizeable step toward creating the state of utter deprivation that Frodo finds himself in at the end of the films. Frodo and Gandalf debut together and have several conversations involving no other character, so the emotional pay-off increases with the changes that the filmmakers enforce.

The White Wizard

> ***Which part did you prefer playing: Gandalf the Grey or Gandalf the White?*** *To act, I preferred Gandalf the Grey. He's more complicated than Gandalf the White. He had enormous strength, resilience, intelligence and determination, passion and generosity. He was also very human, very frail, in the sense that he liked to drink, he liked to smoke, he liked to laugh, he liked to play. He also was human in the sense that he was worried he wasn't doing the job properly—that he'd somehow let Middle-earth down by not anticipating Sauron's revival. He had to really organize himself. That was a fascinating character to play.*
>
> ***And Gandalf the White is more straightforward?*** *When he comes back, there's no question he knows what he has to do. It's just getting on and doing it. I wouldn't like to suggest that Gandalf the White isn't an interesting person. He is. But for the actor, he's not quite as complicated or difficult a part.*
>
> —Ian McKellen, from http://www.lordoftherings.net/ film/exclusives/editorial/gandalf.html

Toward the end of the third book, Merry corrects Pippin for suggesting that the resurrected version of Gandalf has not changed at all, pointing out not only that Gandalf is now the most powerful of the wizards — having broken Saruman's staff and dismissed the former head of the White Council from his company — but also that he seems more forthcoming, not to mention both sadder and merrier (*Towers* 249). The bulk of the evidence does seem to bear Merry out, the new white wizard still something of a self-congratulatory and rather self-righteous know-it-all, still responsive and concerned, but also rippling with energy and purpose and clarity, divining still more thorough knowledge of everyone and everything around him. At one point shortly after the wizard reappears to Aragorn, Legolas, and Gimli in Fangorn Forest, Aragorn jokes that Gandalf has not changed, at least in his habit of speaking to himself in ways that no one else present can understand, prompting the wizard to reply that it is a habit of the old to limit their conversation to the wisest person present — in this case, himself (*Towers* 127). As the white wizard, he seems both readier to answer questions (always in ways that confirm the vastness and superiority of his knowledge) and more remote, an otherworldly emissary sent back "for a brief time," until his "task [is] done" (*Towers* 135).

More subtly, though, Tolkien's Gandalf the White is much more solely a creature of the spirit than of the body, an angel briefly clad in mortal form to rally and inspire the mortal creatures of Middle-earth to resist the will of Sauron, a fellow (though fallen) spiritual creature.[19] When he reveals himself to the three hunters in Fangorn, Gandalf informs them that none of their weapons could harm him in this new form (*Towers* 125); he seems to exist more in a spiritual than a fleshly dimension. He has transcended a state in which physical battle, received or waged, matters. So, although he still carries Glamdring,[20] never does the narrative record his using the sword after the battle with the Balrog. When, riding Shadowfax, Gandalf rescues Faramir from the winged Nazgûl before the gates of Minas Tirith, the wizard reveals himself unmistakably as the "good" counterpart to their spiritual evil, forcing the wraiths back with a shaft of light that seems to rise from his upraised arm (*Return* 100). This scene comprises the only one after his return when Tolkien's Gandalf closes in quasi-physical contest with Sauron's forces; even during the final battle before the Black Gates, the narrator finds Gandalf merely standing atop the hill where the forces of the West are under attack (*Return* 278–9). Gandalf the White's physical body, in fact, is apparently almost insubstantial; the eagle Gwaihir declares him light as a feather when he bears the resurrected wizard from Zirak-zigil to Lothlórien (*Towers* 135). And when he begs another aerial ride from the Dagorlad to Mount Doom to rescue Frodo after the destruction of the Ring, Gandalf ensures his benefactor that he will find the wizard little more of a burden to bear than in the flight from Zirak-zigil (*Return* 280). He is the enemy of Sauron, so that the salleys he delivers and the defenses he mounts take place much more on a spiritual than an earthly plane.

Gandalf the White's perspective and interests and perceptions have expanded as well. As he bears Pippin on Shadowfax through Minas Tirith to rescue Faramir from the pyre Denethor would burn them both upon, Gandalf speaks in terms that would simply not be possible for almost anyone else — and perhaps not even himself in his earlier, more fleshly incarnation — noting how the shadow of Sauron's will lies upon the city still and how the deed that Beregond has committed in slaying the guards of Rath Dinen to save Faramir is really the work of Sauron himself, the delight of a creature of pervasive spiritual malice (*Return* 154–5). In the books, Gandalf the White is not only a guide and counselor, but also a philosopher, one who consistently connects the literal developments around him to underlying spiritual insights and truths. When Denethor angrily denounces the decision to send the Ring to the fire in the humble hands of a Hobbit, Gandalf's lengthy reply concludes on a note that is not only defiant, but expansive, informing the Steward of Gondor that he is a steward too, urging the other congenital know-it-all of Middle-earth to perceive the limits of his knowledge and Gandalf's superior status (*Return* 33–4). It is the rebuke of a guru, a spiritual mentor, one whose mind seeks out the broadest perspective as a matter of course.

Not surprisingly, the films' depiction of Gandalf the White tends to reduce the spiritual nature of his actions and being in favor of physical prowess. Gandalf the White wields unmistakably great power in the films, but in keeping with the films' general approach, even the magical flourishes tend to take forcefully tangible form. From the exorcism of Théoden to the rescue of Faramir from the pyre, Gandalf the White is more an action hero than an otherworldly counselor or philosopher. This transformation represents not only a strategy but also, to some degree, an inevitable effect of the process of filming, which necessarily fixes a character in physical form to be experienced visually and sensually in a way that no literary character can be experienced from the printed page alone.

The exorcism of Théoden offers an excellent example of the latter film's reification of Gandalf's actions and powers. Initially, Aragorn, Legolas, and Gimli walk beside the wizard as he approaches the haggard, invalid king slumped on his wooden throne at the far end of the hall. But soon, Gandalf's three companions resort to fisticuffs to ward off the minions of Wormtongue, who would stop Gandalf from reaching the king. All the while his companions fight off the attackers, Gandalf walks steadily and slowly toward the king, oblivious to the strife all about him. The implication is clear: the battle that

Gandalf is about to engage will take a different, less literal form, a spiritual contest to wrestle his rival wizard from the mind and soul of the wasted king. But the exorcism itself plays out as a remarkably physical process — a continuation, really, of Gandalf's battle with Saruman in Orthanc in the first film, in which each pummels the other with blows delivered from afar with swinging and viciously thrust staffs. Gandalf similarly throws Théoden back against his chair with several thrusts of his staff and holds it forward against invisible resistance to keep the king's body pinned. When Théoden, still in Saruman's possession, forces himself up to stride menacingly toward Gandalf, the wizard delivers a decisive thrust that does not touch the king but sends him hurling back into his chair and prompts the camera to cut to a full frontal shot of the body of Saruman hurling backward against the black-stone paving of the same chamber in Orthanc in which he and Gandalf have dueled in the first movie. The next shot of Gandalf shows him breathing heavily and gathering himself slowly from the palpably physical ordeal of drawing his rival forth from Théoden "like poison from the wound."

Gandalf's confrontation with the Lord of the Nazgûl takes similarly much more tangible form in the movies than in the book. Tolkien's written treatment of this scene represents perhaps the masterpiece of his complicated chronological interweavings and subtle perspective shifts for dramatic effect as he shifts first from Pippin's flight down through the levels of the city to find Gandalf to a focus on the seemingly inexorable progress of the malefic battering-ram Grond that the Witch-king uses to destroy the gates and enter the city no foe had ever managed to breach and then finally to a remarkable still-point description of Gandalf astride Shadowfax athwart the Witch-king's path, defying him in terms similar to those he uses with the Balrog, but here ending in no physical clash because of the timely appearance of the long-awaited Rohirrim, signaled by the blowing of their horns. Appearing at the end of the long chapter called "The Siege of Gondor," the confrontation makes for an extraordinary nadir, the inevitable breach coming after a dramatically prolonged devastation of the city's defenses. Tolkien gradually builds a mood of hopelessness and despair to accompany the Lord of the Nazgûl as he goes in through the ruined gates, trampling bodies slowly underfoot, an almost Miltonic or Spenserian figure of all-consuming death and destruction. In other words, the effect depends not at all on physical confrontation or heroism, but on a masterfully achieved accumulation of utter despair against which Gandalf offers the only resistance. Gandalf shines white amid the gloom, but the gloom is pervasive and overwhelming; his speech alone constitutes the only possible antidote.[21]

The third film's treatment of this scene offers a remarkable humbling of

Tolkien's wizard angel, but once again with important benefits for other characters and developments later on. Pippin is already riding with Gandalf back up into the city to rescue Faramir when the Witch-king, in the film already astride his fell winged beast, alights upon a deserted courtyard some way up the mountain. Gandalf and his foe exchange defiance in terms lifted partly from their dialogue in the books, but Gandalf then finds his staff bursting asunder in his hands (just as he has made Saruman's staff burst asunder at the beginning of the third film) and is thrown with Pippin from the back of Shadowfax to the stone paving. The singles of Gandalf that follow emphasize his defeat, showing him at a loss and frightened, looking up helpless at his mastering foe, who has made good on his promise, shown earlier in the film just before the assault on Minas Tirith begins in earnest when he informs his lieutenant that he will "break" the white wizard. When the horns of the Rohirrim sound in the film, the Rohirrim are not so much rescuing the whole city of Minas Tirith, as is the case in the books, as they are saving Gandalf himself (even in his white incarnation) from imminent death at the hands of the Witch-king. The film's scene not only elides the carefully layered build-up from the books, but also handles the whole confrontation rather summarily and simply — merely a demonstration of the Witch-king's superiority even to Gandalf.

The chief benefit of these changes becomes apparent in the subsequent scene of the Witch-king's own defeat and death at the hands of Éowyn and Merry. Especially for anyone who might not have been familiar with the original account, the bravery and valor of the Hobbit and the young shieldmaiden can only take on grander dimensions in light of the Witch-king's apparently easy vanquishing of Gandalf. This is the trade-off for the humbled Gandalf: a more magnificently heroic Éowyn and Merry.

The film's Gandalf makes a similar sacrifice of power and authority for the sake of another character's ascendancy in the parley before the Black Gate with the Mouth of Sauron. In the book, Gandalf is clearly the spokesperson for the forces of the West, taunted by Sauron's emissary but asserting his superiority in his ability to put the lieutenant at a momentary loss when he demands the return of Frodo, whom Sauron would trick them into thinking he holds captive. Although Pippin fails to perceive the truth implicit in the hesitancy and groping of the Mouth of Sauron in response to Gandalf's clever demand, it is nevertheless clear that Gandalf submits the demand precisely to determine whether, in fact, Sauron really does hold Frodo captive, in which case the ensuing battle would be in vain. By putting Mordor's emissary at a loss, Gandalf wins some doubt for the contest to ensue, opening up the possibility that the sacrifice he has persuaded Aragorn and the others to make in hopes of distracting Sauron from the mortal threat creeping through his very realm will not necessarily have been in vain. The parley before the gates in the books represents Gandalf the White at the peak of his wits and powers securing a ray of hope from an otherwise irredeemably grim revelation.[22]

But the third film puts Gandalf at a loss in this scene, another moment (as with the Witch-king in Minas Tirith) when the new white wizard's power does not hold up before the overwhelming evil of Sauron and Mordor. When the Mouth of Sauron produces Frodo's mithril-shirt, Gandalf sinks back into unmistakable horror and sadness, unable to respond at all, much less in a fashion that would put his taunting counterpart at a loss. Moreover, the Mouth of Sauron dismissively tosses the shirt at the wizard in the film — a stark departure from the book, in which Gandalf throws his grey cloak aside and seizes the shirt and Sam's sword from the helpless messenger immobilized by the wizard's mastery (*Return* 205). If his fall before the Witch-king's power is humbling, this scene reduces the scope of Gandalf's power much further, leaving him helpless and wordless before the taunting of Sauron's representative.

What compensates Gandalf's loss is Aragorn's simultaneous gain. When Gandalf essentially shrinks back, helpless before Sauron's messenger, Aragorn rides forward with a stern look and, with a back-hand stroke, decapitates the emissary. From one standpoint, it is a dubious gain, for Aragorn seems to have allowed his anger and bitterness to dictate his actions in a way that would be almost unimaginable for the stern but wise and merciful captain and king-in-waiting that he embodies in Tolkien's original treatment. But this action is clearly devised to show Aragorn's resolve in the face of a hopeless situation, a prelude to his stirring speech to the forces of the West as the vastly greater forces under Sauron's command issue from the Black Gate and surround their beleaguered foes. If even Gandalf proves helpless and teary-eyed before the potent lies of Sauron's messenger, how much must Aragorn have grown to act so summarily and decisively. The implications for Aragorn's growth into a commanding figure in his own right are clear.

Make It Real?

> We wanted to create a feeling that we'd gone to Middle-earth and were able to shoot on authentic locations.... The mantra of our design work became "Make it real."
>
> — Peter Jackson in an interview[23]

An examination of the films' transformation of Gandalf for their own purposes strongly suggests that Peter Jackson's drive for verisimilitude extended well beyond the design work to characterization as well. Even after his return in the more powerful form of the white wizard, Gandalf remains more human — more humble and more vulnerable — than in the books. Gandalf does place the crown upon the newly returned king's head in the final film, even quoting a bit of the speech Tolkien gives him in the books, but the movie — understandably, given its extraordinary length for a feature film aimed at a wide popular audience — omits the crucial recognition that Aragorn honors Gandalf within the books, asking him to place the crown on his head because the triumph over Sauron really represents Gandalf's personal triumph (*Return* 303–4). Gandalf in the books is, as he says at one point, the "Enemy of Sauron" (*Return* 308) — the uncorrupted power sent by the Valar to contest the Dark Lord's will and salvage as much of the vision of Ilúvatar as is possible from Sauron's ruinous campaign for dominion. But in the films, Gandalf is much more a captain, perhaps even a champion, uniquely powerful among the forces that resist Sauron, but still vulnerable, still vanquishable. When Frodo awakes for the final time in Minas Tirith, Gandalf's eyes brim with unmistakably humble gratitude — suggesting that he has not necessarily expected to secure victory, to see Frodo achieve his impossible quest, and therefore can accept the outcome only as a kind of hoped-for but unlikely instance of grace. Gandalf in the third film gets to fell a troll in battle inside the breached walls of Minas Tirith, but in the books, he gets to best Sauron himself with his strategies and inspiring presence.

Many other characters benefit from Gandalf's subtle diminution, ranging from Frodo and Aragorn to Wormtongue, to whom the screenwriters transfer one of Gandalf's most inspired insights: his evocation of the horror of Éowyn's lot as Théoden fell further and further under his treacherous counselor's power.[24] But the films as a whole benefit also by fostering a greater sense of equality and dramatic possibility, not only endowing a Frodo or an Aragorn with greater initiative, burdens, and exploits, but also emphasizing the collaborative nature of a victory that the films labor mightily to make apparently impossible. Philosophically, in fact, one might say that Gandalf's diminishment paves the way for a liberalization of the story, a philosophical opening up to more egalitarian possibilities, Gandalf serving as one of the ensemble instead of the needful and commensurate counterpart to Sauron's evil. Gandalf corrects Pippin at one point for imagining that he will control the fate of the bested Saruman, declaring that he does not "wish for mastery" (*Towers* 243), a line that does not survive into the films, but which could plausibly express the films' approach to his characterization: Gandalf is powerful, uniquely authoritative, and indispensable to the final victory, but he finally exerts little or no real mastery.

In the mastery he exerts in the books, Gandalf finally embodies the much greater conservatism that prevails in Tolkien's sensibility than in Jackson's. The philosophical conservatism of Tolkien's story reveals itself in various ways, but perhaps nowhere more subtly or pervasively than in the uncorrected authoritarianism of Gandalf's tone, posture, and comportment. He is always right, always more knowing, always more commanding than anyone else. And everything in the respect, even the deference, that his companions and even his fellow Ring bearers, Elrond and Galadriel, show to Gandalf confirms the rightness of his exalted station. In the books, in fact, Aragorn often serves as something of Gandalf's herald, informing the Hobbits and others of the reach of Gandalf's powers and the magnitude of his achievements.[25] One of the most philosophically conservative statements in *Lord*—"the old that is strong does not wither"—therefore applies at least as much to Gandalf as to its intended honoree, Aragorn. All but the last two lines of this poem, in fact, which specifically invoke the reforging of Narsil and the coronation, apply at least as well to Gandalf as they do to Aragorn. Gandalf's characterization, in Tolkien's hands, bespeaks a fundamental faith in the unassailable rightness of the oldest forms, creation in its original state, an embodiment, therefore, of what is—in its very timelessness—untouchable, invulnerable to corruption or, ultimately, question.

Gandalf's quasi-infallibility is part of what makes him—at least within certain traditions of novelistic characterization—a remarkably "unrealistic" character. It is telling that he alone of the five Istari sent by the Valar into Middle-earth to contest the will of Sauron never falls away from his purpose. One of the clear implications of the otherwise unanimous fall of these messengers is that embodiment in flesh—a choice made to keep the Istari from seeking dominion over the other creatures of Middle-earth—is the harbinger to a fall, a sign of the futility of mortal existence. Gandalf's triumph is, therefore, one of the factors that seriously delimit the plausibility of labeling Tolkien's narrative a novel,[26] at least in the modern European tradition, beginning with Cervantes, as Milan Kundera has described it:

> The novel's spirit is the spirit of complexity. Every novel says to the reader: "Things are not as simple as you think." That is the novel's eternal truth, but it grows steadily harder to hear amid the din of easy, quick answers that come faster than the question and block it off. In the spirit of our time, it's either Anna or Karenina who is right and the ancient wisdom of Cervantes, telling us about the difficulty of knowing and the elusiveness of truth seems cumbersome and useless [Kundera 18].

With Gandalf, Tolkien managed, in fact, to create an either/or choice: either Gandalf is right or Sauron is right, and the work, of course, consistently and entirely validates the former. Gandalf is not infallible strategically (although when he scolds himself for not pursuing the true origins of Bilbo's Ring aggressively enough, Elrond immediately exonerates him, so that even

Gandalf's mistakes hardly seem such),[27] but he *is* infallible morally, making him not only a character who cannot abide long in Middle-earth, but also one who does not fit the tradition of ambiguity in the European novel. He truly *is* the answer to the problem of Sauron, his choices and advice (especially after his return as the white wizard) proved right over and over again as the Ring finally finds its way into the fire, ending the evil of Sauron.

The uncertainty and complexity that the tradition of the European novel enshrines, according to Kundera, adapts much more closely to the movies' delimitation of Gandalf's authority and powers. In Kundera's characterization, in fact, this spirit of complexity in the novel lends itself to the rise not just of the fabled middle class (a connection between the genre and middle class values and experience has long been a critical commonplace), but also with the rise of democracy as a form of government that validates collective will and initiative over inherited and centralized power. This more egalitarian philosophy, on the whole, in fact prevails in the films' insistence on spreading the decisions and the heroism around, removing from Gandalf the responsibility of sole planner, the one who would, in Aragorn's phrasing, "rule us all" (*Return* 169). It is perhaps telling that Gandalf does not shrink from this extraordinary proposal, one that theoretically would install him in a position similar to the one that Sauron seeks, if for very different purposes. In the films, such a statement, to say nothing of Gandalf's apparently unremarkable acceptance of it, is literally unimaginable.

The final image of Gandalf subtly crystallizes his more humble, more human, more available status in the films. Just as he debuts in the first film, Gandalf bows out of the final film in close companionship with Frodo. After Frodo makes his good-byes with Merry, Pippin, and the devastated Sam, he heads toward the waiting ship into which Bilbo, Elrond, Celeborn, and Galadriel have already disappeared for the journey into the West. But Gandalf waits for Frodo at the edge of the gangplank and takes his hand for the actual boarding. Though he has offered verbatim the farewell that Tolkien gives him in the books, this Gandalf remains more a companion — perhaps a fatherly or grandfatherly one — but nevertheless one closer to the Hobbits and the other creatures of Middle-earth than he is in the books. It is a poignant and appropriate touch, certainly, one entirely in keeping with Gandalf's comparatively humbling pilgrimage on screen.

Appendix: (Walter) Gandalf & Moria

The two chapters in Book II of *Fellowship* called "A Journey in the Dark" and "The Bridge of Khazad-Dum" show Gandalf in his most magnificent, even heroic capacity, the setting of Moria calling upon him to exercise his powers and authority at their peak to convey the Fellowship through. The table below charts the primary changes to Gandalf's motives and actions that the films make to achieve a variety of different narrative and characterization effects especially the minimization of his special, otherworldly authority.

Gandalf and Moria

Tolkien	*Jackson*
Aragorn persuades Gandalf to try Caradhras first before even mentioning the possibility of Moria to the Company.	Gandalf forces the Company to attempt Caradhras, but fails to negotiate or counteract Saruman's storm.
After the failed attempt on Caradhras, Gandalf urges the alternative route through Moria, which Frodo reluctantly supports (with the wolves' appearance an added incentive).	Gimli suggests Moria, Gandalf resists, and Frodo decides (Gandalf fearfully declaring, "So be it").
Gandalf finds the almost lost path, notes the oddity of the stream's silence.	Gimli announces their arrival at the walls of Moria (apparently easy to find).
Gandalf directs Sam to free Bill, offering words of wisdom and guidance.	Aragorn declares Moria no place for a pony and releases Bill.
Gandalf solves the door riddle (with an innocent hint from Merry).	Gandalf is stumped by the doors; Frodo solves the riddle.
	Boromir declares Moria a trap, orders a rerouting through the Gap of Rohan.
Gandalf divines but keeps to himself the reasons for the Watchers seizing on Frodo.	
The narrator describes Gandalf as indispensable, and Aragorn urges complete confidence in him.	
Gandalf keeps Merry and Pippin from rushing into the guard-chamber and falling down the well.	
After Pippin drops a stone in the well, Gandalf makes him take first watch, but soon excuses him kindly, smokes, and solves the crossroads riddle, watching all alone for six hours and explaining his rationale at length.	Stumped at the crossroads, Gandalf discusses Gollum with Frodo and lights on the correct passage merely by "following his nose."

Tolkien	Jackson
Gandalf twice notes the correctness of his passage choice and leads the way into the Chamber of Mazarbul.	Gandalf follows as Gimli leads the way into the Chamber of Mazarbul.
Gandalf extrapolates from the book the Company's position with respect to the gate, notes that his presence makes escape possible, and challenges the attacking Orcs at the door.	Gandalf hangs back by the Hobbits as other non-halflings form the first line of defense; Boromir peers out the door.
	Gandalf dispatches a final pair of Orcs in an impressive sword-and-staff flurry after the troll skewers Frodo (a sequence paired with Sam's similarly maddened flurry to get to Frodo).
Gandalf divines the secret of Frodo's mithril shirt on the fly, sends the Company down the stairs while waiting behind himself to put a shutting spell on the door.	Gandalf recognizes the appearance of the Balrog and issues the comic command "Run!"
Gandalf gives precise orders for the safest crossing of the narrow bridge.	
Gandalf breaks the bridge but is caught by the Balrog's whip and pulled over, crying, "Fly, you fools!" while falling.	Gandalf breaks the bridge but is caught by the whip after lowering his guard and turning to follow the Company; he repeats the "Fly, you fools!" command from the book but while desperately clinging to the bridge, his eyes wide in fear, his voice weak and unconvincing because of his own imminent fall.

NOTES

1. Carpenter, *Letters*, 202.
2. Ibid., 119.
3. See Carpenter, *Letters*, 216–7.
4. In a 1964 letter to Bretherton, Tolkien explained the whole creation of the Necromancer as a plot convenience to remove Gandalf from the Dwarves' and Bilbo's quest: "To be the burden of a large story [the ring] had to be of supreme importance. I then linked it with the (originally) quite casual reference to the Necromancer ... whose function was hardly more than to provide a reason for Gandalf going away and leaving Bilbo and the Dwarves to fend for themselves, which was necessary for the tale" (*Letters*, 346).
5. See *The Treason of Isengard*, 7–9.
6. See *The Treason of Isengard*, 70–3, for Saruman's initial appearance within the complex redraftings of what would become the Fellowship.
7. Tolkien, *Return*, 455.
8. Please see the epigraph at the beginning of this essay for this quotation.

9. See *Fellowship*, 49.

10. In making this distinction between a film's story and its plot, I am following Bordwell and Thompson's distinction in *Film Art: An Introduction*. A film's plot comprises simply the events that transpire on screen, whereas its story can comprehend a much greater span of time and events referred to in the course of the film's unfolding. The classic example that Bordwell and Thompson cite is that of *Citizen Kane*, whose plot consists of the reporter Thompson's quest for the meaning of "rosebud," the cryptic final one-word utterance of the eponymous character, but whose story comprehends the entire decades-long life of Charles Foster Kane. (See *Film Art* 82–102.) To apply this distinction to the long-expected party, then, the plot consists only of the partying, the speech, and Bilbo's inexplicable disappearance, whereas the story incorporates the complex evolution and climax of Bilbo's relationship with Frodo, Gandalf, all his fellow Hobbits, and the Shire itself, as he makes a decisive break with all of them that only Gandalf recognizes. Gandalf's presence and urgent response, then, inform the greater impact of the plot events for the overarching story line than they could have in his absence.

11. See *Fellowship*, 57–8.

12. See *Fellowship*, 374–5. The narrator emphasizes Frodo's relief that Aragorn prevails upon Gandalf not to take the mysterious route that Aragorn so earnestly seeks to avoid.

13. See *Fellowship*, 397–402.

14. See *Fellowship*, 405–6. Among other things, the narrator emphasizes that the vast intricacy of the mines is far beyond even Gimli's comprehension or appreciation, and that Gandalf always decides the Company's course.

15. Gandalf bluntly favors the Company's chances for survival based on his mere presence: "I was not here then" (*Fellowship*, 420).

16. See *Fellowship*, 389–91.

17. For a detailed breakdown of changes the film makes to key aspects of the Moria chapters, please see the appendix, "Gandalf & Moria."

18. See *Fellowship*, 368–9.

19. Tolkien described the resurrected Gandalf in such terms in a note to himself while redrafting portions of the story: "[Gandalf] has thus acquired something of the awe and terrible power of the Ringwraiths, only on the good side. Evil things fly from him if he is revealed — when he shines. But he does not as a rule reveal himself" (*The Treason of Isengard* 422).

20. The index records two references to the sword after Gandalf's return, first among the weapons laid at the doors of Edoras and second near the very end when Gandalf returns to Bree with the four Fellowship Hobbits; see *TT* 147 and *ROTK* 336.

21. See *Return*, 123–6.

22. See *Return*, 201–6.

23. Magid, "Imagining Middle-earth," 60–9.

24. Gandalf delivers his speech in the Houses of the Healing to make Éomer see his sister's life and plight in a new light; see *Return*, 174–5. Wormtongue inflicts an abbreviated version of the speech on Éowyn in the second movie, just before Gandalf and his three companions arrive at Edoras.

25. See, for example, *Towers*, 133, when Aragorn declares Gandalf "our captain and our banner."

26. Shippey plausibly argues that *Lord* manifests a variety of genres, the novel just one of five that he detects, at least in part, in the work. See *Tolkien: Author of the Century*, 221–5.

27. Please see *Lord*, 244, where Elrond releases the wizard from blame: "'We were all at fault,' said Elrond, 'and but for your vigilance the Darkness, maybe, would already be upon us.'"

WORKS CITED

Bordwell, David, and Kristin Thompson. *Film Art: An Introduction.* 7th ed. Boston: McGraw Hill, 2004.
Carpenter, Humphrey, ed. *The Letters of J.R.R. Tolkien.* Boston: Houghton Mifflin, 1981.
Kundera, Milan. *The Art of the Novel.* New York: Harper & Row, 1986.
Magid, Ron. "Imagining Middle-earth," *American Cinematographer* 82, no. 12 (December 2001).
Shippey, Tom. *J.R.R. Tolkien: Author of the Century.* Boston: Houghton Mifflin, 2000.
Tolkien, J.R.R. *The Fellowship of the Ring.* New York: Ballantine, 1984.
_____. *The Lord of the Rings.* Great Britain: HarperCollins, 1991.
_____. *The Return of the King.* New York: Ballantine, 1984.
_____. *The Return of the Shadow.* Boston: Houghton Mifflin, 1988.
_____. *The Treason of Isengard.* Boston: Houghton Mifflin, 1989.
_____. *The Two Towers.* New York: Ballantine Books, 1984.

Jackson's Aragorn and the American Superhero Monomyth[1]

JANET BRENNAN CROFT

Even the most ardent fan of Peter Jackson's *The Lord of the Rings* movies must admit, if they have any familiarity at all with J.R.R. Tolkien's original books, that Jackson made many changes to the characters Tolkien created. Arwen, Faramir, Denethor, Théoden, Treebeard, Gimli, even Frodo, Sam, and Gollum, are all demonstrably different from the characters in the books in their personalities as well as their actions. Whether one considers these changes to be unimportant, an improvement, or a desecration, the question of why Jackson made these changes is an interesting one. The amount of money riding on a major Hollywood production like this means that the answer does not depend solely on the director's artistic vision, but is also overwhelmingly influenced by the anticipated profitability of the final product to the studio and other stakeholders. Taking this into account, the question might be better phrased thus: why did Jackson and his backers feel that these changes would make Tolkien's characters more accessible and marketable to a worldwide audience? Why did Jackson think that the characters as written, in spite of their demonstrated popularity in print, would probably not translate profitably to the screen without fundamental changes?

Part of the answer may lie in the uniquely American revisioning of Joseph Campbell's heroic "monomyth" described in John Shelton Lawrence and Robert Jewett's *The Myth of the American Superhero* and its worldwide influence through exported American cultural products. Campbell developed his theory of the monomyth in *The Hero with a Thousand Faces* by examining myths, legends, and stories from all over the world and teasing out their common elements. As Campbell summarizes it, in the broadest outline of the monomyth, there is a basic pattern of separation, initiation, and return: "A hero ventures forth from the world of common day into a region of supernatural wonder: fabulous forces are there encountered and a decisive victory is won: the hero comes back from this mysterious adventure with the power to bestow boons on his fellow man." (Campbell 30). Lawrence and Jewett similarly examined many iconic American works of literature and film (for example, westerns like Owen Wister's *The Virginian* and action films like *Jaws*) and discovered a typical pattern which makes some fundamental changes to the Campbellian monomyth. The outline they developed describes the American variation this way: "A community in a harmonious paradise is threatened by evil; normal institutions fail to contend with this threat; a selfless superhero emerges to renounce temptations and carry out the redemptive task; aided by fate, his decisive victory restores the community to its paradisiacal condition; the superhero then recedes into obscurity." (Lawrence and Jewett 6).

Note that in the latter version the hero is already separate from his community when the journey begins, either because he originates from outside or is an idealistic loner within but not of the community: "[H]is motivation is a selfless zeal for justice.... [H]e seeks nothing for himself and withstands all temptations. He renounces sexual fulfillment for the duration of the mission, and the purity of his motivations ensures his moral infallibility in judging persons and situations" (Lawrence and Jewett 47). His victory, however, brings no guarantee of return to or acceptance by the community.[2]

Lawrence and Jewett find that this pattern is especially well-represented in film, and "the American monomyth has become a dominant paradigm for world movie-goers" (Lawrence and Jewett 204). It's not all that surprising that a New Zealander brought up on American films would be influenced by this meme.

The Hybrid Pattern

Working with an established story that in most particulars fits the Campbellian model quite closely, there were elements that Jackson could not alter. Thus what we see in the films is a hybrid of these two mythic patterns.[3]

In the original, we follow Frodo on his Campbellian hero-journey as he accepts the call to adventure, leaves the familiar sunlit world of the Shire, and ventures into the confusing and dangerous world outside its borders. But instead of a decisive victory, we have the more ambiguous moment of eucatastrophic failure and redemption at the Cracks of Doom. The destruction of the One Ring, which is Frodo's boon to Middle-earth, is veiled in obscurity and loss. But Tolkien does an interesting thing with the two major heroes of his story, as Verlyn Flieger points out in her classic essay "Frodo and Aragorn: The Concept of the Hero." At the beginning, Frodo is clearly the fairy-tale hero, the ordinary little man who "stumbles into heroic adventure and does the best he can" (Flieger 41), while Aragorn is the classic epic/romance hero, larger than life and "equal to any situation" (Flieger 41). But as Flieger demonstrates, Tolkien had Frodo and Aragorn cross story-threads and roles at several points throughout the story. Typically, the fairy-tale hero wins the princess and the kingdom, while the epic/romance hero faces an end of tragedy and disillusionment—"the stark, bitter ending typical of the *Iliad*, *Beowulf*, the *Morte d'Arthur*" (Flieger 42). In contrast, Aragorn, who appears fully formed as the Campbellian helper-figure at Bree instead of being called to adventure from his safe village, in the end wins a decisive victory over supernatural forces and brings back the boon of a restored and peaceful kingdom. Frodo is transformed into the tragic epic/romance hero; and while his actions are more important than the battles Aragorn wins, they are less publicly recognizable as a boon to the world.

In Jackson's movie, we see the Shire established almost from the beginning as the American monomyth's harmonious paradise threatened by evil. The medium of film and Jackson's emphasis on horror and violence make the threat more visceral; consider the panicked, haphazard packing and headlong flight of Frodo in the movie (*FOTR*, scene 10), the vicious death by trampling of the gate-warden at Bree (*FOTR*, scene 16), and the ratcheted-up violence of the encounter with the Black Riders at Weathertop (*FOTR*, scene 19). Contrast this deliberate intensification of menace to the same incidents in the book, where Frodo and his friends remove from Bag End to Crickhollow with calm deliberation and thorough planning, where the Black Riders don't actually harm anyone physically until the attack on Weathertop, and where Bree is a safe and civilized haven on the way.

Additionally, normal institutions are presented as even more powerless and weakly led in the film than in the book, where the restoration of right rule is a prelude to reenergized resistance to the enemy. For example, Théoden, even after his healing by Gandalf, is an ineffective leader in the movie. In the book, his first thought is to oppose Saruman, and he immediately makes plans to lead his own troops against him, sending only the women and children to refuge in Dunharrow. Jackson's Théoden instead says, "I will not bring further death to my people. I will not risk open war" (*TT*, scene 23), and leads all of his people, including the warriors, into hiding at Helm's Deep for safety. He seems more concerned not to lose precedence to Aragorn than to consider strategy. Denethor, unlike the tragic but noble figure in the book, ignores his city's urgent needs in his sorrow over Boromir's death; in the movie, Gandalf must remind him of his duty to set aside his grief and defend his city (*Return*, scene 11). In the book Gandalf observes that Denethor "uses [his] grief as a cloak" while questioning Pippin, and never swerves from his highest purpose, "the good of Gondor" (Tolkien, *Return* 30). Even Elrond is less in control of his stronghold, allowing his Council to devolve into an undignified shouting match, in contrast to the calm and deliberately paced committee meeting depicted in the book.

Sexual Renunciation

Following the classic pattern established in countless Westerns, the Aragorn of Jackson's movies must renounce love in order to do his job. Aragorn thus wins his series of decisive victories after separating himself from Arwen. He gains the throne rather than receding into obscurity — an event Jackson could not alter; but as Diana Paxson points out, Aragorn in the movie "accepts the crown almost as one condemned to it" (Paxson 97). Aragorn could only think Arwen was dead, her "life tied to the fate of the Ring," as her father told him (*ROTK*, scene 30) and Sauron showed him in the *palantír* (*ROTK*, scene 60), and he was doomed to a sterile and lonely reign without her.

This renunciation of sexual and romantic love by the hero is one of the major characteristics of the American monomyth which Lawrence and Jewett examine in great detail and which is particularly applicable to Jackson's Aragorn. In Campbell's monomyth, one of the most frequently recounted episodes on the hero's journey is the meeting and union with a goddess or a temptress at the nadir of the journey, and another is the divine marriage at the end of the tale. In many cases the goddess figure may be both the object of the quest and its reward. But in the American version of the monomyth, the emphasis is on woman as temptress, luring the hero from his duty, whether as a distraction, by outright seduction from his purpose, or by the tragic fact that his love for her can make her a strategic pawn to be used against him by his enemies. Sexual and romantic entanglements with women are therefore to be rejected until the hero's duty is done.

Consider the archetypal example of the *Superman* movies, where Clark Kent is attracted to Lois Lane but must remain celibate or lose his superhuman powers, or *Star Trek*'s Captain Kirk, who over and over again affirms that he is "married to his ship" and cannot afford to be distracted by love. And as Lawrence and Jewett point out, "judging from the fatalities that befall the fiancées of Ben, Joe, and Hoss Cartwright in TV's popular *Bonanza* series, merely planning to marry a fictional redeemer may be the riskiest job in America" (Lawrence and Jewett 43). Small wonder, then, that we see Aragorn rejecting Arwen's love because he doesn't want to put her in harm's way, telling her she must go over the sea with her kinfolk, as her father wishes, rather than face the dangers of Middle-earth by his side.

Tolkien's Aragorn has as his ultimate goal the union with the goddess in the form of Arwen, whose promise he won in the early stages of his quest and whose marriage to him at the end, uniting Elf and Man, is even more the sign of his rightful kingship than his coronation. He is never in doubt of their pledge; it sustains him both emotionally (at Cerin Amroth in Lorién after Gandalf's death, the "grim years were removed from his face" as he recalled meeting there with Arwen (Tolkien, *Fellowship* 366–7) and symbolically (the banner which Arwen sends with the Dúnedain, the sign of the goddess's approval of his path and a clue to the direction it must take after Helm's Deep (Tolkien, *Return* 48). Arwen is never a temptress or a weakness keeping him from concentrating on his quest — she is an inspiration and a source of strength. When Tolkien's Aragorn encounters woman as temptress in the person of Éowyn, his unquestioned commitment to and faith in his relationship with Arwen helps him pass the test.

Jackson's Aragorn reacts to both women to some degree as at least distractions if not outright temptresses. He initially tries to reject the gift of Arwen's pendant (*FOTR*, scene 26), though as she points out on several occasions it is her gift to give. Under pressure from Elrond, Aragorn tells Arwen to go over the sea with the rest of her people and tries to return the pendant (*TT*, scene 33). Concern for her would be only a distraction from his quest; like Spiderman/Peter Parker, who rejects Mary Jane's love out of concern for her safety, Aragorn doesn't allow Arwen the independence to make her own decision about whether she wishes to risk her life or not — even when Arwen has already been established as a quite capable swordswoman and outstanding rider who can take care of herself. Arwen does not send the banner she made to publicly affirm her faith in him and his quest — Elrond brings the sword to Dunharrow instead and does not bother to mention that it was Arwen who demanded its reforging (*ROTK*, scene 30). Jackson's Aragorn is even rather harsh towards Éowyn's infatuation, saying bluntly, "I cannot give you what you seek" (*TT*, scene 31), whereas in the book, with great delicacy of care for her feelings, Aragorn speaks only of their respective duties to their peoples (Tolkien, *Return* 56–9).

Distrust of Established Democratic Institutions

Another theme which Lawrence and Jewett find intriguing in the American monomyth is the rejection of democratic processes and the depiction of established institutions as helpless in the face of the threat to the community. The hero is a loner, an outsider who instinctively knows what needs to be done even though the community thinks he is wrong. Compare this to Tolkien's Aragorn. Though a Ranger and therefore an outsider to the community he now guards, this was not always the case. As a younger man, Aragorn underwent extensive military and political training as a member of several communities in Middle-earth; he was fostered in Rivendell and was a close companion to Elrond's two sons and later served in the armies of Rohan and Gondor. It is not through any quarrel with any of these societies that he has hunted Gollum alone or served with the Rangers, his kinfolk, as one of the unthanked guardians of the north; it is simply where his matured talents were needed at the time (see Croft 87–91). While most of this information is revealed in the appendix, his status as an insider in several communities is shown in the text in his interactions with the Elves of Rivendell and with the Dúnedain when they join him in taking the Paths of the Dead. And Tolkien's Aragorn has no quarrel with the orders of the entirely capable Théoden at Helm's Deep.

Jackson's Aragorn is closer to the classic loner of the American monomyth, who typically rejects democratic discussion and decision-making and favors instead independent action without accountability. Jackson's version of Aragorn takes its cue from our initial glimpse of Strider in the inn at Bree. Tolkien's mature Aragorn may lead by consensus, but Strider is a loner. As Flieger observed, when we first meet him he "evoke[s] a character out of the mythic American west—the stranger in town—cool, alert, alone" (Flieger 43); but as we see him transform from Strider, the enigmatic, advice-giving guide (Campbell 72–3), into Aragorn, the competent and charismatic king-to-be, he loses some of these qualities, which he tends to retain in Jackson.

Throughout the movies, there is less depiction of the consensual leadership style which is so essential to Aragorn's character. In the book, Aragorn constantly seeks the advice and agreement of his companions (Croft 90), calling them together for meetings at important turning points in their path. For example, at Parth Galen, before the disastrous attack by the Uruk-hai, Aragorn leads a discussion of the Company's goals and asks Frodo to make the decision about whether to go to Minas Tirith or Mordor. Instead, Jackson's Aragorn brusquely insists on his chosen path straight into Mordor from the north, rejecting Gimli's advice and insisting, "That is our road" (*FOTR*, scene 43).

In the book, the Last Debate before the attack on the Black Gate is a formal meeting similar to Elrond's Council in its reasoned debate of the courses open to the allies. The princes and leaders of the armies meet to advise Aragorn, and he makes his decision with their consent. In the movie, this debate is informal; Éomer is the only other battle leader present, and there is basically no discussion (*ROTK*, scene 59). As Judith Kollmann points out, Gandalf "offers no military insights," nor do any of the other advisors gathered there (Kollmann 168).

The elimination of the Scouring of the Shire from Jackson's film serves to underscore solitary outsider leadership as well. For one thing, the returning Hobbits do not get to have their version of "riding into town to save the day," reinforcing Aragorn's uniqueness as the lone hero. But more important, the Scouring is very much an example of group action by established democratic (though loosely established) institutions with leadership by consultation and consensus; as such, it goes against every trope of the typical film based on the American superhero monomyth.

The pivotal moment where Aragorn takes the Paths of the Dead is characteristic of Jackson's reinterpretation of Aragorn's leadership style to meet the demands of the American version of the monomyth. Tolkien describes a leader growing into his power of command, firm in his decision but willing to listen to the advice of others and leading the Dúnedain and their horses into the caverns through his charisma and the sheer "strength of his will" (Tolkien, *Return* 60). Jackson's Aragorn wants to go alone and in secret, and only accepts Gimli and Legolas as companions because they force themselves on him (*Return*, scene 31).[4] In the book, while Aragorn "summons" the Dead to a meeting at the Stone of Erech, he does not then command or force them to serve him; he instead offers them the opportunity to fulfill their broken oath to Isildur (Tolkien, *Return* 62–63). In the movie it is necessary for Aragorn to confront and physically defeat the King of the Dead, then proceed from commanding to pleading before being routed by an avalanche of skulls (*Return*, scene 35).

Diminishment and Its Implications

Jackson's Aragorn can strike the reader familiar with the book as strangely diminished from Tolkien's Cambellian and epic/romance hero. One early reviewer commented on Jackson's "systematic removal of all traces of nobility and faith from the most noble and faithful characters, and the concomitant angstifying [of Aragorn] and wimpifying [of Frodo]" (Hostetter). Frodo is diminished by the fact that the movies are more focused on Aragorn and Arwen's story than the "hobbito-centric" books (Chance 178), but these very additions to Aragorn's story diminish him as a character even as he becomes more central to the movie.

Jackson claimed that the writers tried to make Aragorn's character "more complex" (*FOTR*, scene 25, writers and director commentary). Presumably the original character, devoid of any debilitating internal conflicts, is simply not interesting enough. Timmons points out that the difference between the Frodo of the film and the Frodo of the book is that the original was someone we could admire and aspire to be like, someone a little better than us; the movie version is designed for a mass audience to relate to and even feel superior to (Timmons 147). This applies as well to Aragorn. We are meant to relate to and pity his self-doubt, soul-searching, and lack of faith in love — instead of admiring and aspiring to the original Aragorn's clarity of purpose, self-assurance, and confidence in Arwen's promise.

Northrop Frye's taxonomy of literary modes provides us with an applicable terminology. Tolkien's Aragorn is the typical hero of *romance*, who is "superior in *degree* to other men and his environment ... whose actions are marvelous but who is himself identified as a human being" (Frye 33). Frodo is more the hero of the *high mimetic* mode, "superior in degree to other men but not to his natural environment" (Frye 33–4). As a recent paper by Anthony Burdge and Jessica Burke demonstrates, Tolkien was adept at incorporating a wide range of both heroes and villains from all of Frye's modes into a seamless story, even at times bridging modes within the same character (Burdge and Burke 138–9). Jackson, however, has eliminated these nuances and bumped nearly all the characters down to the *low mimetic* mode, where the hero is "superior neither to other men or his environment," so that "we respond to a sense of his common humanity" (Frye 34).

But these humanized movie heroes can somehow seem less soul-satisfying than their idealized literary predecessors. Kayla Wiggins observes that by diminishing Aragorn and Frodo, "the effect is not to bring us closer to these characters but to shove us further away. We can't know them with the fundamental recognition that is part of our primal consciousness, the part of ourselves that reaches out to myth ... as essential truth" (Wiggins 121). Campbell understood this basic human need for heroes and concluded that many of the heroes in the stories we tell share the same path because it speaks to something in our souls. By internalizing these stories, we discover meaningful patterns in our own lives and gain understanding of our own paths.

What similar needs does the American monomyth serve? Lawrence and Jewett feel that it may actually be harmful, as this mythic pattern undermines confidence in democratic and community principles and can lead to pathologies like those exhibited by Theodore Kaczynski (the "Unabomber") and Timothy McVeigh — both known fans of certain popular culture products which particularly embodied the American monomyth (Lawrence and Jewett 167–76).[5] Jackson likewise does a disservice to the audience by buying into this dominating mythic pattern and discarding the democratic and community-affirming aspects of Tolkien's Aragorn and his acceptance of love as an integral part of the hero's life.

But is this revision of Tolkien's characters actually one of the keys to the financial success of the movies? Does the "Americanization" of the hero and the plot serve to create a movie experience that resonates more deeply with a worldwide audience by hitting the notes so familiar to them from countless other movies? At this point it may be instructive to take a brief look at two other attempts to film *The Lord of the Rings*— Ralph Bakshi's 1978 *LOTR* and Rankin-Bass Studio's 1979 *The Return of the King*. Bakshi's film, which takes the story up through the battle at Helm's Deep, was penned by Peter S. Beagle, who stuck quite closely to the books in most ways. But even here the chronological rearrangement of the story, which necessitates the early introduction of Saruman as a heretofore unsuspected traitor, emphasizes the threat to paradise at an earlier point than in Tolkien's original, reinforcing the American monomyth pattern. However, Aragorn has no opportunity to reject romantic entanglements in this film, as Arwen neither appears nor is alluded to and Éowyn has only one nonspeaking scene with no personal interaction with Aragorn. This greatly weakens how this film maps onto the pattern. The Rankin-Bass cartoon, created for a much younger audience and departing quite radically from the source material, even more deliberately avoids the question of romantic entanglement. In part it does this by concentrating almost entirely on Frodo's story, but also by similarly leaving out Arwen and greatly reducing Éowyn's role. But this unbalanced concentration on the Ring-story rather than the king-story takes the cartoon even further away from the American monomyth pattern.

Both films are highly unsatisfactory as examples of either the Cambellian or the American monomyth patterns, ending in mid-story without resolution in one case and muddling the whole tale beyond salvation in the other. Is it possible that the reasons for the lack of commercial success and critical regard for these films may rest to some degree on their lack of adherence to a monomythic story-pattern, in addition to their other more obvious flaws?

Jackson wrote his screenplay for Hollywood's lowest common denominator, an audience that is expected to respond only to the pathos of the low-mimetic mode (Burdge and Burke 157) and the irresistible power of the

American version of the monomyth. Jackson's films massage and flatter this rather adolescent desire to see oneself as the lone redeemer, riding into town, rejecting emotional entanglements with self-sacrificing drama, saving the day, and galloping off into the sunset. Money, after all, follows the well-worn path of least resistance and easy, short-term success. Tolkien challenges us instead to emulate timeless characters of a higher mode than ourselves and to respond to the ancient call of the original monomyth that has patterned humanity's stories for centuries.

Notes

1. This paper was originally presented at the Popular Culture Association/American Culture Association Annual Conference, San Diego, March 2005.

2. Think about *Blazing Saddles*, for instance, which parodies every cliché of the western while following the pattern nearly perfectly. The black sheriff is the ultimate outsider, and he saves the town which initially rejects him from corrupt institutions which normally should be working for its benefit. He rejects an emotional entanglement with a temptress sent to distract him. In the end, in spite of the town folk begging him to stay, he leaves because he is bored, riding off into the sunset.

3. Or perhaps we should say that Jackson's films belong to the subset of the American monomyth which depicts the restoration of a hereditary monarchy as the ideal ending — consider *The Lion King* or *Star Wars* as examples — which is an unusual ideal for a democratic society to espouse, but still quite a common theme.

4. This pattern of rejecting a leadership role is more typical of Frodo in Tolkien's books, who often attempts to steal away alone and is forestalled. For him, it is appropriate and essential to reject power (Croft 83–87); for Aragorn, who should slowly be proving his fitness to be king and lead ever-larger armies, these defeats his purpose.

5. But they do see hope in some of the stories which came out of the 9/11 terrorist attacks, celebrating the heroism of people who worked for and within the community, like firefighters, and who took communal action, like the passengers who diverted the plane headed for Washington and crashed in Pennsylvania (Lawrence and Jewett 362–3).

Works Cited

Burdge, Anthony S., and Jessica Burke. "Humiliated Heroes: Peter Jackson's Interpretation of *the Lord of the Rings*." *Translating Tolkien: Text and Film*. Ed. Thomas Honegger. Zurich: Walking Tree Publishers, 2004. 135–64.

Campbell, Joseph. *The Hero with a Thousand Faces*. 2nd ed. Princeton: Princeton UP, 1973.

Chance, Jane. "Tolkien's Women (and Men): The Films and the Book." *Tolkien on Film: Essays on Peter Jackson's the Lord of the Rings*. Ed. Janet Brennan Croft. Altadena CA: The Mythopoeic Press, 2004. 175–94.

Croft, Janet Brennan. *War and the Works of J.R.R. Tolkien*. Contributions to the Study of Science Fiction and Fantasy. Westport: Praeger, 2004.

Flieger, Verlyn. "Frodo and Aragorn: The Concept of the Hero." *Tolkien: New Critical Perspectives*. Eds. Neil D. Isaacs and Rose A. Zimbardo. Lexington: UP of Kentucky, 1981. 40–62.

Frye, Northrop. *Anatomy of Criticism: Four Essays*. Princeton: Princeton UP, 1957.
Hostetter, Carl F. *Digest Number 1086*. 2003. Mythsoc discussion group. Available: http://groups.yahoo.com/group/mythsoc/message/7188. 6 January 2003.
Kollmann, Judith. "Elisions and Ellipses: Counsel and Council in Tolkien's and Jackson's the Lord of the Rings." *Tolkien on Film: Essays on Peter Jackson's the Lord of the Rings*. Ed. Janet Brennan Croft. Altadena CA: The Mythopoeic Press, 2004. 149–71.
Lawrence, John Shelton, and Robert Jewett. *The Myth of the American Superhero*. Grand Rapids: Eerdmans, 2002.
The Lord of the Rings. 1978. Dir. Ralph Bakshi. Warner Brothers, 2002.
The Lord of the Rings: The Fellowship of the Ring. Special Extended DVD Edition. Dir. Peter Jackson. New Line Productions, 2002.
The Lord of the Rings: The Return of the King. Special Extended DVD Edition. Dir. Peter Jackson. New Line Productions, 2004.
The Lord of the Rings: The Two Towers. Special Extended DVD Edition. Dir. Peter Jackson. New Line Productions, 2003.
Paxson, Diana. "Re-Vision: The Lord of the Rings in Print and on Screen." *Tolkien on Film: Essays on Peter Jackson's the Lord of the Rings*. Ed. Janet Brennan Croft. Altadena CA: The Mythopoeic Press, 2004. 81–99.
The Return of the King. 1979. Dir. Arthur Rankin Jr. and Jules Bass. Warner Brothers, 2001.
Timmons, Daniel. "Frodo on Film: Peter Jackson's Problematic Portrayal." *Tolkien on Film: Essays on Peter Jackson's the Lord of the Rings*. Ed. Janet Brennan Croft. Altadena CA: The Mythopoeic Press, 2004. 123–48.
Tolkien, J. R. R. *The Fellowship of the Ring: Being the First Part of the Lord of the Rings*. 2nd ed. Boston: Houghton Mifflin, 1965.
_____. *The Return of the King: Being the Third Part of the Lord of the Rings*. 2nd ed. Boston: Houghton Mifflin, 1965.
Wiggins, Kayla McKinney. "The Art of the Story-Teller and the Person of the Hero." *Tolkien on Film: Essays on Peter Jackson's the Lord of the Rings*. Ed. Janet Brennan Croft. Aladena CA: The Mythopoeic Press, 2004. 103–22.

Neither the Shadow Nor the Twilight
The Love Story of Aragorn and Arwen in Literature and Film

Richard C. West

There is a striking scene in the book version of *The Lord of the Rings* (Appendix A, section I, part v) where Aragorn and Arwen stroll together on a midsummer evening, walking barefoot through lush grass and flowers to the top of the fair hill named Cerin Amroth in the Elvish land of Lothlórien (depicted in both the book and the movie as an extremely beautiful region). To the east they can see the Shadow lying over the land of Mordor, representing the threat of Sauron against which both of them, along with their respective peoples, are struggling. In the opposite direction it is twilight as the sun sets, representing the waning of the Elves, who are destined to sail west over the sea to the somewhat Eden-like earthly paradise of Valinor, abandoning Middle-earth to live under the protection of the Valar (angelic beings in Tolkien's invented mythology) in the Undying Lands. It is in this time and place, both of them determined to maintain the fight against the Shadow and Arwen declining to escape into the Twilight where Aragorn cannot go, that the lovers engage to be married: "they plighted their troth and were glad."[1]

The scene encapsulates the essence of the relationship between these two characters, as representatives of Human and Elf within the history and mythology of Middle-earth and as star-crossed lovers who are "glad" of each other and of their betrothal despite the enormous obstacles they face. The setting is also important to the story and to the characters. Unraveling how Tolkien got them to this point, and its aftermath, will tell us a great deal about his narrative methods. The substantially different treatment of their love story in the film adaptation will also tell us much about how the art forms of literature and drama differ even when treating related material.

Some readers of this collection of essays will be familiar with both the book and the film based on it, while others may know only one of them. Especially to those who have seen the movie trilogy but not read the book, it must be said that the two are very different works of art. The artistic use of moving pictures is not the same art as the artistic use of written language. The former uses not only action and speech but also lighting, costuming, musical background, the angles from which a scene is filmed and cutting between scenes, pacing, and, not least, the performances of the actors to present a gripping drama. The latter uses the power of words to speak to our imaginations.

J.R.R. Tolkien was both a student and a master of language — of his native English in all periods of its history and many of its dialects, as well as of other languages both old and modern. He also invented many languages, both as a hobby and as a study in the workings of linguistics, and from this went on to spend decades creating a fictional world with a multiplicity of cultures and millennia of history in which those tongues could plausibly evolve and be spoken. His sources were primarily Germanic and Celtic but he also drew on mythology and history worldwide. His Elves and Dwarves, for example, are not Victorian or Disney but tap more primal wellsprings and are creatures of power and dignity. Tolkien spent several years writing and revising *Lord,* a long narrative that depicts a world with many plot threads carefully interlaced into a majestic tapestry. Still, there was much background that could not be included in the main narrative, and he added half a dozen appendices not only to satisfy readers who asked him for things like alphabets and details of the languages and family trees of the characters, but also to fill out backstories and side stories and the aftermath of events. As good as *Lord* is on first reading, it is even better with rereadings when one has absorbed the background material.

Tolkien once told a student who was writing a master's thesis on Tolkien's work that he had a "general idea" of the overall story of *Lord* from the first draft of the second chapter ("The Shadow of the Past") in the late 1930s and that he made notes and synopses for himself on how he planned to develop it. But, he said, the story mostly just "unfolded itself" and it took "constant re-writing backwards" to tie the narrative strands together.[2] This is quite a good, as well as a concise, description of how he wrote, as we can see, since it is all laid out for us by his son Christopher Tolkien in the volumes of his

History of Middle-earth series dealing with the evolution of *Lord*. These show how that crucial second chapter (in which Gandalf explains the background of the One Ring to Frodo) went through numerous drafts, contain many of the author's notes (such as his often asking himself, "Who is Strider?"), and take us down the many byways that Tolkien partially explored before settling on the main courses of the story.

It took considerable time during the writing for a major character who started out as a Hobbit to become (Tolkien decided) a man, and then a man of royal descent. Names were important to Tolkien, and the character's name changed to match his situation as the rather plebeian-sounding Trotter was replaced by the more gallant Strider and then by Aragorn (a name that means "royal tree" in Sindarin, one of Tolkien's invented Elvish languages, indicating he is of kingly lineage). Finding him a suitable mate took the author even longer, so that Arwen (whose name in Sindarin means "royal maiden," indicating she is a fitting consort for one of kingly lineage) was a quite late development whose appearances in earlier sections had to be added in the revisions (rewritten backwards, so to speak). It is the final version of the story as published (which was the source for the filmmakers) that concerns us here.

It is typical of Tolkien's writing that he rarely abandons story or character elements but often just keeps adding to them. Thus Aragorn always remains a wanderer skilled in woodcraft who is helpful to Frodo; but as the character evolved he drew to himself the powerful myth of the dispossessed but rightful king whose restoration to the throne will usher in better times. To achieve this, Tolkien drew on (and further developed) his earlier, then-unpublished writings about the fall of the majestic human realm of Númenor in an Atlantis-like flood and the establishment by the survivors of related kingdoms in Arnor and Gondor, in order to provide a throne to which Aragorn can eventually be restored.

It is another characteristic of Tolkien to set up parallels between characters and between events (for one small example, Merry entering the service of Théoden and Pippin of Denethor). So he also drew on one of his oldest stories, that of Beren and Lúthien in the First Age,[3] as a parallel tale of a Man and an Elf-maiden deeply in love but long kept apart by a father who disapproves of the match while they are at the forefront of the struggle against the Dark Lord of their time.

We see both of these strands used in Tolkien's depiction of the first meeting of Aragorn and Arwen in Appendix A.[4] Aragorn is twenty years of age and his foster father, Elrond, gives him the heirlooms of his house, which is royal among Men, and the task to continue his father's (Arathorn) part in the ongoing fight against Sauron. One of these heirlooms is the Ring of Barahir

(Barahir was the father of Beren), and a token of friendship between Elves and Men. (Aragorn will later use this as his engagement ring.) It is while Aragorn is feeling happy about coming to his majority and is singing a lay of Beren and Lúthien that he has his first sight of Arwen walking in the woods of Rivendell, much as Beren and Lúthien themselves first met in the woods of Neldoreth in her father's realm. She has been away in Lothlórien for what in Elvish terms was a relatively short visit but happens to encompass all of Aragorn's life to this point, so they have not had a chance to meet heretofore. He at first assumes from her apparent youth and beauty that they are of similar age, but she is an Elf and is indeed more than 2,000 years older than he.[5] He tries hard to impress her, blurting out his noble lineage and all his titles, and does amuse her, mostly by comparing her to her ancestor Lúthien, whom she is said to resemble. She is kind to him, he falls head over heels in love with her, and soon Elrond advises him to go away and get some life experience.

Their shared interest in the story of Beren and Lúthien is one of the things that brings them together. Arwen presciently says that "maybe my doom will be not unlike" Lúthien's, while Aragorn notes that it is his fate to have "turned my eyes to a treasure no less dear than the treasure of Thingol that Beren once desired."[6] Tolkien draws the parallel between the two sets of lovers who unite Elf and Human but suffer death. One significant difference, however, is in the fathers concerned.

It is an ancient trope for a disapproving father to set a difficult brideprice for an unwelcome suitor, often with the hope of compassing his death. Such might have been the result when King Thingol sent Beren to take a Silmaril from the iron crown of Morgoth had Beren not received a lot of help, not least from Lúthien herself. But in the case of Elrond, Tolkien adds a new twist. Elrond is a very caring father, not at all cruel, and by insisting that Arwen "shall not be the bride of any Man less than the King of both Gondor and Arnor"[7] he is only giving his foster son incentive to achieve what it is his hereditary duty to attempt anyway, while also making the best provision he can for his daughter if she does choose to relinquish her Elvish immortality. Elrond loves them both. And, moreover, a successful outcome will be to the good of all of Middle-earth. Aragorn accepts the condition and the challenge and prepares himself to be a good ruler through study with Gandalf. He campaigns with Arwen's brothers and with the Rangers, who are the last remnant of the magnificent Númenorean people, travels across Middle-earth and serves in many lands, including Rohan and Gondor.

When the two meet again by chance (or fate) in Lothlórien he is fortynine years old, still youthful in Númenorean terms but matured by his experiences, and he has been dressed by Galadriel like an Elf-lord. Arwen chooses her future husband and accepts the consequences. On the one hand she will be of great help to someone who will be mighty in the overthrow of Sauron and they will have a long and good life together; but on the other she will be separated from her father and family and friends, all of whom she loves deeply, and her life will be drastically shortened, for she has relinquished the immortality of the Elves for the mortality of human beings. She will help defeat the Shadow but, ironically, she who is called Arwen Evenstar will not have the Twilight.

It might seem that the iconic image of the betrothal used by Tolkien should be a gift to a filmmaker: the two lovers on the flower-strewn hilltop at dusk, looking in one direction to the Enemy who must be overcome and in the opposite direction to what must be sacrificed. But the image that is returned to several times throughout the film trilogy by Peter Jackson and his collaborators is of this movie's depiction of Aragorn and Arwen holding both hands and facing each other as they pledge their love. That the figures are almost in silhouette is romantic lighting rather than that of an evocation of evening upon Cerin Amroth, and indeed they could be anywhere. This illustrates the difference in the two art forms. Tolkien's scene is so striking and powerful because he has developed the mythic background as well as making it personal, so that every detail is deeply evocative. In a work of literature he not only has the room to do so, but also the nature of the work calls for it. Jackson's team might have filmed such a scene but could not have achieved such depth without similar development that would have digressed from the main story line (even Tolkien puts it in an appendix) and unduly lengthened an already long movie. But the image the team chose instead is immediately recognizable as lovers gazing at each other and works very well as a leitmotiv in a film.

That Peter Jackson and his co-scriptwriters, Fran Walsh and Philippa Boyens, put so much focus on the love story of Aragorn and Arwen is to their credit, for to Tolkien this was a very important thread in his interlaced narrative. It might be tempting for a screenwriter simply to excise Arwen. As we have already noted, she was a late addition; and while Tolkien inserted some crucial references to her, they are relatively few.[8] Therefore an adapter might find it easier to leave her out. The Jackson team, in order to keep the audience mindful of the relationship throughout all three movies released years apart, had to mine most of Tolkien's references and invent others.[9] Their depiction of the love story has significant differences from that of Tolkien, however.

That the parallel with the story of Beren and Lúthien is almost entirely omitted is nearly a foregone conclusion, for the filmmakers had background material about the history of the One Ring to fit in that was extensive enough without also delving into the First Age. Yet there is one very telling reference. In *FOTR*, as the Hobbits are encamped in the marshes, a wakeful Frodo hears Aragorn singing and is told that it is "the Lay of Lúthien, an Elf-maid who gave her love to Beren, a mortal." When Frodo asks what happened to her, Aragorn says sadly and simply, "She died."[10] He is clearly thinking of what Arwen's end will be if they marry. This is a much abbreviated version of the book—where Aragorn, while the party is camped on Weathertop, sings part of the song and tells the story at some length[11]—but its very brevity makes it affecting.

It is of interest to the nature of film adaptation that this brief scene was not in the theatrical release but added in the later, extended edition in videotape and DVD formats. The versions of movies shown in theatres are of necessity more limited by time constraints and tend to focus on action and lose character-oriented moments such as this one. Many are the laments from people in the film industry of good scenes that ended up on the cutting-room floor. But Peter Jackson early averred that he "intended to reedit scenes, change the sound track, and make something far more elaborate than the usual director's cut. The extended edition, "he repeatedly declared," was for the serious fans, while more casual viewers would stick with the theatrical version."[12]

That the movie also uses the myth of the dispossessed but rightful king might seem more surprising, but, as can be seen from as recent a popular example as Disney's *Lion King* (1994), this myth retains its appeal even in our democratic times. While history has examples of people born to be king who made a good job of it (in part because they were, of course, trained for it from a young age), there are also plenty of real-world examples of those with impeccable royal credentials who turned out to be quite unsuitable (and not a few of whom it might be said that they botched the job royally). Yet the desire and the hope remain and in fiction can be gratified. There is also a submerged democratic aspect in the dispossessed king growing up in straitened circumstances and learning empathy with all levels of society. Tolkien's long-struggling Aragorn is shown to be worthy of his crown, and, to a lesser extent (for we cannot see as much of his development), so is Jackson's.

Probably the most major change is in the characterization of Aragorn. In the book he accepts the task of winning the throne of Gondor and Arnor as soon as he learns that his lineage has fated him to try—feeling it to be his duty in the struggle against the menace of Sauron—and the need to win the hand of Arwen gives him a powerful added incentive. It will be an almost insurmountable task because a stranger is not likely to be accepted by many people, least of all by Denethor the Steward, who would have to give up enormous power should a king be restored. While Aragorn willingly puts his life at risk time and again, thereby taking the chance of losing everything, what this shows is that he is ready to sacrifice himself in the service of the higher good, as a true king and worthy ruler would. He never swerves from his path.

But Aragorn in the movie adaptation is depicted as highly reluctant to seek the throne that is his inheritance. When Gandalf asserts to Elrond that there is one who could reclaim the kingship of Gondor and unite the disparate factions of Middle-earth to fight Mordor, Elrond replies that "he turned from that path a long time ago."[13] Aragorn tells Arwen that he fears that the weakness whereby Isildur succumbed to the lure of the One Ring flows in his blood too, and she reassures him that the Shadow does not lie on him (nor on her) and she is confident that he will not fail as his ancestor did.[14] He vacillates about this throughout the film trilogy. This could make him seem less resolute a man than his counterpart in the book, but for many in the movie audience his doubts will make him a more acceptable candidate for his eventual kingship. When considering whom to place in a position of power, people are wary of someone who seems too eager for it, feeling a reluctant person is more likely to wield power responsibly. It is fitting that, shortly after the coronation of the movie's Aragorn, one of his first acts is to pay homage to the four ordinary Hobbits who have accomplished so much.[15]

Peter Jackson and his team in their dramatic adaptation of the book mostly chose to use and even extend action sequences, which are well suited to a visual medium. Aragorn remains a mighty warrior in both versions, and it was even considered that at the climax of the film it might be a good idea to have him fight Sauron in single combat.[16] This would have echoed the scene at the beginning of the movie trilogy where Isildur cuts the ring-finger from Sauron's hand. So one can see that such an artistic parallel might be tempting. But really it would not do. Besides being a major change from the book, it would have lessened the nature of Sauron too much (in the mythology of Middle-earth he is a diabolical being, a fallen angel) and weakened what is the main point: that the big battles may look more glamorous and glorious, but what is really important is more commonly a smaller thing such as the forlorn little Hobbits getting the Ring to the volcano. Jackson, like Tolkien, did a lot of revising as he worked, but it was a wise decision to retain Tolkien's carefully planned ending.

The character of Arwen is also changed in the film. When first introduced, she might be, like Strider, a Ranger, a guardian patrolling wild places to protect civilized areas from Orcs and other dangers. "What's this, a Ranger caught off his guard?" she asks jokingly as she holds a sword to Aragorn's throat. She is shown to be a superb rider and expert with a sword, as she carries the wounded Frodo on horseback from Weathertop to the Ford of Bruinen where she defies the pursuing Black Riders ("If you want him, come and claim him!") and disperses them by summoning enchanted floodwaters.[17] This is an example of compression common in movie adaptations of literary works. In the book, Frodo is carried on the horse of the Elf-lord Glorfindel (a character of some importance but still a minor one and as such was excised from the film), but it is Frodo himself who brandishes a sword and defies the Black Riders from across the river ("You shall have neither the Ring nor me!") and Elrond and Gandalf who are responsible for the magical flood.[18] This revision introduces Arwen earlier than in the book and as a force to be reckoned with. The filmmakers had originally intended that the character continue in this shield-maiden vein (she was to go to Helm's Deep in the second movie to take part in that battle, for instance), but objections in online fan forums to altering the character so much as to be "Arwen, Warrior Princess" persuaded them against this.[19] Yet she remains Aragorn's helpmate and inspiration. Since in the main plotline they are nowhere near each other, her appearances occur by cutting to show what is happening elsewhere or in flashbacks and dream sequences where she and Aragorn can be together. One significant difference is that the movie Arwen does yield to her father's entreaties and sets out for the Undying Lands, only turning back when she has a prescient vision of a future in which she and Aragorn will marry and have a son.

The movie Elrond is also a sterner figure than his counterpart in the book. There is no mention of his being the loving foster father of Aragorn who urges him to seek the kingship, and indeed Elrond seems not unhappy whenever Aragorn turns from that path. There is some antagonism between them arising from Elrond's fear of what might happen to his daughter if they marry. Part of Aragorn's ambivalence is that he fears that he ought to give up his beloved Arwen in order to extend her life, though she repeatedly tells him that she freely chooses mortality with him over immortality without him.

In the movie this culminates in a mysterious illness which will kill Arwen unless the Ring is destroyed (there is no counterpart to this in the book). Elrond therefore relents, has the broken sword of Isildur reforged, and takes it to Aragorn as the token that will bring him safely over the Paths of the Dead with an army to lift the siege of Minas Tirith. (In the book, the Sword-That-Was-Broken is reforged at the start of the quest before the Fellowship leaves Rivendell,[20] and Elrond's sons come to advise Aragorn to take the Paths of the Dead.[21]) With the destruction of the Ring and overthrow of Sauron, Arwen's health returns, and Elrond is happy to consent to her marriage to Aragorn. Thus, for all the earlier talk of their eventual deaths, it is a happy ending to their love story that the movie provides.

Tolkien, too, depicts their happiness when they are wed on Midsummer's Day in the year 3019 of the Third Age,[22] thirty-nine years to the day after they plighted their troth on Cerin Amroth in 2980,[23] and they reign together for more than a century. But Tolkien's concerns are mythic and deeply philosophical, and he goes on to show the tragedy of their eventual separation at the mortal Aragorn's ineluctable death at the age of 210. Arwen returns to Cerin Amroth — now long abandoned by Galadriel and all the Elves, who have sailed to Valinor, to die a lonely death in the place where she was once so happy. We recall that this hill in Tolkien's mythology was named for Elvish lovers who were separated and could not reunite. (But might there be a reunion in an afterlife that these pre–Christian people would not know about? Tolkien, a devout Catholic, hints at it.)[24]

As a scholar, Tolkien knew that in the Middle Ages stories were considered common property that different artists could revise and reshape to give them different emphases. The modern world has a very different conception. Yet Tolkien did intend that in his legendarium he would "leave scope for other minds and hands, wielding paint and music and drama."[25] The adaptation of Peter Jackson and his collaborators borrows heavily from, but is very different from, Tolkien's literary masterpiece. But the paint and music and drama they have wielded has resulted in a distinct work of art that is worthwhile in its own right.

NOTES

1. *The Lord of the Rings*, 1060–1061.
2. Letter to Caroline Whitman Everett dated 24 June 1957, *Letters*, 258.
3. Most concisely told in ch. 19 of *The Silmarillion* (1977).
4. *Lord*, 1057–1058.
5. Tolkien considered different dates, but settled on Arwen being born in Third Age 241, Aragorn in 2391, per *Lord,* Appendix B, 1085, 1089.
6. *Lord*, 1058, 1059.
7. *Lord*, 1061.
8. Detailed in West, *passim*.
9. Cathy Akers-Jordan has a careful listing of all Arwen's appearances onscreen in "Fairy Princess or Tragic Heroine? The Metamorphosis of Arwen Undómiel in Peter Jackson's *LOTR* Films," Croft, 195–213.
10. *FOTR-EE*, Part One, Scene 17, "The Midgewater Marshes."
11. *Lord*, 191–194.
12. Thompson, 214.
13. *FOTR-EE,* Part One, Scene 24, "The Fate of the Ring."
14. *FOTR-EE*, Part One, Scene 25, "The Sword That Was Broken."
15. *ROTK-EE*, Part Two, Scene 74, "The Return of the King."
16. *ROTK-EE*, The Appendices Part 5: The War of the Ring, "Abandoned Concept: Aragorn Battles Sauron."
17. *FOTR-EE*, Part One, Scene 21, "Flight to the Ford."

18. *Lord*, 209–215.
19. *TT-EE*, The Appendices Part 3: The Journey Continues, "From Book to Script: Finding the Story."
20. *Lord*, 276.
21. *Lord*, 775.
22. *Lord*, 1095.
23. *Lord*, 1090.
24. West, 325–327.
25. Letter to Milton Waldman late in 1951, *Letters*, 145.

WORKS CITED

Croft, Janet Brennan, ed. *Tolkien on Film: Essays on Peter Jackson's The Lord of the Rings*. Altadena, CA: The Mythopoeic Press, 2004.
Everett, Caroline Whitman. "The Imaginative Fiction of J. R. R. Tolkien." M.A. thesis, Florida State University, 1957.
Ford, Judy Ann and Robin Anne Reid, "Councils and Kings: Aragorn's Journey Towards Kingship in J. R. R. Tolkien's *The Lord of the Rings* and Peter Jackson's *The Lord of the Rings*," *Tolkien Studies* v. VI (2009): 71–90.
Foster, Robert. *The Complete Guide to Middle-earth*. London: HarperCollins, 2003 [copyright 1978].
Hammond, Wayne G. and Christina Scull, *The Lord of the Rings: A Reader's Companion*. Boston: Houghton Mifflin Company, 2005.
Honegger, Thomas, ed. *Translating Tolkien: Text and Film*. Zurich and Berne: Walking Tree Publishers, 2004. DVD.
The Lord of the Rings: The Fellowship of the Ring: Special Extended DVD Edition. New Line Home Entertainment, Inc., 2002. DVD.
The Lord of the Rings: The Two Towers: Special Extended DVD Edition. New Line Home Entertainment, Inc., 2003. DVD.
The Lord of the Rings: The Return of the King: Special Extended DVD Edition. New Line Home Entertainment, Inc., 2004. DVD.
Thompson, Kristin. *The Frodo Franchise: The Lord of the Rings and Modern Hollywood*. Berkeley, Los Angeles, London: University of California Press, 2007.
Tolkien, J. R. R. *The History of Middle-earth. Vol. VI: The Return of the Shadow: The History of The Lord of the Rings, Part One*, ed. Christopher Tolkien. Boston: Houghton Mifflin Company, 1988.
_____. *The History of Middle-earth. Vol. VII: The Treason of Isengard: The History of The Lord of the Rings, Part Two*, ed. Christopher Tolkien. Boston: Houghton Mifflin Company, 1989.
_____. *The History of Middle-earth. Vol. VIII: The War of the Ring: The History of The Lord of the Rings, Part Three*, ed. Christopher Tolkien. Boston: Houghton Mifflin Company, 1990.
_____. *The History of Middle-earth. Vol. IX: Sauron Defeated*, ed. Christopher Tolkien. Boston: Houghton Mifflin Company, 1991. Includes "The End of the Third Age," *The History of The Lord of the Rings, Part Four*.
_____. *The Letters of J. R. R. Tolkien*, ed. Humphrey Carpenter with the assistance of Christopher Tolkien. Boston: Houghton Mifflin Company, 2000 (with expanded Index compiled by Christina Scull and Wayne G. Hammond and first published in 1995).

_____. *The Lord of the Rings,* fiftieth anniversary ed., 1 vol. Boston: Houghton Mifflin Company, 2004.

_____. *The Silmarillion*, ed. Christopher Tolkien. Boston: Houghton Mifflin Company, 1977.

West, Richard C. "'Her Choice Was Made and Her Doom Appointed': Tragedy and Divine Comedy in the Tale of Aragorn and Arwen," *The Lord of the Rings 1954–2004: Scholarship in Honor of Richard E. Blackwelder*, ed. Wayne G. Hammond and Christina Scull (Milwaukee, WI: Marquette University Press, 2006), 317–329.

Concerning Horses
Establishing Cultural Settings from Tolkien to Jackson

JANICE M. BOGSTAD

While there are many members of the nonhuman world with seeming power to communicate, or even sentience, in Tolkien's fiction — eagles, other birds, Fell Beasts, warg/wolves, and even a sort of "tree" called Ents — horses seem to have a multitude of narrative functions, functions with more significance than merely forwarding of the plot by moving people (Elves, Dwarves, Men, Nazgûl, etc.) about. In Jackson's films, the horses are foregrounded in many of these functions, while many of the other animals function in much reduced roles. Aside from the Ents, or tree-herders, who are central to the plot of Peter Jackson's *The Two Towers*, none of them speak onscreen, only a form of crow, Fell Beasts and eagles, and what appears to be a moth, respond to some sort of communication, largely from Gandalf or Saruman. This would seem to imply, in the films at least, that these other nonhuman creatures are accessible only to wizards like Gandalf and Saruman, where as they have a wider narrative function in Tolkien's original books. So while eagles talk in Tolkien's books, they rescue Gandalf in *FOTR* and Frodo and Sam in *ROTK* and appear at battles in *ROTK*; but they don't talk and we don't experience the civilization Tolkien created for them. On the other hand, in both books and films, many horses are referenced in many settings and of many types. The most invisible are mundane and iconic for a level of cultural development; the most notable are interpersonal, sentient, talking beings and the most numerous are found in battle scenes, where again the horses become part of an iconic representation of technological levels of a society. And in *TT* and

ROTK they also represent a benchmark in the use of computer-generated imagery (CGI), both in improvements in motion-capture technologies that allowed for real-time motion-capture and in software like Massive, developed specifically for the films.

Horses are pivotal to the plot in both renditions of Middle-earth.[1] I argue here that a narrative centrality of horses was not only perceived but also greatly expanded in the films, through efforts of physical and virtual design. Thus the horses — which function as more than conveyance and seem to exist as both non-sentient and sentient beings, function at mythic/mystical levels such as that of Shadowfax and Arwen's horse and the ancestral Mearas, as well as at more mundane levels. Jackson's scripts (by Jackson, Boyens, and Walsh) foreground several narrative functions for horses. Interpersonal functions, where some sort of special bond, sometimes one that we recognize as mundane and at other times as mystical, reflect on the character of Elves, Dwarves, Hobbits, Men, Wizards, and Nazgûl, especially. In some cases, it is clear that the horses utilize a high level of communication with the sentient beings around them; although in no case do the horses talk "out loud." They also function in the broadest sense to reinforce the overall cultural and economic level of Middle-earth, the preindustrial one so prized by Tolkien himself. Further, horses serve as more specific cultural icons much more centrally in the films — for example the Rohirrim and their horse-based societal systems — and, especially in the films, as icons of the late-medieval technology of warfare used by both humans and the forces of evil, of Mordor and Sauron or Isengard and Saruman.

It is my intention in establishing this list to demonstrate Tolkien's knowledge of and attention to horses as actors in the drama of the Ring. They are ever Elves, Men's and Hobbits' helpers and companions, except when perverted by Mordor and the Ringwraiths to do their bidding. I will further illustrate these additional narrative functions — functions of characterization, iconography, and visual spectacle; but for purposes of length, this paper will foreground the interpersonal and cultural. Details on horses and warfare will need to wait for another study. Even a quick catalog of the horses in both text and film demonstrates that both Tolkien and Jackson took horses very seriously and indeed made some effort to highlight their best qualities. One might be tempted to attribute the interest and skill with which Tolkien depicted some horse-human relationships solely to his experience in World War I, where he was responsible for breaking horses for the cavalry.[2] But one can specifically trace many techniques which brought horses so centrally into play in Jackson's films to a group of talented individuals responsible for training, managing and riding the over 250 horses used in the film, as well as to the CGI experts who used actual horses to create the multiplicity of mounted warriors as special effects for war scenes, especially those of battles at Helm's Deep, with its heroic charge of Théoden and Aragorn, and the penultimate one of Pelennor Fields so central to both Tolkien's and Jackson's plots.[3] In Jackson, however, the battle scenes are much more expansive, evocative not only of the war technology of later-medieval and early-modern Europe but also of the massive spectacles in the early history of film.

Since we make assumptions about the historical level of Middle-earth's culture, it is easy to reduce the importance of horses to mere background noise, there merely to establish the rustic nature of the historical period or the preindustrial level of the cultures. The general technological and social level of Middle-earth is established by the use of horses in peace and war. Included are ponies in Hobbiton, Gandalf's cart horse as Gandalf arrives in Hobbiton in *FOTR*, and Gandalf's normal riding horse as Gandalf leaves Hobbiton, cart horses in Bree, Strider's pack pony as Strider leaves Bree with the four hobbits, Boromir's horse as Boromir arrives in Rivendell, white horses ridden but not raised by Elves — seen first as Frodo and Sam encounter them at a distance and then as Arwen's (or Gar's *Fellowship*) fast horse — and especially the horses of the Ringwraiths and the horse-shapes in the water of the Anduin when the wraiths are drowned by Arwen. And then there are the many warhorses, in both virtual and physical form, in the films, as well as those in the books.

This overriding narrative function — the establishment of preindustrial but post–Iron Age culture — is so common a trope in fantasy as to be missed in Tolkien criticism. In fact, some writers have speculated that the socioeconomic level of Middle-earth is anywhere from the 14th century to the 17th century. Tolkien[4] himself relates the Hobbit culture to the pastoral English countryside of his early youth despite the fact that England had already moved far into an industrialized and colonial period by the late 19th century.[5] Jackson preserves this function of horses as he creates the basic setting for the films.

First, the overall cultural level of Middle-earth is preindustrial, but it can also be seen as at least late medieval, with horses being central to that technological level. Much has been written in the critical literature contrasting preindustrial, pastoral culture in the humanistic Middle-earth, with the industrialized destructiveness of both Saruman and Sauron/Mordor. But Saruman and Sauron both enact their successes persuading or enchanting humans, producing masses of soldiers — the Westrons, Southrons and Easterlings, humans somehow seduced to the support of Mordor and the quest for the One Ring — as well as debased but marginally sentient beings like Orcs, Uruk-hai, and goblins, and messenger-birds, wargs (*TT*) and the Nazgûl-ridden Fell Beasts

(*TT* and *ROTK*). Even among the war technology of Sauron and Saruman, there are no mechanical vehicles, only permutations of trebuchet and battering rams. So Jackson, following Tolkien, reinforces this preindustrial realm, backed up by a few creatures with supernatural evil qualities like Shelob, a few flying Fell Beasts, cave trolls, and the preternaturally evil beast who kills Gandalf in the first book in the mines of Moria — the Balrog.

The Nazgûl[6] horses, never fully explained in the films, are another example of the mystical: Mearas captured from Rohan and trained to tolerate the Nazgûl. In *Fellowship*, the eagle Gwaihir defends Rohan against rumors that it pays a tribute of horses to Mordor.[7] Even those examples take on a greater significance when it comes to establishing both characterization and iconic cultural referents for Rohan (this will be discussed later). Of course there are the more mundane functions of horses in rural settings, with the attendant ability to call upon readers' store of cultural expectations. Thus, in early sequences of the *Fellowship* and *FOTR*, Gandalf arrives in Hobbiton in a cart drawn by a horse, the method of conveyance common in most parts of the world until the advent of the train and even after that in more remote areas up to the present day, but pervasively into the early 20th century.

Other horses appear on the screen in all films, along with pigs, cows, sheep and goats, in the village of Hobbiton. Carts and horses in Bree, riding horses used by Hobbits and humans throughout film and fiction, and even the horses of war, form a basic referent to call up an entire cultural construct. (Horse-level technology was pervasive in Europe during Tolkien's childhood.)

To date, most attention given to horses in the critical and laudatory literature on *Lord* has been focused on Shadowfax,[8] king of all horses and old friend to Gandalf, and secondarily on the culture of Rohan, whose horses are seemingly debased descendents of the numinous Mearas. These descendents of Felaróf— of which Shadowfax seems to be in both books and films the last full-blooded representative in Middle-earth — are suggested as being behind the sensitivities between Rohirrim and their horses. For horse-mad young people (of which I was one), even Shadowfax becomes an entrée into the books, as well as a confirmation of what such young people already know about horses. In written narrative and visual representation, such relationships are attractive to a sector of the audience; and, for many horse lovers, the American cultural-iconography is obvious. Shadowfax was one of my first loves in the Tolkien books; but Bill, the most mundane of ponies, was also important to me. The opportunity to see the horses has sparked great interest in the filmic audience and has resulted in the creation of many Websites and other Web manifestations discussed below. Each horse has a Web presence.

While one could detail the many mundane appearances of horses throughout *Lord* and Jackson's films, comparing and contrasting them, I will rather devote my attention to several interpersonal relationships between human, Hobbit, Elf, wizard and specific horses as examples of the different qualities of characterization represented by these functions. Human/Hobbit and horse relationships that stand in for those one could associate with normal functions are many in the books and films. This assertion can be somewhat controversial, depending on the belief system of individuals with regard to animal intelligence as ranking lower on a hierarchy of being (the sociological view prevalent in the preindustrial and industrialized world up through the mid-to-late twentieth century) or as simply of a different order — another "other" to add, especially to those of race and gender.[9] I will appeal to that referent, as it is relevant to the vast majority of both Tolkien's and Jackson's audiences. On the other hand, such works as Haraway's — as well as many less abstract scientific explorations of "animal intelligence" and activism of animal rights groups — have transformed the thinking along these lines of a significant social sector, especially in the industrialized world. So let me add that I sit somewhere in the middle of these extremes in my belief system — agreeing that horses and humans, as well as humans and some other animals, can share a special bond but not that they can communicate on the level that seems to be implied by Gandalf and Shadowfax's relationship in books and films and by Aragorn's relationship with Brego, one that was totally invented, or perhaps extrapolated, for the films. So the sympathy built up between the pony Bill and Samwise Gamgee, throughout *Fellowship*, is of that more mundane order — that humans and animals can establish a bond of sympathy. To a certain extent, this same perspective on human-horse relationships becomes part of the culture of Rohan in *Towers* but not the war technology of *Return*. In the latter, horses are not semi-sentient in either books or films. They are a technology of war and somewhat historically particular, a sort of shorthand to help audiences of both books and films get their bearings.

Although Sam and Bill the pony, who share a sympathetic relationship in the journey to the Mines of Moria, represent a non-fantastic, recognizable iconography, other examples of close bonds with horses in books and films do not. In an only more slightly fantastic sense, some of the bonds between Rohan's riders and their horses are of a comparable order and can be seen as representative of the types which develop between humans and their horses when the humans are intimately and consistently dependent on the horses for enhancing their quality of life. The ambiguity in Rohan is maintained, however, by a mythos of the Mearas. Felaróf is introduced only briefly in Tolkien's novels as the ancestor of Shadowfax, and Mearas are a special kind of horse. The liminal Mearas are referenced in the films in *TT* when Gandalf refers to

Shadowfax as "lord of all horses."[10] But Mearas become a full minor theme in Tolkien's books. The many scenes from the films that consist of long shots of Gandalf riding Shadowfax (well, with McKellen's stunt double riding Shadowfax) are an ambivalent substitute for Tolkien's narrative details. Of course these long camera shots feature the stunning landscapes of New Zealand still of interest to tourists But there are other interpersonal relationships between horse and human, Elf, wizard, and even, for a short periods, Hobbits. And each of these provides both obvious and subtle sociocultural cues about the characters.

Little if any explanation is given as to why those contemporary-with-the-main-narrative time stream — nonetheless high-quality in the hierarchy of horses with which we are mostly familiar — horses of Rohan are not all as seemingly liminal as Shadowfax. Examples abound in the books of Shadowfax's ability to communicate with these horses, but the only major scene which alludes to this quality of Shadowfax is in *TT* where Gandalf calls Shadowfax with a whistle and then returns bringing with him the Rohan horses Arod and Hasufel, which were loaned to Legolas the Elf and Aragorn the Man.[11] Shadowfax can communicate in some form with Gandalf and with other horses. Most humans and other sentient beings cannot do so in the films, despite the eagles' representation in the books where Gandalf relates a conversation with the eagle Gwaihir when describing his escape from Saruman in "The Council of Elrond." Gwaihir responds to his question: "How Far can you bear me?" with "Many leagues, ... but not to the ends of the earth. I was sent to bear tidings not burdens" (*Fellowship* 255). Then the eagle goes on to offer Shadowfax, Mearas of Rohan, as the answer to Gandalf's needs. Tolkien has established a lineage for Shadowfax more directly back to Felaróf— originally brought to Middle-earth from the mystical home of gods (Valinor)— a relationship not foregrounded in the films. But Shadowfax also functions as an element in the characterization of Gandalf, a liminal being, who forms a close personal bond with another liminal being, a Mearas.

While the difference between Shadowfax and other horses of Middle-earth is maintained in the films, it is extended to some level to include Brego, the horse that rescues Aragorn from his seeming death in *TT*. Brego was both such a surprise for Tolkien enthusiasts and such an icon of the fantastic for the more enthusiastic film viewers that he, like the otherwise insignificant Elf affectionately known as Figwit, has his own Web pages. But consider Brego's contribution to characterization of Aragorn in the films. He elevates the divine or liminal nature of Aragorn, as in the sense of "divine right of kings," to some degree as Shadowfax elevates that of Gandalf. He is a filmic "happy accident" establishing parallel powers for Aragorn in Jackson's films that just aren't there in the books. Jackson identifies another plot-driven function for Brego, in the Tolkien universe the name of the long-ago king who built the hall of Meduseld in Rohan. The battle of the wargs, which takes up so much narrative time and causes plot restructuring in the films, is both a vehicle for Jackson to display wargs and Orcs, humans and horses battling each other, and also a vehicle for Jackson to reintroduce the Elf Arwen, long-time love of Aragorn, to viewers. The rescue scene at the river is invented for the films, but it is not wholly unprecedented in the fantastic underpinnings of the books. It is an extension of concepts already in Tolkien's fiction — and also somewhat reinforces a reconstructed characterization for Aragorn that other critics have identified as more central to the films than the books. This leads us to the depiction of Rohan, referenced first in Tolkien's *Fellowship* but not until *TT* in Jackson's adaptation.

What of the many cultural referents reinforced by the horses in Tolkien? In the cultures of both Rohan and Minas Tirith, Jackson has again extended concepts in Tolkien's written work. Minas Tirith in *TT* and *ROTK* is not so centrally based on management of horses, although statues of them create a visual iconography, and the famous/infamous charge of Faramir in *ROTK* cements a technological level that includes horses. Rohan, on the other hand, is a horse culture and some scholars have used both the reference to historically horse-based cultural groups like the Anglo-Saxons, complete with many physical trappings like helmets and armor, to attempt a one-to-one correspondence between Rohan and one of Tolkien's areas of linguistic expertise — the language and culture of the primary surviving Anglo-Saxon text, *Beowulf*. This referentiality when examined closely in Tolkien — as is argued most convincingly by Shippey and in this volume with more detail by Drout in the context of films as well as written fiction — is only that. It is reference not reproduction.

In Tolkien's narrative, the horse culture of Rohan is incorporated into the iconography as well as into the socioeconomic sphere of Théoden King, Théodred, Éowyn and Éomer, the nobility of that culture. For example, while Tolkien mentions Celtic-type knotwork representations on the pillars of the golden hall, Meduseld, in *Towers* and also the pale blond youth riding a horse in a banner inside the hall, Jackson's technical team extends this iconography to many banners of horses, none of them with riders (although there is a tapestry with a horse rider in one scene), around the throne of Théoden. There are also crossed horse heads on outside roof beams of Meduseld and other buildings and horse heads on the arms of Théoden's throne, to name a few. They appear on helmets and on other horse gear. Some of this iconography is probably inspired by our increased knowledge of Anglo-Saxon culture in the early 20th and 21st century with the discovery of buried hoards of precious materials from Sutton Hoo and a few other archeological sites and the many decades of sophisticated research that has been done in the interim between Tolkien's writing of the books and the creation of the films. This perspective was suggested by Anglo-Saxon scholars. The decorations on buildings, weaponry, pillars, walls and even clothing incorporated in Jackson's films perhaps are more evocative of Anglo-Saxon culture than Tolkien intended, but they also bring to mind the Scythians[12] of the Northern European plains, a long-dead culture known only for its many horse-related artifacts found preserved in burial mounds in northeast Europe.

A quality of horse-sentient relationships possessed by Elves as well as Gandalf is also worth mentioning, as it posed certain technical problems for producers of the films. This quality is the ability of Elves to communicate like Gandalf with all horses so well that they did not use saddle or bridle. As verified in one of the "making of" films on the *ROTK-EE* (disk five) "liberty-trained horses" and unusually skilled riders were needed to create this visual effect of grace and transcendence for Legolas and Arwen — sole representations of the Elf-horse communication in the films — Gandalf, and to some extent Aragorn. Gandalf and the Elves in Tolkien's works did not use saddle and bridle to control the horses. Jackson preserves this effect.

But for my purposes, the significant adaptation in the films is Brego, the horse that creates a parallel liminality for Aragorn in the films to that of Gandalf in the novels. In some ways, the inclusion of Brego casts Aragorn's "divine right of kings" into a mold reminiscent of Gandalf as a higher order of being and, in the complexity of the visual experience for the audience, may even reduce Gandalf to the order of being of Aragorn. This is an ambivalence more tolerated, by modern audiences, than the concept that Gandalf is a real wizard with real transcendent powers originating in "another place." This particular difference between film and novel, one of character development, significantly changes the cinematic representation of liminality of a hierarchy which in Tolkien's legendarium/mythic superstructure is fixed but in Jackson's films is largely rendered irrelevant. Does the foregrounding of Aragorn as a warrior, king, liminal being, and partner with an Elf-maiden in a love story anchor Jackson's Middle-earth in a less hierarchical mythos? This is the question to which my answer would be an emphatic "Yes!" — an answer supported by the horses.

Notes

1. As co-producer Rick Porras notes: "When you read the Lord of the Rings, you know these horses are also characters. "Home of the Horselords" in "The Appendices, Part Five: War of the Rings," *ROTK-EE*.

246   II. Techniques of Character and Culture

2. In Hammond & Scull's chronology, part of their *Tolkien Companion and Guide*, describes Tolkien's work breaking horses for the cavalry in 1911.

3. The many individuals involved in training and recruiting horses and riders are described in a film entitled: "Home of the Horselords" in The Appendices, Part Six, *LOTR-EE*.

4. Tolkien refers to nostalgia for the pastoral in his *Letters*.

5. Tolkien talking about rural Hobbiton

6. In the Tolkien books, there is some description suggesting that the Nazgûl horses were sold to them by the Rohirrim and much is made the Rohirrim denials that these horses were given willingly. See *TT*.

7. In "The Council of Elrond," Gandalf relates this information when summarizing his conversation with Gwaihir. (*Fellowship* 255).

8. See The Horses of Middle-earth. http://www.tuckborough.net/horses.html. And Encyclopedia of Arda. http://www.glyphweb.com/arda/s/shadowfax.html

9. Works such as Haraway's *Simians Cyborgs and Women*, and the works of Gary Steiner question the Enlightenment understanding of the hierarchy of being and the cultural implications of that hierarchy. Haraway suggests that gender norms are infected with the misused hierarchy. There are websites devoted to sentience, sapience and animal rights all over the internet and too numerous to list.

10. Gandalf's explanation to Aragorn, Legolas and Gimli is "Shadowfax is the lord of all horses and he has been my friend through many adventures" (*TT-EE*), and Jane Abbott, the stunt rider for Arwen notes: "My horse was Dublin. "The Appendices, Part Five: War of the Rings," *ROTK-EE*.

11. In fact it would be impossible for me to even mention all the horses by name that ARE in both the books and films, but these have been cataloged in many places, and briefly in online in *The Thain's Book*, under "Horses of Middle-earth."

12. See *Oxford Illustrated Prehistory of Europe* under "Scythians." There are also many websites that picture their preserve-artifacts as well as imaginative representations in the plastic arts.

Works Cited

Bill, Cunliffe. *Oxford Illustrated Prehistory of Europe*. Oxford: Oxford University Press, 1994.

Carpenter, Humphrey. *The Letters of J.R.R. Tolkien*. Boston: Houghton Mifflin, 1981.

Encyclopedia of Arda. 1998,2001. http://www.glyphweb.com/arda/ (accessed July 11, 2010).

Hammond, Wayne, and Christina Scull. *J.R.R. Tolkien Artist and Illustrator*. First. Boston, Massachusetts: Houghton Mifflin Company, 2000.

_____. *J.R.R. Tolkien Companion and Guide*. Boston: Houghton Mifflin, 2006.

Haraway, Donna. *Simians, Cyborgs, and Women: The Reinvention of Nature*. New York: Rutledge, 1991.

Horses in World War I : History Learning Site. http://www.historylearningsite.co.uk/horses_in_world_war_one.htm (accessed July 9, 2010).

Jackson, Peter, Fran Walsh, and Philippa Boyens. *The Lord of the Rings: The Fellowship of the Ring*. DVD. Directed by Peter Jackson. Produced by Barrie Osborne. New Line Cinema, 2004.

_____, _____, and _____. *The Lord of the Rings: The Fellowship of the Ring*. DVD.

Directed by Peter Jackson. Produced by Barrie Osborne. New Line Cinema, 2001.
_____, _____, and _____. *The Lord of the Rings: The Return of the King.* DVD. Directed by Peter Jackson. Produced by Barrie Osborne. New Line Cinema, 2004.
_____, _____, and _____. *The Lord of the Rings: The Return of the King.* Directed by Peter Jackson. Produced by Barrie Osborne. New Line Cinema, 2003.
_____, _____, and _____. *The Lord of the Rings: The Two Towers.* DVD. Directed by Peter Jackson. Produced by Barrie Osborne. New Line Cinema, 2004.
_____, _____, and _____. *The Lord of the Rings: The Two Towers.* DVD. Directed by Peter Jackson. Produced by Barrie Osborne. New Line Cinema, 2002.
Shippey, T. A. *J.R.R. Tolkien: Author of the Century.* London: HarperCollins, 2000.
_____. *The Road to Middle Earth.* Boston: Houghton Mifflin, 1982.
*Spartacus Educational*http://www.spartacus.schoolnet.co.uk/. http://www.spartacus.schoolnet.co.uk/FWWhorses.htm (accessed July 09, 2010).
Steiner, Gary. *Anthropocentrism and its discontents : the moral status of animals in the history of Western philosophy.* Pittsburgh: U of Pittsburgh Press, 2005.
The Thain's Book: Encyclopedia of Middle-earth and Númenor. Horses of Middle-earth. 2003–2010. http://www.tuckborough.net/horses.html (accessed July 11, 2010).
Tolkien, J.R.R. *History of Middle Earth.* Edited by Christopher Tolkien. Boston: Houghton Mifflin, 1985.
_____. *The Annotated Hobbit.* Edited by Douglas A. Anderson. Boston: The Annotated Hobbit, 2002.
_____. *The Fellowship of the Rings.* Boston: Houghton Mifflin, 11994 (1955).
_____. *The Hobbit, or There and Back Again.* London: Unwin Paperbacks, 1981.
_____. *The Return of the King.* Boston: Houghton Mifflin, 1994 (1955).
_____. *The Silmarillion.* Edited by Christopher Tolkien. Boston: Houghton Mifflin, 2001.
_____. *The Two Towers.* Boston: Houghton Mifflin, 1994(1955).

The Rohirrim, the Anglo-Saxons, and the Problem of Appendix F
Ambiguity, Analogy and Reference in Tolkien's Books and Jackson's Films

MICHAEL D.C. DROUT

In Appendix F, section II, "On Translation," J.R.R. Tolkien develops the conceit that *The Lord of the Rings* is a translation from the Red Book of Westmarch: "In presenting the matter of the Red Book, as a history for people of today to read, the whole of the linguistic setting has been translated as far as possible into terms of our own time" (*The Return of the King*, Appendix F, ii, 411). The Common Speech, or Westron, tongue of Middle-earth is rendered as English and therefore "the mannish languages that were related to the Westron" are turned into "forms related to English" (*Return*, Appendix F, ii, 414). Thus the language of the Rohirrim was translated into Old English and "the still more northerly language of Dale" given in Old Norse forms (*Return*, Appendix F, ii, 415). But, Tolkien asserts, linguistic correspondence should not be taken as cultural correspondence: "This linguistic procedure does not imply that the Rohirrim closely resembled the ancient English otherwise, in culture or art, in weapons or modes of warfare, except in a general way due to their circumstances: a simpler and more primitive people living in contact with a higher and more venerable culture, and occupying lands that had once been part of its domain" (*Return*, Appendix F, 414 n. 1). Similarly, in Letter 211, Tolkien writes that "the Rohirrim were not 'mediaeval,' in our sense"

(280–81).¹ And in an unsent response to the American poet and translator Burton Raffel, Tolkien writes that "no one would learn anything valid about the 'Anglo-Saxons' from any of my lore, not even that concerning the Rohirrim; I never intended that they should."²

These dicta have long been a problem for Tolkien studies. On the one hand, we have Tolkien's explicit disavowal of the equivalence of the Rohirrim and the Anglo-Saxons. On the other hand, the Rohirrim undeniably speak Anglo-Saxon,³ and specifically the Mercian dialect of Anglo-Saxon.⁴ Not only are characters and places named in Anglo-Saxon, but also characters speak untranslated Old English — for example "Wes thu hal" and "fer thu hal" ("be you well" and "fare you well"). Lines from the famous Old English poem *The Wanderer* are the source of the "Where is the horse? Where is the rider?" poem that Aragorn "translates" from the language of the Riders to the Common Speech (*Towers*, III, vi, 112).⁵ The Rohirrim bury their dead in barrows, pass mead-cups at events of significance and recite alliterative poetry (in flawless Anglo-Saxon meter). As Tom Shippey notes, in saying that the Rohirrim are not in any way Anglo-Saxon except in language, "Tolkien was stretching the truth a long way ... to say the least!"(*Road* 94).

The compositional history of *The Lord of the Rings* also does not suggest that Tolkien followed the schema in Appendix F, at least in the earlier stages of composition. The Rohirrim first enter Tolkien's first drafts of *Lord* as the "Horse-kings," who were in the service of Sauron; but at this first stage of the development of the story they are not Anglo-Saxon (*Shadow* 422 and see 434 n. 22). The Old English name "Riddermark" first appears in a revised draft of "The Council of Elrond," at almost the same time that "Orthanc" is used to describe Saruman's tower — formerly "Irongarth" (*Treason* 130–35) — and it may be at this stage of revision that Tolkien first thought to use Old English as the language of Rohan.⁶ Reasonably soon thereafter in the process of composition the Rohirrim start to become more Anglo-Saxon. In a sketch at the beginning of the draft of the chapter "The Riders of Rohan," Tolkien begins with the Rohiroth being "relations of the Woodmen and Beornings, old Men of the North. But they speak Gnomish — tongue of Númenor and Ondo,⁷ as well as [?common] tongue." However, two lines later he begins making the Riders onomastically Anglo-Saxon, with a list of possible names such as Marhad, Marnath, Marhelm, Marhun, Marhyse, and Marulf, all built on the Old English word "mearh" ("horse") or its Gothic cognate, "mar."⁸ He then writes, "Éowyn Elfsheen daughter of Éomund" (*Treason* 390). In the first draft of the chapter, the place name of the Entwade River is used (*Treason* 392), soon followed by the name Éomer son of Éomund.⁹ At this point, Tolkien appears to have settled on the device of making the Riders speakers of Anglo-Saxon (*Treason* 393), because there is a gradual increase, followed by an explosion, of Anglo-Saxon words into the text as if, having decided to employ Old English, Tolkien reveled in the possibilities of the many words he could use.

Tom Shippey has long held that "nothing could be more provocative to Tolkien than a word without a referent," and lists *emnet* as one of those words (*Road to Middle-earth* 181). This is a word that survives as a place-name in Norwich whose antecedent would be reconstructed as *emnæ?*, a steppe or prairie (*Road to Middle-earth* 100). We see here some additional support for Shippey's interpretation: immediately after making the decision to have the Riders speak Anglo-Saxon, Tolkien begins to put Old English words into the text, beginning with a word that is a matter of reconstruction and interpretation (*Treason* 398). And indeed we find that *éored* enters the text soon afterwards (*Treason* 399). This word is a problem in the Old English poem *Maxims I*, where the manuscript reads "Eorl sceal on eos boge, worod sceal getrume ridan" (lines 62–63a).[10] This reading in itself makes little sense: "An earl should go on the back of a war-horse, an infantry guard must ride as a group." "Infantry" (*worod*) would obviously not be riding (*ridan*), so scholars emend *worod* to *eorod* (mounted troop), and in doing so assume that they, as philologists, know more than the scribe of the passage (Shippey, *Road to Middle-earth* 16, 96). A bit later in the manuscript, in "The King of the Golden Hall," we find another Anglo-Saxon word that is linked to a crux in Old English poetry: *ides*, which is the source of the name of Théoden's daughter Idis (*Treason* 447). *Ides* is a crux because, although the word — which means "maiden" — has basically positive connotations, it is applied to Grendel's mother in line 1259 of *Beowulf* (*ides aglæcwif,* "monster-woman maiden?").[11] Furthermore, it is part of a problematic and extremely interesting phrase, *ides ælfscinu*, in the poem *Judith*. What "elf-shining" means in this context is a disputed question in Anglo-Saxon studies,[12] and it is a question that interested Tolkien, as we know from his poem *Ides Ælfscyne*, written in Old English and originally published in *Songs for the Philologists*.[13] Thus we see Tolkien, once he has decided to use Anglo-Saxon, immediately using words which have philological significance.

In the draft of "The Riders of Rohan," the majority of the words that first enter the text are place names (*Eastemnet, Westemnet, Entwade*) and personal names (*Eomer, Théoden, Thengel, Eothain*). Tolkien also explored using different variants for important places, for instance writing *Meodarn, Meduarn, Winseld* in *Eodor* for what eventually became *Meduseld* in *Eodoras* (*Treason* 402). But it is in the draft of "The King of the Golden Hall" that Tolkien uses a substantial number of Anglo-Saxon words, including passages of Old

English much longer than those he uses in the published version. An example is when the guardsmen at the Golden Hall challenge Gandalf, Aragorn, Legolas and Gimli thus:

> Hwæt sindon ge, lathe othethe leofe, the thus seldlice gewerede ridan cwoman to thisse burge gatum? No her inn gan moton net wædla ne wæpned mon, nefne we his naman witen. Nu ge feorran-cumene gecythath us on ofste: hu hatton ge? hwæt sindon eower ærende to Théoden urum hlaforde?
>
> Stay, strangers unknown! Who are ye, friends or foes, that have come thus strangely clad riding to the gates of this town? None may enter here, neither beggarman nor warrior, if we know not his name. Now, ye comers from afar, declare to us in haste: what are ye called? What is your errand to Théoden our lord? (*Treason* 449 n. 5, translation by Christopher Tolkien).

Anglo-Saxon enters not only into the text of the Rohan chapters but also into the larger story. In plot notes titled by Christopher Tolkien "The Story Forseen from Fangorn," Tolkien discusses the upcoming war between Mordor and the West, noting that "the whole of Rhûn the Great, the endless East, is in motion" and that from the South come the "fierce dark men of the South, the Haradwaith (Harwan Silharrows Men of Sunharrowland Men of Harrowland)" (*Treason* 435). "Silharrows" seems to be a variation on "Sigelhearwan," an Anglo-Saxon word that Tolkien investigated in a two-part essay published in 1932 and 1934.[14] "Sigelhearwan" is used in Anglo-Saxon literature to translate the Latin Æthiops (Ethiopians), and Tolkien appears here to be adapting it to describe the "fierce dark men of the South." In this passage, Tolkien puts the words into the mouth of Théoden, which would explain the use of Anglo-Saxon; but it also appears that at this point he had a idea that the name of the people who eventually became called the Haradrim would be an Old English word.

We see, therefore, that there is a great deal more Old English in the drafts edited by Christopher Tolkien in *Treason* even than there is in the published text of *Towers*. It is difficult to square this textual history with the assertion that the Rohirrim speak Old English mainly to illustrate a relationship between the Common Speech and the language of the Riddermark.

Similarly, the decision by Tolkien to render the names of dwellers in the north of Middle-earth — the Dwarves, Men of Dale and Beornings — appears to have been forced by his original use of Old Norse names in *The Hobbit*. Tolkien took the names of most of the Dwarves and of Gandalf[15] from the "Dvergatal," a list of Dwarf names included (but often thought to be an interpolation) in the Old Norse poem *Völuspá*. "I don't much approve of *The Hobbit* myself," wrote Tolkien to a friend in 1937, "preferring my own mythology (which is just touched on) with its consistent nomenclature ... and organized history, to this rabble of Eddaic-named Dwarves out of Völuspá, newfangled hobbits and gollums (invented in an idle hour) and Anglo-Saxon runes" (*Shadow* 7). But once the Dwarf names were fixed by the publication of *The Hobbit*, Tolkien was forced to incorporate them into the long-promised sequel.

As early as 1938, however, he seems to have been some way along to formulating the Appendix F schema. Tolkien notes in Letter 25 that the Dwarves "have been given Scandinavian names, it is true; but that is an editorial concession. Too many names in the tongues proper to the period might have been alarming." Tolkien followed this editorial procedure because "dwarvish was both complicated and cacophonous. Even early elvish philologists avoided it, and Dwarves were obliged to use other languages, except in entirely private conversations." If we did not have Appendix F, it still might be possible to determine from this statement that the Dwarves had secret names in Dwarvish and used other names in conversation, but the conceit of these names being *translated* into Old Norse does not yet exist.

"The language of hobbits was remarkably like English, as one would expect" (30–32), Tolkien writes. And from this we can reconstruct the schema at this time: Hobbits spoke something remarkably like English; Dwarves spoke another language entirely, so that their names were translated into the language of the Hobbits in Middle-earth. The specific reason that Tolkien used Old Norse for these names is not yet explained. Thus at this stage (1938), Tolkien had not yet adopted the conceit that the Common Speech itself needed extensive translation, and so the equivalence of Old Norse with "northern" speech in Middle-earth and Anglo-Saxon with the tongue of Rohan was yet to be developed, as Rohan would not be conceived in any detail until at least 1942 (*Treason* 1). As his tale grew in the telling, so did his linguistic plan. When Tolkien did recognized that he could interpret his own work (and, presumably, develop and revise *Lord* in line with the conceit) is not obvious from the *History of the Lord of the Rings* volumes. Thus we can conclude that, in terms of composition and obvious interpretation, Tolkien's assertion in Appendix F is to a very significant degree a post hoc rationalization. However, it is a post hoc rationalization with an important kernel of truth.

Although the Rohirrim speak Anglo-Saxon, and their culture resembles that of the Anglo-Saxons "down to minute details" (Shippey, *Author* 117), not everything is an exact match. First, there is the well-remarked point that the Anglo-Saxons avoided fighting on horseback (the poem *The Battle of Maldon* depicts the warriors as sending their horses away before the battle), while the Rohirrim are the "Horse-kings" or "Horse-lords" (Shippey, *Author* 126–27). Tolkien describes the Riders of Rohan thus: "They are proud and willful but they are true-hearted, generous in thought and deed; bold but not cruel; wise but unlearned; writing no books but singing many songs, after the matter of the children of Men before the Dark Years" (*Towers*, III, ii, 33). This cannot be a description of the historical Anglo-Saxons, who, at least after their conversion to Christianity, wrote many books (although they still sang many songs) and cannot fairly be described as "unlearned."

One answer to this problem was devised by Shippey: Tolkien's Rohirrim were Anglo-Saxons before they came to England, the Anglo-Saxons of song and legend, depicted in *Beowulf* (*Road* 94). Or perhaps they are the ancestors of the Anglo-Saxons, Gothic cavalry on the plains of Europe (Shippey *Road* 97–98).[16] This is certainly a plausible interpretation, particularly when we note that in his translation of line 225 of *Beowulf*[17] Tolkien rendered the lemma "Wedera leoda" (Land of the Weders) as "Gothland" (*Monsters and Critics* 63), suggesting a connection between the Goths and the Anglo-Saxons. But there are some philological problems with this approach, the most significant being that the ancestors of the Anglo-Saxons, when they were living on the Continent before the migration, would not have spoken Anglo-Saxon in the forms that Tolkien uses in *Lord*. It would have been a fascinating exercise if Tolkien had applied a few sets of sound changes to shift the speech of the Rohirrim to postulated pre-migration forms. Tolkien certainly had the philological skill to do so, but he did not do this and instead, probably because he loved the West Midland speech of Warwickshire,[18] converted West Saxon words to Mercian forms. The Rohirrim therefore cannot be the ancestors of the Anglo-Saxons linguistically, and they cannot be the Anglo-Saxons themselves culturally, though they speak Old English and there are many cultural similarities.

The relationship between the Rohirrim and the Anglo-Saxons, therefore, is asymmetric. Knowing about the Anglo-Saxons can tell us something about the Rohirrim, but knowing about the Rohirrim does not tell us much about the Anglo-Saxons. Although knowing about the Rohirrim may also tell us something about what Tolkien thought about the Anglo-Saxons — for instance, their possible ancestral relationship to the Goths,[19] and this *is* matter of significant interest in the history of medieval studies — it is not the same thing as learning about the Anglo-Saxons themselves through *The Lord of the Rings*. However, despite these problems, and despite Tolkien's protestations in Appendix F, a great many readers (critics and others) are influenced in their understanding of the Anglo-Saxons by the Rohirrim: once the connection is made, however subtly, it cannot but help influence the interpretation.

Peter Jackson's film version of *LOTR* complicates further the problem of seeing the Anglo-Saxons in and through the Rohirrim and vice versa, but this is not entirely due to Jackson's directorial decisions. The power of visual representation has created a closer connection between the Rohirrim and the Anglo-Saxons than is present in Tolkien's original text.[20] There is a certain ambiguity inherent in even the most detailed description of face or scene or landscape that is impossible to maintain in a work of visual culture. For example, Aragorn's battle standard is described thus: "there flowered a White Tree, and that was for Gondor; but Seven Stars were about it, and a high crown above it, the signs of Elendil that no lord had borne for years beyond count. And the stars flamed in the sunlight, for they were wrought of gems by Arwen daughter of Elrond; and the crown was bright in the morning, for it was wrought of mithril and gold" (*Return*, III, vi, 123). When converting this description to a design for a prop, a director cannot retain the ambiguity of the stars flaming in the sunlight. They may be wrought of gems, but the director must choose *which* gems (which colors, what kind of faceting, etc.) and arrange them in some way. Likewise, there are many, many ways to imagine trees: a reader can hold many different trees in the mind's eye and perhaps may not even settle on one single, constant image. But a film requires one particular type of tree (even if the original choice of tree is not particularly circumscribed), one kind of stylization, one set of colors. Thus even a director who deliberately sets out to present a literal interpretation of a work of prose fiction will end up changing an important aesthetic effect by reducing or eliminating the ambiguity inherent in prose that is used to describe sensory data.

Prose also has the capability of communicating the ideas of "immeasurable" or "impossible to describe" or "the most beautiful" or "the most terrifying thing in the world." These concepts are impossible to present in film because once depicted, no actual image can be "immeasurable" or "impossible to describe." For example, Arwen is described as being so beautiful that "such a loveliness in living thing Frodo had never seen before nor imagined in his mind" (*Fellowship*, II, i, 239), a neat rhetorical trick, but one impossible to capture in film where a particular actress must be chosen to be the most beautiful of all living beings, "in whom it was said that the likeness of Lúthien had come on earth again." Even the specific description of Arwen — "young she was, and yet not so. The braids of her dark hair were touched by no frost; her white arms and clear face were flawless and smooth, and light of stars was in her bright eyes, grey as a cloudless night" (*Fellowship*, II, i, 239) — is ambiguous from the beginning ("young ... and yet not so"). All of that ambiguity is lost once Arwen is represented by a mortal actress, no matter how much craftsmanship is lavished on prosthetic ears, costume and makeup.

This reduction of ambiguity is a inescapable property of the change from prose to visual culture, and it fundamentally changes the ways the work can be understood. Aspects of the narrative that are presented ambiguously — for example, Galadriel "seeming now tall beyond measurement, and beautiful beyond enduring" (*Fellowship*, II, viii, 381), or Théoden calling in a voice "more clear than any there had ever heard a mortal man achieve before" (*Return*, V, vi, 112) — must be portrayed in concrete terms. However tall the director chooses to depict Galadriel, it will not be beyond measurement; however clear the voice of Théoden, there may be some voices, in the experience or imagination of the audience, that are more clear. This forced move, the reduction of ambiguity to concreteness, may be one of the many reasons that so many critics feel that the films are inferior to the books[21]: one of Tolkien's aesthetic effects is the superlative nature of descriptions at key moments — tall beyond measurement, more clear than mortals have heard. The inability of a film to live up to these descriptions indicates a fundamental aesthetic difference between prose and film, not (necessarily) a failure on the part of director or actor or script.[22]

The reduction of ambiguity forced by the visual medium of film interacts with the asymmetry of the relationship of Rohirrim to the Anglo-Saxons in the film portrayal of the Riders of Rohan. The costumes, props, sets and script of the film all combine to make the Rohirrim far *more* Anglo-Saxon than does the text of *Lord*, and the two phenomena (disambiguation and asymmetry) in places reinforce each other. In the prose *Towers,* the Riders, when they first appear in "The Riders of Rohan" chapter, are not visually Anglo-Saxon in their dress or armaments, at least in any particular sense (their long, "flaxen-pale" hair in braids is more continental Gothic than Anglo-Saxon, as is the horse-tail crest on Éomer's helmet). The first Anglo-Saxon word in the chapter is the name of Eorl the Young said by Aragorn; the first Old English word spoken is Éomer son of Éomund's name and the first non-name in Anglo-Saxon is *éored*, given in italics and not translated but easily interpretable from the context (*Towers*, III, ii, 33–37).

The first mentions of material culture are in Legolas' description of Edoras (an Old English word meaning "the courts"), when Tolkien adopts part of the description of the great hall, Heorot, noting that the hall is thatched with gold and "the light of it shines far over the land." The Anglo-Saxon source is line 311 of *Beowulf*: "lixte se leoma ofer land fela,"[23] which can be translated as "the light shines over many lands" and which is quoted by Tolkien in "*Beowulf*: The Monsters and the Critics" (33). Tolkien then describes the grave mounds covered with the flower *simbelmynë*, translating this word as "Evermind" (*Towers*, III, vi, 115). With the adapted lines from *The Wanderer* and the interchange with the door wardens that is based on *Beowulf*, the Anglo-Saxonization of the Rohirrim is complete.[24]

When Aragorn, Legolas, Gimli and Gandalf enter Meduseld, the reader encounters more of the material culture of Rohan: a roof upheld by mighty pillars, these richly carved and hung with tapestries. Although this description could certainly be of an Anglo-Saxon hall, in literary terms it is very obviously taken from William Morris' *The House of the Wolfings*, even down to specific details and words (14)[25]:

> As to the house within, two rows of pillars went down it endlong, fashioned of the mightiest trees that might be found, and each one fairly wrought with base and chapiter, and wreaths and knots, and fighting men and dragons; so that it was like a church of later days that has a nave and aisles: windows there were above the aisles, and a passage underneath the said windows in their roofs. In the aisles there were the sleeping-places of the Folk, and down the nave under the crown of the roof were three hearths for the fires, and above each hearth a luffer or smoke-bearer to draw the smoke up when the fires were lighted. For sooth on a bright winter afternoon it was strange to see three columns of smoke going wavering up to the dimness of the mighty roof, and one maybe smitten athwart by the sunbeams.

Compare this passage with Tolkien's description of the interior of the Golden Hall:

> The hall was long and wide and filled with shadows and half lights; mighty pillars upheld its lofty roof. But here and there bright sunbeams fell in glimmering shafts from the eastern windows, high under the deep eaves. Through the louver in the roof, above the thin wisps of issuing smoke, the sky showed pale and blue. As their eyes changed, the travelers perceived that the floor was paved with stones of many hues; branching runes and strange devices intertwined beneath their feet. They saw now that the pillars were richly carved, gleaming dully with gold and half-seen colors. Many woven cloths were hung upon the walls, and over their wide spaces marched figures of ancient legend, some dim with years, some darkling in the shade. But upon one form the sunlight fell: a young man upon a white horse. He was blowing a great horn, and his yellow hair was flying in the wind. The horse's head was lifted, and its nostrils were wide and red as it neighed, smelling battle afar. Foaming water, green and white, rushed and curled about its knees....
> Now the four companions went forward, past the clear wood-fire burning upon the long hearth in the midst of the hall. Then they halted. At the far end of the house, beyond the hearth and facing north towards the doors, was a dais with three steps; and in the middle of the dais was a great gilded chair (*Towers*, III, vi, 116).

The images are not precisely the same, but they are similar enough to see the influence of Morris' Wolfings upon Tolkien's description of Meduseld. Morris' Wolfings are not Anglo-Saxons, and so here we have in Tolkien — if only through literary reference — a brief deviation, perhaps, from the unequivocal Anglo-Saxonism of the previous few pages. The subtle invocation of Morris makes the equivalence of the Rohirrim with the Anglo-Saxons at least slightly ambiguous here.

Contrast the way the culture of the Riders of Rohan is introduced in Jackson's adaptation. The first appearance of Rohan is in scene six of *The Two Towers*, "The Burning of the Westfold," but the people in the scene are merely generic medieval peasants and the architecture (though later we will see that it has some affinity with the more elaborate Edoras sets) is unremarkable. The only hint of Anglo-Saxon is the name of the male child, Éothain, said by his mother. As this is obviously a name and used only once, viewers will not notice anything particularly Anglo-Saxon about the scene. In scene seven, "Massacre at the Ford of Isen," we get glimpses of helmets that are like the once recovered from the Anglo-Saxon ship burial at Sutton Hoo (discussed in more detail below). However, the helmets are seen only very briefly and Éomer, the main focus of the scene, does not wear a helmet for any close-ups. In any event, "Massacre at the Ford of Isen" is only part of the extended DVD version of *LOTR* and was not shown in the movie theaters.

Scene eight, "The Banishment of Éomer," is the first to give viewers detailed examples of Anglo-Saxon material culture. The first significant image is that of the carved pillars at Meduseld. These are decorated with an elaborate zoomorphic interlace, which calls to mind either Anglo-Saxon or Celtic (but not continental Germanic or Gothic) designs. It is at this point most viewers will begin to make a connection to Anglo-Saxon England, though the interlace invokes as much the generic "North" as it does the particular culture of England before the Conquest. In fact, even though there is action within Meduseld in scene eight, the material culture is not clearly visible (beyond the pillars) to further disambiguate the visual reference. It is not until scene eleven, "The Riders of Rohan," that viewers see Éomer wearing what is clearly a variant of the Sutton Hoo helmet, the single most iconic image of Anglo-Saxon culture. Éomer's helmet has a horse-head crest as a nosepiece whereas the Sutton Hoo helmet is decorated with boars, but the appearances of both helmets are extremely similar. It is at this point that the Rohirrim become Anglo-Saxon and the ambiguous notes of culture that have previously been free to be interpreted as "Northern" or "barbaric" are now fixed as Anglo-Saxon (even though there are variations). It is useful to contrast the close-up of Éomer in the helmet with another scene, later in the film, where an Easterling warrior wearing a face-covering helmet is also shown. This latter image communicates cultural tropes of veiling and Orientalism, with the Easterling's lower face hidden not only by the helmet itself but also by a mask worn beneath the steel. Éomer's helm, in contrast, displays most of his face between the cheek-guards. The "barbarian" face is less threatening and more open than that of the "oriental."

After the introduction of the iconic image of the adaptation of the Sutton Hoo helmet, the imagery of the film becomes much more Anglo-Saxon. Scene twenty-one, "The Funeral of Theodred," though not part of the theatrical release, includes Éowyn singing a dirge in passable Anglo-Saxon. The funeral itself is Anglo-Saxon but not Beowulfian: riders stand silently as the body is interred, as if for a Christian funeral, and there is no pyre or sacrifice of treasure or the circling of riders around the barrow, as there is in Tolkien's depiction of Théoden's funeral in *The Return of the King* (*RK*, VI, vi, 254–55). The next scene, number 22, "Symbelmynë on the Burial Mounds," depicts Théoden at the barrow of his son, invoking to at least some degree the Anglo-Saxons.

In the commentary on the extended edition DVD of *TT-EE*, Jackson and the designers of the costumes, sets and props comment that they believed Rohan, for Tolkien, fulfilled the role of a mythology for England. Jackson states that he envisioned the culture of the Rohirrim as "Norse, Scandinavia, Northern Europe civilizations." Designers thought of the Rohirrim as "Vikings of the Plains," a less specific vision than Anglo-Saxons. However, the designers (Allan Lee and John Howe) then discuss the ways that they wanted the material culture of Rohan to be consistent with Anglo-Saxon archeology and to specifically invoke the context of Sutton Hoo. Théoden's helmet "feels like it could go in an exhibit with the work of Sutton Hoo and wouldn't be out of place." Thus we see again the same disambiguating move, from generic Northern culture equally well (or poorly) described by the adjectives "Norse," "Scandinavian" and "Celtic," to a much more specific Anglo-Saxon culture invoked through the iconic image of the Sutton Hoo helmet.

Such is the power of a visual icon that once Jackson has presented the image of the helmet the culture of Rohan is no longer of indefinite (if Northern) affiliation but is instead connected to that of Anglo-Saxon England. Similarly, once Tolkien made the decision to have his Rohirrim speak Anglo-Saxon, they became linked to the Anglo-Saxons (despite his protestations in Appendix F). My point is not to go heedlessly down the path of "The Death of the Author"[26] and ignore Tolkien's or Jackson's intentions, but instead to point out that certain imagery, be it linguistic or visual, is so powerful that it can override the author's intended ambiguity and force a depiction that is meant to be individual, even unique, into a cultural pigeonhole. This effect occurs differently in different media, with film being more susceptible to disambiguation than prose, but it happens as soon as things within the text refer in a one-to-one correspondence with things outside the text.

Tolkien could avoid using direct similes in his fiction. He never explicitly says in *Lord* that the Númenóreans are like Egyptians in, for example, their fondness for monumental building in stone. Within the circumscribed bounds of the story this is not problematic. But once the reader makes an analogy to the Egyptians, some of the individuality of the Númenóreans is lost, just as some of the specific individuality of the Riders of Rohan is lost if they are analogized to Anglo-Saxons. This analogizing does not occur consciously for every reader: those unaware of Anglo-Saxon material culture and who do not recognize Old English, for example, are not influenced by the extra-textual reference in the same way as those who do recognize the allusions and influences. But, conscious of the references or not, the reader is caught up in the web of words (and the web of images), and that web is made up of links between words and words and between words and ideas — links that influence reading and interpretation even when they are not consciously recognized. For example, a viewer might not directly recognize the reference to the Sutton Hoo helmet, but the contrasting iconography of Éomer's helm with that of the Easterling taps into a set of conventions and ideas about West versus East, Northern versus "Oriental." Tolkien's Middle-earth is the richest and most complex fantasy world ever constructed; but because it must be encountered through language (and, in film, through imagery) it is not self-contained, and it participates in the real world — just as its author intended, to one degree or another. Thus authorial ambiguity becomes reduced to analogy even without the further disambiguation of visual culture.

This same process occurs when critics read the Rohirrim in light of the Anglo-Saxons or teachers use *Lord* to spark interest in Anglo-Saxon culture among their students. The free play of the text in the individual mind is limited, the range of possible interpretations narrowed and the possibly insightful "strong misreadings"[27] partially eliminated when the text is matched specifically to something outside the text. No longer can a pit be immeasurably deep or a voice more clear or a ring more perfect than all others; visual representations and critical interpretations move ideas constructed in prose from forms to shadows. In a sense, it is not possible to read without making many similar moves, circumscribing the immeasurable, converting a multivalent idea into a single image. Our own personal images limit texts: if I see the hythe in Lothlórien one way, I cannot see it another, but only at that particular time. We can, in reading a text, change our minds, reread the description and reconsider our earlier perception, see something in nature that replaces a preexisting conception. Such readjustment is much harder to do when a large and detailed equation of Middle-earth to a specific historical culture has been established, and since so much of Tolkien's aesthetic effect is based on the artful use of ambiguity (immeasurable, more clear, and others), the connection of the Rohirrim to the Anglo-Saxons, the depiction of landscape or character or material object, lessens a reader's aesthetic appreciation of Tolkien's work. Making connections has its own reward: we understand more of Tolkien's work when we read the Old English speech of the Rohirrim and understand the meanings of their names, and there is additional pleasure, both intellectual *and* aesthetic, in recognizing allusions, references and sources. But we should not forget the price we pay for linking Middle-earth and England, and at times we may want to mitigate the shaping effect of the correspondences between what is in the text and what we bring from outside. Likewise, we can step away from the films and return to the text to recapture, albeit in a form forever changed, our pre-film and pre-visual imaginative engagement with the text. Therefore we might, with profit, reread Appendix F, not as a discussion-ending dictum, but as a gentle nudge back towards the freer play of imagination, personal interpretation and invention that is part of the aesthetic effect of not only Tolkien's work but all great prose fiction.

Notes

1. Here Tolkien is directly addressing a question by Rhona Beare about the style of dress of particular peoples of Middle-earth, but note that if the Rohirrim are not "mediaeval" then they cannot be Anglo-Saxon, since the Anglo-Saxons were most definitely medieval.

2. MS, Oxford, Bodleian Library, Tolkien A 30/1 f. 121. Quoted in Stuart D. Lee and Elizabeth Solopova, *The Keys of Middle-earth*, 2005 (201–2), and quoted at greater length and discussed further in Stuart D. Lee, "J.R.R. Tolkien and *The Wanderer*: From Edition to Application," 2009 (189–211 at 204–205).

3. John Tinkler, "Old English in Rohan." In *Tolkien and the Critics*. ed. Isaacs and Zimbardo. (Notre Dame: University of Notre Dame Press, 1968), 164–69.

4. T.A. Shippey, *The Road to Middle-earth* (London: Allen and Unwin, 1982), 94. See also *Letters* 65, where Tolkien says that he is tempted to speak only "Old Mercian."

5. For more detailed discussion see Michael D.C. Drout, "Transformation," 2004: ME 101, 1–22, and http://www.literaturecompass.com/viewpoint.asp?section=1&ref=437

6. For the entry of Anglo-Saxon into *The Hobbit*, see Anderson, "R.W. Chambers" (2006), 137–47, and John D. Rateliff, ed., *History* (2007), 228–92.

7. This name would eventually become Gondor.

8. See *Unfinished Tales* (311) West Saxon forms in Old English have been subject to "breaking," in which "a" is "broken" to form the diphthong "ea." The West Saxon word for horse is "mearh"; the Mercian form would be "mar." Similarly, the West Saxon spelling for the Mercian forms "Saruman" and "Arkenstone" would be "Searuman," (crafty man) and "Eorclan-stan" (precious stone).

9. Christopher Tolkien notes that Éomer's name is at this stage of composition unaccented.

10. Old English text from Krapp and Dobbie, eds. *The Exeter Book*, vol 3 (1936). Translations are my own.

11. Old English text from Fr. Klaeber, *Beowulf and the Fight at Finnsburg* 3rd ed. (Lexington, MA: D.C. Heath, 1950).
12. For the current state of the question of the meaning of ælfscyne, see Alaric Hall, *Elves in Anglo-Saxon England* (2007), 88–95.
13. Printed and translated by Shippey in *Road*, 229–30.
14. J.R.R. Tolkien, "Sigelwara": Part 1 (1932), 183–96; "Sigelwara": Part 2 (1934), 95–111.
15. In the first drafts of *The Hobbit*, Gandalf is the name of the head Dwarf, who will later be named Thorin Oakenshield. The wizard's name is not Gandalf, but Bladorthin.
16. For further discussion of the connection between the Rohirrim and the Goths, see Drout "A Mythology for Anglo-Saxon England," ed. Chance (2004), 335–62.
17. Printed in the essay "On Translating *Beowulf*," which was originally published as "Prefatory Remarks on Prose Translation of 'Beowulf'" as part of John R. Clark Hall's revised edition of C.L. Wrenn's *Beowulf and the Finnesburg Fragment: A Translation into Modern English Prose*.
18. See Letter 163, where Tolkien writes "I am a West-midlander by blood (and took to early west-midland Middle English as a known tongue as soon as I set eyes on it)" (*Letters* 213).
19. See Shippey, "Goths and Huns," in *The Medieval Legacy*, ed. Haarder, et. al. (1982), and Drout, "Mythology."
20. My argument here is similar but not identical to that made by Tolkien in his section on Fantasy in *On Fairy-stories*, though Tolkien is making a distinction between drama and literature. Tolkien notes that "Men dressed up as talking animals may achieve buffoonery or mimicry, but they do not achieve Fantasy" (61), and this is an important critique, though perhaps requiring modification, as special effects have become more and more capable of fooling the eye and mind.
21. It is difficult to disentangle how much the negative reaction by Tolkien scholars to Jackson's films is based on actual missteps in the films and how much is motivated by the inescapable process of disambiguation. For examples see many of the essays in Croft's *Tolkien on Film*, 2004. No actress could fit the mental image of Arwen, as inchoate as it is, as created by Tolkien's prose.
22. At some points the films avoid the problem by substituting an entirely different special effect: Galadriel does not grow tall but instead enters into the visual context that elsewhere indicates the wraith world. At other times it seems as if the director was very aware that once an image was captured on film the underlying idea would be less terrifying. Thus the shot of Barad-dûr that travels slowly along a massive tower only to pan back and show that the tower is only one small excrescence on the even vaster main body of the Dark Tower seems an attempt to counter the inevitable disappointment of the audience when something described as "towers and battlements, tall as hills, founded upon a mighty mountain-throne above immeasurable pits; great courts and dungeons, eyeless prisons sheer as cliffs, and gaping gates of steel and adamant" (*Return*, VI, iii, 224) has to be made into an image that can be contrasted with other images (perceived and imagined) and is therefore not immeasurable.
23. Text from Fr. Klaeber, ed., *Beowulf*, 1950.
24. For discussion see Shippey, who notes that "The King of the Golden Hall" is "straightforwardly calqued on *Beowulf*" (*Road* 94–98).
25. Morris calls his Wolfings "Folk of the Markmen." In a forthcoming essay I

discuss the extreme similarity between Morris' description of the hall of the Wolfings and Tolkien's Meduseld.

26. The *loci classici* for discussions of the problem of authorial intention are Foucault, "What Is an Author?" in *The Foucault Reader*, ed. Paul Rabinow (1984), 101–20; Barthes, "The Death of the Author," in *Image, Music, Text*, trans. Heath (1977), 142–8. For a different approach, see Drout, "I am Large, I contain Multitudes: The Medieval Author in Memetic Terms," forthcoming.

27. See Bloom, *Anxiety*. 1997. 3–5.

Works Cited

Anderson, Douglas A. "R.W. Chambers and *The Hobbit*." *Tolkien Studies* (2006): 137–47.

Barthes, Roland. "The Death of the Author." *Image, Music, Text*. Translated by Stephen Heath. New York: Hill, 1977.

Drout, Michael D.C. "I Am Large, I Contain Multitudes: The Medieval Author in Memetic Terms." In *Tradition and the Individual Talent: Modes of Authorship in the Middle Ages*. Edited by Slavica Rankovic. Toronto: Pontifical Institute of Medieval Studies, 2011.

_____. "A Mythology for Anglo-Saxon England." In *J.R.R. Tolkien and the Invention of Myth*. Edited by Jane Chance. Lexington: University Press of Kentucky, 2004.

_____. "The Problem of Transformation: The Use of Medieval Sources in Fantasy Literature." *Literature Compass* (2004): 1–22.

Foucault, Michel. "What Is an Author?" In *The Foucault Reader*. Edited by Paul Rainbow. New York: Pantheon, 1984.

Jackson, Peter, dir. *The Two Towers*, Extended Edition DVD. New Line Home Entertainment, 2003.

Fr. Klaeber. *Beowulf and the Fight at Finnsburg*. 3rd ed. Lexington, MA: D.C. Heath, 1950.

Lee, Stuart D. "J.R.R. Tolkien and *The Wanderer*: From Edition to Application." *Tolkien Studies* (2009): 189–211.

Lee, Stuart D., and Elizabeth Solopova. *The Keys of Middle-earth*. London: Palgrave Macmillan, 2005.

Morris, William. "The House of the Wolfings." In *More to William Morris: Two Books that Inspired Tolkien, The House of the Wolfings and The Roots of the Mountains*. Edited by Michael W. Perry. Seattle: Inkling, 2003.

Shippey, T.A. *The Road to Middle-earth*. London: Allen and Unwin, 1982.

_____. "Goths and Huns: The Rediscovery of the Northern Cultures in the Nineteenth Century." In *The Medieval Legacy: A Symposium*. Edited by Andreas Haarder et al. Odense: Odense University Press, 1982.

Tinkler, John. "Old English in Rohan." In *Tolkien and the Critics*. Edited by Neil D. Isaacs et al. Notre Dame: University of Notre Dame Press, 1968.

Tolkien J.R.R.. *The Annotated Hobbit*. Edited by Douglas A. Anderson. 2nd ed., revised. Boston: Houghton Mifflin, 2002.

_____. "*Beowulf*: The Monsters and the Critics." In *The Monsters and the Critics and Other Essays*. Edited by Christopher Tolkien. London: George Allen & Unwin, 1983; Boston: Houghton Mifflin, 1983.

_____. *The History of the Hobbit*. Edited by John D. Rateliff. Part 1: *Mr. Baggins*. Boston: Houghton Mifflin, 2007.

———. *The Fellowship of the Ring*. 2nd ed., revised. Boston: Houghton Mifflin, 1987.
———. *The Two Towers*. 2nd ed., revised. Boston: Houghton Mifflin, 1987.
———. *The Return of the King*. 2nd ed., revised. Boston: Houghton Mifflin, 1987.
———. *The Return of the Shadow*. Edited by Christopher Tolkien. London: Unwin Hyman, and Boston: Houghton Mifflin, 1988.
———. *The Treason of Isengard*. Edited by Christopher Tolkien. London: Unwin Hyman, and Boston: Houghton Mifflin, 1989.

Filming the Numinous
The Fate of Lothlórien in Peter Jackson's The Lord of the Rings

JOSEPH RICKE AND CATHERINE BARNETT

The beauty of words and the beauty of a cinematic image are two different things, even if they are the same kinds of things. Rendering compelling verbal images into film calls for close attention not just to the "original" ideas, words, and "word pictures" but also to the special languages, the grammars, and the aesthetics of film art. Historically, rendering the beautiful, awful, and transcendent experience sometimes termed the "the numinous" has proven particularly challenging and sometimes ridiculous on film.[1] A select group of classic film directors, such as Carl Theodore Dreyer, Robert Bresson, and Andrei Tarkovsky, have famously, as one critic (writing of Tarkovsky) has noted, "strained to portray the numinous" (Hancock 136).[2] None of these directors would ever be confused with the director of an action film like, say, *King Kong*.

On the other hand, many action-packed heroic fantasy films (the original *Star Wars* being the obvious example) do, especially through certain spine-tingling scenes, make some attempt at rendering a numinous-like experience. Peter Jackson, in his *LOTR* trilogy of films, faced the difficult task of "translating" J.R.R. Tolkien's vision and version of the numinous, especially as expressed in the life of the High Elves and in the realm known as Lothlórien. Although primarily a *Silmarillion* theme, the numinous "charge" of the High-Elven realm lives on in *The Lord of the Rings* in that enchanted dream-like forest—"the heart of Elvendom on earth," as Aragorn calls it (342). In his first Middle-earth film, *FOTR*, Jackson had to balance the challenging process of representing Tolkien's numinous Lothlórien with the much simpler process (given the computer graphic imaging [CGI] capabilities and, perhaps more important, the tastes of contemporary cinematic audiences) of depicting the heroic action story which Tolkien had also imagined. Although it would be impossible to calibrate the exact degree of success with which Jackson accomplished this balance, it is worth paying critical attention both to Tolkien's literary version of the numinous and Jackson's attempt not only to "translate" Tolkien's words but, as Maureen Thum writes, to "transmute" those materials "from words into filmic images"— that is, into a world of his own "subcreation" (231).

This essay argues that Lothlórien is central to Tolkien's mythology and that, in the novel, it provides the most obvious link to the larger visionary realm elaborated especially in *The Silmarillion*. As such, Lothlórien is the vehicle of a different order of experience —"the numinous"— as characters (and perhaps readers and viewers) are challenged and inspired by suggestions of something awesome and transformative made accessible if not entirely comprehensible. After establishing this weight of significance, we consider Jackson's own creative vision and stylistic choices both to represent Tolkien's numinous Lothlórien and, further, to make his own Lothlórien, serving the purposes of his own similar but different secondary epic.

We Brake for Elves (or Make Magic Not Gore)

Waxing nostalgic for a moment — and like most nostalgia, these *ubi suntish* memories have a slippery relationship to the facts — many of us (including one of the coauthors of this piece) discovered the works of J.R.R. Tolkien right at the end of the 1960s and the beginning of the 1970s. Whether this was the dawning or the waning of the Age of Aquarius we leave to the prophets, the popular culture scholars, postmodern mythographers, and the next generation (represented by the other coauthor). At least in the fuzzy, hallucinogenic-influenced memory of some of us, we were just about arriving for our first visit to Lothlórien as we were munching on magic mushrooms, toking on Longbottom Leaf, and seriously starting to distrust anyone over eleventy-nine. This is not to idealize the popular understanding that Tolkien is of interest primarily to those with such a weak hold on so-called reality that they need the kind of cheap escape offered by drugs, skinny dipping by moonlight, songs around a campfire and elven epiphanies.[3] It is, however, to highlight a way of seeing (and perhaps a way of being) provided by Tolkien which meant something to a great many once upon a time. For a variety of reasons, Tolkien's narratives of escape, consolation, and recovery reverberated with a generation which, for all its many faults, found itself in great need of re-enchantment.

This might be one of the reasons that many of us pretty well raced past many of *Lord*'s scenes of battle, derring-do, and Orc-slaughter (we'd had enough of Vietnam War-era body counts) to get ourselves back into the woods, on to the trail, under the moonlight, beneath the waterfalls, under the influence of Elves, and perhaps even, as Tolkien suggests in "On Fairy-stories," in touch with the Lord of it all (78). It is possible, of course, to write this off as Tolkien's appeal to hippies, escapists, mystics, and ecologists (although that seems like quite a lot to write off). But perhaps it is more. *Lord*, for many of us, really was a kind of liminal experience, taking readers, by means of literary enchantment, to the threshold of a place, a feeling, a way of being, which might be termed "transcendent" or, more specifically in the language of the philosophy of religion, "numinous." Tolkien himself seemed to think so and claimed it was one of the purposes of his kind of fantasy, "to open a door on Other Time, and if we pass through, though only for a moment, we stand outside our own time, outside Time itself, maybe" ("On Fairy-stories" 48).

For both of us (coming from very different backgrounds) the essence of the "transport" provided by the Tolkien experience was found in the Lothlórien section of *The Fellowship of the Ring* (Book 2, chapters 6–9). Placed structurally between the darkness of Moria and the fragmentation of "The Breaking of the Fellowship," the Lothlórien section is surely the single most enchanting and enchanted (and most chanted, given its many songs) extended passage in Tolkien's magical book. It is also, if anything, one of the most over-determined passages in Tolkien's dripping-with-backstory narrative. In Lothlórien, we enter a unique place, extraordinarily full of history and depth and beauty and sadness; we catch a glimpse of how all the stories of Middle-earth are somehow linked to the story at hand; and we discover that many of the overarching themes — hope, loss, nostalgia, self-sacrifice, and language — converge. The many ways that Lothlórien is significant to the larger work, and the larger "Tolkien world," not to mention the stated importance attached to it by Tolkien himself, make it nearly impossible that Peter Jackson's film version could have "lived up to" or even approached the expectations or wishes of devoted fans of Tolkien in general and fans of Elves and Lothlórien more specifically. By first analyzing the significance, purposes, and "meanings" of Lothlórien to Tolkien's vision, especially his depiction of the numinous, and then by considering Jackson's own treatment of the Lothlórien material, we hope both to defend some aspects of Jackson's treatment from some of his detractors and to criticize some problems arising from Jackson's approach. To be fair to Jackson, such criticism must go beyond the simplistic standard list of cinematic practices found offensive by bibliophiles of all sorts (especially, recently, fans of Jane Austen and Tolkien)—like compression, elision, and casting, since most readers come to a film version with an idealized, personalized vision of their favorite characters. Some of the problems do arise, however, from Jackson's deeply rooted attraction to and proficiency in depicting action and violence. On the other hand, in our conclusion we nevertheless suggest some ways that, though he does "miss" certain "Tolkienish" experiences, it is Jackson who actually attempts to provide his audience a numinous or numinous-like experience, whereas Tolkien is more prone to describe a character having that experience.

The Elven as a Category of Value

For structural reasons within the larger work, as well as for the depth of reference to the larger mythology, the significance of the Lothlórien section to the overall effect of *Lord* seems obvious. Further, from more specific documentary evidence, we know that Tolkien saw Lothlórien and its Elves as profoundly important. In one of his letters, Tolkien states that the end of the chapter "Lothlórien" (almost completely cut from the film) is one of the most moving passages in the entire work (*Letters* 376). Interestingly, in another place, he also expressed very specific concerns as to how Lothlórien might be represented or misrepresented in film. In a letter written in 1958, he resentfully attacks a film "treatment," a workup for a potential script of the novel, partly for ignoring his "descriptions [of Lothlórien] that are obviously central to the tone and style of the book!" (274). Despite such a dire need of money that he had, in fact, suggested that his publisher cut a deal, with the Hollywood devil itself, if the money was right, Tolkien announces, "I will in no circumstances accept this treatment of Lórien" (274).

Although Tolkien came rather late to the idea of Lothlórien and its significance, once he developed the story into something like its final version, he invested the Golden Wood with a suggestiveness of greater and higher things beyond and behind the foregrounded plot. Obviously, the very manner in which Tolkien narrates the "crossing over" of the Ring bearer and the fellowship into the realm of Lothlórien marks it as a liminal space, a threshold into another way of being and seeing. Hammond and Scull note that Tolkien tries to capture the "air of timeless enchantment" (308) by bringing his characters into the realm gradually, emphasizing its other-world, even other-time, dimension. Even blindfolded as he is, Frodo feels a sense of both awe and attraction: "As soon as he set foot upon the far bank of Silverlode a strange feeling had come upon him, and it deepened as he walked on into the Naith. It seemed to him that he had stepped over a bridge of time into a corner of the Elder Days, and was now walking in a world that was no more. In Rivendell, there was memory of ancient things; in Lórien the ancient things still lived on in the waking world" (*Fellowship* 340).

Tolkien, in this one brief scene, uses physical description, a rather simple description of an extraordinary state of consciousness, a wonderfully apt figure—"bridge of time" reminds us that he is, in fact, crossing a river but also crossing into a different order of existence—a paradox, and a compact analogy to Rivendell, which seems to function to Lothlórien as Lothlórien does to the Elder Days. This richness of development, mostly by indirection, suggests a powerful but almost indescribable experience, one both deeply meaningful and mysterious. Tolkien would have been well acquainted with a similar pattern, in which a traveler in a strange world feels not estranged but spiritually energized, by his experience from his friend C.S. Lewis's science fiction novel, *Out of the Silent Planet* (1938), in which the protagonist has a variety of numinous experiences that enrich and transform his life. In fact, not only that novel but also Lewis's extended discussion of "the numinous" in his *The Problem of Pain* (1940) would have been first read aloud to Tolkien and other friends in the late 1930s before publication.

Although numen and "the numinous" can simply refer to a god, the divine realm, or the supernatural in the language of the philosophy of religion, especially since Rudolf Otto's classic *The Idea of the Holy*, it primarily has been used to refer to a specifically human experience of that other realm, the human perception of some spiritual presence, an elevated or transcendent but still human or "creaturely" state. More specifically Otto equates the "feeling of the numinous" with the experience of what has been translated as the "wholly other," but might also be translated the "quite different" or the "radically strange." It is that experience of the other which specifically "transcends or eludes comprehension in rational or ethical terms" (Otto xvi). This "beyond our grasp" quality does not mean we cannot talk about it or that it has no ethical claim on us. In fact, Otto argues emphatically for the "holy as a category of value," something that we experience and testify to as valuable whether or not we completely understand why (50–59). In later editions of *The Idea of the Holy*, he takes pains to clarify that the numinous should be thought of as "non-rational," not "irrational." That is, in his words, it is an experience with a "mysterious overplus surpassing all that can be clearly understood or appraised" (xviii). Numinous experience can be profound, alien, awe-inspiring, strange, uplifting, and even transformative. It is the "mysterium tremendum" (Otto 12–24), characterized by awfulness, generating a response of fearful reverence, overpoweringness or "majestas" in which, one might say, we recognize that we are not in control, and energy or urgency, the idea found in such texts as "God is a consuming fire."

It is important to note, however, that the "numinous" is not *just* scary, although it can be that. Even when it induces fear, it is a "category of value," unlike a ghost or a Balrog. Although Moria inspires dread, its specific experience of fear and trembling has more to do with fear itself. The "Other" in Moria is dangerous and destructive, something to avoid if one can but to be faced if necessary to heroism. Lothlórien, on the other hand, is a place that should not be avoided, although some — like Boromir in the book and, for some reason, Gimli in the film — might think it more "safe" to do so. It may be an awe-full experience, but one that ultimately enriches rather than terrifies, transforms rather than destroys. When we are our best selves, we welcome, albeit with fear and trembling, such experience. According to Otto, the numinous is also an experience which can be rendered, or at least approximated, by certain artistic works, especially those characterized by what is often called "the sublime."

As mentioned previously, during the time when his friendship with and influence on Tolkien was inarguably deep and close, C.S. Lewis made the numinous (and an extended explanation of it) a major part of the introduction to his *The Problem of Pain,* and almost certainly Tolkien heard Lewis' discussion of the numinous read aloud. Certain passages in *Problem of Pain* seem to be specific references to ideas Lewis gleaned from Tolkien, especially those discussed in their famous "long night talk" which led to Lewis' conversion (Carpenter 42–45) and similar ideas appearing in Tolkien's "On Fairy-stories" lecture at St. Andrews. Similarly, some of Tolkien's ideas in "On Fairy-stories" as well as *Lord*, including Lothlórien, appear to be influenced by Lewis' explanation of the numinous. In that respect, it may be significant that Frodo's passage into Lothlórien is described as a passage into "the Elder days" (304). One of the specific examples Lewis uses to describe the numinous in *Problem of Pain* is Virgil's reference to the palace of Latinus: "awful (*horrendum*) with woods and sanctity (*religione*) of Elder Days" (Lewis 7). Whether the combination of woods, awe, and Elder Days was coincidental, an unremembered borrowing, or homage to Lewis (or Virgil or both), the concept of the numinous, here expressed through artistic elements of sublimity, helps us interpret Lothlórien's mysterious otherness in a context relevant to Tolkien's own thinking at the time of the development of the story.

In addition to being experienced in the "wholly other" and encountered in the sublime, the numinous might be, but need not be, linked to other religious indicators such as cult, mythology, sacrifice, etc. It is ironic, then, as others have previously noted, that Tolkien's majestic, perhaps even sublime, novel is for all practical purposes "religion-less," especially in details of gods, cult, mythology, ritual actions, and the like. There is little evidence of overtly religious practices, such as worship, prayer, asceticism, and almsgiving, in *Lord*. Similarly, the pantheon of "gods" so important to Tolkien's *Silmarillion* remains for the most part almost completely out of the picture. On the other hand, the story plays out in a haunted world and landscape, with the definite sense that in the so-called background powerful higher powers exist and are in mysterious ways involved in the action. This is true not only of the powerful forces of evil whose malice towards the creatures of Middle-earth lurks always in the narrative's shadowy places, it is true also of the majestic and awful powers of good, analogous to if not specifically symbolic of the Divine Power(s) of Tolkien's own Catholic faith. Despite the surface appearances, Tolkien himself claimed, in a letter comparing the Lady Galadriel to the Virgin Mary, that *Lord* is "a fundamentally religious and Catholic work" in which "the religious element is absorbed into the story and the symbolism" (172).

For Tolkien, and Lewis, the "numinous" is not simply "the holy" or "the divine realm," as in heaven. It is more the divine or holy experienced on earth by earthly creatures. The experience of God's presence by the redeemed in heaven would not necessarily be "numinous" because it would be the given, the expected, even "the usual." Instead, they seem to understand the numinous in a Wordsworthian way, as fleeting glimpses, momentary impressions or experiences within this faded and fallen world. For Lewis, it means something like the "Joy" he had been surprised by as a child and had been in search of ever since (see especially his discussion in *Surprised by Joy* and *The Pilgrim's Regress*). It is an "out of this world experience" in this world experienced by those who are still "of the world." In other words, even though the path to paradise or heaven or Valinor is buried in terms of direct and complete connection, some taste of the other is still available to all "with ears to hear and eyes to see," especially in moments of virtuous action, religious vision, spiritual receptivity, and heightened connection to nature. More accurately, given the nature of numinous "majestas," one might say such experience is available whenever the ineffable, incomprehensible, and unconstrained Holy chooses to make it so by burning its way into our human consciousness.

Perhaps the most profound "numinous" moment in *Lord*—except possibly for certain parts of the conclusion at the Grey Havens—is the description of the "unveiling" of Lothlórien by the uncovering of Frodo's eyes. If the "secret passage" into Lothlórien serves to "numinize" the place, the response to the fuller revelation, once it is given, seems intended to suggest the awful, ineffable, and valuable "Other." When Frodo's eyes are finally uncovered, he "caught his breath" (341), not from exhaustion but from his astonishment at this first vision of a world beyond what he had known—a world, as David Bratman has pointed out, rather more colorful than Jackson's dark-hued realm (29). In Lothlórien, Tolkien has moved a world away from the "cute" Elves and Elvish realm of *The Hobbit*. In fact, it is the drawn out, reverent "crossing over" into Lothlórien that serves as the great divide in our understanding of Elves and perhaps of what Tolkien is actually up to in *Lord* as opposed to *The Hobbit*.

This new understanding is, of course, anticipated but not nearly as fully developed in the Rivendell episode a few chapters prior to this. And Lothlórien signifies much more than Tolkien's mature vision of Elves. It stands as the inscrutable but wonderful remainder and reminder of a heightened life, a life both more divinized and yet somehow, ironically, more "natural" than that experienced by the other folk in and on Middle-earth. It is a taste of the other, a trace of the glory of the One, a place apparently still untouched by the ravages if not the temptations of Time—something Frodo senses upon his first glorious experience of it:

> The others cast themselves down upon the fragrant grass, but Frodo stood awhile still lost in wonder. It seemed to him that he had stepped through a high window that looked on a vanished world. A light was upon it for which his language had no name. All that he saw was shapely, but the shapes seemed at once clear cut, as if they had been first conceived and drawn at the uncovering of his eyes, and ancient as if they had endured forever. He saw no colour but those he knew, gold and white and blue and green, but they were fresh and poignant, as if he had at that moment first perceived them and made for them names new and wonderful. In winter here no heart could mourn for summer or for spring. No blemish or sickness or deformity could be seen in anything that grew upon the earth. On the land of Lórien there was no stain [*Fellowship* 341].

Despite its difference, its numinous strangeness, this place "upon the earth" yet "a vanished world" is somehow, ironically perhaps, more natural than anything outside its borders. When Frodo touches one of the trees, "never before had he been so suddenly and so keenly aware of the feel and texture of a tree's skin and of the life within it. He felt a delight in the wood and the touch of it, neither as forester nor as carpenter, it was the delight of the living tree itself" (342). Here, as elsewhere in Tolkien and other writers in the so-called Inkling tradition, the significance of hyper-nature takes us beyond Otto's basic premises about the numinous into a more specifically sacramental understanding in which the "holy" inheres in the natural in ways that can only be called revelatory. Interestingly, in light of references by Otto, who relates it to the numinous, and Tolkien, who relates it to "Faerie," the "lower" (or at least smaller) characters in the novel try to account for this numinous/sacramental charge by reference to "magic."

In fact, multiple references to magic occur in the Lothlórien section, primarily as a topic for Hobbit discussion. About the magic in Lothlórien, Sam says, "Nothing seems to be going on.... If there's any magic about, it's right down deep, where I can't lay my hands on it" (351). Frodo, who has grown "deep" himself both on the way to and within the Golden Wood, responds wisely, "You can see and feel it everywhere" (351). Colin Duriez relates this "deep magic" (a term popular with C.S. Lewis in his Narnia books) to Tolkien's "deeply theological" and "sacramental" understanding of nature. According to Duriez, Tolkien's Elves, who represent a quasi-divine higher order of being, are "tied up with the natural order" (175). After the Hobbits discuss magic, Galadriel appears "as if she came in answer to their words" and gently mocks Sam with the offer of some "Elf magic" — as if her mind-reading were not already magic enough. To Sam's bumbling answer, the Lady responds "with a gentle laugh" (353). Just before her appearance, Sam had said, "I don't reckon these folk can do much more to help us, magic or no" (352). This statement, of course, is rendered ironic by the visionary gift Galadriel provides. Yes Sam, there is magic here. And, yes, it can help. That gift as well as the further "natural magic" of Galadriel expressed in the later gift-giving scene (cut from the theatrical release of the film) certainly does "much more to help" the Fellowship.

Indeed, another important aspect of the numinous reality experienced in Lothlórien, especially as "naturalized" or "sacramentalized" by Tolkien, is this purposeful and providential giving of blessings and gifts. (Theologically, such would be understood as gifts of grace, or "charismas.") After drinking the parting glass of blessing with the Fellowship, Celeborn and Galadriel impart individualized and meaningful gifts to each of its members. None is particularly supernatural or "magical" in Sam's older sense, except perhaps the phial of the light of Eärendil's star given to Frodo. But each carries with it something of the unique combination of natural rootedness, surpassing beauty, and skillful work that is the special magic of the realm of Lothlórien. As Galadriel herself says to Sam, "I have only a small gift.... Earth from my orchard, and such blessing as Galadriel has still to bestow is upon it" (366).

Responding in 1971 to a reader who claimed that he had created a world "in which some sort of faith seems everywhere present but without a visible source" (*Letters* 413), Tolkien wrote: "You would [not] perceive it in these terms unless it was with you also. Otherwise you would see and feel nothing, or (if some other spirit was present) you would be filled with contempt, nausea, hatred. Leaves out of the Elf-country, gah! Lembas — dust and ashes, we don't eat that" (*Letters* 413). In other words, "those who have eyes to see and ears to hear" may recognize the numinous otherness in Lothlórien specifically or *Lord* more generally, even if the work itself does not locate those religious ideas and symbols in exactly an "orthodox" way or even in any very exact way at all. Like C.S. Lewis' character Elwin Ransom — almost certainly modeled on Tolkien — who wants his readers to "convert" from a narrow-minded "faith" in empty space to an acceptance of the ancient idea of "the heavens" (in other words, that ultimate reality is characterized by life, light, and meaning), Tolkien seems to have invested his Lothlórien, — and through it his entire work, — with a rather vague but still powerful notion of "a presence that disturbs me with the joy of elevated thoughts" felt by Wordsworth at Tintern Abbey (line 94) or, in Tolkien's own words in another context, "a fleeting glimpse of Joy, Joy beyond the walls of the world, poignant as grief" ("Fairy Stories" 75).

The question, then, about Jackson's film, at least in terms of the numinous quality of Tolkien's Lothlórien episode, is not so much whether it mirrors Tolkien's incidents and descriptions, something all but impossible when moving from text to film (Thum), but whether that same "spirit was present" which was "with" Tolkien and which is such an integral part of his sub-creation. Or, to put it in more practical terms, whether Jackson succeeded, as a scop standing on the shoulders of Ents, of rendering some of that same numinous atmosphere that, at least to some degree, differentiates Lothlórien from other stops along the way in the *Lord* landscape.

Jackson's Lothlórien Lost and Found

Although we have found it difficult — well, actually impossible — not to reference Jackson's film before now in order to point out some specific and significant contrasts with Tolkien's book, we hope to have shown that Jackson's film deserves it own analysis apart from simplistic criticisms of what he left out or changed from the novel and that Jackson's achievement (and, in him, that of his massive cast and crew) stands or falls primarily on cinematic terms. Despite some restatement of those earlier comments, this final section is more than a summary of scattered criticisms from the first part of the chapter. Instead, we have tried to group the many interesting aspects of Jackson's treatment of Lothlórien into just a few concepts. Having said that, we apologize especially to film fans and experts for the absence of many important elements worth consideration. A shot by shot analysis of the Lothlórien section(s) (including the Extended Edition), although not the purpose of this essay, would be a very interesting window into Jackson's vision and method, both as adaptor and as auteur.[4]

Our own journey in writing this chapter has taken us from a position highly critical and almost obsessed with Jackson's bent towards horror and massive battle scenes to a grudging admiration for the ways he at times restrains those tendencies, though not nearly enough to translate Tolkien's mythology or to make a truly great work of his own. When he does so, he shows himself wonderfully capable of rendering a place, a class of being, and an experience which can be truly "Other" without necessarily being monstrous. Of the many ways Jackson works to adapt the Lothlórien material, both to "translate" Tolkien's work and to make his own, several "big idea" approaches stand out: especially omission/compression of material; interpretation of material, especially by casting, acting style, and mise-en-scène; and technical treatment, especially music, editing, coloring, etc.

Omission/Compression of Material

Jackson has never been a director given to reflection, lyricism, and slow pacing. Such being the case, we should perhaps expect the intense pressures of pacing to contribute to severe elision and even omission of material in the Lothlórien section. For the theatrical release, Jackson reduced Tolkien's three chapters depicting Lothlórien to twelve minutes of screen time. And, perhaps worried that even those twelve rather quiet minutes might "lose" his action-oriented audience, he intercut yet another scene of ugly Orcs — in this case Saruman's creation and commissioning of his most ugly Uruk-hai. Along the way, almost all of chapter six, "Lothlórien" (which, as we said, contains what Tolkien himself thought was one of the work's most beautiful passages), is missing, as are Gollum, the encounter with Elves in the trees, the blindfolded "crossing-over" scene, the gift-giving scene, four (!) songs — which does not include the lament for Gandalf sung by the Elves — and much more.

Still, Lothlórien makes up only three chapters of Tolkien's vast work. Why even worry about such a "brief encounter"? One obvious reason, in addition to the points that have already been made in earlier sections, is that *Lord* is, for the most part, composed of just such encounters. Although it can be described in many ways, the novel is, at the very least, a quest narrative. It involves many stops and starts of various duration, all of which are significant to the whole regardless of the length of the literary passage or running time of the film. In that regard, the time spent in Lothlórien is equal to or longer than the usual "stops along the way" (such as those in Bree, Rivendell, the house of Tom Bombadil, etc.). And, in this special place, Tolkien compresses an amazing and more than usual amount of significant background story and "deeper meaning." Even the friendliest critic must conclude that Jackson, whether by necessity or disposition, has omitted most of that material. This is not to fault Jackson for failing to supplement his story with massive amounts of information from the *Silmarillion*, although the later publication of much of the mythological materials would exert an unfair pressure on all adaptors/translators to do so — unfair especially, since Jackson was legally barred from using any material not found in *Lord*. Further, some of that material is contradictory, such as the Galadriel myth which Tolkien was revising and reinventing right up to his death, redundant at least in cinematic terms — one enchanted Elven realm of rest and refocus may seem as good as another — or just unnecessary, such as Gollum in Lothlórien.

We do, however, think Jackson leaves himself open to criticism for his severe condensation of the Lothlórien section, with almost complete omission of most of its scenes, dialogue, and characterizations, in light of other choices he made to dilate, embellish, and simply add material. More important, some of his changes not only compress or speed up the narrative; at times, they also work to reduce the overall vision of *Lord*. This especially grates considering the expansive treatment Jackson gives to the Moria section which precedes it. Although crude quantifying does not exactly prove anything, it is worth noting that the Moria episode takes up two chapters in the novel (thirty-six pages), yet runs approximately twenty-eight minutes in Jackson's film. Obviously, there is a great deal of action in the great hall of Moria under the mountain, and, to be fair to Jackson, one could easily make a case for the validity of this expansive, or at least "less compressive," treatment. By comparison, however, and to be fair to Jackson's critics, the Lothlórien section covers forty-six pages in the book but runs only twelve minutes in the film. Unfortunately, Lothlórien has no Balrog nor any heroic action, at least not of the traditional cinematic variety.[5] Perhaps due to this lack of action, Jackson found this to be an obvious section to cut, shortening the film (the cynical might say saving more space for his Orcs and Orc-designers) while keeping the plot basically intact. For all the beauties of Jackson's films, this degree of compression to the point of losing Lothlórien, though somewhat understandable given Hollywood's expectations and Jackson's tendencies, seems unfortunately to reinforce Bratman's contention that Jackson's film is far away from Tolkien "in spirit and tone" (29). In light of Lothlórien's great importance to Tolkien's world and vision, this narrows the appeal and achievement of Jackson's work as well, making it much more of an "epic" and much less of an "elegy" on Tolkien's own terms.[6]

We are not the first to note Jackson's love for and comfort with action and horror over against reflection, elegy, and lyricism. One biographer claims that precisely this tendency towards action and away from reflection and lyricism doomed his depictions of Elves generally and the Lothlórien section of the novel specifically:

> Their [the Elves'] uninspired, overly-abbreviated treatment is the price we pay for a director more in his element when the Elves are on horseback or firing arrows. Jackson's strengths are not ethereal moments but the darker, more immediate qualities of caves overrun with orcs and monsters, and the unearthly cries of approaching Black Riders.... When it comes to Tolkien's elven characters, *Fellowship* stalls when it should soar.... The film's quasi-mystical low point is found in the forests of Lothlórien, with the appearance of flowing-haired Galadriel (Cate Blanchett) and a jug of water. For a rare moment, you sense a director who has lost his way [Pryor 308].

Of course, Tolkien himself writes action-packed fiction with strong epic-like characters. Tolkien's characters, however — like the narrative in which they exist — pause often for reflection, lamentation, poetry, song, moral inventory, refocusing, wrestling with their consciences, and debating their commitment to the mission before them. This is especially true of the "stops along the way" places in *Lord*, which make up so much of the story. In fact, it is a common misinterpretation of heroic literature and film that heroic "tests" are those which occur *in* battle (fighting hoards of really ugly Orcs, for example). Indeed, this was not Tolkien's understanding, in literary theory or practice.[7]

Obviously, then, with his bias towards the epic, and especially film epic, Jackson's treatment of lyrical Lothlórien is abbreviated. That cannot simply be rationalized by the need for compression, since comparison with other sections, Moria, for example, suggests that Lothlórien really is cut beyond reason. My argument is that this not only comes close to gutting Tolkien's story of its numinous/spiritual center, but it also aligns Jackson's film firmly with the action film tradition rather than with something more profound and, finally, more daring, which clearly was within his grasp. Valente claims that the film features a general "toning down of majesty" and eliminates "fundamental moral and philosophical concerns" (35). It is rather like an adaptation of *War and Peace* that omits peace. Without a time for peace, the brief film section fails, or mostly fails, to render Lothlórien as a place of much needed rest, for audiences as well as characters. Neither does it give time for the kind of reflective, even transformative, experience undergone by Tolkien's Frodo in the Golden Wood. As a further effect of this, whatever numinous-like experiences are included in Jackson's Lothlórien tend to be, with some exceptions, of the more immediate, frightening, and monstrous variety, such as Frodo's horrific vision in Galadriel's Mirror and his even more horrific vision of monstrous

Galadriel a few minutes later. This is not just quibbling with a bad special effect (I will do that in minute). The point is that, clearly, Lothlórien represents the "Other" place, and "Other Time" in Tolkien's words; but this particularly valuable "Other" is experienced as much more terrifying and horrifying than it is in Tolkien's novel and more than it should be in the film if it is to be distinguished from other more terrifying, less "holy" "Others" like Balrogs, Black Riders, and Dark Lords. Whether, though, Jackson's treatment is on the whole "uninspired," and Jackson is out of his "element," and, in fact, the treatment represents the film's "quasi-mystical low point" depends on whether he manages, by other means, to help his audience to experience some inkling of the numinous, in spite of the aforementioned shortcomings of his adaptation.

Interpretation of Material

Since they did not completely omit Lothlórien from their film, Jackson and his cast and crew had to make specific interpretive decisions as to how they would "show" Lothlórien through costuming, sets, casting, acting style, and music. Obviously, this "showing" overlaps with technical decisions such as photography, editing, and musical background, although, for the most part, we will deal with them separately. These interpretive choices were clearly very important to the making of the film, and numerous little documentaries, many included with the DVDs, testify to the thought and effort that went into such decisions. The most obvious element necessary to a depiction of the Golden Wood of Lothlórien was that natural or "hyper-natural" place itself. Our first glimpse of Lothlórien in the theatrical film occurs when Aragorn, running out ahead of the devastated but stumbling forward company, sees it shimmering in the distance, or, at least, with the help of an online script and the aid of hindsight, one might guess that the place he sees in the distance is meant to be an establishing shot of Lothlórien. It would not be obvious otherwise.

In the next shot, the company is moving on through a forest landscape. Despite what one might expect, the leaves are not particularly golden, the trunks of the trees are not exactly silvery, and the forest floor is not strewn with Lothlórien's characteristic winter-blooming yellow flowers (341). It did look like a nice forest, though, with very tall trees and steadily falling leaves to underscore the elegiac theme. From that point, after the "arrest" of the Fellowship by the haughty Haldir, the film's depiction of Lothlórien soars, expressing the "numinous" theme in a rather spectacular, even sublime, manner. The music switches from the somewhat ominous non-diegetic electronic music that underscores the entrance into Lothlórien leading up to Gimli's boastful warning and the "capture" of the Fellowship by what we gradually come to understand are Elven voices—which are off-screen but in the story, or diegetic—chanting an ethereal music in words we do not understand.[8] That music's mysterious beauty yet incomprehensibility—to us and to most of the members of the Fellowship, we assume—provides a wonderful counterpoint to the visual elements of the scene. Especially in this scene, as the company ascends to Caras Galadhon, but generally throughout the rest of the Lothlórien section, the mise-en-scène is composed, sometimes aided by filters, of dark hues, especially dark blues and greys, splintered by lights which pierce but never really light up the darkness. And the tall trees of the forest entrance give way to magnificent cathedral-like shapes—moving from tall, to taller, to tallest—composed in a dizzyingly high crane shot from above and another from the distance to the side and tilting up. As the music continues, we see delicate shapes like Gothic tracery work, and the entire scene has a hushed, even reverent, quality rather unlike anything else in the film up to that point.

After the meeting with Celeborn and Galadriel, throughout the rest of the section, shades and tones continue to be dark and pale, sometimes even bleached out of almost all color, such as the beautiful filtered shot of Boromir and Aragorn's discussion. More diegetic chant is heard. This time we know it is sung by Elves—presumably in the trees but out of the picture—because of Legolas' reference to it. And, as if in church, the characters tend to speak in whispers. Further, whatever Elves are there seem to be huddled together in little groups whispering to themselves or doing whatever Elves do in Jackson's Lothlórien. Nobody runs. Nobody talks loud. Nobody snores (in this version at least!). Interestingly, too, there is very little interaction between the Fellowship members and the inhabitants of Lothlórien. This is rather unlike Tolkien's account; but, to my thinking, it works effectively to show Lothlórien and its inhabitants as "Other" without necessarily showing them, in this case at least, as particularly frightening or monstrous—that is, except for Galadriel, who, it seems to me, almost but not completely undoes whatever numinous effect Jackson achieves by setting, sound, and shot in the rest of the scene.

Obviously the depiction of Galadriel could be the topic for a chapter in itself, especially since she is given the non-"Tolkienish" responsibility of voice-over narrator for the entire story, a choice as puzzling as any number of Jackson's other additions, like the decision to turn Gimli into a lovable buffoon. Further, one might find grounds to disagree with the Jackson biographer who claims that the Lothlórien section and its Elves are a total disaster, while agreeing that Cate Blanchett's Galadriel in conception, performance, and as technically "enhanced" is both intentionally and unintentionally a monstrosity. That her character does not completely ruin Jackson's Lothlórien, given Galadriel's significance and the percentage of screen time she is given, speaks of the quality of his "making" in the rest of the section. Amazing and distressing upon first viewing (at the obligatory midnight opening) as the Jackson/Blanchett version of Galadriel was, it has only gotten worse with time.

This is not just because of the over-reliance on seriously time-bound special effects, which grow cheesy almost immediately upon first being exposed to air. In fact, some critics, including Thum and Valente, give high marks to the "Galadriel effects" (see Thum 240 and Valente 36). More problematic is the fact that Jackson seemed to develop his understanding of Galadriel (or perhaps Blanchett did and Jackson allowed it) from a misinterpretation of the "temptation scene" which became, for them, the "transmogrification scene," and worked outward from there to understand and depict the character. Galadriel in the film is obviously supposed to be awe-inspiring and almost always terrifying. Although this can be a fine line, and although there are several such "unveiling" scenes in the novel in which we wonder, at least for a moment, about the true motives of mysterious character, the Jackson/Blanchett Galadriel is distant, edgy, dangerous, and not particularly loving. This starts with her annoying voice-over comments to Frodo. These prove to be more fear-inducing magic than warnings (if they are warnings, of what?). "Frodo ... [y]our coming to us is as the footsteps of doom. You bring great evil here, Ringbearer" (*ROTR*). Despite an occasional smile of sorts, this is a Galadriel who is "Other" but to whom one responds primarily in fear. And, of course, in her big "all shall love me and despair" scene, she not only channels the spirits of Hollywood horror flicks, but, as befits this misinterpretation, she specifically does not laugh before or after her demon-possession-like fit, whereas Tolkien's Galadriel laughs twice in this scene.

Of course, to some degree Galadriel's haughty and downright weird demeanor, including what might be called her "stork walk" towards the Mirror, is Jackson and Blanchett's way of expressing her "Otherness." And, in that way, she is linked to the other Elves of Lothlórien, who are, from our first vision of Haldir and his blonde band of Elf brothers, rather strange. They are oh-so-stern, haughty, distant, and bleached out in both hair and skin. Although Tolkien's Lothlórien Elves are more lively and friendly than Jackson's, the "haughtiness" of Jackson's Elves actually works to suggest an important difference, especially from the Elves of *The Hobbit* or from the cute Elves of myth and legend and cookie commercials. As such, Jackson's interpretation works both to show the diversity of the creatures in Middle-earth and to suggest the "numinous." Yet Jackson pushes this to an absurd extreme — especially in the speech patterns of Celeborn and Galadriel, who seem not just formal or royal but remind one of really awful Shakespearean actors. Of course,

Tolkien's "high speech" sometimes has the sound of bad imitations of Shakespeare or the Bible. Harold Bloom compares *Lord* to the Book of Mormon, and he's not intending that to be a positive (Bloom 2). This, however, is more than a matter of the written lines. Delivering their lines, Celeborn and Galadriel, especially Galadriel — perhaps because she communicates through voice-overs much of the time — do not look at the people to whom they are speaking. And they speak as if they are not speaking to a real person but to ... well, to a film audience expecting something really strange and affected. The subtext seems to be "I am now talking like a very anxious High Elf."

In one of the many short documentaries which accompany the DVD, Blanchett, Elijah Wood (Frodo), and Jackson all talk about their understanding of the character. Instead of focusing on her majesty or her connection to "elder days," each of them stresses the "terrifying" or "dangerous" side of Galadriel (all in a two minute clip). Blanchett claims that there is "an edge of danger" about Galadriel. Wood says that she is "incredibly creepy and possibly dangerous." At another point, he claims that it is "ambiguous as to whether she is a positive or negative force." Of whom are they speaking? The character Tolkien suggested was modeled, at least in part, on the Blessed Virgin Mary. And Jackson, as quoted earlier, speaks of her twice as "terrified."

Undeniably, as even Tolkien pointed out in his criticism of the earlier film treatment, the temptation of Galadriel is of great importance. Significantly, especially in light of Jackson's film, he adds that "the disappearance of the temptation of Galadriel is significant" and complains that "practically everything having moral import has vanished from the synopsis" (274). Whether or not someone connected with Jackson's film was familiar with this letter, Jackson clearly does not ignore this aspect of the story. If anything, his treatment of Galadriel's temptation, including the now infamous "transmogrification" effect, has been generally viewed as over-the-top and excessive. However we take it, Jackson clearly wanted to emphasize this part of the Lothlórien material, whether because he saw it as central to the story or because it provided the opportunity for another terrifying special effect, especially in a rather slow section without Orcs or Balrogs. In one of the many extra documentary features included with the original DVD version, Jackson says that Galadriel "is terrified of the temptation of this ring" and that "she knows that she will have to face the incredible test of being tempted by [it]" (Jackson). But to work outwards from that event — which, by the way, is never configured by Tolkien as necessarily "terrifying" to observers but only to her, if even that — to create this edgy, anxious, rather bitchy Lady of the Golden Wood seems to have been one of those "strong choices" by actors and directors that ends up a weak link in an ensemble work. Further, the specific not-very-special effect, that turns Galadriel into a giant ghost figure but certainly not "beautiful beyond enduring" (but nearly beyond enduring for other reasons), complete with cheesy electronic voice manipulation, is a good example of the kind of film "magic" which loses its effect almost as soon as it is created. Partly this is a problem of film form, but it has been handled — and is handled by Jackson in other places — more successfully. Usually this involves greater subtlety, with more suggestion rather than direct close-up of the effect, and by reflection of the "terrifying" or "majestic" Other in the eyes and on the face of the one being terrified or humbled. One thinks of Boromir's response in the meeting with Galadriel scene (but we'd have to say that Sean Bean gets just about everything perfectly right in this film).

Other Technical Choices

Finally, there are some positive comments to make about certain technical choices, especially as to how Jackson uses those choices to suggest the numinous. Interestingly, whether he was familiar with *The Idea of the Holy* or not, his techniques are strikingly similar to those Otto discusses when he turns to the question of how artists can and do try to reflect the numinous. We have already mentioned color and lighting as part of the overall look of the film, features which can be both "set up" to be filmed (mise-en-scène) and manipulated technically. In any case, it seems to us that the rather dark tones, flecked with light, work beautifully throughout the section. Similarly, Howard Shore's music, once we get past the ominous electronic sounds just before the capture, hit just the right notes of sadness, otherness, and holiness. The chant-like quality reminds one of ancient religious ceremonies. The ethereal voices suggest the difference of Elves, and especially of Lothlórien, from what we and most of the characters know. And performing the songs in other (Tolkien-like) languages works for both characters and audience to suggest not only "the feeling of antiquity" but to "transport [us] into another world" (Shore in Jackson).[9] Before the initial viewing of the film, some were wary of a heavily synthesized New Age soundtrack, given the well-publicized involvement of Enya. But the choice of human voices, singing in "other tongues" in chant-like songs, which, by turns, suggest the uplift of inspiration and the downward movement of lament, worked excellently, especially for the numinous theme which, we argue, is central to Lothlórien. Although Peter Jackson "knows nothing of music," according to himself, his choice of Howard Shore and their basic decision to "put Tolkien's songs back into the film," as Shore says, worked importantly to create a Lothlórien that, although radically cut, still suggests a place like that which Frodo experiences in his great revelation scenes.

As mentioned, Jackson's handling of these elements is eerily similar to the way Rudolf Otto describes how the numinous might be and often has been represented in artistic expression. Interestingly, Otto distinguishes between the "magical," which connects with certain "effects" that might appear to be numinous, and the "numinous itself:" "Now the magical is nothing but a suppressed and dimmed form of the numinous, a crude form of it which great art purifies and ennobles. In great art the point is reached at which we may no longer speak of the 'magical,' but rather are confronted with the numinous itself, with all its impelling motive power, transcending reason, expressed in sweeping lines and rhythm" (67). How, though, is this numinous quality embodied in art? Traditionally, Otto says, through "the sublime." Clearly, for Otto, the sublime signifies the lofty and the exalted, as well as something suggesting unconstrained boundlessness. More specifically, and significantly in light of the perpendicular theme of Jackson's Lothlórien imagery, Otto claims that "to us of the West the Gothic appears as the most numinous of all types of art" (67).[10]

Finally, though, Otto admits that in neither the sublime nor the magical "effective as they are, has art more than an indirect means of representing the numinous" (68). He then considers what he calls the "only two" more "direct" methods available to Western art — darkness and silence. Interestingly, the following extended passage from Otto sounds incredibly like a "treatment" written for certain elements of Jackson's Lothlórien as described earlier:

> The darkness must be such as is enhanced and made all the more perceptible by contrast with some last vestige of brightness, which it is, as it were, on the point of extinguishing; hence the "mystical" effect begins with semi-darkness. Its impression is rendered complete if the factor of the "sublime" comes to unite with and supplement it. *The semi-darkness that glimmers in vaulted halls, or beneath the branches of a lofty forest glade, strangely quickened and stirred by the mysterious play of half-lights, has always spoken eloquently to the soul*, and the builders of temples, mosques, and churches have made full use of it [68, emphasis mine].

Similarly, silence — or, as in Jackson, a quiet, hushed quality — further adds to the impression of the numinous "Silence is what corresponds to this in the language of musical sounds.... With prophet and psalmist and poet we feel the necessity of silence from another and quite independent motive. It is a spontaneous reaction to the feeling of the actual *numen praesens*.... Not even music ... has any positive way to express 'the holy'"(69–70). Otto seems to mean that the kind of music necessary is one that suggests silence or "declines into silence." He praises Bach's "Incarnatus" section in his "Credo" saying, "The effect is due to the faint, whispering, lingering sequence in the fugue structure, dying away pianissimo.... All this serves to express the mysterium by way of intimation, rather than in forthright utterance" (70).

One especially beautiful and meaningful scene in this regard is the one that is bracketed by the two "offensive" scenes of "creepy Galadriel" and "monstrous Galadriel." The film cuts away from the Galadriel's scary eyes after she has just said something in her scary voice-over voice about "The Eye" to a view high up into one of the lofty Gothic pillar-like mallorns. The camera slowly tilts down along the line of the tree, then pans right as Legolas walks into the picture and by a flowing fountain and is finally framed in a profile. We are now on the pavilion floor where the Fellowship members are reclining in different states of rest or restlessness. A new chant has begun (immediately after the cut); it is the lament of the Elves for fallen Gandalf. The gentle sound of the fountain, perhaps many fountains, is heard throughout. Speech, color, music — all tones are hushed and delicate. Legolas turns, looks up and says, "A lament for Gandalf." As in the book, he declines the request to translate the words. "I have not the heart to tell you. For me, the grief is still too near." While Legolas gives a perfectly fine explanation for his silence, much like the one provided in the novel (*Lord* 348), the film, you might say, gives its own explanation in its own terms — or in Otto's. Some things are untranslatable, "surpassing all that can be clearly understood or approved" (Otto xviii). But they can be felt and appreciated. The picture cuts to a view of Frodo's face, resting perhaps, but still devastated.

This is followed by Jackson's beautiful added scene of a discussion between Aragorn and Boromir, part of the expansion of that character throughout the film. The Elven lament continues as Boromir, near to tears, as he was earlier in the presence of Galadriel, speaks first, quietly as do all in Lothlórien, of what he heard Galadriel say to him of hope and despair for the future. Then he memorializes Gondor in one of the most beautiful poetic passages in Jackson's film: "Have you seen it, Aragorn? The White Tower of Ecthelion, glimmering like a spike of pearl and silver, its banners caught high in the morning breeze ... have you ever been called home by the clear ringing of silver trumpets?" All this is underscored by the sound of a rushing wind, which provides the audio transition to the mirror scene which follows, and Shore's subtle horn-dominated orchestral music — non-diegetic now, the diegetic Elven chant having died out, on cue, as Boromir begins to speak of the restoration of Gondor.

We like to think that this almost ecstatic passage, regardless of its theme, sums up the effect of Lothlórien on Boromir just as surely as the tears he sheds. Of course, this quiet, reflective, meditative passage is spoken by a warrior and, to some degree, evokes martial imagery. But, like Jackson, one more skilled in "making" war than reflection and poetry, Boromir here symbolizes the way that Jackson's *LOTR* can both be different and yet capture some of the same "spirit" that is in Tolkien's novel: the elegiac, the lyrical, the Elven, even the numinous. In fact, as we have suggested in this concluding unscientific postscript, where Tolkien, on the page, gives serious attention to representing the numinous experience of his characters, especially Frodo, Jackson ignores the depiction of Frodo's transformation. Instead, the film's use of the sublime, the play of darkness and light, and the "ancient" reverent music, both diegetic and non-diegetic — which in Otto's terms "declines into silence" — suggests, and perhaps even provides, the vehicle for a brief but meaningful numinous experience for his human audiences — like Boromir, the most recognizably human character in the Fellowship and arguably the protagonist of Jackson's version of *FOTR*.

Notes

1. The concept of the numinous was popularized in Otto's *The Idea of the Holy* (first published in 1917) and was an important concept in the thought of Tolkien's friend and colleague C. S. Lewis. Tolkien would have heard Lewis's discussion of the numinous in *The Problem of Pain* (1940), first read aloud and later dedicated "To the Inklings."

2. For an introduction to Tarkovsky's attempts to render the numinous on screen, see D'Sa. For a larger study of the issue, see Schrader.

3. Bloom, one of the greatest of Tolkien pooh-poohers, sees *Lord* as "a giant Period Piece" (1) and patronizingly concludes that "Tolkien met a need, particularly in the early days of the Counter-culture" (2).

4. This essay considers only the original film New Line Cinema released in the U.S.

5. Although Jackson does try to "heroize" even Lothlórien by expanding the significance of Boromir and by intercutting a scene depicting the creation and commissioning of Saruman's horrific Uruk-Hai.

6. Beowulf is not an 'epic' but "rather [an] 'elegy'" (Tolkien, "Beowulf" 31).

7. In his "Beowulf" essay, Tolkien insists that "we must not view this poem as in intention an exciting narrative or a romantic tale" (29); in fact the "heroic" legendary material is "mainly on the outer edges or in the background" (31). In his interpretation of *Sir Gawain and the Green Knight*, Tolkien focuses on the "more neglected" but "more fundamentally important" (than the more obviously "heroic" material) third section of the poem, detailing the temptation and confession of Sir Gawain ("Sir Gawain" 73).

8. Diegetic sound is sound made by characters or objects (including musical instruments) in the space of the story. Non-diegetic sound is sound, like "background music" or narrator's commentary, presented as if it is coming from outside the space of the story.

9. This sounds amazingly like what Tolkien says about the uses of "antiquity" to create a "mythical or total (unanalysable) effect," by which we are transported to "Other Time" ("Fairy Stories" 48).

10. We have borrowed the concept and phrase "perpendicular theme" from Lewis' *Out of the Silent Planet* (48 and 53), which, as we suggest, was profoundly influential on Tolkien's Lothlórien.

WORKS CITED

Bloom, Harold, ed. *J.R.R. Tolkien's "The Return": Modern Critical Interpretations.* Philadelphia: Chelsea, 2000.
Bratman, David, "Summa Jacksonica: A Reply to Defenses of Peter Jackson's *The Lord of the Rings* Films, after St. Thomas Aquinas." In *Tolkien on Film: Essays on Peter Jackson's" The Lord of the Rings."* Edited by Janet Brennan Croft. Altadena, CA: Mythopoeic, 2004.
Carpenter, Humphrey. *The Inklings.* London: George Allen and Unwin, 1978.
D'Sa, Nigel Savio. "Andrei Rublev: Religious Epiphany in Art." *Journal of Religion and Film* 3, no. 2 (1999) *http://www.unomaha.edu/jrf/saviodsa.htm*. (Website accessed 11 January 2010).
Hammond, Wayne G., and Christina Scull. *"The Lord of the Rings": A Reader's Companion.* Boston: Houghton Mifflin, 2005.
Hancock, Stuart. "Andrew Tarkovsky: Master of Cinematic Image. *Mars Hill Review* 4 (1996): 136–146.
Lewis, C.S. *Out of the Silent Planet.* London: John Lane the Bodley Head, 1938.
_____. *The Problem of Pain.* London: Centenary, 1940.
_____. *Surprised by Joy: The Shape of My Early Life.* New York: Harcourt, 1956.
Jackson, Peter, dir. *The Lord of the Rings: The Fellowship of the Ring.* New Line Home Video, 2002. DVD.
Otto, Rudolf. *The Idea of the Holy.* 2nd ed. Translated by John W. Harvey. London: Oxford University Press, 1950.
Pryor, Ian. *From Prince of Splatter to Lord of the Rings.* New York: Thomas Dunne, 2004.
Schrader, Paul. *Transcendental Style in Film.* Berkeley: University of California Press, 1972.
Thum, Maureen, "The 'Sub-Subcreation' of Galadriel, Arwen, and Éowyn: Women of Power in Tolkien's and Jackson's *The Lord of the Rings.*" In *Tolkien on Film: Essays on Peter Jackson's "The Lord of the Rings."* Edited by Janet Brennan Croft. Altadena, CA: Mythopoeic, 2004.
Tolkien, J.R.R. "Beowulf: The Monster and the Critics." In *The Monsters and the Critics and Other Essays.* Edited by Christopher Tolkien. Boston: Houghton Mifflin, 1984.
_____. *The Letters of J.R.R. Tolkien.* Edited by Humphrey Carpenter. Boston: Houghton Mifflin, 1981.
_____. *The Lord of the Rings.* One-vol. ed. Boston: Houghton Mifflin, 1994.
_____. "On Fairy-stories." In *Tolkien on Fairy-stories:* Expanded ed. with commentary and notes. Edited by Verlyn Flieger and Douglas Anderson. London: HarperCollins, 2009.
_____. "Sir Gawain and the Green Knight." In *The Monsters and the Critics and Other Essays.* Edited by Christopher Tolkien. Boston: Houghton Mifflin, 1984.
Valente, Claire. "Translating Tolkien's Epic: Peter Jackson's Lord of the Rings." *Intercollegiate Review* 40, no. 1 (2004): 35–43.

About the Contributors

Janice M. Bogstad is the Head of Technical Services and a professor in the McIntyre Library at the University of Wisconsin–Eau Claire, where she also teaches women's studies and English. She received her PhD in Comparative Literature at the University of Wisconsin–Madison for Anglo-American, French and Chinese literature. She reviews books for publications including the *SFRA Review, Collection Building, JFA,* and *Medieval Feminist Forum,* among others. Her reference book articles have appeared in titles including *Oxford Encyclopedia of Children's Literature, Brill Encyclopedia of Pilgrimage* and *Women in Science Fiction and Fantasy.*

Catherine Barnett received her BS in English Education from Taylor University, where she served on the C.S. Lewis and Friends Society committee and presented research at the 2006 and 2008 Colloquia on C.S. Lewis and Friends. In January of 2008, she studied "Faerie (in) Literature" with Sarah Shaw in Oxford and presented a paper on Tolkien and George MacDonald (previously published in the *Saint Austin Review*) to the Oxford C.S. Lewis Society. She received the Sigma Tau Delta Midwestern Regent's scholarship in 2008 and the Phillip Christopher Schrum Prize for Literary Analysis at the Making Literature Conference in 2009.

Janet Brennan Croft is Head of Access Services at the University of Oklahoma libraries. She is the author of *War in the Works of J.R.R. Tolkien* (Praeger, 2004; winner of the Mythopoeic Society Award for Inklings Studies), of *Legal Solutions in Electronic Reserves and the Electronic Delivery of Interlibrary Loan* (Haworth, 2004), and of articles on Tolkien, J.K Rowling, and Terry Pratchett in *Mythlore, Mallorn, Tolkien Studies,* and *Seven,* and is editor of two collections of essays: *Tolkien on Film: Essays on Peter Jackson's Lord of the Rings* (Mythopoeic Press, 2004) and *Tolkien and Shakespeare: Essays on Shared Themes and Language* (McFarland, 2006). She is the editor of *Mythlore* and book review editor for *Oklahoma Librarian* and serves on the board of Mythopoeic Press.

Michael D.C. Drout is the William C.H. and Elsie D. Prentice Professor of English and chair of the English Department at Wheaton College, Norton, Massachusetts, where he teaches Old and Middle English, medieval literature, fantasy and science fiction. The author of *How Tradition Works,* Drout edited *J.R.R. Tolkien's Beowulf and the Critics,* which won the 2003 Mythopoeic Society Scholarship Award for Inklings

Studies. His book *The Tower and the Ruin: Explorations in Tolkien's World*, will appear in 2011. A founder and coeditor of the journal *Tolkien Studies*, Drout has published widely on Anglo-Saxon literature and culture, Tolkien and fantasy literature. A graduate of Carnegie Mellon University, he received his PhD in 1997 from Loyola University Chicago after earning degrees from Stanford (journalism) and the University of Missouri–Columbia.

Dimitra Fimi is a lecturer in English at the University of Wales Institute, Cardiff (UWIC), where she teaches 20th-century literature, fantasy, science fiction and myth in literature. She has published a series of articles on Tolkien's roots in Victorian and Edwardian visual and literary culture and on Tolkien's creative use of Celtic mythological and folklore material. Her most recently published book is *Tolkien, Race and Cultural History: From Fairies to Hobbits* (Palgrave Macmillan, 2008). She is a graduate of the University of Athens (Greece) and earned her PhD from Cardiff University in 2005.

Verlyn Flieger has published widely on Tolkien's fiction. Her books include *Splintered Light: Logos and Language in Tolkien's World*, *A Question of Time: J.R.R. Tolkien's Road to Faërie*, and *Interrupted Music: The Making of Tolkien's Mythology*. She edited the critical edition of Tolkien's short story *Smith of Wootton Major*; and with Douglas A. Anderson she edited the critical edition of Tolkien's essay "On Fairy-stories." With Carl Hostetter, she edited *Tolkien's Legendarium*, a collection of essays on *The Silmarillion*. Together with Douglas A. Anderson and Michael D.C. Drout, she is coeditor of *Tolkien Studies*, the only scholarly journal devoted entirely to the work of J.R.R. Tolkien.

Judy Ann Ford is a medieval historian who specializes in popular religion in medieval England. She teaches medieval history as well as introductory courses on the scope and methods of history. She has published an essay on the parallels between Rome and Tolkien's ideas of Minas Tirith in *Tolkien Studies* (vol. 2, no. 1). Dr. Ford and Dr. Robin Anne Reid are colleagues at Texas A&M University–Commerce. They codirected two N.E.H. Summer Institutes on Tolkien (2004, 2009) and regularly team-teach courses on Tolkien on both the graduate and undergraduate levels. Their essay "Councils and Kings: Aragorn's Journey towards Kingship in J.R.R. Tolkien's *The Lord of the Rings* and Peter Jackson's *The Lord of the Rings*" appears in *Tolkien Studies* 6 (July 2009).

Philip E. Kaveny is an independent scholar at the University of Wisconsin–Eau Claire. He completed an MA and a CAGS in library and information studies at University of Wisconsin–Madison and is currently studying religion and economics through the Philosophy and Religion Department at UW–Eau Claire. He has also collaborated with Janice M. Bogstad on many conference presentations and published book reviews alone for *New York Review of Science Fiction*, *SFRA Review*, and *Midwest Review of Books*, among others. He has also written poetry and fiction for small press publications.

Yvette Kisor is an associate professor of literature at Ramapo College of New Jersey. She has various publications on Tolkien, *Beowulf*, and medieval literature to her credit, including recent essays in *Tolkien Studies* and *Mythlore* as well as multiple entries in *The J.R.R. Tolkien Encyclopedia: Scholarship and Critical Assessment*, edited by Michael Drout (New York: Routledge, 2006).

About the Contributors

John D. Rateliff spent many years researching Tolkien's manuscripts at Marquette University, as well as at other archives. Out of this work grew *The History of the Hobbit*, his two-volume edition of Tolkien's original manuscript of *The Hobbit*. He holds a PhD from Marquette. His dissertation was on the short stories of Lord Dunsany, and he has a special interest in the history of fantasy and in the Inklings. Among his other publications are contributions to *Mythlore: The Rhetoric of Vision* (1996), *Tolkien's Legendarium* (2000), *The Lord of the Rings 1954–2004: Scholarship in Honor of Richard E. Blackwelder* (2006), *Tolkien Studies* (2009), and the online Classics of Fantasy series (2002–2004).

Robin Anne Reid's area of scholarly interest is speculative fiction. She regularly presents papers on Tolkien at the annual International Congress on Medieval Studies and the mythopoeic conferences. She also presents papers on Tolkien at the International Conference for the Fantastic in the Arts (ICFA). Her teaching fields are creative writing and critical theory. She is the editor of the *Women in Science Fiction and Fantasy* encyclopedia (Greenwood), and is working on an anthology of gender theories and the fantastic. She is a professor in Literature and Languages at Texas A&M.

Joseph Ricke is a professor of English at Taylor University. He studied with Jane Chance at Rice University, specializing in medieval and renaissance literature, and now researches and writes on early drama, including a forthcoming chapter in the *MLA Approaches to Teaching* "Taming of the Shrew." He teaches the Tolkien section of a C.S. Lewis and Friends Seminar and World Cinema at Taylor. He is presently working on a longer study of the significance of "the numinous" to Lewis, Tolkien, and the Inklings, on the pre–Shakespearean stage history of "shrews," and on the depiction of gender and sexuality in the Inklings.

E.L. Risden is a professor of English at St. Norbert College. He has published thirteen books on subjects ranging from Beowulf to film criticism and including fiction, poetry, a translation, and a textbook. His current projects include a study of narrative subversion in medieval and Renaissance literature, a consideration of the transition from the medieval to the Renaissance mind, a series of essays on structure and theme in Tolkien's literary and critical work, and an analysis of the idea of the problem play in Shakespeare.

Sharin Schroeder is a PhD candidate at the University of Minnesota. In addition to her scholarship on nineteenth-century British fantasy, she has presented work on Tolkien's mythology and style at Tolkien 2005 and the Congress for Medieval Studies in Kalamazoo, Michigan. She has taught Tolkien's works in her Tolkien: Medieval or Modern? and Modern Fiction courses.

Kristin Thompson is an honorary fellow in the Department of Communication Arts at the University of Wisconsin–Madison. Her most recent book is *The Frodo Franchise: "The Lord of the Rings" and Modern Hollywood* (University of California Press, 2007). She has contributed a number of books to the study of film and film theory, most recently including *Herr Lubitsch Goes to Hollywood: German and American Film After World War I* (2005).

Brian D. Walter is an assistant professor of English and the director of convocations at the St. Louis College of Pharmacy. His scholarly and professional work has appeared in *Boulevard, The Southern Quarterly, Nabokov Studies, Essays in Literature,* and the *St. Louis Post-Dispatch,* among others. His areas of scholarly and professional interest include modern English and American literature, the novel, film and literature, and children's film and literature.

Richard C. West holds graduate degrees in English and Library Science and has a background in medieval English, French, and Scandinavian literature, modern science fiction and fantasy, and librarianship. A member of the Science Fiction Research Association and the International Association for the Fantastic in the Arts since their inception, he is on the board of advisors of the Mythopoeic Society and the editorial board of *Tolkien Studies.* His bibliography *Tolkien Criticism: An Annotated Checklist* was published in two editions (Kent State University Press, 1970, 1981), and he has published articles on Tolkien, Lewis, T.H. White, Beagle, and Peake. He is currently a senior academic librarian and Head of Serials at the Kurt F. Wendt Library, College of Engineering, University of Wisconsin–Madison.

Robert C. Woosnam-Savage studied art history at the University of Manchester before becoming curator of European Arms and Armour at Glasgow Museums (1983–97). He has been Curator of European Edged Weapons at the Royal Armouries Museum, Leeds, since 2001, where he co-curated (with Richard Taylor) the highly successful exhibition *Arms & Armour from the Movies: The Wonderful World of Weta* (2008). He has visited Weta Workshop twice and spoken with many of those involved in the making and building of the arms and armor produced for *The Lord of the Rings* motion picture trilogy. He is currently working on a book on arms and armor in the movies and another on medieval battles on film.

Index

Abraham 17, 189
absence 2, 12, 34, 37, 47, 54, 55, 57, 59, 61, 62, 63, 65, 66, 103, 177, 198, 214n10, 273
Academy Awards 157
Achilles 72
Ackerman, Forrest J 5, 6, 7, 27
action films 6, 59, 67n9, 141, 217, 264, 276
Adam 120, 130
The Adventures of Robin Hood (1938) 149
Aegnor 97, 99n23; *see also* Figwit
The Aeneid 72
afterlife 17, 170, 172, 173, 177, 179, 180, 255
Ainulindalë 123
Ainur 16, 120, 174
Alexander Nevsky 7
Allen and Unwin 5, 6, 260n4
alliterative poetry 249
Altdorfer, Albrecht (1480–1538) 158, 160
Alte Pinakothek 158
American monomyth 18, 19, 217–219, 221, 223, 224, 225n3
Amon Hen 109, 144, 164n117
Anderson, Bob 151, 156
Anderson, Douglas 189, 192n11, 260n6
Anduin 15, 240
angels 120, 130, 204, 207, 233, 241
Anglo-Saxons 256–60, 260n1, 260n6, 262n12, 262n16, 288
animal rights 242, 246n9
animals 20, 73, 157, 238, 242, 246n9, 261n20; *see also* animal rights; eagle; horse; pony
Anna (Karenina) 210
Anthony, Marc 189
anthropomorphism 126–129
Appleton, Matt 161
Aragorn 11, 13, 14, 17–20, 29–31, 37–39, 41, 42, 43n11, 51, 58, 60, 65, 66, 71, 74, 75, 78, 79, 81, 91–93, 102, 103, 106, 107, 108, 111, 135n17, 169, 172, 175, 187, 188, 198–200, 203–205, 207–211, 212, 214n12, 214n25, 216, 218–224, 225n4, 227, 229–235,
235n5, 235n16, 240, 243–245, 246n10, 249, 251, 254–256, 264, 277, 278, 283
archeology 245, 258
archery 38, 146, 153, 156
Arda 246n8
Argonath, Gates of 31
armies 28, 39, 108, 139, 157–160, 221, 222, 225n4
armor 1, 2, 14, 15, 16, 139–151, 153–160, 161n1, 161n10, 244
Arnor 229, 230, 232
Arod 243
arrow 88, 126, 145, 152, 153, 160, 276
art 6, 28, 46, 47, 79, 89–91, 96, 132n2, 135n17, 142, 154, 158, 186, 190, 214n10, 228, 231, 235, 248, 264, 282
Arthurian Vulgate Cycle 13, 102
artisans 139, 143
Arwen 11, 17, 19, 20, 30, 31, 39, 41, 42, 43n11, 60, 65, 90, 96, 143, 161n4, 174, 179, 216, 219, 220, 223, 224, 227, 229–234, 235, 235n5, 235n9, 239, 240, 244, 245, 246n10, 254, 261n21
Astin, Sean 133n8, 141, 148, 161n7, 162n49
Astor, Mary 53
Auden, W.H. 117, 129, 133n6, 133n9
Aule 121, 122, 126
Austen, Jane 267
authority 85, 177, 195–203, 207, 209, 211, 212
axe 48, 150

Bach ("Incarnatus") 282
Bag End 32, 34, 74, 77, 197, 218
Bakshi, Ralph 5–7, 10, 56–59, 61, 67n9, 67n12, 86, 224
Balin 116, 163n58
Balrog 38, 44, 71, 86, 126, 135, 184, 200, 201, 204, 206, 213, 241, 269, 275, 277, 280
Barad-dûr 261n22
Barahir 229, 230
Baranduin 39
barbarians 154, 257

291

292 Index

barrow 11, 12, 29, 55–65, 66n3, 67n16, 70, 81, 108, 176, 245, 249, 258
Barry Lyndon (1975) 156
Batman & Robin (1997) 156
Batman Forever (1995) 156
battle 6, 14, 16, 19, 21, 25, 30, 33, 38, 39, 41, 44n13, 65, 71, 73, 78, 81, 82, 83, 93, 94, 105–109, 119, 122, 131, 135n16, 139, 141, 144, 146, 152, 155, 157–160, 163n93, 169, 171, 177, 183, 184, 187, 190, 191, 200, 204–207, 209, 218, 222, 224, 233, 234, 235n16, 238, 240, 244, 252, 254, 256, 261n22, 266, 274, 276; *see also* war
Battle of (Alexander at) Issus 152, 159
Battle of Britain (1969) 160
The Battle of Maldon (poem) 73, 74, 252
Bazin, André 110, 111
BBC 56, 58, 59, 66n9, 67n10, 143
Beagle, Peter S 7, 56, 57, 59, 67n12, 224
Beagle/Bahski 56, 57, 59
Bean, Sean 16, 114, 144, 163n65, 281
The Beatles 6
Ben-Hur 159
Beorn 34
Beornings 249, 251
Beowulf (man) 117, 133n6, 258, 261n17, 284n6, 284n7
Beowulf 12, 13, 21, 50, 72, 102, 112n2, 117n2, 117, 118, 132n5, 134n16, 218, 244, 250, 253, 255, 261n11, 261n17, 261n23, 261n24
Beowulf: The Monsters and the Critics 117
Bercilak 73
Beregond 205
Beren and Luthien 19, 181n5, 229, 230, 231
Berkshire 51
betrayal 135, 203
betrothal 227, 231
Bible 80, 82, 119, 120, 135n16, 180, 189
Bilbo 16, 17, 31, 32, 34, 40, 51, 52, 28, 72, 77, 78, 136, 155, 174, 175, 177, 178, 183, 188, 189, 190, 194, 196, 197, 198, 210, 211, 213n4, 214n10
Bill (the Pony) 9, 74, 90, 199, 212, 240, 241, 242
birds 20, 53, 95, 238, 240
birthday party 31, 34, 72, 194
Black Gate 18, 30, 66, 106, 204, 207, 208, 222
Black Rider 39, 56, 57, 61, 62, 67n13, 67n15, 78, 89, 106, 109, 188, 195, 218, 234, 276, 277
Black Speech 188
Black Years 188
Blanchett, Cate 276, 278–280
The Blind Dead (1971–1975) 156
blizzard 201
Blood of Kings 183, 190
Bloom, Harold 280, 284n3
Bloom, Orlando 37, 135n17, 153
Bolger, Fatty 56
Bombadil, Tom 2, 7, 11, 12, 19, 21, 29, 48–52, 55, 57–59, 61, 63, 64, 66, 66n6, 67n10, 68n12, 70, 72, 74, 76–79, 108, 164, 169, 174, 176, 177, 274
Bonanza series 220
Bondarchuk 159, 164n107
Book of Mormon 280
Boorman, John 6, 56, 57, 59, 60, 66n7
Bored of the Rings 57
Boromir 15, 37, 38, 47, 52, 71, 74, 113n14, 119, 124, 126, 135n17, 144, 200, 201, 212, 213, 219, 240, 269, 278, 281, 283, 284, 284n5
Boyens, Phillipa 54, 55, 59, 61–63, 65, 66n1, 66n2, 67n17, 118, 119, 125, 127, 128, 231, 239
braids 254, 255
Bratman, David 132n3, 161n4, 271, 275
Braveheart 143, 149, 159
Bree 29, 57, 59, 62, 65, 67n13, 77–79, 214n20, 218, 221, 240, 241, 274
Brego 9, 20, 242–245
Bresson, Robert 264
Brodax, Al 5
Bucklebury Ferry 61, 62, 67n13, 67n15, 67n16
Burdge, Anthony 223, 224
Burke, Jessica 223, 224
burnt offerings 189
butchers' gloves 150

Caesar, Julius 50, 189
camera 35, 36, 54, 96, 125, 144, 155, 197, 198, 201, 206, 243, 283
Campbell, Joseph 18, 75, 216–219, 221, 223
Canton-Jones 143
Captain Kirk 219
Caradhras 199, 201, 202, 212
Caras Galadhon 278
Carpenter, Humphrey 5, 43n7, 43n9, 44n16, 172, 173, 175, 181n3, 213n1, 213n3, 269
Cartwright (*Bonanza* family) 220
cathedral 12, 71, 79–81, 278
Catholicism 171, 172, 235, 270
Cavalry 158, 159, 239, 246n2, 253
Cave troll 15, 116, 118, 119, 124, 126, 128, 135, 135n22, 241
Celeborn 211, 272, 278, 279, 280
Celebrimbor 40
Celtic Revival Movement 13, 88–91
Celts 13, 21, 85, 87, 88, 90, 91, 97, 98n8, 99n10, 181n2, 228, 244, 257, 258
Central Otago 37
Cerin Amroth 220, 227, 231, 235
Cervantes 210
Chamber of Mazarbul 200, 213
Chamberlain, Neville 27
chaos theory 75
chiaroscuro 71, 80
Christianity 73, 80, 121, 131, 171, 172, 180, 181n2, 189, 235, 253, 258
Chronicles of Narnia 142, 150
church 80, 81, 172, 256, 278, 282
Círdan 177

Index   293

City Gates 177
Cobb, Ron 5, 6
Cold War (Great Britain) 185
coloring books 186, 187
Commando (1985) 156
Common Speech 248, 249, 251, 252
computer-generation 10, 11, 35, 43, 47, 49, 53, 126, 132n1, 142, 153, 156, 157, 159, 160, 191, 239, 265
computers 28, 47, 153, 157, 159, 191
Conan the Barbarian 154
Conklin, Chris 7, 57, 67n12
conspiracy 55, 57, 61, 62, 202
coronation 42, 172, 210, 220, 233
corpse 33, 94, 124, 134n16, 160
Council 26, 95, 204, 219, 222
Council of Elrond 25, 52, 67n13, 95, 191, 243, 246n7, 249
Cracks of Doom 106, 189, 190, 191, 218
Crickhollow 11, 55–57, 59, 61, 62, 66n3, 74, 76, 77, 218
Croft, Janet Brennan 2, 5, 8, 18, 19, 43, 43n1, 66n7, 104, 216, 221, 225n4, 235n9, 261n21
crowd replication system 157
culture 2, 9, 20, 21, 86, 97, 117, 123, 132n4, 156, 185, 186, 192n9, 216, 238–244, 246n9, 248, 253, 257, 258
The Curse of Frankenstein (2002) 117, 119, 124, 125; *see also Frankenstein* (Whale's)
Cushing, Peter 124
Cymric 73

Dagorlad 204
Dale 248, 251
dance 48, 49, 50, 194, 196
Dane 117, 134n16
Dante 12, 73, 2
Dark Lord 51, 72, 173, 209, 229, 277; *see also* Sauron
darkness 32, 33, 37, 47, 81, 88, 107, 108, 109, 118, 120, 123, 125, 126, 132n4, 135n16, 169, 179, 180, 184, 185, 187, 189, 190, 199, 200, 211, 215n27, 251, 253, 254, 266, 271, 278, 281, 282, 284
Dead Marshes 130
death 19, 21, 31, 38, 41, 47, 71, 72, 74, 75, 78, 80, 81, 108, 118, 127, 122n9, 177, 179, 181n5, 183, 184, 189–191, 194, 206, 207, 218–220, 230, 234, 235, 243, 258, 262, 275
Decipher's *The Lord of the Rings* Trading Card Game 97
design team 40, 90, 93, 94, 99n14, 99n17, 99n19, 99n22, 163n68, 163n74, 163n82, 163n94
democracy 221, 222, 224, 225n3, 232
demon 81, 134n16, 134n16, 135n16, 279
Denethor 18, 30, 64, 136n27, 144, 155, 175, 205, 216, 219, 229, 232
de Ossorio, Amando 156
Dernhelm 108
despair 78, 103, 107, 108, 130, 206, 279, 283

DeVries, Kelly 161
Dewey, James 3
disembodiment 126, 127, 130
Disney 40, 48, 86, 228, 323
Docherty, Jason 93
dragons 40, 72, 78, 117, 120, 136n25, 159, 196, 197, 256
dreams 53, 75, 109, 128, 141, 169, 176, 177, 179, 234, 264
Dreyer, Carl Theodore 264
drink 49, 68n17, 79, 83, 194, 203, 272
Duncan, Cameron 180
Duncan, John 89, 90, 161n6, 163n73, 163n79, 163n84, 164n102
Dúnedain 40, 220–222; *see also* Ranger
Dunharrow 106, 108, 218, 220
Duriez, Colin 272
DVD 7, 8, 9, 12, 43n4, 55, 57, 67n16, 86, 89–91, 93, 95, 116, 232, 252, 258, 277, 280
Dvergatal 251
Dvořák, Max 79
dwarves 2, 15, 48, 49, 89, 121, 123, 150, 154, 199, 200, 202, 113n4, 228, 238, 239, 251, 252, 261n16
Dwimorberg 92

eagles 20, 81, 204, 237, 241, 243
Eärendil 109, 175, 272
Eastemnet 250
Easterling 130, 240, 257, 259
Eco, Umberto 170, 192n4
Edda 93, 252
Edoras 198, 214n20, 255, 257
Egypt 42, 258, 259
El Cid (1061) 149
Elder Days 268, 269, 280
elegy 275–277, 284, 284n6
Elendil 14, 66, 254, 177, 179, 181n5, 220, 227, 229, 230, 232, 234, 242–245, 250, 272, 279, 280; *see also* Elves
Elision 12, 19, 54, 55, 59, 267, 274
Elrond 11, 16, 19, 26, 30, 38, 29, 41, 52, 67n13, 92, 95, 172, 175, 177, 178, 191, 210, 211, 215n27, 219, 220, 229, 230, 233, 234, 243, 246n7, 249, 254
Elves 2, 13, 16, 17, 19, 20, 25, 38, 39, 44n13, 49, 61, 67n13, 72, 78, 85–92, 95, 96, 97, 99n1, 107, 109, 120, 121, 123–125, 129, 133n16, 134n16, 153, 154, 157, 160, 164n101, 172–179, 181n5, 221, 227, 228, 230, 231, 235, 238–240, 245, 261n12, 264–267, 271, 272, 274–276, 278, 279, 281, 283–284
emnet 250
Emyn Muil 109
Ents 29, 11, 238, 273
Entwade 249, 250
Enya 91, 281
Eodoras 250
Éomer 74, 111, 141, 214n24, 224, 249, 250, 255, 257; banishment of 257
Eorl the Young 255

Index

eorod (mounted troop) (250
Éothain 250, 257
Éowyn 31, 105–110, 113n11, 198, 207, 214n24, 220, 224, 249, 258
Erebor 38
eternal truth 210
Ethiopia 251 (Latin Æthiops)
eucatastrophe 81, 106, 110–112, 181n2, 218
Eucharist 81
Europe 2, 13, 85, 94, 147, 210, 211, 245
evil 14, 15, 17, 18, 47, 71–73, 77, 78, 89, 83, 97, 118–122, 124–127, 129–131, 133n6, 133n9, 134n14, 134n16, 135n16, 136n23, 142, 147, 169, 171–173, 175, 179, 184, 185, 192n8, 192n9, 204, 208, 210, 211, 214n19, 217, 218, 239, 241, 267, 270, 279
Eye of Sauron 51

faerie 13, 89, 271
Faerie Queene 73
fairy stories 75, 80, 85–87, 89, 90, 120, 129, 218, 235n9
faith 10, 31, 37, 38, 58–60, 73, 79, 110–112, 125, 155, 170, 173, 176, 210, 220, 222, 223, 270, 272, 273
Falconer, Daniel 147, 154, 162n43, 163n89
fandoms 1, 13, 44n17, 86, 87
Fangorn Forest 45, 63, 204
fans 1, 2, 7–10, 13, 17, 27, 28, 31, 42, 43, 49, 56, 57, 70, 71, 83–86, 95–98, 124, 150, 153, 160, 188, 216, 224, 232, 234, 266, 267, 273
Fantasy 2, 7, 35, 39, 41, 46, 47, 84, 85, 87, 97, 98, 120, 121, 133n6, 134n14, 142, 1456, 154, 160, 170, 188, 192n9, 240, 259, 261n20, 264, 266
fantasy film 25, 97, 264
Far Green Country 169, 176, 177
Faramir 74, 113n14, 133, 160, 164n119, 164n120, 177, 195, 204, 205, 207, 216, 244
fate 1, 38, 43n11, 78, 122, 173, 174, 201, 209, 217, 219, 230, 232, 235n13, 264
Fate of Frankenstein (1823) 122
Fearless (2006) 158
Felarof 241, 242, 243
Fell Beasts 28, 106, 238, 241
the Fellowship 7, 11, 31, 32, 37, 38, 42, 43n4, 43n13, 44n17, 60, 62, 81, 102, 103, 118, 129, 131, 144, 185, 199–202, 212, 213n6, 234, 266, 272, 278, 283, 284
The Fellowship of the Ring (*Fellowship*; *FOTR*; *FR*) 3, 6, 7, 11, 15–19, 25, 27, 31, 32, 37, 38, 42, 43n4, 43n13, 44n17, 49, 51, 52, 56, 59, 63, 66n1, 66n4, 67n11, 67n13, 67n16, 68n18, 68n20, 70, 88–91, 95, 98n2, 98n7, 99n9, 99n11, 102, 104, 116, 118, 119, 121, 123, 124, 125, 126, 131, 131n1, 132n3, 133n8, 135n17, 139, 157, 161n1, 161n10, 162n36, 162n41, 162n42, 162n48, 162n50, 162n52, 162n53, 162n58, 163n58, 163n65, 163n82, 164n98, 170–171, 173–176, 185, 192n5, 195, 198–200, 202, 211, 214n9, 214n11–n16,

214n18, 218, 220, 221, 223, 235n10, 235n13, 235n14, 235n17, 238, 239, 240–244, 246n7, 254, 255, 264, 266, 276, 284
festivities 194
fighting styles 156, 157
Figwit 96, 97, 243; *see also* Aegnor
Finarfin (Finduilas; Fingolfin; Fingon; Finrod; Finwë) 96
fireworks 32, 34, 196
First Age 16, 87, 173, 229, 232
Fisher, Terence 123, 161n1
Flieger, Verlyn
flowers 49, 51, 64, 227, 231, 254, 255, 277
folklore (technique) 1, 13, 84–98, 99n12, 99n20
Ford of Bruinen 57, 234, 235n17, 257
fountain 110, 283
Frankenstein 15, 117–128, 131, 134n13; myth 14, 116, 117, 120
Frankenstein (Shelley) 116, 119, 120, 129, 132n3, 135n18; adaptations 14, 117, 118, 122, 123, 130, 131, 132n3
Frankenstein (Whale, 1931)) 117, 121, 125, 132n3, 135n19; *see also Curse of Frankenstein* (2002)
Frankenstein, (Baron) Victor 121, 124, 130
Fraser, George MacDonald 143, 161n14
The Frighteners 65, 94
Frodo 6, 8, 11, 14–18, 20, 27, 29, 30, 33, 35–39, 50, 52, 53, 57, 58, 60, 61, 64, 65, 67n16, 70–77, 81, 88, 104, 105, 108–111, 113n13, 113n14, 199, 124, 128–131, 135n17, 136n23, 136n26, 142, 144, 169, 170, 172, 174, 176, 177–181, 183, 187, 188, 190, 191, 192n1, 195–197, 199, 200–209, 211–213, 214n10, 214n13, 216–219, 222, 223, 225n4, 229, 232, 234, 238, 240, 254, 267, 269, 279, 281, 282, 284; journey 67n16, 77, 169, 170, 176, 203
Froud, Brian 89
Frye, Northrop 223
funeral 47, 73, 189, 258

Galadriel 11, 14, 19, 21, 33, 34, 38, 39, 47, 87, 99n23, 108–110, 112n13, 128, 172, 173, 175–178, 210, 211, 230, 235, 255, 261n22, 270, 272, 275–279, 281, 283; mirror 173, 178, 276
Galahad 72, 81
Gandalf 6, 7, 14, 18, 19, 26, 27, 29, 30, 32, 33, 34, 39, 40, 42, 43n13, 47, 51, 52, 58, 60–62, 64, 65, 66n9, 67n13, 71, 81, 86, 109, 111, 115, 131, 136n27, 159, 174, 175, 177–179, 181n2, 183, 184, 187, 188, 192n1, 192n5, 196–212, 213n4, 214n10, 214n12, 214n14, 214n15, 214n17, 214n19, 214n20, 214n24, 217–219, 222, 229, 230, 233, 234, 238, 240–243, 245, 246n7, 246n10, 251, 256, 261n15, 275, 283
Geats 117, 134n16
gems 33, 254

Index 295

genocide 184
ghosts 13, 93, 94, 99n15, 176, 269, 281
Gibson, Mel 143, 180
Gildor 61, 88, 89
Gillies, Rob 161
Gimli 11, 13, 24, 26, 37, 47, 48, 53, 74, 92, 102, 103, 106, 200–202, 204, 205, 212, 213, 214n13, 216, 221, 222, 246n9, 251, 256, 269, 277, 278
Glorfindel 39, 179, 234
Gnomish-tongue 249
goblins 120, 133n8, 240
God 15, 17, 73, 79, 80, 120–122, 125, 125n18, 131, 140, 159, 269, 270
goddess 219, 220
gods 127, 171, 174, 243, 268, 270
gold 8, 52, 53, 107, 108, 254–256, 271
Goldberry 11, 48, 49, 51, 53, 56, 57, 63, 64
Golden Hall 244, 250, 251, 256, 261n24; *see also* Meduseld
Golden Wood 267, 272, 276, 277, 281; *see also* Lothlórien
Gollum 6, 15, 17, 25, 26, 35–37, 44n14, 72, 76, 105, 109, 110, 116, 124, 126, 128–131, 132n3, 136n26, 183, 185–187, 188–192, 192n4, 212, 216, 274, 275; *see also* Smeagol
Gondor 37–40, 60, 75, 81, 108, 135n17, 136n27, 144, 145, 146n32, 167n33, 169, 172, 175, 181n2, 205, 206, 219, 229, 230, 332, 233, 260n7, 283
good (moral) 3, 15, 17, 35, 43, 71, 72, 78, 79, 81, 95, 129, 130, 133n9, 141, 142, 169, 171, 172, 179, 180, 184, 185, 189, 204, 207, 214n9, 219, 231, 233, 270
Gothic 71, 79–81, 132n3, 249, 253, 255, 257, 278, 282, 283
Gothic cathedral 12, 79, 80, 81
Gothmog 123
grace 16, 37, 39, 49, 81, 89, 90, 172, 209, 245, 272
grasslands 37, 49, 51, 108, 227, 271
Grealish, Michael 146, 161, 162n35, 162n44
Greco–Roman 171
greed 53, 53n1, 136n26
Green, Warren 147
Green Knight 73, 88, 284n7
Greenstreet, Sidney 53
Grendel 117, 126, 132n5, 133n5, 133n6, 134n16, 250
Grey Havens 16, 31, 44, 72, 81, 113n12, 172, 174, 177, 178, 180, 270
grief 41, 87, 90, 200, 203, 219, 273, 283
Grond 206
guide (person) 51, 113n14, 199–203, 205
Gwaihir 204, 241, 243, 246n7

Haldir 277
halflings 85, 129, 213
Hamlet (Zeffirelli, 1991) 143
Hammer Horror series 118, 124
Hammett, Dashiel 153

Haradrim 129, 251
Haradwaith 251
Haraway, Donna 242, 246n9
Harlow, Dr. Harry 190
Harry Potter 8
Harryhausen, Ray 118
Harvey, John 150, 153, 161
Hasufel 243
healing 78, 190, 214n23, 218
heirarchy 80, 129, 132n4, 242, 243, 245, 246n9
Hektor 73
Hellboy 142
helmet 21, 107, 142, 144, 155, 244, 255, 257–259; *see also* Sutton Hoo
Helm's Deep 184, 187
Henry V (1944; 1989) 143, 149
Heorot 118, 255
heraldry 154, 155, 158
The Hero with a Thousand Faces (1973) 217
heroism 12, 18–20, 30, 41, 56, 72, 73, 75, 77, 87, 93, 113n11, 136n26, 142, 143, 150, 199, 200, 205, 206, 207, 211, 212, 217–219, 221, 222, 223, 225n5, 235n9, 240, 264, 265, 269, 276, 284n7
hierophany 80
High Elves 88, 264
high fantasy 188, 192n9
History of Middle-earth 8, 10, 103, 170, 188, 191, 192n3, 229
The Hobbit (1937; 1951) 1, 5–8, 33, 34, 40, 43n10, 68n5, 68n9, 71, 75–77, 85, 89, 155, 171, 185, 187–189, 192n3, 192n11, 195, 199, 251, 260n6, 261n15, 271, 279
Hobbits 2, 15, 17, 18, 20, 29, 32, 35, 36, 41, 47–49, 51, 55–59, 62, 63, 64, 65, 66n1, 67n13, 67n15, 68n20, 72, 77, 79, 81, 83, 89, 122, 132n4, 136n26, 145, 172, 173, 175, 178, 180, 187, 188, 190, 191, 192n1, 194–197, 201, 205, 207, 210–213, 214n14, 214n20, 222, 229, 232, 233, 239–243, 246n5, 252, 272; *see also* Halfling
Hollin 200
Homer 72, 188
Horace 82
horn 206, 207, 256, 283
Hornburg 29, 163n72, 163n107
horror 33, 74, 79, 94, 95, 97, 116, 118, 124, 131, 133n9, 160, 208, 209, 218, 274, 276, 279
horse-heads 245, 257
Horse-Kings/horse lords 20, 249, 252; *see also* Riders of Rohan; Rohirrim
horses 7, 9, 16, 20, 21, 48, 89, 92, 113n7, 134n10, 146, 156, 157, 159, 160, 162n30, 164n114, 198, 222, 234, 238, 240–245, 245n4, 246n3, 246n6, 246n8, 246n9, 246n10, 246n11, 249, 250, 252, 255–257, 260n8, 276
hound of Sauron 200
The House of the Wolfings 256

Howard, Ron 155
Howe, John 26, 161, 162*n*40
Hughes, Shuan 183
humans 2, 15, 17, 18, 20, 49, 50, 53, 57, 72, 73, 77, 94, 103, 111, 117, 120, 121, 126, 127, 132*n*2, 133*n*5, 133*n*6, 134*n*10, 135*n*16, 139, 144, 156, 171, 172, 180, 181*n*5, 188, 191, 194, 203, 209, 220, 223, 227, 229–232, 239–243, 268, 270, 281, 284
Huston, John 53, 53*n*1, 67*n*9
Hwaet sindon ge 251
hythe 259

I, Robot (2004) 158
icons 6, 19, 20, 63, 65, 142, 153, 154, 186, 187, 190, 217, 231, 238, 239, 241, 243–244, 257–259
The Idea of the Holy 268, 281, 284n1
Ides Aelfschyne 250 (elf shining)
The Iliad 72, 188, 218
Ilúvator 16, 120, 122, 123, 124, 209
imagery 6, 11, 12, 16, 19, 21, 28, 35, 41, 47, 48, 78, 85, 87, 94, 98, 106–110, 121, 122, 135*n*16, 135*n*18, 136*n*23, 142, 156–158, 170, 176, 177, 179, 186, 187, 190, 192*n*7, 194, 195, 197, 198, 203, 231, 254, 256–259, 262*n*21, 262*n*22, 262*n*26, 264, 265, 282, 283
imagination 16, 32, 46, 47, 49, 53, 54, 72, 76, 79, 81, 88, 117, 141, 160, 228, 255, 260
immortality 136*n*24, 181*n*5, 230, 231, 234
incarnation 76, 77, 79, 117, 127, 131, 134*n*14, 179, 194, 196, 205, 207
Indiana Jones 118
Indonesia 190
Ingeld 117
Ingram, Stephen 153, 162*n*31
Inklings 192*n*9, 271, 277, 284n1
inscriptions 52, 53, 155, 163*n*89, 199, 200
internet 96, 97, 246*n*9
Iron Age 90, 91, 99*n*8, 240
iron crown of Morgoth 230
Iron Mask 188
Irongarth 248
ironsmith 148
Isaac 17, 189
Isengard 26, 102, 103, 111, 113*n*15, 125, 139, 148, 161*n*1, 176, 213*n*5, 214*n*19, 239, 251
Iser, Wolfgang 104
Isildur 11, 17, 29, 66, 91, 92, 173, 177, 189, 190, 192*n*1, 222, 233, 234
Istari 194, 195, 210
Ithaka 72
Ithilien 35
Ivanhoe 143

Jackson, Peter 2, 3, 5, 7–15, 17–22, 25–28, 34, 35, 39–41, 41*n*14, 47–51, 54, 55, 57–66, 66*n*3, 66*n*4, 67*n*9, 67*n*11, 67*n*15, 70, 71, 82–88, 90, 92–98, 102–112, 112*n*5, 113*n*13, 113*n*14, 113*n*15, 116, 117, 119, 122–131, 131*n*1, 134*n*14, 135*n*16, 135*n*17, 136*n*26, 139, 141, 145, 146, 151, 153, 155–161, 161*n*8, 162*n*30, 163*n*57, 163*n*58, 163*n*72, 163*n*86, 163*n*87, 93, 164*n*107, 164*n*112, 164*n*115, 164*n*121, 170, 172–177, 179, 180, 181*n*2, 183–188, 191, 192*n*2, 192*n*7, 194–198, 208, 209, 212, 213, 216–219, 220–225, 231–233, 235, 235*n*9, 238–245, 253, 254, 257, 258, 262*n*21, 264–267, 271, 273–284, 284*n*5; films 13, 14, 20, 65, 86, 102, 119, 225, 225*n*3, 238, 239, 242, 244, 245, 248, 261*n*21
Jaws 217
Jeanne D'Arc (1899) 149
Jewett, Robert *see* Lawrence and Jewett
Johnson, Stu 147, 161
journeys 29, 41, 59, 66*n*3, 67*n*18, 74, 78, 81, 103, 109, 162*n*38, 162*n*43, 163*n*83, 176–178, 180, 181*n*2, 199, 203, 211, 212, 218, 219, 236*n*19, 242
jousting 147, 162*n*46
joy 273
Judith (poem) 250

Kaczynski, Theodore 224
Kalevala 85, 87
Kay, Guy Gavriel 188, 192*n*10
Khazad-Dûm 38, 199, 211
King Kong 116, 142, 264
King of the Dead 92, 142, 222
Kingdom of Heaven (2005) 143, 150
Kingdom of Men 60
kingship 11, 18, 19, 30, 81, 220, 233, 234
Kollmann, Judith 222
Koven, Michael 84, 86, 94, 99*n*20
Krempe, Paul 125
Kubrick, Stanley 156, 159
Kundera, Milan 210, 211
Kurosawa, Akira 158

Lady of Shallot 66
Last Alliance 39, 92
Last Debate 222
The Last Samurai 142
Latin cross 80
Lawrence and Jewett (Lawrence, John Shelton and Jewett, Robert) 18, 217, 219–221, 223, 224, 225*n*5
Lay of Luthien 91, 232
Lee, Alan 13, 16, 26, 89–91, 146, 147, 161*n*11, 161*n*30, 164*n*101, 188, 258
Lee, Christopher 63, 68*n*18, 70, 89, 124, 125, 134*n*12, 134*n*13
Legendarium 8, 19, 33, 39, 40, 87, 97, 170, 181*n*2, 185, 187, 188, 192*n*3, 235, 245
Legolas 16, 27, 36, 39, 74, 86, 92, 102, 103, 106, 145, 153, 198, 200, 201, 204, 205, 222, 243, 245, 246*n*10, 251, 255, 256, 283
Lembas 272
Lennox, Annie 17, 279, 181*n*2

Letters (of J.R.R. Tolkien) 13, 27, 48, 51, 56, 64, 65, 66n3, 66n6, 104, 118, 136n24, 189, 213n1, 213n2, 213n4, 235n2, 236n25, 246n4, 260n4, 261n18, 267, 272, 273
Lewis, C.S. 120, 192n9, 268–270, 273, 284n1, 285n10
Li, Jet 158
Lion King (1994) 225n3, 232
The Lion, the Witch and the Wardrobe (2005)142, 150, 158
Lois Lane 219
Longman, Wolfson 122, 133n7
Lord of the Nazgûl 105, 108, 173, 206
Lord of the Rings (Lord; LOTR) 1, 3, 5–9, 11, 13–16, 19, 20–22, 24, 26–28, 31–34, 37–43, 43n4, 43n8, 43n10, 44n15, 46, 47, 49, 51, 54, 56, 60, 64, 66n2, 66n5, 67n16, 70–72, 74–82, 84–90, 92–97, 102, 103, 111, 112n6, 116, 117, 120, 122, 123, 129, 132n3, 132n4, 134n129, 139–142, 145–147, 148n11, 149, 151, 154, 156, 157, 159, 160, 169, 171, 172, 174–176, 180, 181n2, 183–184, 187–191, 192n3, 192n11, 194, 195, 199, 201, 214n26, 215n24, 216, 224, 228, 229, 235n1, 235n6, 235n7, 235n9, 235n11, 236n19, 236n20, 236n21, 236n22, 236n23, 241, 242, 245n1, 246n3, 248, 249, 252, 253, 255, 258, 259, 264, 267, 269, 271, 273–276, 280, 283, 284, 284n3
Lords of the West 194
Lorre, Peter 53
Lórien 34, 108–110, 175, 220, 268, 271
Lothlórien 2, 7, 11, 12, 17, 21, 38, 39, 76, 78, 87–89, 91, 204, 230, 259, 264–269, 271–284, 284n5, 285n10
Lurtz 15, 122, 123, 125–131, 134n13, 135n17, 135n19
Lúthien 19, 91, 181n5, 229, 230, 231, 232, 254
Lyon, Peter 16, 139, 144–147, 149–152, 155, 156, 161, 161n10, 162n21, 162n22, 162n27, 162n46, 163n91

Mabinogi (Mabinogion) 73
Macbeth 47, 50
mace 106
MacLeod, Fiona 89
magic 33, 34, 51, 60, 72, 85, 88, 153, 157, 158, 189, 199, 200, 234, 265, 266, 272, 279, 281, 282
Mahy, Warren 94, 154, 156
mail 148–150, 163n51
Major, Grant 146, 162n32
Maker 116, 121, 123, 133n6, 137, 149, 150
Maltese Falcon 53
Mandos 173
maps 29, 40, 62, 67n14, 67n16, 74, 75, 76, 103, 190
Marhad, Marnath, Marhelm, Marhun, Marhyse, and Marulf 249
Massacre at the Ford of Isen 257

Massive (Multiple Agent Simulation System in Virtual Environment) 157, 158, 164n102, 239
material culture 90, 140, 255–259
Matériel 139, 142, 147, 155
Maxims I 250
Maxwell, Kirk 150, 156
Mayes, Bernard 58, 64
Mays 5
McCallum, Tris 161
McKellen, Ian 27, 135n22, 203, 243
McKenna, Shaun 60
McVeigh, Timothy 224
Mearas 20, 239, 241–243
medievalism 2, 12, 13, 20, 72–74, 78, 80, 88–91, 93, 97, 112n2, 146, 147, 149, 152, 156, 158, 170, 171, 239, 240, 248, 253, 257, 260n1, 261n19, 262; see also Middle Ages
Meduseld 21, 194, 244, 250, 256, 257, 262n25
Meet the Feebles 95
Méliès, Georges 146
Melkor 14, 120–123, 125–127, 131, 134n11, 174
Meodarn/Meduarn/Winseld 250
Mercian 249, 253, 260n4, 260n8
Merry (Meriadoc Brandybuck 190) 11, 26, 61, 62, 65, 67n13, 67n14, 74, 81, 102, 103, 105–109, 113n7, 177, 178, 187, 188, 194, 196, 197, 199, 204, 207, 211, 212, 229
Middle Ages 73, 94, 147, 235; see also Medieval
middle class 211, 211
Middle English 87, 88, 192n6, 261n18
Middle-earth 2, 8, 10, 12–14, 16, 18–20, 26, 31, 32, 40–42, 47, 62, 64, 67n16, 71, 72, 74, 76, 78, 79, 87, 88, 90–92, 96, 98n2, 99n9, 99n12, 99n18, 103, 112n2, 116, 129, 131, 132n4, 134n6, 139, 142, 143, 145, 154–158, 161n1, 161n10, 162n36, 162n41, 162n42, 162n48, 162n50, 162n52, 162n53, 162n55, 163n61, 163n65, 170–176, 179, 180, 183, 184, 188, 191, 194, 195, 203–205, 208, 210, 211, 214n8, 214n12, 250–252, 259, 260n1, 260n2, 260n4, 264, 270, 271, 280
Midgewater Marshes 91, 235n10
military 146, 159, 184, 221, 222
Milton, John 206
Minas Tirith 18, 30, 38, 40, 64, 158, 159, 172, 175, 204, 205, 207, 208, 221, 234, 244
Miramar 147
Mirkwood 155
Mithril 14, 105, 136n23, 150, 208, 213, 254
monsters 14, 15, 17, 25, 72, 97, 116–131, 132n1, 132n3, 133n7, 134n12, 134n13, 134n14, 135n17, 135n18, 135n19, 135n26, 250, 255, 276
moon (light) 175, 179, 265, 266
Moore's Law 191, 193n12
morality 9, 73, 91, 119, 123, 136n23, 172, 185, 211, 219, 276, 280
Mordor 7, 14, 15, 18, 37, 52, 64, 70, 71, 75,

298 Index

81, 96, 106–111, 135n20, 139, 177, 187, 191, 207, 208, 221, 227, 233, 239–241, 251
Morgan, Tracey 161
Morgan le Fay 73
Morgoth 133n9, 134n11, 173, 175, 230
Morgoth's Ring 120, 122, 129, 131, 133n9, 134n11, 134n16, 136n24, 181n5
Morgul/Nazgûl Blades 148, 188
Moria 27, 32, 33, 38, 48, 49, 66n3, 86, 116, 118, 131n1, 122n8, 135n27, 142, 147, 163n82, 199–203, 211, 212, 214n17, 241, 242, 266, 269, 275, 276
Morning Star 120
Morris, William 21, 256, 261n25
mortality 41, 168, 181n5, 231, 234; *see also* immortality
Morte d'Arthur 218
Mortenson, Vigo 16
Mount Doom 30, 71, 204
Mouth of Sauron 14, 18, 207, 208
Müller, Axel E.W. 161
mushrooms 57, 61, 78, 162n28, 265
music 5, 31, 60, 80, 89, 91, 99n10, 99n11, 107, 113n11, 179, 228, 262n26, 274, 275, 277, 281, 282, 284, 284n8
"The Music of the Ainur" 120
Mythopoeia 133n6
Mythopoeic (Society) Conference 186, 192n9

Naith 268
The Name of the Rose 170
Napoleon 158, 159
Napoleon (film) 159
Narsil 11, 151, 187, 210
Nasmith, Ted 26, 86
National Public Radio 58
Nazgûl 57, 105, 108, 113n7, 136n23, 147, 163n, 93, 188, 204, 206, 238, 239, 241, 246n6
Neldoreth 230
New Age 91, 172, 281
New Line Cinema 185, 188, 284n4
New Zealand 1, 9, 27, 47, 64, 100, 139, 140, 141, 146, 148, 192n2, 217, 243
1960s 6, 85, 190, 265
1970s 5, 95, 156, 265
Norman Conquest 257
"Note on the Shire Records" 170
Novik, Naomi 159
Númenor 19, 20, 40, 169, 175, 181n4, 229, 230, 249, 258, 259

Odinic wanderer 195
Odyssey 72
Old English 73, 134n16, 248–251, 253, 255, 259, 260, 260n3, 260n8, 260n10, 261n11
Old Forest 11, 29, 54, 55, 57, 59, 61–64, 65, 66n3, 67n15, 67n16, 67n17, 77, 79
Old Man Willow 50, 55, 56, 63, 68n17, 70, 72, 77
Old Norse 13, 85, 88, 93, 248, 251, 252

Olivier, Laurence 143
optimism 17, 170, 180
orcs 2, 15, 28, 37, 38, 47, 62, 111, 118, 119, 121–126, 128, 129, 131, 132n4, 132n6, 132n8, 133n9, 134n10, 134n11, 134n16, 134/5n16, 135n17, 135n20, 136n23, 136n24, 136n26, 137n27, 139, 141, 142, 146, 151, 157, 159, 160, 173, 184, 200, 213, 233, 240, 244, 274, 276, 280
Orientalism 257, 259
Original Sin 73
Orthanc 30, 124, 206, 249
Osborne, Barrie M. 142, 161n10, 162n53, 164n104
Oscars 25, 97
Osgiliath 111, 160, 177
the Other 269, 271, 274, 277–279, 281
other-time 266, 267, 276, 284n9
Otherworld 88–91, 204, 205, 212
Otto, Rolf 268, 269, 271, 281–283
Out of the Silent Planet (1938) 268, 285n10
Outer Sea 174
Oxford 5, 6, 51, 134n12, 171, 184, 185, 192n9, 246n12, 260n2

Palantír 40, 175, 219
paradise 19, 217, 218, 224, 227, 279
Paradise Lost 120
Parth Galen 221
Parthian Shot 156
The Passion of Christ 181
path of least resistance 225
Paths of the Dead 13, 26, 91–93, 95, 103, 163n94, 221, 222, 234
Payne, Carl 149
Peake, Richard Brinsley 122
Pelennor Fields 107, 108, 111, 146, 158, 159, 177, 187, 191, 240
penance 73
The Peoples of Middle Earth (book) 129
Petritksy, Anatoly 164n117
photography 47, 277
The Pilgrim's Regress 270
pillars 21, 34, 244, 245, 256, 257, 283
Pipeweed 6, 56
Pippin (Peregrine Took) 7, 26, 29, 61, 62, 65, 67n13, 67n14, 71, 74, 81, 102, 103, 175–178, 181n2, 187, 188, 194, 196, 197, 200–202, 204, 205–207, 209, 211, 212, 219, 229
Pirates of the Caribbean 93
poetry 102, 175, 249, 250, 276, 284
Poll, Dallas 161
power 17–19, 30, 35, 36, 50, 51, 64, 72, 76, 78, 85, 89, 92, 97, 109, 120, 121, 125, 127, 129, 132n3, 132n5, 152, 173, 177, 179, 189, 192n1, 194, 195, 200, 204, 205, 207–209, 211, 214n19, 217, 222, 224, 225n4, 228, 229, 231, 232, 233, 238, 258, 270, 273, 276, 282
The Prancing Pony 74, 77
prayer 80, 81, 270
Prince Caspian (2008) 150

The Problem of Pain (1940) 26, 269, 284*n*1
profit 13, 216, 260
The Promise (2005) 158
prophet 256, 282
props 12, 15, 28, 31, 142, 143, 144, 145, 146, 154, 255, 258
PVC alkathene pipe 149
Pwyll, Prince of Dyfed 73
pyre 205, 258

Quenya 175
quest 73, 75–78, 81, 134, 143, 183, 189, 195, 209, 213*n*4, 214*n*10, 219, 220, 234, 240, 241, 274
Quest of the Holy Grail 72, 73

Raffel, Burton 249
rain-curtain 169, 176, 177
Rangers 13, 92, 199, 221, 230, 233, 251; *see also* Dunedain
Rankin and Bass 7, 41, 67*n*9, 224
Ransom, Elwin 273
Rath Dinen 205
Red Book (of Westmarch) 248
Red Cliff (2008) 158
red dragon explosive 196
Redhorn Gate 199
reenactment groups 147
Regulous, Stephen 157, 158
religions 16, 17, 78, 79, 135*n*16, 169, 170–172, 181*n*2, 189, 190, 266, 268, 270, 273, 281
Remington, Barbara 57
Renaissance 73, 158
The Return of the King (*Return*; *ROTK*) 3, 9, 11, 13, 14, 19, 25, 35, 39, 41, 42, 43*n*4, 43*n*8, 44*n*15, 56, 64, 72, 73, 90, 93, 96, 99*n*13, 99*n*14, 99*n*16, 99*n*17, 99*n*18, 99*n*19, 99*n*21, 99*n*22, 105, 117, 123, 127, 128, 136*n*23, 136*n*26, 137*n*27, 158, 159, 162*n*25, 162*n*32, 162*n*33, 163*n*93, 163*n*94, 164*n*114, 164*n*115, 164*n*120, 169, 172, 173–179, 171*n*1, 187, 191, 204, 205, 208, 209, 211, 213*n*7, 214*n*20, 214*n*21, 214*n*22, 214*n*24, 219, 220, 222, 224, 235*n*15, 235*n*16, 238, 241, 242, 244, 245*n*1, 245*n*10, 258, 261*n*22
Rhun the Great 251
Riddermark 249, 251
Riders of Rohan 37, 74, 156, 159, 249–251, 253, 255, 257
Ring 9, 16–19, 29, 30, 34, 36–39, 50, 53, 55, 60, 64, 70–73, 80, 83, 93, 96, 105, 108, 113*n*14, 131, 136*n*25, 144, 164*n*98, 178, 183–185, 187–191, 192*n*1, 192*n*5, 196–199, 201, 202, 204, 205, 210, 211, 213*n*4, 218, 219, 224, 229, 230; destruction of 17, 18, 29, 30, 34, 71, 81, 204, 234
Ringbearer 60, 108, 109, 183, 187, 189, 191, 199, 202, 210, 267, 279
Ringwraith 65, 72, 79, 120, 135*n*21, 136*n*23, 145, 188, 204, 214*n*19, 239, 240, 261*n*22
ritual 81, 82171

Rivendell 11, 12, 21, 39, 44*n*13, 66*n*3, 67*n*14, 74, 76, 78, 89, 90, 91, 97, 136*n*26, 195, 199, 221, 230, 231, 233, 234, 240, 168, 271, 274
Road to Middle-earth 2, 74, 83, 112*n*2, 134*n*16, 250, 260*n*4
Rob Roy 143
Robin Hood (1928) & (2010) 143, 149, 150
Rodger, Tania 161, 162*n*48, m *n*60, 163*n*74
Rogers, Deborah 190
Rohan 20, 30, 39, 60, 155, 156, 201, 212, 230, 241, 242, 244, 249, 251, 252, 256–259, 260*n*3
Rohirrim/Rohiroth 1, 2, 20, 21, 71, 142, 145, 146, 159, 164*n*114, 194, 206, 207, 239, 241, 246*n*6, 248, 249, 251, 253–255, 257–260, 260*n*1, 261*n*16; *see also* Riders of Rohan
Roman culture 49, 72, 82, 171
romance 4, 8, 12, 31, 72, 74, 75, 78, 82, 88, 90, 91, 97, 102, 103, 112*n*2, 218, 219, 223, 224, 231
rope, Elven 109
Rotten Tomatoes 25, 43*n*2
Royal Armouries, Leeds 15, 15, 143
Royal Guard (of the Rohirrim) 142
Runes 252, 256

Sackville-Baggins, Lobelia 77
Salo, David 40, 155
Salvation 73, 171, 235
Sam 6, 9, 11, 12, 15, 16, 35–37, 53, 57, 58, 61, 62, 64, 65, 67*n*13, 68*n*19, 71, 74–76, 78, 81, 88, 104, 105, 108, 109, 111, 113*n*14, 128, 130, 131, 136*n*26, 141, 169, 176–9, 180, 188, 199, 200, 208, 211–213, 216, 238, 240, 242, 272
Saruman 15, 19, 30, 38, 43*n*13, 51, 61, 64, 65, 67*n*13, 70–72, 79, 121, 123–129, 131, 133*n*8, 134*n*11, 134*n*13, 135*n*8, 201, 202, 204, 206, 209, 212, 213, 218, 224, 238–243, 249, 260*n*8, 274, 284*n*5
satan 86, 120
Saul Zaentz Company 6
Sauron 14, 15, 18, 30, 38, 39, 51, 54, 57, 64, 66, 71, 72, 79, 92, 121, 126, 127, 134*n*10, 136*n*23, 136*n*24, 139, 159, 160, 169*n*1, 173, 176, 184, 191, 192*n*1, 194, 195, 200, 203–211, 227, 229, 231–234, 235*n*16, 239, 240, 242, 249, 277
scabbard 144, 152, 155
scale (weapons) 75, 76, 144–146, 159
scale double 145
Scandinavia 40, 171, 252, 258
Science Museum, London 141
Scott (Ridley) 143
Scythians 245, 246*n*11
Second Age 16, 17, 91, 172, 173, 174
secondary world 49, 116, 132*n*2, 181*n*2, 183, 184
Seven Stars 254
Shadow 64, 106, 120, 134*n*14, 205, 227, 231, 233, 242, 243, 246*n*8

Shadowfax 9, 183, 204, 205, 236, 237, m 239, 241, 246n3, 246n10
Shakespeare, William 76, 279, 280
Shelenkov, Aleksandr 164n117
Shelley, Mary 14, 116–120, 122, 123, 125, 127–130, 132n2, 132n3, 133n7, 135n18
Shelob 14, 15, 33, 37, 82, 105, 108–110, 113n12, 126, 128, 136n23, 136n26, 173, 241
shield-maiden 113n7, 207, 234
shields 106, 107, 144, 148, 150, 154
Shippey, Tom 26, 27, 28, 31, 43n5, 43n6, 43n11, 44n14, 74, 76, 77, 87, 103–105, 111, 112n2, 112n3, 134n16, 136n23, 171, 180, 184, 192n3, 214n26, 244, 249, 250, 252, 253, 260n4, 261n13, 261n19, 261n24
ships 16, 34, 41, 106, 108, 111, 113n8, 158, 174, 178–180, 211, 221, 257
Shire 2, 19, 21, 29–31, 34, 41, 62, 64, 71, 72, 77, 78, 81, 83, 88, 110, 119, 170, 173, 176–178, 194, 195, 214n10, 217, 218, 222, 253; scouring of 2, 19, 29, 30, 71, 72, 81, 83, 173, 177, 222
Shore, Howard 91, 179, 281, 283
Sibley, Brian 5, 58, 59, 61, 63, 67n12, 67n16, 161n8, 102n39, 163n64, 163n78, 163n80, 163n86, 163n87, 163n88, 163n90, 164n102, 164n112, 164n121
Sidhe 13, 89, 98n5
silence 282
Silharrows 251
silicon mold 148, 153
Silmaril 230
Silmarillion 8, 16, 50, 71, 87, 120, 123, 171, 173–175, 181n3, 181n5, 185, 192n3, 192n10, 235n3, 264, 265, 270, 275
silver 108, 120, 150, 169, 176, 177, 179, 283
Silverlode 268
simbelmynë 255
Sindarin 96, 229
Sir Gawain 73, 88, 285n7
Sir Orfeo 188
skateboard wheels 153
skulls 93, 222
Sméagol 17, 35, 36, 44n14, 109, 110n14, 130, 131n1, 183, 185; *see also* Gollum
smoke rings 34
Songs for the Philologists 250
Spartacus 160
spiders 155, 173
Spielberg, Steven 118
spirit 2, 10–12, 16–19, 31, 33, 51, 57, 64, 78, 81–82, 88, 91, 93, 94, 110, 125, 130, 132n5, 154, 169, 170, 172, 173, 176, 179, 180, 181n2, 189, 196, 204–206, 210, 211, 268, 270, 272, 273, 275–276, 279, 284
Stagecoach (1939) 159
Star Trek 8, 220
Star Wars 222n3, 264
stars 41, 64, 78, 108, 109, 120, 144, 179, 227, 254, 272
Steward of Gondor 144, 175, 205, 233

Stone of Erech 92, 99n15, 222
Stoor Hobbit 187, 190
Streeter, Ri 161
Strider 20, 25, 55, 57, 62, 169n10, 184, 195, 221, 229, 233, 240; *see also* Aragorn
string theory 186
Sturrock, Emily-Jane 161
Superman 219
Surprised by Joy 270
Sutton Hoo 21, 145, 257, 258, 259
Swoboda, Karl Maria 79
swords 11, 16, 35, 55, 68n20, 92, 107, 108, 119, 128, 139, 142, 144–148, 150–153, 155, 156, 160, 161n4, 161n10, 162n46, 163n89, 187, 200, 201, 204, 208, 213, 214n20, 220, 233, 234, 235n4; *see also* weapons

Tarkovsky, Andrei 264, 284n2
taunting 202, 208
Taylor, Richard 16, 85, 93, 95, 141, 146, 47, 150, 152–155, 161, 161n5, 162n25, 162n26, 162n29, 162n36, 162n37, 162n41, 163n59, 163n61, 163n66, 163n68, 163n75, 163n84, 163n94
Te Papa Tongarewa 141
Templars 156
temptation 34, 48, 217, 219, 220, 225n2, 271, 279, 280, 284n7
Teutons 88, 91
Thengel 251
Théoden 19, 38, 39, 107, 113n7, 142, 155, 162n25, 198, 205, 206, 209, 216, 218, 240, 244, 250, 251, 255, 258
Theodred 244, 258
theology 120, 121, 131, 133, 171, 183, 189, 192n1, 192n8, 272
TheOneRing.net 9, 10, 44n17, 95, 97
Thingol 230
Third Age 16, 19, 30, 92, 134n11, 170, 172, 235, 235n5
Thorin (Oakensheild) 32, 40, 67n9, 21n15
threat 18, 29, 31, 92, 128, 131, 192n5, 202, 207, 217, 218, 221, 224, 227, 257
Thum 265, 273, 279
Tiller, Terence 5, 56, 59, 60, 64
Tolkien, Christopher 46, 131, 134n11, 171, 174, 181n5, 188, 228, 251, 260n9
Tolkien, J.R.R.: death 8, 188; narrative 12, 71, 74, 104, 105, 111, 112, 180, 198, 199, 210, 243, 244, 266; posthumous work 188; songs 281; story 8, 10, 13, 55, 58, 60, 62, 65, 66n5, 70, 196, 209, 276
Tom Bombadil *see* Bombadil, Tom
tombs 80, 81, 83, 93, 116, 163n58
Toronto Star 97
transmogrification 279, 280
Trawpe 73
The Treason of Isengard 213n5, 213n6, 214n19, 249–252
Treebeard 25, 63, 68n17, 74, 81, 216
trees 21, 29, 41, 46, 48, 49, 51, 57, 67n15, 77,

79, 175, 228, 229, 238, 254, 256, 271, 274, 277, 278, 283; *see also* White Tree
trolls 15, 28, 49, 66, 78, 116, 118, 119, 124, 126, 128, 129, 135*n*22, 209, 213, 241
Troy (2004) 158
Tuatha Dé Danann 87
2001: A Space Odyssey (1968) 156
The Two Towers (*Towers*; *TT*) 3, 6, 9, 14, 19, 25, 29, 35, 36, 38, 41, 43*n*4, 48, 56, 63, 67*n*14, 67*n*17, 68*n*17, 127–130, 131*n*1, 133*n*9, 136*n*23, 137, 162*n*38, 162*n*43, 163*n*57, 163*n*68, 163*n*72, 163*n*83, 164*n*96, 164*n*107, 164*n*119, 174, 175, 195, 204, 209, 214*n*20, 214*n*25, 218, 220, 236*n*19, 238, 240–245, 246*n*6, 246*n*10, 249, 251, 253, 255–258
Two Trees of Valinor 174, 175

United Artists 6, 7, 8
Unwin, Rayner 6
Unwin, Steve 149, 151, 161
Urban, Karl 141, 161*n*12
urethane 145, 148, 149, 152, 153
Urquhart, Robert 125
Uruk 133*n*6, 144, 156, 158
Uruk-hai 2, 15, 38, 67*n*14, 71, 121, 122, 124–127, 128, 129, 133*n*6, 133*n*8, 135*n*20, 139, 144, 145, 156–158, 164*n*117, 184, 221, 240, 274, 284*n*5

Valar 16, 40, 174, 175, 179, 209, 210, 227
Valente 276, 279
Valhalla 93
Valinor 17, 41, 88, 96, 168, 173–177, 227, 235, 243, 279
vampires 94
victory 18, 106–108, 111, 117, 158, 182, 187, 191, 209, 217–219
Vikings 21, 258
villains 15, 29, 30, 126, 135*n*17, 233
Virgil 72, 269
Virgin Mary 270, 280
The Virginian 217
Völuspá/Völuspá 251, 252

Walsh, Fran 35, 54, 55, 61, 65, 66*n*2, 118, 119, 125, 127, 128, 179, 231, 239
The Wanderer 249, 255, 260*n*2
war 6, 20, 30, 38, 41, 67*n*16, 78, 79, 83, 133*n*9, 136*n*23, 154, 157–160, 174, 184, 185, 213, 239–242, 248, 250, 251, 266, 276, 284
War and Peace (1968) 160, 176
War of the Rings 18, 19, 30, 28, 139, 160, 176, 191, 235*n*16, 245*n*1, 246*n*10
The Warlord (1995) 149
warriors 18, 38, 65, 77, 94, 156, 157, 219, 233, 234, 240, 245, 251, 252, 257, 283

Watcher in the Water 116, 132*n*1
Watchers 212
water lilies 49
waterfalls 56, 144, 266
Waterloo (1970) 159, 160, 164*n*107
Waterloo (battle) 159
weapons 1, 15, 16, 29, 67*n*16, 141, 142, 144–147, 150, 151–157, 170, 200, 204, 214*n*20, 245, 248; *see also* swords
Weathertop 55, 65, 78, 218, 232, 234
West Saxon 253, 260*n*8
Westmarch 248
West-midlander 261*n*18
Westrons 240, 248
Weta Tenzan Chainmaille 150
Weta Workshop 15–17, 87, 93, 98*n*2, 140, 141, 146, 148, 150, 151, 159, 161*n*11, 161*n*36, 162*n*31, 162*n*42, 162*n*48, 162*n*52, 162*n*53, 162*n*55, 163*n*61, 163*n*65
Whale, James 123
White Tower of Ecthelion 283
White Tree 169, 175, 181*n*2, 254
Wiggins, Kayla 223
Wilde, Lady 89
Wilderland 40
Willow (1988) 155
windows 80, 256, 271, 274
winter 41, 92, 188, 189, 256, 271, 277
Wister, Owen 217
Witch-king (of Angmar) 106–108, 163*n*93, 188, 206–208
Withywindle 50, 51, 57, 64
wizards 17, 20, 30, 33, 34, 72, 85, 126, 131, 174, 183, 194–198, 200–208, 211, 215*n*27, 238, 239, 242–245, 261*n*15
Wizards (film) 7
wolves 199, 200, 212, 238
women 20, 89, 124, 142, 143, 218–220, 246*n*9
Wood, Elijah 133*n*, 8, 280
Woodmen 250
Wootten, Ben 154
Wordsworth 270, 273
Wormtongue (Grima) 51, 79, 198, 205, 209, 214*n*24

X-Men: The Last Stand (2006) 158

Yates, Jantry 143

Zeffirelli, Franco 143
Zimmerman, Morton Grady 5–7, 27, 56, 58, 59, 64, 66*n*3, 66*n*6, 66*n*7, 67*n*15
Zirak-zigil 204, 205
zombies 14, 92–95, 98
zoomorphic interlace 257

www.ingramcontent.com/pod-product-compliance
Ingram Content Group UK Ltd.
Pitfield, Milton Keynes, MK11 3LW, UK
UKHW041916140426
5217IPUK00013B/177